The
Book of Mychal

The
Book of Mychal

The SURPRISING LIFE *and* HEROIC DEATH
of FATHER MYCHAL JUDGE

Michael Daly

THOMAS DUNNE BOOKS
ST. MARTIN'S PRESS   NEW YORK

THOMAS DUNNE BOOKS.
An imprint of St. Martin's Press.

THE BOOK OF MYCHAL. Copyright © 2008 by Michael Daly. All rights reserved. Printed in the United States of America. For information, address St. Martin's Press, 175 Fifth Avenue, New York, N.Y. 10010.

www.thomasdunnebooks.com
www.stmartins.com

161-7863

Library of Congress Cataloging-in-Publication Data

Daly, Michael, 1952–
    The book of Mychal : the surprising life and heroic death of Father Mychal Judge / Michael Daly. — 1st ed.
        p. cm.
    "Thomas Dunne Books."
    Includes index.
    ISBN-13: 978-0-312-30150-7 (alk. paper)
    ISBN-10: 0-312-30150-2 (alk. paper)
    1. Judge, Mychal, 1933–2001. 2. September 11 Terrorist Attacks, 2001—Biography.
3. Catholic Church—United States—Clergy—Biography. I. Title.
    BX4705.J767D35   2008
    282.092—dc22
    [B]   2008019635

First Edition: September 2008

10 9 8 7 6 5 4 3 2 1

To my father, Charles U. Daly,
and my brother, Douglas Daly

Acknowledgments

This book would not have been possible without the generous help of Mychal's sisters, Dympna and Erin, as well as the full spectrum of his many friends. I thank among many others Vina Drennan and young John and Adrienne and Justine and Jessica, Gladys Andersen, Steven and Patti Ann and Conor McDonald, Al Alvarado, Mike and Janet Brown, Tara Stackpole, Keith and Ellen McLaughlin, Beth Hatton, Jimmy Boyle, the Siedenburg family, the Valentino family, the Johnson family, Michael Walker, Addie LaPiedra, Connie Smith, Randi Wylie, Maura Lener, Brian Mulheren and John Mulheren, Michael Angelini, Michael Mulligan, the Smurr family, Craig Monahan, Chris Waugh, Father Chris Keenan, Father Pat Fitzgerald, Father Ron Pesci, Father John McNeill, Father Brian Jordan, Father Hugh Hines, Jean Willis, Kevin Shea, Bobby Burke, Pete and Rita Hayden, Liam Flaherty, Tim Brown, Jim Elison, Tim Grant, Steve Gonzalez, Steve and Danny Browne, Peter Michaels, Mickey Kross, Brendan Fay and Tom Moulton, Michael and Susan Madden, Mychal McNicholas, Tom Ferriter, Joe Bryant, the Carven family, Sister Pascal Conforti, David Dinkins, Sister Mary DeSales, Rev. Everett Wabst, Jimmy Gilfeather, Gerry Whelan, Gerry Adams, Cristyne Lategano Nicholas, Everald Brathwaite, Hillary Clinton, Rudy Giuliani, Brian Carroll, Mike Currid, Pat Kowalski, Al Fuentes, Tom Nerney, Mike Moran, John Ryan, Howard Safir, Tom Von Essen, and Steve Shlopak.

On the editorial side, I thank the people at Thomas Dunne Books, my determined editor, Rob Kirkpatrick (who kept the faith), as well as Lorrie McCann and Meg Drislane. I am forever grateful to Marianne Patridge for her editorial and spiritual guidance. I also thank the wise Dinah Prince Daly, Douglas Daly, Sinead Daly, Bronagh Daly, and the great Nancy Cardozo.

And Flip Brophy proved once again that not all agents are in it just for the money.

And the biggest thanks go to the surprising one Mychal sometimes called "the Boss."

Preface

I had been up with the dawn working on a political story for the New York *Daily News* when a cop friend called to tell me a plane had hit the World Trade Center. I got to the scene as the South Tower collapsed. The North Tower came down twenty-nine minutes later. I ran for my life. I was still alive when the dust cleared.

"How many people died back there?" a firefighter from Engine 353 cried out. "How many were lost?"

The more dedicated and daring firefighters are the ones a city newspaper columnist gets to know, and I was sure many of them had been killed, along with thousands of other innocents. These included two dear friends who had parked their fire rigs side by side at the base of the North Tower. As the dust cleared, I saw that both rigs had been crushed.

I was still not prepared for what I heard when I encountered Deputy Chief Peter Hayden, who had commanded the rescue effort in the North Tower. Hayden said, "Father Judge is dead."

I felt my knees give. A retired firefighter named Jimmy Boyle caught me. I was shamed, for his only son had been in the North Tower just a block from where we stood, and he was rock steady. I said, "I loved Mychal Judge." Hayden said in a reproving tone, "A lot of people loved Mychal Judge."

I had been introduced to Fire Chaplain Mychal Judge in 1994 by one of the steadiest of firefighters, Capt. Patrick Brown. I saw at fire scenes and at FDNY rites and ceremonies how much firefighters loved their Padre. Judge was the one to whom they turned after a tragedy to give it form and meaning. He also was able to get them laughing even at funerals.

On the night of the greatest tragedy ever to strike the city, I walked over the Brooklyn Bridge just as I sometimes had with Judge. My way home took me past the street where he was raised and the church where he said his first Mass. My firstborn had often waved to the religious bas relief out front, saying, "Hi, Mary! Hi, Jesus!" The Dalys only went to church for weddings and funerals.

But I always felt church had come to me when I encountered Mychal Judge, a church of life and love and laughter. I felt this way again the summer after 9/11 when I chanced upon a homeless man sprawled on the sidewalk a half block from the friary where Mychal had lived. The man was bare-chested, but wore three pairs of pants in the sweltering heat, none of which were zipped.

I handed him a neatly folded dollar bill and said, "This is from Mychal Judge."

The man rose from the sidewalk and announced, "Father Mychal Judge was my spiritual adviser."

With that, he scuffled down to a small courtyard adjoining the church and deposited the dollar in a collection box beside a bank of candles. He said not a word as he continued crosstown, tugging up his pants.

Mychal was also my spiritual adviser, and he taught me by example to look for what is best in people. I have sought to do that here for him with considerable help from his friends and fellow friars as well as his twin sister, Dympna. *The Book of Mychal* is also a book for Mychal, my friend Father Mychal Judge, the one and only.

The
Book of Mychal

2

The first surprise was always the size and strength of his hands, hands that at the greeting clasp seemed meant for riveting the high steel or fielding a hot grounder, hands that blessed and anointed as if the spiritual were as actual as honest labor or tender sex. Hands that made the holy real, just as the hands of the firefighters waiting beside him prepared to make the real holy, hefting tools and tugging at air tank straps.

His own hands hung useless at his sides as he now stood on West Street in a Roman collar and a black standard-issue FDNY firefighter's protective turnout coat, gazing from under the brim of his white fire helmet. He and the firefighters around him were witnessing an elemental law of nature by which a falling object accelerates at thirty-two feet per second minus the particular air resistance, be the object a lead weight dropped by Galileo from the Tower of Pisa or a human being leaping from the upper floors of One World Trade Center.

Male or female, young or old, healthy or ill, urban or suburban, black or white or Hispanic or Asian, married or single, parent or childless, straight or gay, rich or poor, generous or miserly, kind or cruel, fierce or meek, virtuous or sinful, dreamy or practical, toned or flabby, Christian or Jew or Muslim or Hindu, all fell at the same ever-increasing rate. The only variants were density and surface area. Mundane business papers wafted gently down, but even the most decent person was soon plummeting at nearly 150 miles per hour.

Those who leapt from the topmost floors of the North Tower fell for as long as nine seconds. The people on the floors closest to where the plane actually hit had maybe seven seconds, still time to think of loved ones and pray to their particular notion of the Almighty. A Roman Catholic, for example, would have been able to say a Hail Mary but not an entire Act of Contrition.

Everybody had time to utter "Oh, God!" or "God, no!" or some other plea even atheists cry at the onrush of death. All likely remained as keenly conscious as skydivers.

Some jumped together, holding hands. Most leapt singly, often tumbling as they fell. At least one man stayed feet first, his red-and-blue tie streaming above him. But most were on their backs as they reached the lower floors, facing the heavens if not necessarily heaven. Their last sight was of the perfect baby-blue sky as they struck the pavement with a velocity that instantly turned a living person into a bright red splatter. The sound was jarring, loud, a body becoming a bomb.

Other sounds, the wailing of sirens, converged from uptown and downtown and crosstown, more sirens than had ever been heard in the city. Engine companies and ladder companies and rescue companies kept arriving, eventually more than 240 FDNY units from all five boroughs. The attack had come just as the firehouses were changing shifts, and many companies arrived with double the usual contingent of five. Anyone who happened to be hanging around came, too. Those who could not cram onto the rigs drove their cars and pickup trucks or commandeered taxicabs. One young firefighter rode the subway from Midtown in full gear, standing amid gawking passengers. Off-duty firefighters reported on their own. One had been golfing. Another had been surfing at Rockaway, riding in to shore when he saw the distant smoke. Another bicycled from Brooklyn. Another hit traffic in the Battery Tunnel from Brooklyn to Manhattan and ran the rest of the way, emerging at the foot of the towers.

The firefighters who did not have equipment rummaged the rigs at the scene. They joined the others in pulling on air packs, grabbing tools, and shouldering thirty-pound hose lengths as they would at a routine tenement blaze. Then they saw the jumpers.

A figure would be tiny and indistinct at first, but grow more and more detailed as it fell closer, its gender and race soon becoming clear, then startlingly vivid, an individual human being in the instant before striking the pavement. The sound of each reminded the firefighters what would happen if one of these bodies struck them. There was none of the usual fire-scene banter as they gazed skyward and tried to gauge when they could dash those final steps into the tower while burdened with fifty-six and a half pounds of gear and whatever tools they carried.

"When I say run, you just run!" a fire officer shouted.

. . .

The F.D.N.Y. CHAPLAIN stenciled in reflecting yellow letters on the back of Father Mychal Judge's turnout coat marked him as one figure unburdened of even the expectation that he dash into danger. He could have stayed at the staging area across from the tower with nobody thinking less of him. The sick and the dying and the bereaved had often said that the touch of his big Irish hands seemed the Almighty's own and that he looked heaven-sent with his warm blue eyes and a marquee-handsome face lined only by his smile. But he could no more save those still trapped above than he could catch those who jumped and landed with such force there was nothing even to anoint. He was a sixty-eight-year-old priest, three years past the age when a firefighter would be forced to retire, and he could pray just as well from where he stood.

Still he had always stood witness at the forward command post as the firefighters battled what they sometimes called the Red Devil. And on this morning when there was only hell on high, absolute evil seemed to be challenging the value of life itself.

Just the day before, Judge had ended a firehouse dedication in the Bronx by placing his big right hand over his heart and singing "God Bless America." He now listened mutely to the unholy detonation of body on pavement, each seeming to be mocking proof that the cosmos was ultimately and absolutely indifferent, that the differences between people were inconsequential because people themselves were of no consequence, that what was real was just real, that if there is a God, then He has no hands at all.

Yet all around him was the manifest grace of firefighters poised to risk everything to save those of whatever persuasion, firefighters who routinely challenged the cosmic indifference of combustion and gravity by placing all lives ahead of their own. They moved as one when the order came to "Run! Run! Run!"

For Judge to have let his fear rule him would have been to shrink before a challenge to all decent people, to have let evil win. He moved with the firefighters, his black lace-up shoes in pace with their fire boots across the field of carnage, crunching on the broken glass and skirting the fresh red splatters.

He was a priest who could make a paraplegic man feel lucky and make a dying AIDS victim feel the kiss on his forehead was the kiss of the Almighty Himself. He was so dashingly handsome, he once arrived in his habit at a party and was mistaken for a male stripper in costume. He was so brash, he made the cardinal sputter, and so devout, he was sometimes lost in prayer for hours. He brought laughter everywhere—to the White House in the wake of scandal, even to grim vigils in the burn unit. He had a genius for saying exactly the right thing in the most extreme circumstances and knew when to say nothing at all. A former mayor called him his best friend, and homeless people listed him as their next of kin. He saw Alcoholics Anonymous as a miracle of wine into water where people struggled to save their own souls. He admired nobody more than those who saved lives, and on other days when firefighters died, he declared their firehouses holy ground, their spirit alive anew with every alarm. In the aftermath of this fire unlike any others, his own spirit would join with theirs to be more powerful than anyone could have imagined and, for a brief time anyway, defeat the evil and affirm all he believed. Those who loved him would remember what he often said of his most passionate love, who was neither man nor woman yet both.

"My God is the God of Surprises."

2

H e knew what he wanted to be before he could pronounce the word.
"I wanna be a *peest*," he would say.

He was maybe three years old and living in working-class South Brooklyn, where people would give not the name of the neighborhood but of the parish, St. Paul's, when telling where they lived. Other Irish mothers would have rejoiced at such a declaration by a boy that age. His mother was of another mind. Mary Ann Judge, born Fallon, viewed her native land as "priest ridden" and the Church as party to the harshness of her upbringing. She felt the people had it hard enough in her home county of Leitrim, whose name derives from *laith druim*, the Irish for "gray ridge." Those who fled from there knew it as a realm of stony ground and grinding poverty.

"My mother was from the stones," her daughter, Dympna, said years later.

Mary Ann considered the priests in her native Drumkeerin to be tyrants as cruel as her own mother, whom she would simply say she hated. Her mother was so heartless she would force her legally blind stepson to sleep outside in the bitterest weather. And when young Mary Ann entered their garden in a contest and won a prize, the mother punished her for drawing attention to the family.

"The harshness of it all," Dympna said.

When she became the first of four siblings to emigrate, at the age of twenty-four, Mary Ann departed without fondness for home, house, town, or Church. She did bring along a sprig of Ireland's green, an ivy cutting from her prize-winning garden that she kept as alive as hope. This improbable sign of sentiment made her all the more memorable to the twenty-two-year-old man she encountered on the eight-day crossing to New York.

Michael Judge was from the same county as Mary Ann and an even smaller town, but he had nothing of the stones about him. He had been raised on a struggling farm on the shore of Keshcarrigan Lake, where the Judges were held to be a little unusual, if not exactly suspect, by the parish. They had built their house, not hunkered down like everyone else's, not sheltered from the biting wind and lashing rain, but atop a rise overlooking the lake, as if a fine view could keep you warm or feed your family.

From this almost scandalously impractical vantage, young Michael Judge could see beyond the lake to a range of hills, most renowned among them Sidh Beag and Sidh Mór, the Small Fairy Hill and the Big Fairy Hill. Sidh Beag was said to be the burial place of Fionn mac Cumhaill, the mythic hero who battled injustice with his Fianna Éireann warriors.

Michael Judge himself was no warrior; he had refused to take up the gun against the British. But he had a spirit akin to the spring at the base of the big hill whose "living water" bubbled from the sullen earth. He brimmed with song and tales of myth and mirth, some concerning the fairies that neighbors swore they saw playing in the three fruit trees planted in front of his family's home. He smiled and laughed like a man who needed no money to enjoy the richness of being alive.

And perhaps that was part of what appealed to Mary Ann when she met him aboard the SS *Celtic* in 1921. She was more the warrior of the two, having served with Cumann na mBan, the women's branch of the Irish Republican Army. She apparently accepted that he was not of similar temperament, that he was simply too much a lover of life to snuff it out.

On landing in New York, Mary Ann went to work as a domestic in Sea Gate, a well-to-do gated community at the western tip of proletarian Coney Island. She slept in a tiny room in a big house, cooking and cleaning and caring for the employer's children. She earned little and sent much of it back to Leitrim via money orders from the Irish Emigrant Society in Manhattan. She began making installments with the White Star Line so her three sisters could also flee mother and homeland.

Michael went to work as a laborer in Providence, Rhode Island, but traveled to Brooklyn every weekend. He spent his Sundays walking up and down in front of the grand house in Sea Gate, not daring to knock on the door, hoping to "chance" into the woman he had met at sea. He finally did.

The eight-day crossing led to an eight-year courtship. They were finally married on August 30, 1929, at St. Anselm's Church on Fourth Avenue in

Brooklyn. He was thirty and new citizen No. 290224540. She was thirty-two and new citizen No. 292525424. All she ever told her children about the wedding was that the priest was late.

Two months later, the stock market crashed and the country tumbled into the Depression. Michael was among the fortunate few, managing to keep a job he had taken at Butler's supermarkets in Brooklyn. They moved into a four-story brick house at 230 Dean Street in South Brooklyn.

Mary Ann had kept tending her bit of ivy, and she of the stones now planted it in the back garden. The sprig of her improbable sentiment thrived and grew in her new life with this magical man from Keshcarrigan, the little town whose name in Irish means "water on rock."

Their first child, Erin, was born the very next year. A boy, Thomas Emmett, arrived the following year, named after Michael Judge's brother. The family's luck took its first tragic turn when the child developed an ear infection that spread to the mastoid bone. He died at fifteen months.

Fraternal twins arrived in 1933. The mother may have set a local record for labor by having a boy on May 11 and the girl twin May 13, the feast day of Saint Dympna. The girl was named Dympna, the boy Robert Emmett, in honor of the great Irish patriot. His family would call him Emmett even after he took the religious name Father Mychal Judge.

As did many in the neighborhood, the parents played the Irish Sweepstakes and the twins had just turned one when a telegram arrived announcing, "YOUR TICKET MB 73234 HAS DRAWN IRISH HOSPITALS DERBY SWEEPSTAKES PRIZE . . . 514 [POUNDS]." The Judges already had a steady income and a house. They were now able to buy a new car.

"It really was the luck of the Irish," their son later said.

When the twins were three, Michael Judge was taken to St. Peter's Hospital on Henry Street with mastoiditis, the same condition that had killed his firstborn son. He was hospitalized for more than three years, undergoing nine surgeries.

Mary Ann visited Michael every day, but the hospital rules barred children. She would sometimes stand Erin and the twins on the corner so they could see their father in the third-story window, smiling down from above, conveying love however he was able without touch or word.

"It was the saddest thing," remembered Sister Mary DeSales, who taught the children at the parish school and visited their father often. "It was a real shock to him he couldn't be with his children. It was a real cross for him, real suffering."

Even in such circumstances, she found Michael witty and charming, "a real Irishman." He was apt to whistle the lilting "Sidh Beag Agus Sidh Mór," written by the blind seventeenth-century harpist Turlough O'Carolan ("the last of the great Irish bards") about a mythical clash at the foot of the two hills beyond the Judge farm. Michael himself could have been a *seancha,* one of the storytellers who traveled with the chivalrous *fianna* warriors. He would speak of magical beings such as the shapeshifters, who could become what you needed most in the moment. He also would tell of how the real-life Saint Patrick passed through the Keshcarrigan area in the sixth century and how the nascent Christians gathered by the well at the base of Sidh Beag and its living water and declared it a *tobar naofa,* or holy place. How beside it rose Cill Tiobraid, the Church of the Well, and beside that a monastic settlement, *conhospitae,* where men and woman cohabited and raised children as they pursued a life of the spirit. How the Celtic Church permitted women to be priests despite official scolding from Rome in the sixth century. How that golden age ended when the Roman Church eclipsed the Celtic one.

He also told of centuries of British oppression, of the Great Famine, of the Penal Laws that prohibited Catholics from practicing their religion, of the fugitive clerics who hid out on Sidh Beag, saying secret Masses on the hill topped by mythic Fionn mac Cumhaill's resting place.

Michael the *seancha,* no doubt would have loved to bequeath his love for the Ireland of lilt and lore to his children, but this is a wealth you can pass on only as you live. And as the surgeries failed to prevent the infection from spreading to his brain, he became so ill he had difficulty even reaching the window.

At home, little Emmett would kneel by his bed every night and pray for the smiling father who was becoming as unseen as any higher being. Emmett would awaken to unanswered prayers and toddle off to school with his sisters while their mother headed for the hospital. The children often returned to an empty house.

On June 2, 1939, the mother came home and spoke four words.

"Your daddy died today."

Emmett left the house without a word. Dympna followed and realized he had not turned left toward the hospital and their school and church and buddies, but right, away from everything they knew. He stopped at the corner and stood silent and still.

Dympna came up beside him. The two remained there at the corner of Dean Street and Nevins Street, six-year-old twins standing mute at the far shore of their lives.

The body of forty-year-old Michael Judge was laid out in the parlor for the three-day wake as nuns told the children again and again, "A saint. Your father was a saint." His remains were then transported to St. Paul's Church. Emmett saved three of the 2½-by-3-inch holy cards given to Catholic mourners. He was just learning to read, but he likely was able to manage the typewritten particulars:

MICHAEL D. JUDGE
✝✝✝ Who Died ✝✝✝
On June 2, 1939

A prayer from St. Ambrose was printed at the top of the card:

> *We have loved him during life; let us not abandon him*
> *until we have conducted him by our prayers*
> *into the house of the Lord.*

The back identified the producer of the cards.

From the Franciscan Fathers.

The hearse swung past the Judge home for a prayer before continuing to St. John's Cemetery in Queens. The family followed in the car that had once been proof of their Irish luck, the mother wearing a black dress that Dympna thought made her look beautiful. The girls wore white dresses, Emmett a white suit with short pants, all bought big enough so the children would be able to wear them at their First Communion.

Their saintly father was now said to reside in a higher place than that hospital window, higher even than the new Empire State Building in Manhattan. The particulars of the afterlife were set forth in the Baltimore Catechism, whose numbered questions and answers his children learned by rote.

> *Q. 1376. Why does Christ judge men immediately after death?*
> *A. Christ judges men immediately after death to reward or punish them according to their deeds.*
>
> *Q. 1379. What is Hell?*
> *A. Hell is a state to which the wicked are condemned, and in which they are deprived of the sight of God for all eternity, and are in dreadful torments.*

The talk of damnation ran deep in Dympna, but the boy who so keenly felt the death of his dad was more taken with the promise of loss turned to bliss.

> *Q. 1395. What is Heaven?*
> *A. Heaven is the state of everlasting life in which we see God face to face, are made like unto Him in glory, and enjoy eternal happiness.*

Under the threat of hell and with the promise of heaven, the twins made their First Communion in the clothes they had worn to their father's funeral.

The Judge children continued to live on Dean Street with a mother already made fierce by her own upbringing and the stringency of her Church. Mary Ann now became only fiercer on her own and the children never knew what to expect. Erin would sometimes make the Sign of the Cross before coming into the house, as if this might protect her. But Dympna could seek no protection or comfort in the Almighty as described by the mother.

"She'd say, 'God sees what you're doing! God sees what you're doing!'" Dympna would recall. "I knew I was going to hell. I didn't know what I was doing to get there, but I knew I was going."

Emmett, however, was able to embrace Our Father as if he were a father, however judgmental and stern.

"He had a different relationship with God than I did," Dympna later said. "He believed in things I couldn't."

He himself would later say, "I've grown up with this God and I've always loved Him. For years I feared Him, but I always talked to Him because there was no father, no uncles, no brothers, no cousins. So God was the man in my life, and very often because He was the man—He was older—I was afraid of Him. But I knew that somehow He would take care of me, and He did."

The connection between Emmett and Our Father was direct and little disturbed by his mother's periodic rages at the Church. She retained an anti-clerical streak not unknown among Irish rebels.

"Too much religion is no good for anybody," she would say.

Emmett did find himself stirred, as well as mystified, by his mother's own direct connection.

"My mother's faith was so simple," he would recall. "It was so strange at times. She'd get upset and mad at the Pope, she'd get mad at the priests and nuns, but then she'd have all her little prayers. She had a great devotion to the Sacred Heart."

The Sacred Heart represents the Son of God's love for humankind in assuming human form and its attendant suffering. Mary Ann's supplications would sail forth on a sigh as a single word.

"Sacred-Heart-of-Jesus-have-mercy . . ."

A deep breath.

"Sacred-Heart-of-Jesus-have-mercy . . ."

Again and again, stirring Judge not with the words but the cadence, one older than the Church, older even than Jesus, something brought from Ireland like the ivy that now filled much of the back garden, an incantation from the time of the ancient Celtic gods.

"There was a rhythm to it, a magic to it," Judge would say. "Somehow it became part of me."

What was harder for Judge to fathom and accept was his mother's anger. He would write about it years later in a private journal.

My constant fear of mother and what I know now—did not know how to describe it then—her rage. She would put the fear of God into the Pope and so she often said, "I'll put the fear of God into you . . ." What a terrible thing to say to a child—what a burden to put on God. I am amazed how well and normal I turned out to be—A poor, innocent, good, hard-

*working kid getting the shit beat out of him over and over—for nothing
at all.*

Her temper could flare up in an instant. She had a frying pan in her hand
when she caught Emmett and his best friend, Jimmy Gilfeather, horsing around
in the basement.

"She smacked him right over the head with the frying pan," Gilfeather recalled. "I can still hear it ringing. Oh, what a shot!"

The twins were in the basement on Christmas when they heard a loud ar-
gument erupt upstairs between Mary Ann and two of her sisters, who were
now married and living in the Bronx. The sisters departed, never to visit
again, taking with them any chance Emmett would have even an uncle in his
life. He responded as he would in later years when circumstances brought out
the worst in people.

"He pretended nothing was happening," Dympna said.

Mary Ann, a widow and the sole support of her family, turned their home
into a boardinghouse. Money was tight, but she never let her children feel
poor, even when the scrumptiously secular bells of the ice cream man summoned those children whose families had a few coins to spare. The matriarch
of 230 Dean Street informed her brood that Judges do not indulge in anything so common and vulgar.

"Judges don't do that," Dympna later said.

Their mother was one of the Irish who, having been "in service," assumed
the airs of those they had served. She moved like gentry through the scruff of
South Brooklyn, maintaining her own sense of class.

"Delicatessen. That word sent shivers through my mother," Dympna said.

When their mother felt the children had departed even slightly from her
notion of decorum, she could be savage. She once turned without warning
outside church and slapped Dympna's face.

"I didn't know what I did," Dympna later said. "I still don't, but I'm sure
I did something."

Her twin found escape from the harrowing harshness at home by delighting in those he saw in the street who seemed untouched by such dark forces.

"He thought great people were the ones who had a good time, [who]
didn't suffer from guilt, who just did what they did every day," Dympna later
said.

Emmett began a lifelong passion for walking the city, seeing more proof each time he stepped outside the door that the face of God had not a scowl but a smile. His buoyed spirit reflexively sought to do the same for those he encountered who were sinking low. He and Dympna were walking on Schermerhorn Street when they were accosted by a panhandler. Emmett took the lone coin in his pocket and set it into the man's outstretched hand.

"What did you do that for?" Dympna demanded. "He's only going to buy beer."

Emmett answered in the patient tone he would always employ in citing a basic truth that seemed so obvious to him.

"It doesn't matter."

He said this with such absolute conviction that Dympna immediately accepted it as so. She had no idea how Emmett knew such truths. "It wasn't insight, it was outsight," she later said. "His faith was intuitive. It wasn't three Our Fathers and three Hail Marys. It had nothing to do with what we learned in school or at home. It came out of him."

Not that anyone at St. Paul's Grammar School seemed much interested. The nuns there were Sisters of Charity who generally viewed a child as a small person who was not so much to be taught as curbed and controlled.

"I was an adult before I was a little kid," Dympna later said.

The sisters did not hesitate to inflict corporal punishment, and the children knew better than to complain when they got home.

"The nun hit you, you didn't dare say anything at home because you got it again," a classmate named Gerry Whelan recalled. "The nun wouldn't have hit you unless you had done something wrong."

Back in Ireland, Whelan had a grandmother known as Mary the Man, renowned for knocking flat a cleric who dared to beat her child. Here in America, Whelan's family was no more likely than Mary Ann Judge to protest when their kids suffered such treatment.

"When you're an immigrant, you don't argue," Whelan said.

The principal, Sister Noleen, walked the halls with the vigorous, athletic stride of doom itself.

"She hit harder than a truck driver," Whelan remembered. "If one of the nuns said, 'Here's a note, go to Sister Noleen,' the boys would have rather run away."

Students, of course, wore uniforms, a white shirt and blue trousers for the boys, a white blouse and blue skirt for the girls. The Judge children always arrived neatly turned out, even if they were not among the kids so rich they always had an extra nickel for chocolate milk. Children of whatever means had either to sit on their hands or hold them behind their backs when they were not working. The school day began with the Pledge of Allegiance and the first period was always religion. There was no science, not even Galileo's least heretical principles regarding falling objects. But there was grammar, grammar, grammar.

When he was called upon to read aloud in class, Emmett would falter repeatedly with a stuttering "Errumm . . . errumm" that was puzzling to Dympna, for he had no trouble at home reading the funny papers. The problem did not seem to be shyness either. To his twin sister it appeared he was suffering less from stage fright than from a chilling of the spirit.

The youngsters were ranked by seating, Dympna always in the first row with the smart ones. Her twin was consigned to the second or third row as "the dumb one." He later wrote in a letter, "I remember when I was going on 11 or 12. No one thought this young man had anything to say and *I did*. And no one heard me."

His standing in class was not for lack of effort.

His friend Gilfeather would recall him practicing his signature at home hour after hour.

"What's that for?" Gilfeather asked.

"I want to get it right," Emmett said.

In keeping with what some considered Brooklyn's true religion, Emmett was a big Dodger fan and would slip into Ebbets Field hours before a game to avoid paying. He cheered himself hoarse when his favorite player, lucky Number 13, pitcher Ralph Branca, was on the mound.

What he loved about baseball was also what made it so daunting. This was not a fluid game where you could develop your skills in the tumult of the scrum. Baseball was a series of individual trials. The pitch, the swing, the catch were all momentary solos, each an opportunity for a great player to electrify a stadium, or for an untutored boy who was not a natural to humiliate himself in front of his friends. Voices that cheered the Dodgers would just as loudly jeer a bumbler, and Emmett saw no other option than to slip away when the boys back at his home parish would start up a sandlot baseball game. A father who was enjoying life everlasting in the Kingdom of Heaven could not show you how to throw and catch and hit.

• • •

But as an altar boy serving the 6:30 A.M. Mass, Michael Judge's only begotten son shone even at that early hour the way other boys shone on a baseball diamond. He had a quality that caught the eye, a spark in the dimness of the unvarying ritual, as bright as the flame of the candle he bore. He would then hurry the seven blocks home for breakfast and dash to school, arriving just in time to begin the day with a lesson in religion as a coda to be memorized like grammar.

The only reprieve would come when he and his fellow altar boy Gilfeather were summoned to serve a funeral Mass. They escaped the stultifying classroom, pulled on the altar boys' black cassocks, and tolled the bells slowly to announce the ritual that Emmett had first witnessed when the person in the coffin was his father.

The boys then joined the procession that escorted the body into the church. Emmett would see the mourning family take the front pew, just as his family had. He would once more listen to *Pater Noster, qui es in coelis . . .*

For Emmett at such moments, religion ceased to be just another lesson to memorize. Religion became a real-life drama where he watched the biggest issues of human existence bear down on individual working people in St. Paul's Parish. Emmett's identification with those in the pews may be what helped him always to see the people, not the church, the figure on the cross, not the crucifix.

After the coffin was escorted out, the undertaker, Harry Quayle, always tipped Judge and Gilfeather each a quarter. The wages of sin might have been death, but the wages of a funeral were enough to get a frappé or a marshmallow sundae. Unless, of course, Emmett happened to encounter a panhandler along the way.

Judge and Gilfeather both loved ringing the church's three bells. They would clamber up the stairs from the basement to the choir loft and then climb the steel spiral ladder to the wooden platform above the organ pipes where the three bell ropes were within easy reach. They grabbed a rope and a young boy's weight translated to a sound that rang out across the whole parish and beyond.

"You could hang on it like the Hunchback of Notre Dame," Gilfeather recalled.

One day, Emmett summoned the courage to climb up past the steel beam from which the bells hung. He reached a small platform maybe ten stories up and peered out a tiny aperture, far beyond the streets of his daily experience. The Statue of Liberty. The Empire State Building, just two years older than he was himself, still a wonder, rising nearly fifteen hundred feet, much taller than any steeple, at the time the world's tallest building. Best of all, the Brooklyn Bridge, stretching from his known world to what he even then felt sure was the very center of the universe, from all that was to all that was possible.

Judge was eight years old on the Sunday in December when the Japanese bombed Pearl Harbor. Many of the older boys in the neighborhood enlisted and were shipped to places far beyond the steeple's view. Judge and Gilfeather built shoeshine boxes from grocery crates and began hopping the subway to Manhattan. They made as much as forty dollars a day shining shoes at Grand Central Terminal and Times Square and Penn Station, looking in particular for sailors home on shore leave who tipped with wild abandon. They also had to keep an eye out for cops, who deemed shoeshine boys a public nuisance.

One day they got caught. The cop took them to a nearby building and then into a freight elevator.

"He said, 'Okay, boys, now let me have your money,' and we took out our money and we gave him the money," Judge would remember.

The cop ended with a warning.

" 'Now, you go back to Brooklyn and you don't come over here to New York anymore.' "

Judge felt as powerless as he indeed was.

"I was a little kid . . . I had no father, no brother, no uncles, no cousins," he would say. "So, that was the end of that. I took my shoeshine box and went back to Brooklyn."

From then on, Judge and Gilfeather shined shoes in their home borough, getting sailor-sized tips from the henchmen who lounged at the Montague Street office of the gangster Frank Costello. The streets around the Judge home had a fair share of tough guys. Exactly a year after the attack on Pearl Harbor a stick-up man fatally shot a cop on the very corner where Judge had stood after learning of his father's death. The bars like Flynn's and Lavin's and Toomey's were crammed with fathers who had a particular measure of success for their sons.

"The biggest thing to brag about was, 'Well, none of my kids went to jail,'" Whelan later said.

Mary Ann would point out Sing Sing prison when driving her children upstate on summer outings. Her feelings regarding priests and religion did not stop her from believing that these gray walls were the destination of all who did not attend a Catholic high school.

"You see that?" she would say. "That's where you'll be."

Back on Dean Street, neighborhood boys cheered Willie "That's Where the Money Is" Sutton after the bank robber was arrested outside a rooming house just down from the Judges'. Emmett's hero became a smiling, bare-toed figure he met while on an errand for the Sisters at St. Paul's.

The nuns had learned of his Manhattan adventures, but rather than chastise him they saw an opportunity to spare themselves some bother. Even after he stopped shining shoes, they continued to ask him to stop by St. Francis of Assisi Church near Penn Station and pick up Mass cards, which are given to the family of the newly bereaved as a pledge that the departed will be remembered in a Mass.

"When someone died, they would put me on the subway," Judge later said.

Judge would get off at Penn Station, cross Seventh Avenue, and start down West Thirty-first to a Romanesque church squeezed among its drab commercial neighbors. Above the doorway was a huge mosaic of a figure in a brown robe holding out his arms in welcome. This was Saint Francis of Assisi, a wealthy merchant's son and onetime troubadour who at the turn of the thirteenth century outraged his father by giving everything in his purse to a beggar in the marketplace just as Judge had given that coin on Schermerhorn Street. Francis subsequently announced he was taking "Lady Poverty" as his bride, and set off barefoot in a peasant's rough tunic cinched by a rope, a joyful example of unencumbered spirit. He founded the Order of Franciscans Minor and it had survived various splits over the centuries to establish far-flung geographical "provinces." Holy Name Province of New York and New Jersey had built the church whose twelve stone steps Emmett now ascended.

He entered to see an even bigger mosaic, the biggest in America. The myriad tiles above the altar depicted the Virgin Mary holding the infant Jesus as she tread upon the serpent of Evil. To the right of the altar was a statue of Saint Joseph with two fatherly hands on the shoulders of a Jesus about the age of Emmett when he lost his dad. A relatively small mosaic above showed

Joseph on his sickbed, as the patron saint of the Happy Death as well as the family.

Along the walls were what Judge would later learn were the busiest confessionals in America. The parish had been just another like Judge's own St. Paul's until the neighborhood turned commercial in the 1920s. St. Francis of Assisi was left a parish without parishioners and became what is known as a shrine church, or a service church visited largely by commuters, shoppers, tourists, and other passersby. The worshippers themselves became a kind of mosaic of nationality and class and race.

Many preferred to confess here rather than to their parish priest, who might give you a certain look later, particularly if the sin was of the flesh and now there you were, stepping up for Communion with your spouse. Here at St. Francis you could confess any sin large or small in true anonymity. And Franciscan friars had a reputation for being less scolding than the average agent of the Almighty.

As a result, more than 800,000 people a year, or 2,000 a day, trooped in. One regular visitor termed St. Francis the criminal court of the Catholic Church. Others said that if Times Square was the crossroads of the world, then St. Francis was its confessional. The place was so busy that a second church had been established in the basement by the time Emmett chanced along. This was the one that captivated him.

The unassuming steps descended to a chamber whose thick, windowless walls shut out the noise of the street. The lower church was dimly lit, almost dingy, but the altar was as simple as true faith and there were no soaring ceilings or imposing statues to dwarf all who entered. This was a house of worship where you were less aware of the building than of those who prayed there, and with this awareness came an intimacy with the whole great variety of them, the diversity itself seeming divine.

Amid this holy hodgepodge, Judge glimpsed a man wearing the same brown robe as the welcoming figure in the mosaic outside. Judge's shoe shining had made him reflexively look at people's feet, and he noticed this very different kind of father was wearing sandals.

The man was Henry Vincent Lawler, but he introduced himself in the Franciscan way simply as Father Henry. He smiled as if it were only natural to do so in church. He spoke in the warm, paternal tones of a boy's ideal dad.

Judge got the Mass card and should have been on his way. He instead found himself trailing behind as Father Henry tended the candles.

"There was something simple and beautiful about him," Judge later recalled. "Watching him, I realized that I didn't care for material things all that much. I would just walk around and follow him and I loved his brown robe and sandals. I knew then that I wanted to be a friar."

At the end of grammar school, Dympna continued on to the well-regarded all-girls Bishop McDonald High School on Eastern Parkway. The place for boys to go if the family could manage it was "The Prep," St. Francis Preparatory School on Butler Street.

"That was one of the classy schools," Whelan later said. "That's where the people with money went."

Judge was able to enroll only because his mother managed to scrimp and save the three-hundred-dollar yearly tuition. He might have imagined the hand of God was at work when he arrived at the school named after the founder of Father Henry's order. The brutal truth came at the hands of brown-robed men who slapped and hit as part of a tradition of corporal punishment brought from Ireland by the two Franciscans who established the school in 1858. The faculty's enduring reputation for brutality was seen as proof of quality.

"The stricter the school, the more you were getting your money's worth," Whelan said.

Emmett and his six hundred fellow students were pummeled with such gusto that outrage would still boil out of him in the last days of his life.

Judge would recount being taught how to conjugate "to love" in Latin.

"It's *amo, amas, amat.* Say it now!" the brother would command.

Emmett would then do his best.

"*Amo . . .*"

"*Amat . . .*"

Bang!

"*Amas . . .*"

Bang!

"*Amat . . .*"

Bang!

"*Amo . . .*"

"*Amas . . .*"

"*Amat . . .*"

Bang!

Emmett quickly learned not to complain to his mother when he got home.

"After they hit me, she'd go after me," he recalled.

She would order him to bend over the couch and she would choose one of her two usual instruments of discipline.

"The strap and the spatula. My father's razor strap," he would remember. She would shout the Irish word for *idiot* as she swung.

"*Amadán!*"

Bang!

"*Amadán!*"

Bang!

"*Amadán!*"

Emmett was then reaching the age when he began to wonder what it was to be a man and how to find his way there and how he might measure up, when he was feeling the first stirrings of urges he could not immediately name. He was turbulent with feelings that are common to all boys but whose very mention would have been branded as shameful and prompted beatings both at home and at school. He later wrote in a letter:

> *Year[s] 13 to 15 were the absolute worst ones of my life. You would not recognize me then. I felt so out of touch because no one under-stood me or knew how to support me. I hated it. No father, no broth-ers, no cousins, no uncles. No one. My poor mother tried, but, being a young widow, there was no one that she could turn to. It was just some time I had to go through and do it alone. We used to call it pu-berty.*

The most feared figure in the school was beefy, six-foot-three Brother Begnicus, who taught religion. Emmett learned in between beatings how a figure on a crucifix had come alive and instructed Saint Francis to "rebuild my church which you see is falling into ruin," and how the crucified Jesus was speaking not of bricks and mortar but of spirit and faith. Emmett quaked as he recited the opening line of the prayer written nearly eight centuries before by the saint these brothers ostensibly followed.

"Lord, make me an instrument of your peace . . . errumm, errumm . . ."

Bang!

Begnicus liked to hoist a boy off the floor by his neck and slap his face. He would remain one person in whom Emmett would have difficulty discerning good.

"Can you imagine getting up every morning and facing that and watching the other kids being beaten up, too?" Dympna later asked.

Emmett worked at his studies only to *errumm* and bumble like a shirker under the threat of a beating. The threat then would be realized with a slap or a punch and he would falter all the more, knowing that any student who failed two subjects was automatically expelled.

Judge would not have been heartbroken to leave, but his mother was spending what was by their standards a fortune to send him there, and she still considered public high school to be the path to prison. The only other alternative was to commit himself to his childhood ambition when he was still not much more than a child. He now sent away for applications to any seminaries that might take him.

In his mother's experience, the priesthood led not to sanctity and grace but to sanctimony and tyranny. She was emphatic in her opposition.

"She didn't like it at all," Emmett would remember. "The story of the Irish mothers wanting their sons to be priests, that was not my mother. She wanted the name to be carried on. She wanted grandchildren."

Emmett went ahead and filled out the applications. His treatment by the brothers at the Prep had not made him forget that other brown-robed figure, Father Henry, at the church on West Thirty-first Street. Emmett told Father Henry that he had decided to apply to the Franciscan seminary in upstate New York. The priest came by the Judge house for dinner.

Emmett must have hoped that Father Henry would have the same effect on his mother as he had on him, but the priest arrived late and was trembling all over when he sat down at the table. Mary Ann no doubt recognized the drink-induced tremens. The priest then sought to excuse his tardiness by saying a woman had come up to the altar and levitated. Mary Ann was left at a rare loss for words.

A letter arrived soon afterward saying that Emmett had been accepted by the Franciscans. Mary Ann was all the more adamant in her opposition. Her son kept after her. She finally relented, perhaps only because he had no other ready options.

"Let him go and let him find out," she said.

• • •

So, on a hot and humid September 11 in 1948, fifteen-year-old Robert Emmett Judge left his house in a black suit carrying a small suitcase that contained among his scant belongings his picture of Dodger Ralph Branca. He continued on to the Nevins Street subway station.

"Bag in hand, flanked by my two sisters, one my twin, I was on the brink of a new life," he later wrote.

Their mother rode the IRT express with them to Pennsylvania Station.

"I was frightened for many reasons, but a big one was that I would be alone without them now."

3

The railroad he would come to call the "weary Erie" carried young Judge and a handful of other young seminarians 129 miles up into the Catskill Mountains and stopped just long enough for them to step off at a depot not much more than a shack. He scuffled with the others through the tiny town of Callicoon in half the time it would have taken him to walk from home to St. Paul's.

"Lovely place, I guess, but as a city boy . . ." he later said. "I don't know how I lasted six years there."

A curving road took them up a steep hill and at the summit stood a gray stone tower topped by a golden cross. St. Joseph's Seraphic Seminary looked stern and improbably huge in so small a town, and it loomed ever bigger as he ascended in the lingering summer heat. He reached a long circular drive and proceeded past a ten-foot statue of St. Joseph holding the son born of his wife but who was not his son. Here he was to undergo the first stage of a thirteen-year ordeal.

Judge would remember reaching the main entrance only to be brusquely told the front was off-limits to seminarians save for special occasions. The new arrivals were directed around to the back, and they entered a realm dedicated to life as conceived by the vibrant, embracing Saint Francis of long ago.

But that Franciscan spirit had been made steely by a considerably more dour Francis, Father Francis Koch, leader of friars driven from Germany by Prince Otto Bismarck's *Kulturkampf* against the Catholic Church. These German friars landed in Newark and founded Holy Name Province in 1901. Koch crossed the Hudson River in 1904 to establish St. Francis of Assisi on

West Thirty-first Street. He spent the last fifteen years of his life founding churches in northwest New Jersey and upstate New York. He died in 1920, supposedly after trudging through a blizzard to hear a confession.

A quarter-century later, the province and its seminary in particular continued to be ruled by Germanic discipline further stiffened by persecution and exile. One friar would later say, "The notion was be hard, be tough. Test your mettle. They weren't necessarily bad guys. I'm sure some of them had a mean streak, and it probably wasn't too difficult for them."

Judge was assigned a bed and a locker in the big open dormitory on the top floor. The walls were the domain of crucifixes and holy pictures, so he propped his Ralph Branca photo on a chair.

The next morning and every morning thereafter, he was awakened by a cowbell rung by the prefect, who walked down the long row of beds. Fifty students filled tin basins from a single spigot and hurried to wash up in time for six A.M. chapel. Being late was not an option.

Breakfast was at seven A.M., overseen by a prefect who sat at an elevated table. They ate in silence unless the prefect said *prosit,* or "as you were," signaling they were permitted to talk.

Classes started at eight A.M. and were rigorous. Judge was further daunted by finding himself in a group so scholastically brilliant that the instructors dubbed it Lux Mundi, "Light of the World." These brown-robed teachers did not resort to physical abuse, but Judge sometimes felt the verbal scolding was aimed less at humility than humiliation.

"They might have been trying to teach you 'You're not doing enough for God,'" he would recall. "What they actually said was 'You're useless. Absolutely useless.'"

He would remember being ruled by a single, all-pervasive emotion, the very one that had governed him at St. Francis Prep and St. Paul's Grammar School.

"Fear, fear, fear," he would write in a journal years later. "Everything is about fear. I was filled with it every hour of every day. They controlled us by fear—Never once a positive word. 'How good you are!' or 'Nice job!' or 'Keep plugging!' . . . Bastards!"

He assumed he was at the bottom of the class and did not learn otherwise until he read his file almost a half-century later.

"I was 12th out of the class of 19," he would write. "Could have sworn I was 18th or 19th. There was no one ever—to affirm or applaud or correct me on the way. So my personal self-value judgments were so off kilter. No one there."

As psychically battered as he felt, Judge did not fail to recognize the extra pressures experienced by the lone African-American student, Ben Taylor, of mean-streeted Jersey City. Taylor had initially applied to several other religious orders, only to be turned away because of his color.

"Put it charitably and say they weren't ready," Taylor would later say.

The Franciscans officially welcomed those of all races, but a number of the friars and students at the seminary proved not so ready, and the belittling suffered by all carried an extra sting for Taylor. The person who constantly sought to buoy him up was Judge, who had learned the power of a positive word by never receiving one.

"He saw people as people," Taylor would later say. "He used to say, 'You're the boy from Jersey City!' In other words, I had a lot of ways of survival."

Judge retained his particular *lux* when he served as a candle bearer at festive occasions. He was told his voice was too untrained for him to be one of the singers, but he was able to join in the informal sing-songs. His joy made up for any lack in ability as he sent Irish ballads ringing off the seminary's austere stone walls.

He formed friendships that had an intensity and intimacy he had not known back in Brooklyn. He would later write, "There were two or three other young boys like myself, and we shared everything, especially our feelings, those of fifteen-year-old boys, and of being away from home and missing our families."

Here he truly was one of the guys. He would write in an article of the complete absence of gals: "Another frequent topic was what being totally cut off from women meant to us, especially in our puberty years. Our final vows of poverty, chastity, and obedience would seal us into being celibate men, and that meant we would need plenty of mutual support to be faithful to our call."

His body suddenly seemed to have a life of its own, and the longing for the dad he never knew was joined by other deep longings whose nature he did not immediately understand, yearnings that stayed with him through the day and the night and the next day, in chapel, during class, at meals, in bed, lying in the darkness, totally alone but so close to his classmates he could hear them breathing. He was not sure exactly what he felt, only that he felt it deeply. He imagined he must be different and sometimes had the wild thought he might not be different if only he had a dad to teach him to be a regular kid. His passions were even wilder, and he was not reckless only because nobody signaled a willingness to be reckless with him. He could speak to the others about the absence of girls, but he could not talk about the presence of boys. And he certainly could not talk to his mother about whatever it was he was feeling. She went into a tizzy if one of his sisters left a slip in the bathroom, saying, "Your brother might see it!"

He would write in a private journal years later, when he had the perspective of time and was reaching a clear sense of his sexuality, that he had been drawn to several of his classmates.

> *I was the only one—so I thought. We never knew, or if we did, we never discussed anything gay. I was madly in love—whatever that meant—with so many students. But I am not sure that I knew what it was all about. I did know that you were thrown out—next train—for being caught in any kind of sexual activity. I did not try it, but I had a boldness and was willing to take the chance if the chance came—Wow! How in God's name did I do 13 years of the celibate existence demanded of us in such a strong, straight and gay manly life? I know I am disciplined—I can do anything I put my mind to—It might be brutal—but—I'll stick to it to the end—Faithful, too.*

On beautiful evenings when other lads his age might have been taking a lover for a romantic walk, he and the other seminarians circled a small pond on the seminary grounds, proving their Franciscan passion by saying seven decades of the rosary where another religious order would have said just five. They then went inside for study hall, followed by lights out at 9:30 P.M.

Each progression in the day was signaled by the cowbell, and Judge became so averse to such unrelenting management of time that to the end of his days he would never wear a watch. He would constantly be giving away watches given to him by those who pitied the poor friar who did not have one. The only watch he ever owned was the lozenge-shaped one that would be found among his personal effects in a small manila envelope on which he had written a single word.

"Daddy's."

The hands were frozen where the watch had unwound to a final tick after his father's death.

Over the summer breaks from the seminary, Judge earned tuition money by digging graves at St. John's Cemetery, where his father was buried. He also worked with Dympna at the Peerless Christmas Lights factory on Atlantic Avenue in Brooklyn. He occasionally dawdled while socketing bulbs into long strings, and the supervisor would bellow, "Get back and screw!" He would just laugh, a bit of a rebel, a bit of a rascal.

"I was thinking, 'Where is he getting the nerve to do it?'" Dympna recalled.

Most likely, the supervisor at her fiercest seemed a coddler compared to some of the friars. Judge appeared altogether untroubled even when he was finally fired, perhaps because he would soon be headed back to where the rules were invoked in the name of a much higher authority than the owner of Peerless.

Not everybody thought Judge should necessarily return to the seminary. He was sitting on his stoop when Whelan decided that duty required him to dissuade his friend from becoming a priest.

"Look, are you doing this for yourself or are you doing this for your mother?" Whelan would recall saying. "You know my mother's in a hole in the ground. In a few years, your mother's going to be in a hole in the ground, and if you're not doing this because you want to do it, you're going to be a very unhappy guy in an organization you may not wish to belong to."

"No, no, no, I'm doing this on my own," Judge said.

Gilfeather returned from the army, and Judge quizzed him about his travels. Gilfeather said he was keeping mum about the girls he met.

"You're going to be a priest, I can't give away my confessions yet," Gilfeather said.

On September 11, 1951, Judge passed from the high school to the college level at Callicoon. Nobody could have foreseen anything like what would occur exactly a half century later. One date he was sure would go down in history was October 3, when Bobby Thomson of the New York Giants hit a ninth-inning home run off none other than Judge's favorite player, Dodger pitcher Ralph Branca. The homer cost the Dodgers the National League pennant and was dubbed "the shot heard 'round the world," news of it reaching even a realm so removed as the seminary. Judge continued to keep the picture of Branca on display and would rattle off facts and figures (three times an all-star, twenty-one wins in a season) that made the Dodgers' Number 13 one of the greats despite that one unlucky pitch.

After six years at Callicoon, Judge proceeded to St. Bonaventure's Monastery, a gloomy and decrepit brick building in Paterson, New Jersey. There he received his first habit, which was frayed and patched. He cinched the waist with a rope that had three knots symbolizing the three vows he would soon be taking. He might have been taken for a friar were it not for "the tail," a strip of cloth that descended a few inches from under his hood down his back. He began what was known as the novitiate.

"You go into a real cloister," Judge later said. "For a year and a day you're locked in."

Any novice who left at any time for any reason would be required to begin all over again the following year. A novice who was a day late for the start because of a storm at sea was told he would simply have to wait a year to begin. One novice whose mother died was told he would get no dispensation to attend her funeral, and he chose to remain in the monastery.

St. Bonaventure's was a sort of boot camp, complete with an intimidating drill instructor known as the novice master who repeatedly asked Judge, "What are *you* doing here?"

The twenty-two novices lived in small individual rooms and the day began at 5:30 A.M. with a knock on the door and the words *"Avé Maria."* The novice was expected to reply immediately, *"Grantia plena."*

Judge literally developed calluses on his knees, for when he was not praying, he and the others were scrubbing floors. They were given brushes about the size they might use on their teeth and instructed to pay particular attention to a two-inch-wide white stripe that ran along the baseboard.

When they washed dishes, they were expected to say the rosary, and they generally did, unless the novice master was away. The night ended with each novice standing in his room, stripped to the waist, the door shut, but the transom open so he could hear the reader in the hallway. Each then commenced what was known as "taking the discipline," meaning to whip his bare back with a small cat-o'-nine-tails. Judge was not one of the novices who generated the necessary sound effect by whipping their pillow.

At nine P.M. it was lights-out, and on the warm nights Judge would lie awake, his back stinging. He would listen through the open window to the sounds of the surrounding Italian neighborhood, the outdoor parties and boisterous voices and music, what he took to be the true sounds of God.

He would drift off, and the next sound he heard was a knock and a joyless "*Avé Maria*" signaling the start of another day of having his faith tested by religion. He would sometimes seek to lighten his comrades' spirits by rising from his chair as if he had suddenly become some octogenarian friar. His fellow novitiates would burst out laughing, the solemnity of their surroundings making their giddiness all the more uncontrollable and therefore liberating.

At other times, Judge would try to tell a joke, but he would never get through to the end without cracking up. His laughter was so infectious that his comrades would find themselves laughing along at a punch line they never heard.

On August 12, 1955, Judge and the twenty-one others completed the noviciate. He attested to his desire to take the next step in a letter he wrote to his provincial, the friar elected to head Holy Name Province.

> *I ask you for the love of God to admit me to the profession of simple vows in the Franciscan Order in the Clerical State. It is my firm conviction, after having spent six years in the Franciscan Seminary at Callicoon and the year of Novitiate that God is calling me to live the life and Holy Rule of the Friars Minor all the days of my life. It is my firm promise to remain in this Order all the days of my life and after due preparation to be ordained a priest of God thus to save my soul and to be an instrument in saving the souls of others.*

Judge took his "simple vows," the seminarian's equivalent of getting engaged, declaring his intention to live a life of poverty, chastity, and obedience.

"Poverty that you would own nothing," Judge later said. "Chastity that you would lead a celibate life. And obedience that you would obey the will of the community."

He also took a new name.

"We were supposed to be starting a new life," he explained years later.

His first choice was Michael, in memory of his father, but there were already more than three friars named Michael in their province, and the rules prohibited there being another. He added his mother's maiden name, an honor which seemed to give her little pleasure. She had keenly felt the long years of having her son locked away, and now he was no longer to be known as Emmett.

"That killed mother," Dympna later said. "*And to take his name off him.*"

The new Fallon Michael Judge could not shake the desire to take his father's name, and he wrote the head provincial in New York seeking an exception to the rule.

> *I wish to change my name from Fallon Michael to Michael Fallon. The reason is that I am the only son of Michael Judge, who died after suffering for three years. It is due to my devotion to him and the wish to carry on his name that I make this request.*
>
> *Obediently in St. Francis,*
> *Fallon Michael Judge*

Permission was granted. Now seven years into his training, Michael Fallon Judge and the other newly named candidates moved on to the next stage at a former Air Force building turned Franciscan "house of philosophy" in Rye Beach, New Hampshire. He wrote to his family on September 7 of that year.

"It is no picnic."

He reported he was permitted to send only three letters a month. He regretted being unable to respond quickly to a kind note from a friend.

"I would like to write him, but it will take a few weeks before we get paper again."

He concluded by asking his family to pray for him as he took this next step toward priesthood.

"Now I must strive earnestly for the precious goal."

• • •

Judge spent the next three years struggling with philosophy, cosmology, epistemology, Hebrew, sociology, and Latin. He was aware that their superiors periodically met to pass around a box into which each would place either a white or a black ball in judgment of a student. A single black ball meant the student could be asked to leave, never to become a friar, a decade of study and prayer and abnegation come to nothing.

Michael voiced his fears of expulsion as fellow student Cassian Miles was cutting his hair.

"You know, Michael, they won't push you out," Miles would remember saying.

In truth, Miles was not so sure. He was certain that Judge would be a truly stellar priest if he got the chance to become one.

"I was praying they would never dismiss him," Miles later said.

Judge was still there at the end of the third stage and joined the others in solemnizing their vows, pledging to observe them for life. The fledgling friars spent the next three years at Holy Name College in a northeast corner of Washington, D.C., studying dogma, theology, liturgy, and homiletics. Everybody's favorite class was a church history course taught by a friar who had a fondness for the untold story.

"The Council of Trent and the bishops coming with their girlfriends and concubines," Miles later said. "All the inside stuff."

The students began what amounted to pastoral internships. Judge spent a few hours each week at St. Elizabeth's mental hospital, feeling the effects of his own confinement.

"We had no training with people at all," he later said. "Everything was internal, schools and books."

He assembled a group of patients to say the rosary, and a somewhat subdued woman served as the leader, announcing the series of "mysteries," or events in Jesus' life, and beginning the particular prayers for everyone else to join in. The limits of the therapeutic effect became apparent when he returned the following week.

"Working at St. E's Hosp—Going into the lockup cell alone with padded walls and quiet lady who week earlier was 'Rosary Leader,'" he wrote in a note to himself.

He discovered that the asylum was one venue where his singing was actually appreciated. He particularly delighted in "Frankie and Johnnie," singing as one who had lost love before he ever had it, crooning on through the end, his voice resounding off the madhouse walls.

Twice a week the students were eligible to ask (for the love of God) for a WIC (a walk in collar, pronounced "wick") or a WIH (a walk in habit, pronounced "wee"). They would then go "rolling," which consisted of standing at the curb and holding their black fedoras out in such a way as to alert motorists in the know that they needed a ride downtown. The students' prayers to get back in time for evening prayer were often far more fervent than the evening prayer itself. The smaller mysteries of their faith came to include always returning with at least seconds to spare.

"I guess the guardian angels were with us," Miles later said.

In the chapel, students from all three years would sit in stalls facing one another. They would chant the Breviary, the book of daily prayer in Latin.

"It was a great sound," Miles said. "We didn't understand too much of what we were saying. Especially in the first year."

On January 20, 1961, Judge and his comrades were permitted to WIC in their black overcoats and fedoras through the freshly fallen snow and biting cold to the Capitol for John F. Kennedy's inauguration. Kennedy was the first Catholic president of the United States, and Irish as well. But more than that, he was what Judge most admired in people of whatever faith or background: Kennedy was vibrantly alive, driven not by guilt or fear but by the excitement of being. He had youth and wit and charisma and what Dympna described in her twin as "outsight." He summoned what was best in people with that instantly famous call, "Ask not what your country can do for you, but what you can do for your country." He ended his inaugural address by calling to action the faith at the core of all the major religions: ". . . asking His blessing and His help, but knowing that here on earth God's work must truly be our own."

John F. Kennedy then paraded down to the White House to begin his first day as president. Michael F. Judge trudged with his comrades back to Holy Name for the final weeks before his ordination, when he would finally become a *peest*.

On the cold and rainy morning of February 25, 1961, Judge and his comrades trooped up to the Franciscan monastery next to Holy Name College. The monastery is run by a chapter of friars charged with overseeing the sacred sites in the Holy Land, a responsibility the Church had given the Franciscans since the Crusades. The students had nothing to do with the monastery until this, their ordination day, when they entered the main chapel with the vestments of priests over their habits. Ordination could not seem more different than inauguration as they prostrated themselves before Archbishop Egidio Vagnozzi, the Pope's representative in the United States. Vagnozzi happened to be the son of a hero firefighter in Rome.

But for Judge there could have been no higher office than the one he now assumed.

"Archbishop Vagnozzi, the Apostolic Delegate, laid his hands firmly on my head and gifted me with the priesthood," Judge later wrote. "Glorious!"

Michael's own hands, big and thick and strong, were anointed and bound together with a ceremonial cloth that was then presented to his mother. She was in attendance, even though she had urged him to reconsider the night before. Dympna was also present, as was Erin, who had prayed through the entire night as an ordination gift.

Judge and the eighteen other new priests arrayed themselves on the altar and raised their hands to bestow their first blessings on their families before scattering to their home parishes to say their first Mass. Judge arrived back in Brooklyn seeming the real-life version of happy Father O'Malley of the hit forties movies *Going My Way* and *The Bells of St. Mary's*. He was, in the words of one friend, "More Bing Crosby than Bing Crosby." He smiled and laughed and sang as if he had stepped out of some sunny tale rather than from thirteen years of being shut away and constantly told that he was not really friar material.

After more than a decade of scowls from priests and brothers, Judge still saw a grin on the face of God. His tormentors had not dissuaded him from what he intuitively understood as a young boy when he told his sister it did not matter what a drunk did with a coin, that it only mattered that you gave it to him. That God was to be found in goodness just as the devil is to be found in evil.

He had learned in the third row of St. Paul's what it would have meant to have somebody value what he said.

He had learned at St. Francis Prep what it was like to have somebody seize upon only the bad in you.

He had learned in Callicoon that you do not need to be a singer to sing.

He had learned at St. Bonaventure the saving grace of laughter.

All this added up to a true religious education, if not the one that was intended.

He was ready to make God's work truly his own.

Mrs. Michael D. Judge
joyfully announces the
Ordination to the Holy Priesthood
of her son
The Reverend Michael Fallon Judge
of the Order of Friars Minor

First Solemn Mass
Sunday, the twenty-sixth of February
at ten-fifteen o'clock
Saint Paul's Church
Court and Congress Streets
Brooklyn, New York

Enclosed with the invitation were three prayer cards. One invoked his father as well as the object of his mother's veneration.

May the name of my father, Michael, be written in Your Sacred Heart, O Jesus.

Another of the cards had a drawing of Saint Francis. The remaining card bore a Celtic cross and the Hymn of St. Patrick. The back of the card read:

Michael F. Judge
Franciscan
A priest forever

Judge's picture appeared on page 8 of the *Brooklyn Eagle* along with a brief article that read much like a wedding announcement. "Father Judge is the son of Mary A. and the late Michael D. Judge," the paper noted.

At 10:15 A.M. the next day, Judge prepared to step before the altar at St. Paul's as Father Michael Fallon Judge.

He had agonized for days over what he should say in his first homily, but when the time came, he simply spoke his heart, saying whatever came to him, relying on the power of what he truly thought and felt. The particulars of what he said are lost to memory, but not the way he said it. A senior friar who had taught him logic and Latin at Rye Beach was in attendance and later wrote in a letter to him,

> *While I knew you had many good qualities, I did not realize what a terrific speaker or preacher you will be. You have the enviable gift of being able to stand up publicly and talk very honestly, sincerely, and naturally, letting the people know that you like them, and that you like God and that you want them to like Him too. You bowled me over Michael.*

The friar confessed a feeling that in some higher-ranked clergy would later trigger jealousy so intense they seemed to forget their faith: "I'd give anything to be able to do that."

The friar offered a prediction.

"Anyhow because you can do it, you will be able to draw many people to yourself and through yourself to God."

The friar did not fail to note the enthusiasm of the hands, which would not have been so surprising if Judge had been wielding a hammer or a nightstick or a fire hose.

"I was sure you were going to have a charlie horse or its equivalent in both arms from all the blessing you were doing."

The reception was held in Brooklyn Heights at the Towers Hotel, so named for the twin towers atop the building. The boy who never learned to play ball arrived at the hotel for the reception having proven to be a natural of another kind. He had been magnificent, so thrilling that his mother seemed to forget all her misgivings for the moment. The photograph Judge would later hang on the wall of his solitary chamber shows her sitting regally at the center of the elevated dais with her son the priest at the right hand, looking out at tables filled with people of the parish.

"Queen Mary," Judge later said.

4

The newly ordained Father Michael Judge proceeded to St. Anthony's Shrine in Boston, where he was beginning a final year of training that was much like a medical residency at a busy metropolitan hospital. His first official duty was to grind up the empty whiskey bottles so nobody would know the friars drank.

"They used to say the two major things you got back when you were ordained were booze and ice cream," Friar Chris Keenan later said.

The shrine was often packed to capacity, with Masses staggered every fifteen minutes in the upper and lower churches. Judge counseled the troubled and consoled the grieving and heard confession from the guilt-ridden.

"You just went out and started," he said. "You just learned."

Judge's mother remained as fierce as ever, and word came from Brooklyn that his twin had decided to escape after seeing a help wanted ad for a teacher at an Aramco oil company compound in Saudi Arabia. Judge's life was still so regimented that he was required to obtain written permission from the provincial in New York to see Dympna before she departed.

Judge hoped to embark on an adventure of his own as a missionary. The director of this program, Father Lambert Valentine, recognized his gifts and wrote in support of the application. He also wrote to Mary Ann Judge attesting to a change since those seminary days when instructors would ask her son what he was doing there.

> *I am writing this to you to let you know in what high esteem we hold*
> *Father Michael. I know, as his mother, this knowledge will make*

you all the more proud of him. I am still hoping to get him here
on our staff at Franciscan Pilgrimages, so say a prayer for this
intention.

The provincial decided otherwise, as he made known with a letter dated
August 2, 1962. "Enclosed, you will find an Obedience assigning you to
Saint Joseph's Friary . . ."

The embossed enclosure was in Latin, but that made the location of his
first posting seem no more auspicious. "Ad conventum S. Ioseph, E. Rutherford, N.J."

Judge's analysis was pure Brooklyn.

"Jersey is Jersey."

St. Joseph's proved to be an old Franciscan church atop a hill that rose from
the marshlands surrounding the blue-collar town of East Rutherford. The
pastor proved to be the spiritual if not corporal kin to the scowling and punishing Brother Begnicus.

Officially, the Mass was the same no matter who officiated and all the more
so because it was still said in Latin with the priest's back to the congregation. A
priest was only doing what every priest would do no matter where and precisely
so, for the consecration and bestowal was at the very core of Catholic belief.
Those who stepped up to receive Communion could take comfort in doing just
as those who had come before them, just as those who would follow, just as all
who shared their faith everywhere on earth, as it had been, was now, and seemingly always would be. The identity of the particular celebrant should have
been an incidental distraction. What was important was not who gave it to you,
but what you were given, the miraculously transubstantiated Body of Christ.

But when those same words were spoken by Judge, they took on a warm
exuberance even for those who did not understand Latin. He made it seem
truly the language of heaven, ringing not just with duty but with a joy to be
shared wherever God's gift was received.

"He had this special voice," former altar boy Robert Hickey recalled.

At the altar, during confession, in the rectory, on hospital visits, in every
encounter, Judge applied what he had learned despite what he had been
taught. He listened intently to teenagers in particular, no doubt because he
knew what a difference that would have made for him at that age.

Hickey was in the rectory, spilling out some pubescent angst when he got another measure of how different this new priest was.

"He said, 'It sounds like you need to go to confession,'" Hickey would recall. "Let me get my stole."

Father Michael rose and reached for the strip of cloth called "the yoke of the Lord" at his ordination, his badge of office, which, like a cop's badge, should have made it less important who he was than what he was as he performed his duties. He kissed the cross at the center and placed it around his neck as would any priest, but then sat back down, prepared to hear Hickey's sins right then and there, face-to-face. Hickey had never imagined confession being taken anywhere but in the dark booth in the church, a partition separating priest and penitent so they were able to hear but not see one another.

Without even the illusion of anonymity, Hickey could hardly more than sputter at first, but then he began to steady himself in Father Michael's gaze. Judge seemed to be the most inappropriate surname for this priest. Hickey discovered that his sins were suddenly less shameful for being revealed not in cloaking darkness but in the full light of the room.

"You could tell him anything," Hickey later said. "You'd walk away feeling, 'Oh my gosh, I could die today and go to heaven!'"

Judge also had his own notions of penance. He instructed one young woman in the parish to make amends by doing something nice for someone. Whatever she did, she felt it was not good enough, so she kept doing something else.

"Don't you dare ever give me that penance ever again," she told Judge.

Parishioners began appearing at the rectory door and asking the pastor if they could see the assistant pastor, the new priest who actually listened to them, who seemed to look for the goodness in everybody. Hickey would recall, "Judge was the priest in the parish that everyone wanted to go see. If there were other priests, it didn't matter. You went to him because he had that gift to give you what you need."

At least part of that gift derived from offering what he himself had needed, what might have helped him during his own hurts. Hickey was seventeen when his father died, and the fatherless Judge knew just what to do.

"He gave me the best hug I ever had," Hickey remembered.

In his rare idle moments, Judge would sit at the back of the rectory and gaze across the Meadowlands at the Manhattan skyline. Many of his parishioners considered this metropolis on the other side of the Hudson River to be a crime-ridden Sodom. They learned that this was one thing they could not say to the man who was becoming known as the Listening Priest.

"Don't you dare say anything about my city," Judge would warn.

On the even rarer occasions when he could get away, Judge returned to the city to walk the streets and delight in the tumult. He was even then discovering that being the priest everyone wanted was a daily test of his stamina, and one day he stopped into the East Twenty-third Street offices of Charles Atlas. The physical fitness guru was out, but Judge left his name and address. The novelty of a visit by a friar prompted a letter.

> Dear Rev. Judge,
> I'm sorry I was not in when you stopped in to see me. Under separate cover I am sending you my complete Course which I hope will benefit you in many ways. The procedure to follow my lessons is described in the first lesson.
>   With my best personal regards, I am
>
>   Sincerely Yours,
>   (signed)
>   Charles Atlas

The letter was dated November 19, 1962, a month and a week after the Second Vatican Council convened in Rome. Judge began doing the Atlas course of sit-ups, push-ups, and squats every morning to keep in shape for his notion of the priesthood, just as the worldwide gathering of Church officials contemplated changes that would be surprisingly in keeping with his views.

In their seminary days, Judge and his classmates had tried to picture times to come as they read the aspiring Franciscan's answer to science fiction, a book called *The Mass of the Future*. The author spoke of a time a millennium or two away when the Mass would be said in a country's own language.

"This was like in the far 3000s," classmate Miles later said.

The future was on the way to becoming now. Pope John XXIII told the Vatican Council, the first to be convened in almost a century, he wished to "throw open the windows of the Church so that we can see out and the people can see in" and called for "the medicines of mercy rather than the weapons of severity." He died less than a year later, just four months before that other bright figure of hope, President Kennedy. But many of the changes in the Church went through, to Judge's delight.

"He *loved* Vatican II," his twin later said.

The leap ahead was, in fact, an attempt to return the Church to the Jesus of the Bible and the religious orders to the spiritual grace and powers of their founders. And for the parishioners in East Rutherford to see the smiling Father Michael Judge turn toward the pews was for them to see the future and past spark together into the Savior's true message of life and love, a message that was all the more powerful for being in the congregation's native tongue.

"Just to turn around and to be able to face the people and to speak to us in his own language," Hickey would say. "In English he put such life into the prayer. It was so holy. Everything was alive with him. . . . He loved life and all the people in it."

He literally took it a step further, venturing outside the sanctuary rail to stand among the parishioners as he delivered homilies that flashed and bubbled with wit and fun. He imparted a lesson not taught at the seminary or contemplated by the council in Rome.

"It was okay to laugh in the middle of Mass," Hickey would say.

This lesson applied to weddings, even funerals. "How many priests do you know could have you laughing at a funeral Mass?"

Judge declared a one-friar revolution.

"There are no shoulds," Judge said. "There's could or there's might, but there's never should."

Judge seemed as in love with being a friar as Saint Francis himself. His daily encounters left ever more people feeling he was their special friend.

"Once they touched him, they never forgot him," Hickey would say. "Everybody wanted a piece of him. I don't think he ever slept."

Judge organized a bus trip to the 1964 World's Fair in Queens and strolled in his habit through Progressland and the World of Tomorrow. A moving sidewalk at the Vatican Pavilion carried him into the darkened chamber where spotlights shone upon Michelangelo's late-fifteenth-century *Pietà,* the marble sculpture of the Blessed Mother cradling the body of her dead Son.

In his continuingly joyous service to the living Son, Judge inspired a twenty-one-year-old parishioner named Christopher Keenan, who had also harbored early notions of becoming a priest until he encountered a predator in the guise of one.

"I had come off a bad experience with a priest who put a move on me, if you know what I mean," Keenan later said. "Michael just had a way of turning it around."

Keenan spoke with Judge of his renewed sense of vocation, worrying aloud that a working-class lug who unloaded trucks for a living might not be able to cope with the academic demands of Callicoon.

"If I could do it, you could do it," Judge told him.

Keenan's father was there, and he remarked on Judge's surname.

"You know, Judge is an unusual Irish name. In the late twenties and early thirties, I would deliver groceries to a Butler store in Brooklyn that was managed by a Michael Judge," the elder Keenan said.

"That was my father," the younger Michael said.

He said nothing more and stared at the elder Keenan.

"It was almost like with this look in his eye, 'Did you make this up?' " the younger Keenan would remember. "It was as if Michael didn't believe it. Michael looked at him as if it was somebody from outer space."

After all, the elder Judge was not just some guy a trucker could meet at a Brooklyn grocery store. He was an object of epic yearning, a figure who by the constructs of his son's psyche had to be as big as his absence. The son prayed every day, not just to Our Father but his father, who also "art in heaven."

The younger Judge must have feared that the reality would be too mundane to fill the void left by his never having had someone to call Dad. He would wait thirty-seven years, until the elder Keenan was at the end of his life and nearly beyond asking, to inquire what his father was like.

"Just take a look in the mirror," the elder Keenan said.

On the Sunday afternoon before his thirty-first birthday, Judge set off on foot from Manhattan to the borough of his childhood. He was walking across his favorite bridge when he encountered a crowd of nearly a hundred who were gazing up at a young man standing on a cable, threatening to leap to his death.

"Jump! Jump!" some in the crowd taunted.

The police arrived and pushed the onlookers back. Judge was in clerical garb and he persuaded the police to let him talk to the man. The newspaper photographers snapped the young priest standing on the roadway, with both arms upraised.

"You're a good man," Judge said. "Come on down and we'll talk this over."

The man refused, and another priest who chanced on the scene gave it a try. The police commander finally got on a bullhorn. His words would not appear in print.

"If you don't come down, I'm going to shoot you in your balls," said Deputy Inspector William McCarthy.

The man came right down, and of course the priests were credited with the save. Judge awoke the next morning, his birthday, to see his photo in the *Daily News* and the *Journal-American*.

"A Voice Becomes Bridge to Life," read the headline in the *Journal-American*.

Even though Judge was misidentified in both as the other priest on the scene, he liked this first, slight taste of being in the news well enough that he saved two copies of each paper.

The story that began to dominate all the newspapers was the war in Vietnam. Students with deferments in New York and Washington and elsewhere staged ever bigger antiwar protests. Judge watched ever more young men in his working-class parish drafted into the conflict. He began to feel ever more strongly that he should go with them. He sent a letter dated September 7, 1966, to his provincial, Donald Hoag.

> *For the past eight to ten months, I have been doing my very best to stifle a very strong desire to enter the military service. At first, I thought it to be a temptation. It persisted even though I constantly fought it.*
>
> *Over the past three months—seeing so many young men leave the Parish and seeing so many others dying in Vietnam—the desire has reached a point where it is constantly on my mind, day and night.*
>
> *Father, I feel that I am still young enough to give a few years of my Priesthood to my country and the young men who need us.*

*Father provincial, I humbly ask you, in obedience to let me give but
a few years to the military in this time of international crisis.*

The following day, Judge went to the provincial's office in the friary on West Thirty-first Street. Hoag told Judge he was needed at St. Joseph's, and that was that. Judge sent him a second letter later that same day.

*After I left your office I went to St. Patrick's Cathedral to pray.
There is a tremendous desire I think on my part to want to do what
I want to do and not really what God and the Province would have
me do . . . I think God is telling me that I can most likely do more
good in East Rutherford by staying here for the time being than I
could do by going into the military . . . I am sorry I took your time,
Father, and I do appreciate your kind understanding . . . Now I can
get back to the work the Lord has sent me to do.*

Obediently,
Michael Judge

Judge remained in East Rutherford, to the delight of the parishioners if not the half-dozen more senior friars in the house. The pastor, George Riley, in particular seemed to seek any opportunity to belittle him.

"They were so jealous," the younger Keenan would recall. "The people wanted Father Michael for their weddings, for their funerals, for everything. They didn't want this brutal Hell's Kitchen asshole of a pastor."

The pastor treated Judge as if he were, in Keenan's words, "unworthy of being even an altar boy" and demanded that he seek permission for his every move. Judge was accorded no more than three hours of liberty a week.

"There was this terrible thing," Keenan would later say. "In public you were one thing and in the friary you were another. They were just mean. Just mean."

The meanness in the rectory intensified in direct proportion to the devotion Judge inspired in the parish.

"It was almost like he was persecuted for his goodness," Keenan would say.

One morning, Judge awoke to discover he was literally unable to move. He remained paralyzed and was carried from the friary.

"I got sick," he later said. "They took me out of there."

• • •

At St. Clare's Hospital, his paralysis was diagnosed as psychological in origin. A doctor told him, "You have to learn to tell people to go to hell." Judge remained more of a mind to tell people to go to heaven after the breakdown, but his physical faculties returned as he convalesced at a friary in Caparra Heights, Puerto Rico.

He then received a written "obedience" assigning him to the Church of the Sacred Heart in middle-class Rochelle Park, New Jersey. The pastor was none other than Father Henry Lawler, sober after his alcoholism got to a point where he hallucinated that his fingers were poisonous snakes. A fellow friar had placed a chalice and a bottle outside Lawler's door, the message being to choose between his drinking and his priesthood.

Lawler had done such a remarkable job in rescuing himself that his parish became the place that friars in crisis were sent.

"A nice little quiet parish," Judge recalled.

All seemed dreamily ideal at first, with the kindly Lawler welcoming Judge and offering no objection when he started a youth group dubbed the Troubadours. The group was named after the traveling French singers of old who had inspired Saint Francis with their songs of chivalry and the Round Table. Every modern Troubadour meeting ended with them singing a forthrightly corny song Judge had taught them.

> We are Troubadours, walking, walking, walking this land.
> We are Troubadours, walking hand in hand.

Judge's young singers included Nancy Lee Nixon, who on hearing of his death thirty-five years later would be prompted to look up the definition of "troubadour."

"A person who spreads the word of love and peace," Nixon reported in a letter to Judge's sisters.

Love and peace were just the words to be spreading in 1967, but the following year brought the Tet Offensive and the assassinations of Martin Luther King Jr. and Bobby Kennedy. Even the quietest parish was not immune to the tumult of the times. Rochelle Park had a group of concerned citizens clamoring for an end to discrimination in housing. Judge saw it as a simple matter of social justice, and the group decided he would be just the one to present a list of demands to the village council. He did so and the council responded with a demand of its own. It wanted the rabble-rousing priest out of town.

As social change reached even the Franciscans, the friars were given the opportunity to reclaim their names if they so desired. He decided to drop the "Fallon" but keep the Michael.

"I guess I'm really more of a Michael than an Emmett," he later said.

He was sent back to East Rutherford, but thanks to the same spirit of change the old pastor was to be replaced by a "team ministry" of three young friars, all equal. He was made even happier by the news that Christopher Keenan, the young laborer who had worried he might not get through the seminary, was to join the team immediately after his ordination at the start of the new year.

On Christmas Eve, Keenan visited St. Joseph's in anticipation of his first assignment. He had once served as an altar boy with another member of the team, Father Jimmy O'Donnell, who now announced he was leaving the priesthood to get married. A second member of the team announced he also would be leaving the Church, and for the same reason. And hundreds of others in parishes everywhere were responding to the widespread relaxing of the rules not as the freedom to become a better priest but simply as a chance to escape. The concurrence of Vatican II and the swinging sixties had many of the younger priests reacting like men who suddenly had their chains removed.

"It was a shock," Judge later wrote. "[Priests] were going out the door and getting married. People were saying, 'Why are you staying? What keeps you here?'"

He was sure the ultraconservatives would seize upon the defections as proof that reform led to ruin, that a loosening of the bonds simply encouraged people to break away altogether. He also faced the prospect of the priesthood devolving from a calling into a refuge for those who were either too afraid or simply not inclined to run off with a woman, a harbor for the hapless and the homosexual, for the ones who never learned to play ball. He could not turn to the rookie Keenan for bolstering. Keenan was in that youthful stage when celibacy meant simply abstaining from sex. Judge was feeling it mature into the more profound void of not having a family.

"For a man to give up the love of a woman, love of children, and love of his home in order to serve the Church, to 'be all things to all men,' as St. Paul says, is a great challenge," Judge wrote.

Judge was not unaware of his impact on women, of the lingering looks that meant companionship was his for the asking.

"This attractiveness of mine surprises me sometimes and can catch me off guard. . . . Women are drawn to me. It is challenging to them that this man is different: he is sensitive and feeling. They write to me; one writes two or three times a week. When I go into a home after a death, they hold me. I have to be careful not to give a false impression. When I hug or kiss someone or shake hands at the end of the Mass, it comes from the heart and has no other meaning."

He knew that men were also drawn to him and that the prevailing homophobia meant such a liaison would bring an implicit promise of secrecy, that here he could find companionship and release without any expectation of commitment. The temptation was all the more cruel for his being perpetually required to maintain an open, welcoming heart.

"In order to deal with people at their most sensitive moments, death, marriage, illness, you must remain in touch with your own feelings, not shut them off," Judge said.

He had found the only way to cope was through a brotherhood with fellow friars undertaking the same continual challenge.

"A network of celibate friends . . . is essential for this. I have found the contact must be constant. . . . As long as I share my feelings, I am safe and whole."

Through that Christmas week, a time of birth and promise and family joy, Judge had only God to confide in. He had for the briefest time imagined he would be free to become the priest he felt he was born to be and do so while part of a true brotherhood. He would not have felt any better knowing that Vatican II might well have ended mandatory celibacy if Pope John XXIII had lived just a few more months.

Later, Judge described December 31, 1970, as the loneliest, most desolate New Year's Eve of his life. He found himself alone in the rectory as the clock ticked into a new year and he went out onto the back porch to gaze in solitude across the marshlands at the Manhattan skyline. He could see the construction lights of the two towers beginning to rise downtown, towers for which any twin would feel an affinity, which could rouse even such a dejected twin as Judge.

"Marvelous."

5

On September 11, 1971, God's grin began to break through nine months of gloom.

This was the day another friar named Michael, Father Michael Duffy, was ordained. Duffy shared Judge's notion that a priest should create as direct a connection as possible between God and his people. He also had a great sense of fun, and when he joined Judge and Keenan in the new team at St. Joseph's in East Rutherford, they became like the Franciscan answer to Dem Bums, as the Brooklyn Dodgers were known in their glory years.

Judge, Keenan, and Duffy could have been Dem Friars as they formed an arc in front of the sanctuary during Mass, giving in unison a scrappy, spirited rendition of the Our Father. Their homilies were often a jocular back and forth. They would go up and down the aisles giving the sign of peace, shaking hands and embracing parishioners.

At all times, Duffy watched Judge the way a rookie baseball player studies someone he recognizes as one of the greats.

"He was, without knowing it, my mentor, and I was his pupil," Duffy would say years later at Judge's funeral. "I watched how he dealt with people. . . . While the rest of us were running around organizing altar boys and choirs and liturgies and decorations, he was in his office listening. His heart was open. His ears were open and especially he listened to people with problems."

Judge focused totally on that particular human being at that particular moment. Judge would be so intent on whatever the person was feeling that he seemed to feel it, too.

"When he related to a person . . . they felt like he was their best friend," Duffy recalled. "When he was talking to you, you were the only person on the face of the earth."

Duffy, who became known there as Father Mike, remembers one man saying, "Father Mike, my grandfather died. I tried to get Father Michael, but he's busy. Could you do the funeral?"

Judge's appointment book was two inches thick and was indeed filled weeks in advance. He talked to everyone.

"The young kids getting married, the middle-aged with family problems, the elderly. Sometimes, we have three funerals in a week. . . . You're important and you know it, but it wears you down," Judge told a reporter.

He often did not finish until just before midnight. He would be too wound-up just to head for bed, and he would sit with his fellow friars until the early morning, brainstorming and celebrating their fellowship.

"Ripping, roaring, laughing," Keenan recalled.

When Judge would announce he had to go to bed, Duffy knew just the words to keep him up.

"Duffy would say, 'Michael, as soon as you leave here, you know we're going to talk about you,'" Keenan remembered.

Judge would stay, sipping a Tab diet soda, or so it would appear.

"Of course, his Tab can was full of scotch," Keenan recalled.

Not that Judge had any obvious drinking problem. He might as well have been imbibing soda for all the difference it seemed to make. He sipped to no manifest effect until they all finally called it a night.

"Whoever had the seven A.M. Mass, the other guys would fight over who would take the Mass for him so he could sleep in," Keenan said. "'I'll do it.' 'No, I'll do it.' 'Don't be such a martyr.'"

Judge would keep his bedroom door open, and Duffy would see him kneel beside his bed to say his prayers before hopping in.

"Like a little kid," Duffy later said.

Judge's room was the room of a true friar.

"Another aspect, a lesson that I learned from him, his way of life, his simplicity," Duffy said. "He lived very simply. He didn't have many clothes. They were always pressed, of course, and clean, but he didn't have much, no clutter in his room, a very simple room."

In the morning, Judge would do his Charles Atlas routine and bound into another day. He remained especially fond of bestowing blessings. Should a couple tell him they were going to have a baby, he would place his hand on the woman's stomach and call on the Almighty to bless the child.

When a couple was having difficulties, Judge would take the husband's hand in one of his own and the wife's hand in the other. He would draw their hands together as he whispered for God to please end the crisis.

"He was the bridge between people and God, and he loved to do that," Duffy said.

Even in those years, Judge considered a keening siren to be a signal he might be needed, and he would dash off. Duffy walked into the friary one morning to be told by the secretary that Judge had just hurried to a hostage situation.

"Well, I got into the car, drove up there," Duffy recalled. "There was a man on the second floor with a gun pointed at his wife's head . . . and he was threatening to kill her."

The gunman, an ex-convict named James Hyams, was holding his wife at gunpoint, along with their nine-year-old son and six-year-old daughter, in a stand-off with more than a hundred cops. He had served time for manslaughter and assault as well as a sexual attack on a child.

"And where was Michael Judge? Up on the ladder in his habit, on top of the ladder, talking to the man through the window of the second floor," Duffy said.

Judge was holding the hem of his habit with one hand and hanging on to the ladder with the other.

"His head was bobbing like, 'Well, you know, James, maybe we can work this out. You know, this really isn't the way to do it. Why don't you come downstairs, and we'll have a cup of coffee. And talk this thing over,'" Duffy recalled. "Not one ounce of fear did he show."

Then Judge told the gunman, "You're a good man, James. You don't need to do this."

The gunman agreed to allow the children to escape down the ladder. Judge took the younger one, the six-year-old girl, in his arms, carrying her to safety and returning. He said if he ever knew fear it was when he entered the house.

"Can I come in and talk to you?" Judge asked. "You've had enough pain. Let's sit down and talk. We know you want to be heard, so let's hear you."

Judge made a single promise.

"I'll stick by you."

The photos in the next day's newspaper showed Judge carrying down the child, then bringing out the shotgun, and finally emerging with the gunman.

"You do what you have to do in such a circumstance," Judge was quoted as saying.

The brave and handsome friar in his brown robe became a regular in the local newspapers. He who had gone the first three decades of his life without a word of praise started keeping a scrapbook. The articles included one headlined "The Listening Priest" in which a reporter asked him about the "identity crisis" causing an exodus of clergy from the Church.

"Who has time for an identity crisis?" Judge said. "Sure, I've had my pain, my hurt. I sympathize with priests who have an identity crisis, but you know, people need me and I need them."

He spoke of his continuing effort to exorcise the voices of his indoctrination in the seminary.

"Before Vatican II we were always trying to manage people's lives. Do this. Don't do that. Go to Mass. Don't eat meat on Friday. I was brought up in the old school, and I have to remind myself, 'Mike, let people be,'" Judge said.

He called this the hardest lesson he had learned as a priest.

"To let people be themselves."

He described what had carried him through trying times that might have driven him to follow those leaving the priesthood.

"I have a tremendous amount of perseverance. I can wait things out. If I wait, dawn will come."

He saw not a crisis in religion but a blossoming, an escape from dogma and fear.

"I think this is the most exciting time in the history of the Church," he said. "Years ago, the Church was a one-way street, but now there are so many different personalities, mentalities. The human mind is a fascinating thing. How boring the world would be if we all thought alike!"

He never pressured young people to attend Mass.

"Young people are doing it their own way," he said, "They tell me they talk to God and I believe them. . . . God's grace is always there. He'll guide them. . . . We have to leave the kids in God's hands. He has His own way of working."

He felt it was up to the priest to draw people to the Church.

"We have to be versatile in preaching," he told the reporter. "If I'm giving a homily, and a fire truck goes by with ringing siren, I switch my original thoughts and relate to what's happening—the fire."

The pictures accompanying "The Listening Priest" article showed him sitting with a teen on the friary lawn, crouching in the street with a group of younger kids, and chatting with a grave digger in the parish cemetery, his sandaled feet dangling in a half-dug grave. He had grown his hair down over his ears, making clear his affinity with the young.

"As our hair started growing, so did his," Hickey would recall. "We just thought it was kind of cool."

On May 11, 1975, Judge turned forty-two years old. He got a birthday card signed by a group of Siena College students who had visited the parish to see firsthand the life and work of the friars there. One of the students also telephoned, and Judge wrote him a note.

> Dear John,
>
> The older you get, the better you feel—You look back and you see all the people you have touched, the hands you have shaken, the eyes you have looked into, the words you have heard, the hands you have felt, the homes you have visited, the hospitals you have skipped through, the marriages you have witnessed, the dead you have blessed, consoled and buried, the young you have baptized, the ordinary Christians and non-Christians you have met on the street, and on and on and on. John, God has been so good, so very good to me! I just hope you can experience just one-tenth of all of it before it ends.

Judge's stature among all ages was reflected by a prediction Duffy overheard on September 14, 1975, as a parish group boarded a bus for a trip to a ceremony marking the first canonization of a native-born American, Elizabeth Ann Seton, founder of the Sisters of Charity, the very order that had so terrorized the Judge twins at St. Paul's Grammar School.

"Who knows, in twenty years we might be boarding a bus for the canonization of Michael Judge," one of the parishioners said.

Back at East Rutherford, Judge was proving particularly patient with the petty complaints parish priests must always handle. One woman had a screaming fit when a church event was sold out and she could not attend. Duffy wondered at his friend's restraint. Judge explained, "You have to absorb it because someday that woman will need a priest. What's going to happen if her husband gets cancer?"

Judge hated to distract himself with such mundane concerns as budgeting and keeping track of parish finances. He always seemed to conjure up the needed funds at the last minute.

"He'd say, 'You know, I got some money from heaven,'" Duffy recalled. "How did he get that money? I don't know, but he got it."

The parish janitor became increasingly inattentive to his duties, and the friars finally decided they had no choice but to let him go. The task of firing him fell to Judge, who agonized for days before finally going to the man's house. Duffy was at the friary when Judge returned.

"How'd it go?" Duffy remembers asking.

Judge lowered his eyes.

"All right," he said.

"What'd he say?" Duffy asked.

"I gave him a raise," Judge said.

From the back porch, Judge watched with his fellow friars as the towers of the World Trade Center rose to completion. He still considered New York to be his city, and he periodically collected clothes and food to take to Harlem, where his Callicoon friend Ben Taylor had started an outreach program for substance abusers. Judge would then wander on down through Manhattan, energized by the great swirl of races and nationalities.

When time allowed, Judge would cross his beloved Brooklyn Bridge and trek along to Grand Army Plaza. He sometimes cut through Prospect Park, but the Long Meadow and the trees were too much like the country. He more often continued along Flatbush Avenue within sight of the apartment buildings where Ebbets Field had once been, a sign reading NO BALL PLAYING affixed to a wall just about where his boyhood heroes had stepped up to home plate. He would skirt the far side of the park and come to Ocean Parkway, proceeding as far as Coney Island before returning.

One day, Judge stopped into what had to be one of the few surviving tattoo parlors in the city, tattooing having been banned in New York and still decades from legalization. He later showed Dympna the result when they were both visiting Erin's house. Dympna would recall encountering him in the hallway when he was only partly dressed. He hiked up the back of his undershorts and there, tattooed onto his behind, was a small green shamrock.

"I said, 'Is that permanent? You're crazy,'" Dympna recalls.

Judge pulled the shorts back in place and the shamrock disappeared.

Judge also took the occasional road trip with Duffy, the two hopping into a car and just driving, taking whatever route presented itself. They were now the Franciscan answer to the sixties movie *Easy Rider,* only they would say a rosary together as they headed down the highway. The two sought out backroad eateries, always sitting next to an occupied booth in a diner so they could eavesdrop on life as it was lived in that small town.

On a trip to Vermont they saw only gray clouds overhead and decided to keep heading north until they reached blue skies. They ended up in Montreal.

Even on the road, Judge would kneel by his bed at night to say his prayers to Our Father and his father like he was a youngster back home in Brooklyn.

Judge's mother was now in failing health and living near Erin in Maryland. He would make solo trips to see her.

"Hardening of the arteries had completely changed her personality and controlled her life," he later wrote in a pastoral letter.

Her mental balance was knocked further off-kilter by the television that Erin had originally bought her so she could see the St. Patrick's Day parade. A woman raised on a turn-of-the-century Irish farm began watching soap operas that she decided were a window onto modern life. She started imagining that everyone around her was embroiled in affairs and intrigues. She called the principal at the school where Erin taught, saying her daughter was running a whorehouse.

Her imaginings stopped when it came to her son and his fellow priests. The idea that a man of the cloth would engage in scandalous sexual behavior was beyond this mad Irishwoman's most far-fetched fantasies.

Her son was still subject to biting remarks when her fierceness turned to meanness in the concentric confinement of advancing age and failing health. Her reputation for cantankerousness was well known to the friars. They were waiting at Newark Airport to pick up Judge from his latest trip to Maryland, when they saw him come off the plane pushing an elderly woman in a wheel-chair. They stood horrified at the prospect of his bringing his mother to live in the friary.

Just as Judge reached the friars, he told the woman how happy he was to have met her. She was not his mother at all, they realized, only a woman he had offered to help off the plane. He knew full well what they would assume, and laughed all the way back to the friary.

One day a visiting friend and friar named Hugh Hines came into the office when Judge was on the phone. Hines remembers that Judge placed his hand over the receiver.

"It's my mother," Judge explained. "She thinks I stole all her Christmas cards."

Several days later, his mother was hospitalized. Judge traveled down to Washington and slept that night in her bed. The mattress had a lump.

"The damned Christmas cards kept me awake half the night," Judge reported to Hines.

As the mother's condition worsened, her fingers swelled and the wedding band she had worn all these years had to be cut off.

"She did not speak of her feelings about the loss, but I noticed it every time she raised her hand," Judge later wrote. "Somehow that ring of their vows connected me to the dad I never really knew."

Four days after Christmas, Mary Ann Judge died. She remained to the end one of the few to whom he was never able to bring peace. Her son presided at her funeral Mass at St. Joseph's in East Rutherford, which was private in accordance with her wishes. She was buried beside her husband at St. John's Cemetery in Queens.

"She went home to God and our dad," Judge wrote.

Among her effects, fierce Mary Ann Judge had saved cards from Mother's Day that Michael signed in neat script on behalf of Erin, Emmett, and Dympna:

"The Three Musketeers."

The grown "Musketeers" spent New Year's Eve together. They poured champagne and at midnight toasted her and then each other. None of the Judge children had progeny of their own. They would be the next to go, and the line would end with them, but as they clinked glasses Judge seemed as excited as if they were at a beginning, as if there was a newness to all the years to come.

"Now we could let her go," Judge later said. "We were released from her suffering."

Judge spent another two years of busy bliss with Dem Friars in New Jersey. Duffy recalled, "He would say to me once in a while, 'Michael Duffy'—he always called me by my full name—'Michael Duffy, you know what I need?' And I would get excited because it was hard to buy him a present or anything. I said, 'No, what?'"

Judge would repeat the question.

"You know what I really need?"

"No, what?"

"Absolutely nothing. I don't need a thing in the world. I am the happiest man on the face of the earth."

Judge would go on for a good ten minutes, telling Duffy how blessed he felt.

"I have beautiful sisters . . . I have my health. I'm a Franciscan priest. I love my work. . . ."

Judge would gaze heavenward. "Why am I so blessed? I don't deserve it. Why am I so blessed?"

Four months later, Dem Friars marked the nation's two hundredth birthday with a bicentennial Mass. The church was festooned with patriotic banners, and there was patriotic music and a patriotic film clip, and the team was at its ebullient best. A reporter overheard a visitor from Judge's home city offering the ultimate compliment.

"Father, I am a visitor to your church," the man was quoted saying. "I attended Mass all my young life in Ireland. Then I attended Mass in England. And for many years now I've attended Mass in New York, where I still live. I've gone to some of the biggest churches, the cathedral, but I must say this is the best Mass I've ever been at."

The Mass ended with a song that roused the worshippers like none of the everyday hymns. Everyone joined in, including men who usually mumbled and otherwise faked it from the back pews. These men might never have learned the prayers, but even they knew these lyrics.

"God bless America, land that I love . . ."

Judge kept working seventeen-hour days, never sure what surprises the next day might bring. One day he was crossing the parking lot at St. Mary's Hospital to visit a parishioner when he saw a group of priests gathered near a charter bus. A lone cleric sat aboard. Judge ducked his head in to say hello.

"He invited me in," Judge recalled. "He introduced himself as Cardinal Karol Wojtyla."

Judge and the cardinal from Poland sat chatting for ten minutes. Wojtyla explained that he had been in Boston and was now traveling to the Eucharistic Congress in Philadelphia. He had stopped to visit a Polish archbishop who had fallen ill.

Wojtyla asked about the friars in America, and Judge inquired about the difficulties of traveling behind the Iron Curtain. Judge would remember Wojtyla saying, "We are able to negotiate all things."

Judge kissed the visitor's ring and asked his blessing without the slightest inkling that this unassuming, crinkly-eyed cardinal was viewed by the hierarchy as a kind of sex expert. Years later Judge would hear that Wojtyla may have been responsible for the Vatican upholding a chastity vow that had driven so many good men from the priesthood and imposed such anguished loneliness on so many others, all in the name of "the constant tradition of the Church."

In the tradition of the Franciscans, friars remain at an assignment no more than six years. Judge would later explain, "This is part of our vow of poverty, poverty in the broad sense of not identifying with and becoming attached to material things, locations as well as simply not owning anything. When you stay for a long time in one place, you start to feel that it is yours. We must feel free at any time of the day or night to go where God needs us."

Judge was visited by his friend and fellow friar, Hugh Hines, who was now president of Siena College outside Albany, New York. Hines noted that Judge's grueling schedule was beginning to have a noticeable effect.

"It was wearing him out," Hines later said. "Of course, he would never give up. I think it was killing him, to tell you the truth."

Hines offered Judge a job as assistant to the president. Judge himself must have felt he was again nearing a physical and psychological limit. He announced at a Saturday-night Mass in November of 1976 that he was departing St. Joseph's. A good many parishioners burst into tears. Fifteen hundred people showed up at his good-bye party the following week.

"He has done more good for more people than anyone I know," Duffy declared.

Judge arrived at Siena wearing chinos and a blue oxford shirt as if he were the world's oldest freshman. He would have been living most boys' fantasies when he was assigned a suite on Ryan 1-E, the section of the dorm housing freshman girls. He gave over his sitting room as a student hangout and kept for himself only a bedroom tinier than those accorded the students. He was sometimes seen in his habit and sandals, other times in a suede jacket, jeans, and cowboy boots. He had so few socks that he washed out a pair every evening, hanging them at the end of his cot-sized bed to dry. His faith was just as simple.

"God is not an obligation, a burden," Judge was quoted as saying. "God is the joy of my life."

Officially, Judge was an administrator whose duties were, in his words, to "do whatever the president can't do, won't do, or doesn't want to do." Judge was able to employ his charisma to equal effect on everybody from college trustees to local politicians. He proved capable of near miracles when an alumnus would call up irate because his child had not been admitted to Siena.

"When he was done, they were almost happy their son or daughter didn't get in," Hines recalled.

Judge remained more than anything a working priest, and he found his desk was also a comfortable spot to place his feet as he reclined to listen to anyone who needed a listener. He seemed to see goodness in everybody he encountered, and that made them feel it, too. He recognized value where other priests imposed values. He taught as Jesus and Saint Francis and all the great ones did. His living example had a particular impact on an undergraduate named Brian Carroll.

"Exuberance and love and humanity," Carroll would later say. "The vitality. Seeing the folly of God as well as the glory of God."

• • •

Judge was that much more convincing for not pretending to have all the answers. Carroll imagined himself someday donning the brown robe.

"You can't help but get pulled to it," Carroll said.

Another future friar, Brian Jordan, would remember an exchange with Judge at the start of his senior year.

"What are you doing for the rest of your life?" Judge asked.

"I'm thinking of becoming a lawyer," Jordan said.

"Forget about becoming an unhappy lawyer," Judge said. "Become a happy priest."

Judge seemed not at all troubled to discover that many of the students had lapsed so far from their Church that they were ignorant of the most fundamental rituals and traditions.

"They may not know what a novena is . . . but they have a great need and desire to help other people," he was quoted as saying.

Judge became the chaplain of the Siena basketball team, the Saints. He would end a long week doubling as an administrator and campus priest by going on a road trip with the Saints, often not returning until late Sunday night. He would still seek out freshman Lynn Finnegan, whose cousin, Anthony, was in the hospital with Elephant Man's disease.

"As exhausted as I knew he was, he would say, 'Come on, Lynn, let's go. We're going to see your cousin,'" Finnegan recalls.

Judge would drive Finnegan to Albany Medical Center to see the once-handsome football player who had been horribly disfigured by the disease. She remembers that other people would stare at her cousin as if he was a kind of monster.

"Father Michael never saw that. He never saw that in anybody," Finnegan says. "A lot of people were afraid of my cousin. Father Michael almost loved him more because of it."

Judge's intimate connection to the Almighty acquired widespread credence on the campus on a day he set off to visit Michael Duffy's family. He had no sooner driven away from the school than he was pulled over by a cop known as "Shultie," a self-appointed bane of speeders.

As Shultie filled out a summons, Judge sat in the cop's car, asking questions about the radio and the siren and the emergency lights. Shultie answered the queries and seemed duly charmed, but he was not inclined to give even a priest such as this a break.

Judge stepped out with his ticket and started around the back of the patrol car. He stopped.

"You've got a flat," Judge said.

Shultie got out and saw that the car did indeed have a flat tire. The cop's eyes rose toward heaven.

"Oh God, you certainly work fast," he said.

As his first Thanksgiving at Siena neared, Judge caught a ride down to East Rutherford with a student named Jean Willis. He set her so at ease that she confided she was in love with a man who was engaged to another woman.

"I said, 'Why is it wrong to love two people? How can you say one's not love?'" Willis remembers. "He said, 'Well, the only thing I can tell you is that in a situation like that somebody gets hurt, and most of the time everybody gets hurt. So it's better not to put yourself in that situation.'"

Willis broke off the relationship with the engaged man. She became Judge's sidekick, driving him to basketball games and introducing him to her family. She continued to enjoy his counsel and friendship after she graduated, and she invited him to her going-away party before she moved to Los Angeles. The day was sweltering, and the guests were wilting when Judge arrived in his habit, looking cool in the most literal sense. He stood resplendently handsome, not a bead on his brow as those around him dripped sweat.

"Leave it to the Willises to get a stripper dressed as a priest," a guest was heard to say.

Judge was not forgotten by his former parishioners in New Jersey, and he was inundated by more than five hundred cards at Christmastime. He also received letters and phone calls from John Hyams, who was serving a term in

Leesburg prison for charges arising from the day he took his family hostage. One letter read: "You alone have put some meaning in to my life, just the fact that you care. . . ."

Judge wrote back and occasionally visited Hyams, once bringing him a typewriter.

"The day we negotiated I told him I would stay in touch and I mean to keep that promise," Judge would later say.

Judge allowed that he had actually grown fond of Hyams.

"People don't understand our relationship," Judge said. "But that's okay. Neither do I."

Judge was still drinking. While he was no Father Henry, he would sometimes plead fatigue when invited to a movie and instead slip off to the South End Tavern for "a few belts." He reached a point where he needed more than bed-time prayers to sleep. He finally showed up at an Alcoholics Anonymous meeting in Albany wearing Bermuda shorts and tube socks, telling himself he was just there to observe.

During the midmeeting coffee break, Judge spotted Father Charlie M., a fellow Franciscan he knew from Washington, D.C.

"I hear this deep and resonant voice calling out to me and saying, 'Put a Franciscan robe on him and he'd look just like he looked twenty years ago,'" Charlie recalled.

Charlie turned around, and there was Judge, who immediately began explaining that he was not an alcoholic.

"I just like to go and listen to your spirituality," Judge said. "You guys got tremendous spirituality in these rooms."

Charlie's sponsor overheard Judge's remark and shot back a stock AA response to a stock excuse.

"Mike, if you're not an alcoholic, I think you'll do until one comes down the highway."

After the meeting, Judge and Charlie went to a coffee shop. They talked for more than an hour. Judge eventually admitted to Charlie he had to drink himself to sleep every night.

"I am an alcoholic," Judge said.

That night was the first time in months that Judge went to bed sober. That was also the night a senior from Scarsdale was struck and killed by a car while walking home from a party. The college president was away, so Judge had to telephone the parents with the terrible news.

"Oh God, Charlie," Judge exclaimed when he called his friend the next morning. "If it had been a usual Saturday night, I never would have been able to do that. I would have been drunk."

By all accounts, Judge never took another drink. He credited Charlie with "twelve-stepping" him, or leading him to sobriety, an honor his friend was reluctant to claim, citing the AA mantra, "There are no coincidences, just God acting anonymously."

Judge quickly became one of AA's most passionate advocates. He found in AA another sort of fraternity, not of friars giving witness to the Almighty but of souls suffering inner torments as hard to exorcise as the sexual conflicts and hungers he had continued to experience since adolescence. His faith was ultimately a working one, as anchored in day-to-day life as AA's twelve steps to sobriety, integrity, and acceptance. The AA Serenity Prayer, arising as it did from the rawest human failing, was as powerful to him as any prayer of the liturgy.

God, grant me the serenity
To accept the things I cannot change,
Courage to change the things I can
And wisdom to know the difference.

A serious test of Judge's serenity came in the late summer of 1979 when the provincial asked him to depart Siena for a New Jersey parish so rural as to shock a son of Brooklyn.

Judge did as he was bidden, but he arrived in West Milford, New Jersey, feeling as if he had been cast into exile.

"I thought I would die when I arrived—no tall buildings, no streets, no people walking. Oh Lord, I'll die here," Judge later said.

That October, Judge briefly escaped to the city for a Mass at St. Patrick's Cathedral that marked the visit of the new pontiff to New York. The Polish cardinal whom Judge had met in a New Jersey parking lot was now Pope John Paul II. Judge did not fail to recognize the strict orthodoxy underlying the Pope's populist style.

Although he did admire John Paul II's personal warmth, Judge chose to return to his rural parish rather than join the 75,000 who filled Yankee Stadium for a papal Mass. He also chose not to attend the youth rally at Madison Square Garden, where the band from his almost alma mater, St. Francis Prep, played the theme from *Rocky*, the crowd chanted "John Paul II, we love you," and the undeniably charismatic Pope responded, "Wooo, wooo, John Paul II, he loves you."

Judge kept any negative thoughts largely to himself, saying that since the word *pontiff* means "build a bridge," he hoped John Paul II would be like the Brooklyn Bridge, linking people together. Privately, Judge did describe the Pope's tour as "a great show for the deaf."

After a Sunday Mass in West Milford, Judge chatted with a parishioner named Tom Ferriter, who told the new pastor he was going that afternoon to see his mother, Brigid.

"A nice Irish lady from Leitrim," Ferriter recalls saying.

"My mother was from Leitrim," Judge said.

"Was she a little cranky at times?'"

Judge laughed. "At times."

At three P.M., Ferriter and his wife, Noreen, got into their car and were given a fright by a sudden movement in the backseat.

"I'm going with you," Judge said.

Ferriter noted that his mother lived on Long Island, a three-hour drive each way.

"Let's go," Judge said.

Off they went, chatting all the way like old buddies. Ferriter explained that his mother had become increasingly bitter and difficult. She sometimes called to demand he take her shopping, but when he finally got there she would be coming back in a taxicab. She would then indignantly demand to know where he had been.

Judge gave the Ferriters a second surprise when they arrived.

"We walked in the house and he said, 'You and Noreen go to lunch and call me here before you come back,'" Ferriter recalled.

He and his wife gratefully set off for a peaceful meal and called Judge after an hour.

"Not yet," Judge said.

Ferriter waited another hour and called again.

"Not yet."

He tried once more at the end of three hours.

"Okay."

Ferriter and his wife returned to behold the ever cantankerous Brigid Ferriter beaming as if life were only grand.

"She was purring like a kitten," Ferriter recalled. "I saw the rosary beads out on the kitchen table and they were drinking tea."

The mother's good spirits miraculously persisted month after month. Judge had been an *amadan* to his own mother; Ferriter now proclaimed him an *anam cana,* or soul friend, to the Ferriters.

"I owed him my soul," Ferriter said. "I've never seen a change like that in anybody. She gushed about him. She became a Michael groupie like the rest of us."

As in East Rutherford and Rochelle Park, Judge was a particular favorite of the young in West Milford. He announced that he would give a sex talk to the teen boys at the parish school.

"Everybody signed up for that one," Sister Jean Hekker recalled.

Hekker was understandably curious as to how this priest would address the subject. She donned sneakers so she could silently creep up the steps. She reached the door in time to hear him call testicles by the vernacular "balls." She exclaimed, "Oh my God," to herself and retreated down the steps.

"I came back up making noise," she remembered.

Sexual attraction continued to be an undeniable factor in Judge's popularity among the women of the parish. Ferriter would recall a night shortly after Judge arrived when he attended a basketball game at the local high school wearing a gray herringbone sports coat with elbow patches rather than clerical garb.

"Every woman in that place was looking at him," Ferriter would recall. "A few ladies told me after a few drinks they would never cheat on their husbands, but if Michael Judge wanted to put his shoes under their bed, tell him to come over."

At the time, Judge was assisted by two fellow friars, Kevin Daly and Ron Pesci, the latter a rookie who had been sent there by Michael Duffy to learn a different notion of priesthood than was presented in the seminary.

Pesci had been taught to labor long hours preparing a homily, contemplating, writing, memorizing. Judge would simply come dashing in minutes before Mass.

"What's the Gospel today?" Judge would ask.

Judge would then often say how nervous he was. "Oh God, my stomach."

But Judge evidenced not the slightest flutter as he began to address the parishioners, seemingly saying whatever came to him, combining Gospel with actual life, eternity with the here and now.

"Somehow it all made sense," Pesci recalls. "Everybody was mesmerized as he spoke. He was just so natural."

Judge would walk among the parishioners as he spoke, often addressing individuals directly, never hesitating to say, "I love you." Parishioners sometimes came up afterward seeking a concrete record of the homily that had so moved them.

"They would ask, 'Oh, Father Michael, can I have a copy of that?'" Pesci remembered. "He would say, 'Copy of what?'"

Pesci became the latest to realize that Judge oftentimes did not retain what he had uttered any more than a musical instrument remembers a sonata.

"He really didn't know what he had said an hour later," Pesci recalls. "I don't want to say rapture, but . . ."

In some ways, Judge seemed a more traditional Catholic than the seminary's most orthodox instructors. Judge continued his practice of keeping his bedroom door open, and Pesci would walk by as he knelt by the bed in his T-shirt and underwear to say his nighttime prayers.

Judge prayed out loud, as he had a half century before when he was asking for his daddy to get well. His tone remained that of a son speaking to a father. He mentioned person after person.

"He'd say, 'I was with Mary today and she is so concerned. Please take care of her. Give her some peace . . . It's Joseph's anniversary. Give his wife some comfort . . .'" Pesci recalls. "Everyone he encountered. Everyone he had on his mind."

In the morning, Judge would go from person to person as if he were an agent for those prayers.

Judge told Pesci that he had briefly trained as a counselor at the American Foundation of Religion and Psychiatry in New York and had undergone rudimentary analysis, which touched on matters sexual. Judge confided that he had come away unsure whether he was gay or straight, maybe not bi but omnisexual, drawn not so much to men or to women as to all God's adult human creations.

"I didn't know what I was," Judge said, according to Pesci's recollection. "I was this. I was that. I had all kinds of feelings."

Judge was like a man consigned to the desert pondering whether he preferred motorboats or sailboats. Pesci decided that this omnisexuality helped make Judge a great priest. Judge had in some sense never taken complete form as dictated by his needs, and this allowed him to assume the form dictated by the needs of others, what might be called shapeshifting, but what Pesci described as "that chameleon-like ability of his to relate to everybody."

But Judge was again grinding himself down despite grabbing a twenty-minute nap in the afternoon (measured by an egg timer). He seemed in danger of another physical collapse, and his fellow friars insisted on assuming some of the burden.

"Michael, you can't do everything," Pesci told him. "Don't go to the hospital. Don't do home visits."

The other friars assumed those duties, but whoever they visited seemed to have the same question.

"You go up to the hospital and there's little Molly Malone sitting there saying, 'Father, I'm glad you're here. How's Father Michael doing?'" Pesci remembers. "No matter what you did when you were there, it revolved around Michael Judge."

Other friars at other times had been jealous. Pesci found he was not bothered at all, perhaps in part because he had decided on the source of Judge's gift.

"I think it came from God," Pesci later said. "I do."

He added, "Some people are natural athletes. They get up and they throw that ball perfectly the first time. Michael was a priest that way. It wasn't studied. It was just there. He just did it."

Pesci was also a Brooklyn boy, from the Italian stronghold of Bensonhurst, but he enjoyed the country life, to Judge's continual amazement.

"He talked about it like he was stuck in the Rocky Mountains," Pesci recalled. "I said, 'Michael, on a good day you could be in Manhattan forty minutes from now.'"

When pastoral obligations allowed, Pesci would go into Manhattan with

Judge and stroll the streets. Judge rejoiced in the great, swirling mix of humanity. He described it with a single word.

"Alive!"

Pesci was reminded of a story in which Saint Francis invites two young friars to come with him and preach the Gospel. They walk the length of the town and one of the young friars says that he thought they were going to preach the Gospel.

"We just did," Saint Francis tells them.

Judge most often wore the habit that many friars found to be an uncomfortable encumbrance, a barrier to entering modern life.

"He said, 'I don't understand why these guys don't wear it. It took me years to get it. I earned it and I'm going to wear it,'" Pesci recalled.

The robe looked no different from the one worn by Saint Francis in a stone carving of him haloed by a ring of golden birds that Judge discovered over a side door to Rockefeller Center on West Fiftieth Street. The carving is only a half block from St. Patrick's Cathedral.

"Michael always used to point it out," Pesci said. "He would love to say that between the powers of industry and the powers of the Church there's humble Saint Francis."

True, Judge the city boy had no apparent affinity with birds or any other animal, but Pesci was sure that Saint Francis would have loved him.

"I think he would have loved everything about him," Pesci said.

Judge did use the diocesan uniform of a black suit and Roman collar to slip onto the cathedral steps among the powers of the archdiocese on St. Patrick's Day as the marchers paraded by. A front-page photo in *The New York Times* in 1983 showed Judge standing behind Terence Cardinal Cooke as if he belonged there as much as anybody. Pesci heard some of the more conservative priests cite this as evidence of Judge's ecclesiastical frivolity.

"They thought he didn't take it as seriously as they did," Pesci recalled. "They took him as a grandstander."

Pesci had decided that Judge was ultimately more serious than anyone on those steps. Pesci would go so far as to say, "He was an icon of the Church."

Pesci meant the living equivalent of the icons revered by those of the Eastern Orthodox Church.

"It isn't just a picture," Pesci would say. "It's a manifest presence."

• • •

On another St. Patrick's Day, Tom Ferriter said much the same thing, if in a more street-Irish way. He marched that year and made sure he was on the cathedral side of the avenue. Judge was at his usual spot among the personages of the Church. Ferriter waved and called out something to him.

"He couldn't hear what I was saying," Ferriter recalled. "He said, 'What did you say, Tom?' I said, 'You're the only decent one up there.'"

Ferriter had repeated it loud enough for a number of the personages to hear.

"That got their attention," Ferriter said. "It's a good thing he wasn't looking for promotions."

On a subsequent visit to Manhattan when Ferriter and Judge were walking on Sixth Avenue toward a Nedick's for a hot dog, the man Ferriter termed "the perfect priest" offered his own taxonomy of Catholics.

"Some are good and some are bad," Judge said. "You are a good Catholic."

"Really?" Ferriter replied.

"Why are you surprised?"

"When I'm on the Communion line, I'm checking out the ass of the broad in the other line," Ferriter said.

"You, too?"

In May of 1983, a banner went up in front of the church in West Milford.

HAPPY 50TH BIRTHDAY FATHER MICHAEL

The event was marked by a big party in the parish hall with a big cake and candles and singing and a disbelieving guest of honor.

"He used to say, 'I know I'm that old, but I don't know I'm that old,'" Pesci recalled.

The reality of his vanished youth made Judge pine all the more for New York, but he continued to be so successful in West Milford that in 1985 the provincial spoke of making an exception to Franciscan tradition and renewing his assignment there for another six years. Judge was now fifty-two and that would mean his remaining in exile from the city until he was nearing that milestone of undeniable age, sixty. His vow of obedience proved to have its limits.

"I said, 'The hell you are, I'm getting out of here,'" Judge recalled.

A fellow friar had gone on a year's sabbatical at the Franciscan Study Center in Canterbury, England, and Judge decided this might be just the thing for him. He would have a year to do some good for himself, without an official flock, with nobody's immediate needs to attend to save his own. He persuaded the provincial to write a letter of recommendation.

"He is a man of great personal charm and I am sure he will contribute to the élan of the group," Father Alban Maguire wrote. "His approach to the parish ministry has been very personal and somewhat innovative."

Judge was formally accepted in May, and he made a written request to spend the summer months before his departure at the friary on West Thirty-first Street.

"I just need the chance to 'do little or nothing,' and N.Y.C. has the best AA in the world," he wrote.

After six years, Judge returned for a summer in the place of tall buildings.

"God travels by bus and subway," he said.

And, of course, along sidewalks. Judge took a long stroll on September 11, 1985, from the friary to the Nevins Street subway station in Brooklyn.

"Where 37 years ago at age 15 I left for the Franciscan seminary," he later wrote. "They are not accepting them so young these days . . ."

He now stood in his habit on this same platform amid the workday bustle, privately observing the anniversary of when he first left home to become a priest.

"I thought, 'I have no regrets.' How many can say that?"

6

A friar of a different sort on a different sort of pilgrimage arrived at the English town to which Chaucer's pilgrims traveled. The brown habit like that worn by the fictional friar in *The Canterbury Tales* was packed away in his suitcase, and he strode into the courtyard at the Franciscan Study Centre in denims, his graying hair brushed back in a stylish sweep, a tiny golden hoop glinting in his left earlobe. He had decided to have his ear pierced before setting off for Canterbury, and he might have been taken for just another victim of midlife crisis. In truth, he was not so much seeking to recapture his youth as preparing to live it for the first time.

"Wow, this guy's trendy," a seminarian named Anthony McNeill would recall thinking.

Judge's certificate would show that he took courses in Church Liturgy, St. Mark's Gospel, Twentieth-Century Theology, Religion and Culture, Spirituality, Passion Narratives, Christology, Fundamental Morality, Eucharist, and Charisms. But the course that had the most profound effect on him was not listed and certainly had not been available during his previous schooling—an extracurricular modern-dance class taught by Peter Daly, a seminarian who had been with the Folies Bergère.

Daly encouraged and cajoled Judge into overcoming a trepidation about dancing not surprising in a man with a socially deprived adolescence. This may have been accompanied by a deeper fear of revealing too much of himself, of shifting into shapes all and only his own. Judge was perhaps never more Judge than when Daly succeeded in getting him to move to the music, assuming physical forms in accordance with his impulses at the moment, changing from instant to instant, but feeling intensely himself in body and spirit, giving free exercise not just to limbs but to urge, wish, inclination, yen, desire, whim, fancy.

Judge had always transported himself beyond self-consciousness during his unscripted homilies, but he seemed even freer and more energized when it came his turn to say Mass at the center's chapel. He himself became a liberating agent for the fledgling friars.

"It seemed to make the Gospel real," rookie friar Brian Purfield recalled.

Judge often strayed from the prescribed prayers of the Eucharist, yet all but a few of the most orthodox friars recognized that he was not doing this out of rebellion or spite.

"He would take it in himself and change it," the novice McNeill recalled. "He believed everything he was praying. He just believed it. You could see his faith was real. He walked around the altar so natural. It was amazing watching him."

Both in and out of chapel Judge spoke forthrightly about alcohol abuse and his own continuing need to attend AA meetings.

"At the time, alcohol was something you didn't talk about," Purfield remembered. "The subject was seen as taboo. If that was your problem, then out you go."

He held an open AA meeting at the center in which participants spoke of their struggles with the bottle and beyond.

"It was very radical, really," Purfield said. "For him, it was, 'Why not? What's to hide? . . . If you've got a weakness, alcohol or whatever it is, talk about it.' He was very in touch with his own humanity and his own weakness and didn't want people to pretend they were something they were not. . . . He'd say, 'Look, I've made awful messes. I've made terrible mistakes, but I'm still here.' "

Purfield had already been a priest for seven years when he decided to join the Franciscans, and he was older than the other fledgling friars. He noted that a number of the younger ones found Judge to be someone in whom they could confide their private struggle, questioning him about issues they had never discussed in more than whispers for fear of being cast out.

"You didn't talk about sexual orientation," Purfield says. "Young friars struggling with their sexuality found in Michael someone they could turn to. 'Come on, let's talk about this!' "

As in all personal matters, Judge was a listener more than a confider, but many of those who were gay were left with the impression he himself was gay, just as many of those who were straight were sure he was straight. He spoke of being intensely attracted to both men and women during this time.

"All so beautiful," he would say.

He seemed as abrew with urges as a teenager, an impression furthered not just by the earring and the thin "rat-tail" braid he grew down the back of his neck. The perpetual mess in his room would have stunned those who had always known him to live in immaculate orderliness and simplicity.

"There was stuff all over," Purfield recalled. "I don't know how he found his bed."

Purfield could not help but be curious when he saw this very different sort of friar repeatedly return to his room late at night, like a youth who had slipped out to meet a lover.

"Where on the earth has he been?" Purfield recalled asking himself.

Purfield finally decided to follow him one evening.

"Not suspicious," Purfield later said. "Just intrigued, really."

Purfield shadowed Judge to the deserted chapel and entered to see him at the very front, praying before the Blessed Sacrament. Judge seemed oblivious to the other man's presence.

"My impression was he was just lost in his own sort of world," Purfield said.

Purfield later mentioned to Judge that he had seen him in the chapel at night.

"He said, 'Oh, I need to go back to the source at the end of the day, then go to sleep and leave it all in His hands,'" Purfield remembered. "'Whatever happened during the day, you just hand it all over.'"

Purfield understood that Judge was not so much a radical as a kind of essentialist whose relationship with the Father was unmediated by abstractions, as direct as with a father, or perhaps a lover. The liberated and liberating Michael Judge was as viscerally devout and intimately connected as an apostle, but saved from being overbearingly pious by one grace rare even in Scripture.

"He didn't take himself too seriously," Purfield said. "That helped people warm to him."

Notable among those who did not warm to Judge was a friar of the same surname, though in this instance there could have been no more appropriate appellation. Father Urban Judge was implacably and uremittingly judgmental; it was as if Christianity's very survival depended on adherence to Church doctrine. Added to that was a large measure of British rectitude, for this sterner Judge was a former provincial of the English province as well as a canon lawyer.

"Urban was not the touchy-feely type I think it could be safely said," Purfield noted.

Urban seemed to weigh every dogmatic nuance before offering an opinion about anything.

"Michael just came right out with it, calling a spade a spade," Purfield recalled. "I think Urban found that a bit challenging."

Urban seemed the very embodiment of the official Church as he stalked out of the chapel whenever Michael Judge said Mass. Michael Judge seemed determined to win Urban over and would sit right down at the older man's table in the dining room and attempt to make conversation.

"Urban would just not respond," Purfield remembered. "He would quite deliberately shut Michael out. Michael was visibly hurt."

Michael spoke of this hurt repeatedly in telephone calls to Dympna. He told her he had tried to befriend Urban, without success. He recounted an instance when Urban was in the sacristy, attired to concelebrate Mass, when Judge showed up.

"Emmett came in and [Urban] looked at him and said, 'I'm getting out of here,'" Dympna recalled. "He took off his robe and said something that was very direct. It really upset Emmett."

Dympna decided that Urban was just a British version of the priests back home who wore orthodoxy as a cloak for jealousy.

"To me it was pure envy," Dympna said.

The present British provincial, Austin McCormick, described the visiting New Yorker as a loyal nonconformist, reminiscent of one from long ago.

"Like Saint Francis, he found so much good to celebrate because he expected to find it," McCormick was later quoted as saying. "And he went looking for it."

Among the laity, some had been stunned by the sight of a priest with an earring.

"All the old ladies in the church nearly keeled over," a parishioner named

Judith Rosado remembered. "English Roman Catholics are very reserved. They are not quite as poker-faced as the Anglicans, but they are very poker-faced."

The ladies quickly discovered that the earring was accompanied by a finer quality than the brashness they might have expected.

"He had a grace about him; he had a presence about him," Rosado said. "Everyone was drawn to him. He didn't walk into a room without people turning and looking and being attracted and wanting to go and speak to this friar."

Rosado and her family lived on a farm outside Canterbury and she invited Judge to experience another aspect of English life. Judge became a regular Sunday visitor, proclaiming in the Irish way, "God bless this house and all who live here!" Judge introduced the Rosados to the American, if not exactly South Brooklyn, tradition of the cookout. Often, Judge came with Peter Daly. The two shared an exuberant belief in a theological truth.

"You can have fun and everything and still be close to God," Rosado said.

Back at the center, Daly coaxed Judge into one of Britain's secular and not at all stuffy traditions, the pantomime. The theme was Cinderella, and Daly dressed Judge up as the fairy godmother, by one account using carpet glue to stick on false eyelashes. The characters' names were made into spoonerisms, and Judge's getup was completed with a sign reading, GAIRY FODMOTHER. He raised a hand in blessing.

"Bod gless you," he said.

The fun and laughter still stopped when Judge encountered the dour former provincial who shared his surname. The exhilarating promise of what could be was confronted by the stony reality of what could not. And just when rays of liberation were illuminating the very core of the younger Judge, the light was blocked by a scowling figure who represented the institution in which he had to function as a priest if he wanted to continue being a priest at all.

For his part, the elder Judge seemed to see not a loyal nonconformist but an insufferable threat, a symbol of where all the changes in Church and society were leading. He must have felt his judgment confirmed when he learned that during his last Mass in Canterbury the younger Judge asked everyone to hold hands for the Our Father.

"I've waited a whole year to do this," the younger Judge told Rosado afterward.

. . .

The younger Judge was no longer so young and would soon be going back to his old life. He fell into a deep and anxious depression as his fifty-third summer presaged his return.

He was not worried about how his sisters might take the new Michael. He had made a brief trip back home during the year, and he had told them about the discoveries he was making about himself. He had included the possibility that he was gay, news they took as no more earthshaking than if he were that man in the desert announcing he really liked sailboats more than motorboats.

"I was floored, but I wasn't," his twin recalled.

Judge also was not worried about where he would be assigned next. The provincial in New York had called to say he was being sent to a parish in rural upstate New York, and Judge had replied that he would probably end up drinking again. The provincial relented, saying Judge could just come to the friary on West Thirty-first Street.

But the brighter the sun, the darker the shadow. His sisters had embraced his newly liberated self and he would be posted in the city he loved, but there would still be the likes of Urban Judge. There was still the age-old struggle between those who believe in the institution and those who believe in the ultimate nonconformist, between those who adhere to the strictures of the Church and those who follow the example of Jesus. Michael Judge was filled with the fear that his changes would mean more opposition, that being his truer self in the place he felt most alive would only sharpen the conflict, that promise would end in ruin. Judge would later say that the summer solstice in England seemed not just the longest day of the year but of his life.

"The longest and the worst," he would say.

Judge normally would have welcomed the day as the start of summer and its attendant joys, but he saw only the approaching end of his belated youth. He went on a jaunt to London, and there he chanced to see a book sitting atop a trash bin.

The book was *Revelations of Divine Love* by the fourteenth-century mystic Julian of Norwich. Judge retrieved it and saw words that gave him sudden strength.

"All shall be well, and all shall be well, and all manner of things shall be well."

7

The book was in his single suitcase when Judge arrived at West Thirty-first Street on the Thursday before Labor Day in 1986. He was assigned a room on the third floor of the friary adjoining the church that was home to four dozen fellow friars. He had just risen Friday morning when he was approached by Friar Julian Deeken, who served as a chaplain to the New York City Fire Department.

"Do you think you could go to Bellevue Saturday night and say Mass for Officer Steven McDonald?" Deeken asked.

"Sure, I'm free," Judge said. "Who's Steven McDonald?"

"Don't you read the papers and watch TV?"

"I've been out of the country."

Deeken explained that McDonald had been shot in Central Park by a fifteen-year-old and had initially been declared beyond help, but the trauma team at Bellevue Hospital was able to save him. He now lay paralyzed from the neck down. Daily Masses were being said in his room, usually by Msgr. John Kowsky, the police chaplain. Kowsky was off fishing this weekend and Deeken would have filled in were he not also otherwise engaged.

Judge was standing outside the friary at the appointed hour the following evening when a black Lincoln Town Car pulled up driven by an ascetic figure who looked as if he could have been a friar himself. Brian Mulheren was the police detective known as "the Night Mayor," the man who represented City Hall at the scene of every major calamity. Judge settled onto the front passenger seat, fascinated by the console before him, which was crammed with radios set to every emergency frequency in the city. He rode off listening to the crackling voices of the dispatchers along with those of cops and firefighters and ambulance crews responding to calls for help.

At Bellevue Hospital, the night supervisor asked Mulheren to keep Judge in the lobby for a few minutes.

"Don't let him go up," the supervisor said. "The cardinal is coming. He wants to go up for a quick visit."

The supervisor was speaking of John Cardinal O'Connor, head of the archdiocese of New York and therefore one of the two most influential Catholics in America. The other was Bernard Cardinal Law of Boston, who had been named the same week in 1983 as O'Connor. Law and O'Connor were considered conservatives who adhered strictly to doctrine as set forth by the Vatican. They had come to be nicknamed Law and Order, but that did not yet mean anything to Judge when O'Connor now swept in.

"He didn't know me and I didn't know him," Judge would later say.

O'Connor noted only the brown robe.

"I'm glad to see the friars are here," O'Connor said.

The cardinal did not object to the friar and Mulheren accompanying him to Steven McDonald's seventh-floor room. McDonald was a third-generation cop. His maternal grandfather had won the Police Combat Cross in 1936 for chasing down and capturing two gunmen, all the while spitting blood from a bullet wound to the chest. His paternal grandfather had been a police lieutenant. His great-aunt had been one of the first female police officers. His father was a retired police sergeant.

Judge and the cardinal stood on either side of the bed as the latest cop in the McDonald family drifted in and out of a dream world where he played football and walked on the beach and danced with his wife, Patti Ann. She was now sitting at his side, never to dance with him again. She was three months pregnant with their first child.

A patient down the hall went into cardiac arrest and there was a call for a chaplain. O'Connor stayed where he was as Judge hurried to respond. Judge anointed the patient and said a prayer and then returned.

"I'm glad to see you're doing the job well," O'Connor said.

After a few minutes, O'Connor departed. Judge commenced the Mass, and Steven heard a joyful voice that could have been from one of his better dreams. That same joy filled Judge's face and Steven felt himself suffused with a kind of feeling he thought had disappeared with the sensation in his limbs.

"Heavenly," Steven would later say.

At the end of the Mass, Judge broke into song.

And the Lord said let it be,
And the Lord said let it be
Amen, all is well
Let it be.

With that, Judge left.

"We were like, 'Wow, is this okay he's doing this? Is that okay with the Church?'" Patti Ann later recalled.

At the same time, the paralyzed young cop and his pregnant wife sensed an okay of a higher order.

"It was almost like it was all going to be okay," Patti Ann said.

Patti Ann went to the friary the next day to see this remarkable priest with the pierced ear and the tiny braid down the back of his neck. She asked if Judge might come back and say Mass again sometime. He returned day after day, filling in whenever the police chaplain was unable to come.

The chaplain was away on November 7, and Judge arrived to discover that this was the McDonalds' first wedding anniversary. Judge gave an impromptu talk about the joys of love and marriage and soon he was the only one present not in tears. He felt his powers faltering and silently prayed for divine assistance. His eye then fell on a Notre Dame pennant somebody had brought.

He again began to sing.

"When Irish eyes are smiling . . ."

The McDonalds started to laugh through their tears.

During his visits, Judge taught the McDonalds the prayer he had recited at St. Francis Prep under the threat of beatings. He had clung to the meaning through all his trials, and this seemed to give the words that much more power.

Lord, make me an instrument of Thy peace.
Where there is hatred, let me sow love.
Where there is injury, pardon.
Where there is doubt, faith.
Where there is despair, hope.
Where there is darkness, light.
Where there is sadness, joy.

Steven had still not regained his ability to speak. He could only mouth a question.

"What prayer is that?"

"The Prayer of Saint Francis," Judge said.

The words resonated in Steven all the more deeply after his son, Conor, was born. That happened to be the same day Shavod Jones, the teenager who had shot McDonald, was sentenced to a three-to-ten-year prison term. Conor's baptism was approaching when McDonald mutely mouthed words that to Judge seemed shouted from the mountaintop.

"I want to forgive him."

Cardinal O'Connor presided at Conor's baptism, resplendent in his crimson robe as he paused to make asides to the media mob crammed into the Catholic chapel at Bellevue. Patti Ann afterward read a letter from Steven to the City of New York. The letter began by praising Steven's fellow officers and saying he had become a cop to help people.

"On some days when I am not feeling very well, I can get angry. But I have realized that anger is a wasted emotion, that I have to remember why I became a police officer. I'm sometimes angry at the teenage boy who shot me. But more often I feel sorry for him. I only hope that I can turn his life to helping and not hurting people. I forgive him and hope that he can find peace and purpose in his life."

Steven's letter closed with words that must have had a particular ring for the friar who often asked aloud why he was so blessed.

"I believe that I am the luckiest man on the face of this earth. I only ask you to remember the less lucky, the less fortunate than I am who struggle for the dignity of life, without the attention and without the helping hands that have given me this life."

The doctors had declared it a miracle when McDonald survived the shooting, but the cop remained paralyzed below the neck. Even Judge's presence was sometimes not enough to stave off despair.

Then, into the hospital room scuffled another miracle, this a figure in hospital pajamas and a steel back brace. Firefighter Ronald Bucca was with Rescue Co. 1, one of the elite, highly trained units that back up fire companies and take the lead when specialized skill and tools are needed. He had been at a blaze on the Upper West Side when he fell five stories. He had struck a telephone wire and a pair of cables on the way down, but fire officials concluded this slowed his fall only minimally, and they theorized he was saved by his Airborne and Special Forces training he had received in the army. He had landed on his hands and feet like a cat, somehow suffering only a broken back in a fall that doctors would have expected to be fatal.

A broken back is still a broken back, and Bucca must still have been in considerable pain when he learned that a cop who had been shot by a teenager in Central Park was on the same ward. The miracle in the brace made his way down the hall to give his best wishes to the miracle on the ventilator.

Judge had never encountered a member of the FDNY in more than passing, and he could have started with nobody better than this slightly built, mustachioed figure whom Patti Ann would come to call "the Flying Fireman." Judge witnessed at the bedside the pure spirit of the New York firefighter communing with the pure spirit of the New York cop.

In keeping with that spirit, Bucca would ignore those who counseled him to retire with a disability pension. He would also dismiss the specialists who predicted he would never be fit for full duty. He would die on 9/11 after climbing to the seventy-ninth floor of the South Tower, as high as any other firefighter. Not even the Flying Fireman would be able to survive the collapse, although his body would be one of the very few found intact.

In such company, Judge's sense of self seemed to mature. He ceased to wear his earring. He cut off the rat-tail. He kept his room as neat as he always had before his Canterbury interlude. He did engage in a subtler form of rebellion when he changed the spelling of his given, or rather taken, name to Mychal. He said he did so to distinguish himself from other Michaels in the friary.

"Is that the Irish spelling?" people would often ask.

"Yes," Judge would say.

In truth, the Irish would be Mícheál. Judge confided to several friends that the new spelling actually derived from seeing the African-American basketball player Mychal Thompson on television. Judge adopted the name as a kind of inside joke, renewed every time some supposedly devout racist piously addressed Judge as "Father Mychal." The change also afforded the added advantage of placing him after his phonetic brethren in the alphabetic roster of chores.

Judge still enjoyed his priestly duties, working what the friars termed "the schedule." Each day a friar on the schedule said one of the Masses and worked either two ninety-minute shifts in the confessional or one shift in the confessional and ninety minutes of "parlor duty," a sort of spiritual emergency room for people who came in off the street in immediate need of a priest. A fellow friar would write that the confessionals at St. Francis "are spare, small and often cold. In summer, awful odors can linger, a composite of perfume, cologne or spent breath."

Judge continued to prefer face-to-face confessions such as he had always conducted as a pastor, but he understood that a good number of people came to St. Francis because they wanted anonymity. The confessionals had a slot where the friar on duty would slide in his nameplate, and an ever-increasing number of the penitents would look for the one reading FR. MYCHAL JUDGE. He became intimately connected to people he knew only as disembodied voices from the other side of the screen. The new ones sometimes said they had not been to confession for more time than he had been a priest. A few described coming back to West Thirty-first Street again and again until they worked up the nerve. He was able to discern the elderly by the thump of a cane or a groan as they knelt. He honored the sacred bond of confidentiality, though he did allow in the most general terms that many confessions involved sins of the flesh. These generated enough guilt and shame and unhappiness to lighten the burden of the most onerous of Judge's three solemn vows.

"Now, if that doesn't keep you celibate . . ." Judge said.

At seven A.M. on Tuesdays and Thursdays, Judge and fellow friar Pat Fitzgerald set out in search of fifty homeless men in need of clothing. They gave each man a numbered ticket, telling him to come by the friary at nine A.M. Those who did were asked for their size and instructed to return at eleven A.M., at which time they were given a bag of donated clothing.

The items were selected by the friars and their two partners in the effort, a nun named Sister Mary Lawrence Scanlon and a volunteer, Sara Mullen.

They paid particular attention to size and color coordination. Their working philosophy was later summarized by Mullen: "You can't give to the homeless what you wouldn't wear yourself."

The merchants in the surrounding area were hardly thrilled to have that part of town turned into the Brooks Brothers of the homeless. They pressured the Franciscans into scuttling the program. Judge by then knew most of the street people of midtown and they would call out to him as he walked the city.

"Father Mychal!"

"Good evening, James."

"Father Mychal!"

"Hello, Henry."

Jean Willis from Siena and others donated modest stacks of dollar bills that Judge kept in a tin box in his room. He distributed them to James and Henry and the others neatly folded lengthwise, not palmed but extended, the sharp crease a bit of extra care, a sign of respect, enough to make the bill less a handout than a personal gift, a sharing.

As Judge strolled in his habit down Broadway one afternoon, an unfamiliar homeless man stepped out to block his way. The man's eyes were wild, his voice belligerent.

"Bless me!" the man commanded.

Judge took the man's head in his hands.

"In the name of the Father . . ."

Judge pressed his forehead to the man's forehead and the two stood motionless on bustling Broadway. The man was in tears when they parted. Judge smiled. The man smiled back.

"Holy shit," the man said.

"Or something," Judge said.

One gentleman, known as Dutch, had a regular perch on a milk crate outside the old Gimbels department store on the corner of West Thirty-second Street and Sixth Avenue until he succumbed to cirrhosis. Judge and Fitzgerald fashioned a sign from a jumbo-sized brown paper bag and went to Dutch's usual spot. They affixed it to a plywood construction wall, next to a notice reading POST NO BILLS.

The sign read:

DIED, SEPTEMBER 21, 1987

RAYMOND "DUTCH" PARKER

HOMELESS

MAY HE REST IN PEACE.

At the edges of the sign they taped white, yellow, and purple mums. The friars later returned and saw that a passerby had been inspired to add a single red rose.

"Marvelous," Judge said.

Early Friday mornings, Judge worked the St. Francis breadline, which had served more than 2 million people over six decades. He took his own meals in the friary's basement dining room. The walls had a wraparound mural of the life of Saint Francis painted in panels during the 1930s by a woman artist who never got to see it installed because only men were permitted there.

One scene showed Saint Francis centuries before kissing the forehead of a pale, spectral figure. Anyone familiar with Franciscan lore would know this was the day on a road outside Assisi that the order's founder overcame his fear of disease by embracing a leper. A modern scourge had now struck, inspiring such dread that its victims were often shunned by coworkers and abandoned by friends. Many hospitals were reluctant to admit them. At those that did, health-care workers avoided entering the room. And because the disease largely struck male homosexuals, it was commonly called the gay plague, an expression that compounded the fear of contagion with social stigma.

In 1987 the ever-growing list of people with AIDS had come to include Ed Lynch, a caterer with clients such as Henry Kissinger and Barbara Walters. Lynch was a well-known member of AA, and Judge began to visit him regularly at Cabrini Hospital.

At three A.M. one day, Judge was roused from sleep and summoned by phone to Lynch's bedside. Judge dashed there expecting the worst, but arrived to find Lynch lucid and in no apparent crisis.

"You must bring me a plate of scrambled eggs," Lynch said. "You're the only one to do it."

"Why me?" Judge asked.

"Because you're a priest. Who else are they going to let into Cabrini Hospital at three-thirty in the morning?"

Judge laughed and fetched the eggs from an all-night diner. He kept doing what he could for Lynch until there was nothing more to be done but officiate at the funeral. The Requiem Mass was held at St. Francis of Assisi on November 2. The left side of the church was packed with hundreds of Lynch's friends from AA and the gay community. The right side was empty save for a handful of family members.

Such divides were common at AIDS funerals and were seldom bridged by liturgy. Judge was inspired to break with prescribed tradition and ask if any of the mourners had something to say about the deceased. Person after person rose on the crowded side of the aisle and extolled Lynch with the eloquence of grief. An actor declared that he literally owed his life to having Lynch as his AA sponsor.

"I came in like a piece of fruit rotten almost to the core and Eddie picked me up and dusted me off and said, 'You're going to be okay,'" the actor said.

Others offered similar testimony, and the family sat amazed that Lynch had touched so many lives. The end of the Mass saw the two sides converge in the center aisle and file out as one behind Judge and the coffin. The pastor, Fr. Michael Carnevale, witnessed the joining and afterward suggested Judge was just the friar to start a new ministry.

Judge officially began his AIDS ministry on the morning before Thanksgiving, twenty-four days after Lynch's funeral. He started by visiting Sister Pascal Conforti, chaplain at the AIDS ward at St. Clare's Hospital, by coincidence the Catholic institution where Judge had landed after his breakdown two decades before. St. Clare's had since become home to the city's first AIDS ward. The same church that condemned homosexuality as an "intrinsic evil" had nonetheless undertaken to assist victims of "the gay plague" when many health facilities actively avoided treating them.

Sister Pascal met Judge in the lobby and showed him the ward. She immediately decided there was little she could teach him that he did not intuitively understand.

"I felt in some ways he knew more than I did," she would later say. "Whatever that mind of ours does to put everything in columns—this is good, this is bad—he didn't need to do that. There was sort of a breadth about him that just embraced whoever was there."

From Sister Pascal, Judge went to see Rev. Bernie Healy, an Episcopal priest who was doing admirable AIDS work. Healy had a file of people with the disease.

"I picked up a paper with Bill Rizzo's name on it," Judge would write in a hardbound journal he began early the next morning.

The paper reported that Rizzo was at another of the more humane hospitals, Beth Israel. Judge went there only to discover that Rizzo had checked out. Judge went to the man's home on Bank Street in Greenwich Village. Judge wrote: "He was so glad to see me: 'I accept my disease. I accept death, I just pray each night that God will take me peacefully in my sleep . . . I have no bad feelings about anyone . . . I have this great apartment, friends, food every day . . . I am so peaceful.'"

Judge blessed Rizzo but remembered feeling as if he was the one being blessed. Here was a leper who had embraced himself and seemed certain the Almighty would do the same whatever the Church might have to say about his sexuality or anything else.

"Beautiful," Judge wrote.

Judge was inspired to embrace his own whole self, one person he did judge, somebody he had often deemed unworthy, somebody who had been obliged to marginalize his sexuality even before it took form. His torments seemed to assume a purpose, for they made him better able to appreciate what faith had bestowed in Rizzo. Judge was all the more determined to impart such faith to others who suffered the double sting of unjust exile and certain death.

> *I felt no guilt, none whatsoever today—I felt on the train home: "I am at peace finally . . . This is what You want me to do . . . Thank You, Lord."*

That night, Judge went with his fellow friar Pat Fitzgerald to see the huge balloons being inflated in preparation for the Macy's Thanksgiving Day parade. The two friars watched Snoopy, Big Bird, and the others take universally recognized form, the shapeshifter Judge delighting not so much in the characters as in the magic of all the human activity surrounding them. Judge then returned to his single room.

> *1987 Thanksgiving-Morn—1 a.m.*
> *This is really a day to be thankful. I have everything in the world anyone could pray or ask for.*

• • •

Over the days that followed, Judge rose at 6:15 A.M. and set off on what he called "a new priesthood," visiting hospitals, welfare hotels, rooming houses, and drug dens.

Some of the wracked and wasted figures made Rizzo seem almost robust by comparison, but Judge was sure God came in the room with him.

"Even if I don't feel it, I know He's there," Judge would say.

Judge soon discovered that Rizzo had been an exception, that many AIDS patients were in no mood even to see a priest, much less be kissed by one. They often felt ostracized by the Church in their time of greatest need, even though Cardinal O'Connor had approved the AIDS care center at St. Clare's Hospital and had recruited Mother Teresa to staff a fourteen-bed AIDS hospice at St. Veronica's Church in Greenwich Village. O'Connor wrote in his newspaper column of bathing and emptying the bedpans of AIDS patients at St. Clare's Hospital. He professed to be mystified when he flashed "the smile I am told does wonders on television" only to have a young man respond by calling him a "hatemonger."

The reason, as every gay person knew, was that O'Connor still subscribed to official Church doctrine. The Vatican's "Halloween Letter" of October 1986 termed homosexuality a morally unacceptable "objective disorder" and barred gay groups from Church property. The same cardinal who emptied bedpans evicted the gay organization Dignity from the Manhattan church where its weekly Masses sometimes outdrew those at St. Patrick's Cathedral.

O'Connor also joined his Boston counterpart, Law, in opposing a thirty-page position paper issued by the U.S. Conference of Catholic Bishops that proposed teaching in Catholic institutions that condoms could prevent AIDS. The paper emphasized that this should be done only while also teaching sexual abstinence outside of marriage, but O'Connor nonetheless told the press that the bishops had committed a "very grave mistake." He declared there would be no talk of condoms in his "jurisdiction."

Partly as a result of all this, Judge was often met by AIDS patients with a glare or a demand he leave. He approached the most angry and bitter ones by first rubbing their feet.

"Be silent, say nothing, just massage," Judge later advised.

He would then ask a question.

" 'How are you?' The most natural question in the world."

The rare person would speak of fear and certain death. Most often, the person was trying not to think of his fate, much less talk abut it.

"I might say, 'Do you mind if I start out with a prayer?' 'That's okay.' They kind of expect that."

He would thank the Lord for bringing them together on a beautiful day and then seek to make the day exactly that. Neither he nor anybody else had a medical remedy, but he could fight prejudice and fear with the ungloved and unhesitating touch of those big Irish hands.

"If I can, I sit on the side of the bed without disturbing or hurting them and take their hands or stroke their arm," he later said. "It's so important to touch them and sit close to them."

The Church's official scorn made Judge only more determinedly intimate in his ministrations.

"When I pray with them and anoint them I try to make it a beautiful, serious, loving ritual," he reported. "Each time I say, 'I anoint you,' I ask the person being anointed to answer, 'Amen.' By the end, there are tears in their eyes—and mine."

Judge later recalled the sudden spark in one dying young man when asked if he wanted the Sacrament of the Sick again as administered by Father Mychal Judge.

"Of course," the young man said. "I love it."

Judge transformed the city's most forsaken rooms into its most passionate places of worship. He could have been living another scene in the dining room mural, the one where Saint Francis hears a divine voice saying, "Francis, seest thou not that my house is in ruins? Go and restore it for me."

Of course, Saint Francis did not likely receive the request one dying man made of Judge.

"Father, can I give you a blowjob?"

Judge laughed and gently demurred.

On December 11, 1987, Judge visited Rizzo and discovered the man's condition had worsened.

"We had the joy of Communion," Judge wrote.

Six days later, Rizzo died. Judge wrote, "[Rizzo said] The pain is so bad in my stomach at night I pray God takes it away or take me home' . . . His prayer was answered."

Judge let the journal lapse but proceeded through 1988 noting his daily activities in a thick appointment book, just as he had as a New Jersey pastor. The notations for Masses and weddings and baptisms and confessions were joined by as many as four hospital visits a day to young men suffering what the most conservative Catholics considered the wages of sin.

May 18

Larry

Dominic

May 19

2:00 Larry R.I.P.

June 1

Dominic

3:45 p.m.

R.I.P.

Three decades into the priesthood, Mychal Judge still sometimes lamented to friends that he never had anyone to teach him how to play ball and be "one of the guys." The guys he now spent his days with were the guys nobody wanted to be one of, the guys with AIDS. He was seeking more expertise in ministering to them when he visited Father John McNeill, a Jesuit activist and psychotherapist who had been running the Upper Room, a Harlem program for homeless people with AIDS. McNeill knew him by reputation from the friar's own efforts in feeding and clothing the homeless.

"Mychal Judge was doing extraordinary good pastoral work with the poor," McNeill would later say. "Every poor person I knew, knew him."

McNeill quickly discovered that he had little to teach Judge about ministering to people.

"One day he showed up and asked for my help," McNeill said. "I thought it should be the other way around."

McNeill was as amazed as Dympna had been decades before at how Judge just seemed to know certain truths.

"He knew exactly what was needed and was able to provide that," McNeill said. "Anybody whose room he went in really felt blessed."

Judge explained to McNeill how he remained so buoyant while proceeding from bedside to bedside.

"He used to put it to me, if you descend into somebody else's private hell and stand there with them, it ceases to be hell," McNeill recalled. "That's exactly what he did. He would go into their pain and rage and sorrow and share it with them and then both of them would be blessed by that sharing and feel God's grace and presence. He would go away as fulfilled as the AIDS person he visited."

McNeill was suffering a kind of public hell as a result of a book he had published nine years before titled *The Church and Homosexuality*. The book was no sooner published than the American bishops sent it to the Vatican. The book was condemned, and McNeill was ordered not to say or write another public word about such things.

McNeill went on to help found the gay Catholic group Dignity, but he abided by the Vatican's order year after year. He could stay silent no longer after the Halloween letter branded homosexuality an evil and declared that groups such as Dignity could no longer assemble in churches. His first public remarks on the subject in nearly a decade appeared in a newspaper, and he was expelled from the Jesuits, the order where he had spent his entire adult life.

Judge was himself on the way to being as well known among AIDS sufferers as he was among the poor, and the gay community was coming to claim him as one of their own. He had said the occasional Dignity Mass, and he often spoke in the first-person plural at AIDS funerals, though he also used "we" at weddings and baptisms, and later would do so at fire funerals. He made no public declarations regarding his sexuality. He made no direct references to it in his private journal recording the start of his AIDS ministry. He was passionately focused on his work as a priest and he now told the exiled McNeill that his own greatest fear was being forced from the order to which he had devoted himself since he was fifteen.

"That was his nightmare," McNeill said later. "To totally belong and be part of both the Church and the Franciscan order and not hating or repressing his gayness put him in a terrible dilemma."

Judge began seeing McNeill every Thursday at nine A.M., though it was not always clear who was the real therapist. Maybe they both were. McNeill remembers Judge confiding in him the sort of self-doubts patients typically spill to their shrinks.

"He didn't think he was bright, and he really had a low opinion of his intelligence," McNeill recalled. "He treated becoming a Franciscan as a minor miracle, and he wasn't going to waste a minute."

Judge worried aloud that he might someday be expelled from the Franciscans. He was not just connecting with his therapist's hurt over being expelled from the Jesuits, climbing down into McNeill's private hell. The very intensity of Judge's anguish at the prospect of losing his priesthood made clear just how much he treasured it.

"All the strain and pain," McNeill later said. "At the same time, it was part of his sanctity. To become a saint, you have to suffer. He came the closest to sainthood of anyone I knew."

Judge continued his ministry, officiating at AIDS Masses and attending AIDS retreats and AIDS workshops and AIDS support groups and AIDS prayer groups. He recruited fellow AA member Ted Patterson to volunteer.

"I said, 'I don't know what AIDS looks like,'" Patterson recalled. "He said, 'Come on over.'"

Patterson worked an AIDS hotline at St. Clare's Hospital and handed out information to those diagnosed with a disease that still marked its victims untouchable.

"They couldn't get dentists," Patterson said. "Only two funeral parlors in New York would bury them."

The busier of the two was Redden's, where Judge was now going as many as five times in a week. He knew this was how it would soon end for every AIDS patient he visited at the hospital, but he kept striding into their rooms as if he was stopping by a friend's house for a chat.

"He would just go in and say hello and they would talk to him like crazy," Patterson remembered. "He said, 'God's watching over you and I'm going to bless you and everything is going to be just fine.' He never said you have to be Catholic. He said you have to love yourself and you have to love God. When he left, they'd have a big smile on their faces. They all died happier."

• • •

The ministry kept growing, and Judge established an office on the first floor of the friary. He wrote:

> For two years, I was on my own. Funerals and wakes were commonplace each week. I tried to keep it simple (no office, no phone) just a visiting-presence ministry. Being that easy, it could not last. The needs are too many . . . I wanted to keep it simple, but the Lord has other ideas and I have nothing to say about it.

Judge still kept his appointment book, and one name that repeatedly appeared in it was Stephen Smurr. Smurr was from Columbus, Ohio, and the nuns in grammar school had told him he would make a fine priest. He was handsome enough to be a model. He instead chose to become an artist, and he headed to New York to study at the Parsons School of Design, where his work caught the attention of Andy Warhol and Halston.

After graduation, Stephen Smurr had gone to work designing children's clothing, translating his vibrancy into color and fabric. He might well have become another Calvin Klein had he not become infected with the HIV virus. His employer learned of the diagnosis and fired him. His designs were still being sold in the stores, and he would point out children on the street who were wearing his creations.

A seemingly innocuous boil on Stephen's leg signaled that his immune system was breaking down. He was in and out of Beth Israel Hospital with a series of opportunistic infections, and Judge was a regular visitor, giving him Holy Communion and good company. Stephen felt compelled to tell his parents of his illness, which meant also telling them he was gay. Marge and Tom Smurr flew to New York, doubly stunned. They agreed to accompany their son to a gathering of Dignity.

"I was so overwhelmed by this vast group of men," his mother, Marge, would remember. "I knew, but I didn't want to know. I just couldn't bring myself to believe my son was like this."

Then, out of the crowd came a smiling priest.

"He introduced himself, and it just about blew me away because I never dreamed in a million years that someone like that would be there," Marge recalled.

Judge recognized the parents' simple presence as an act of love.

"He said, 'Marge, the great thing you and Tom have done is to uphold your son. So many families can't. You've accepted it,'" she remembered. "I said, 'Well, what choice do we have?'"

Judge was doing what he always did. He was acknowledging what was strong and good in people at a time when they needed that strength and goodness most. He also drew on the saving grace he had learned in the harshness of the novitiate.

"The thing I remember is he could make you laugh," Marge said. "You could be so down and all of a sudden he'd just have you in stitches."

On a day Stephen was out of the hospital, Judge strolled with the Smurrs through Manhattan. People of every persuasion and description called out to Father Mychal. He did not hesitate to embrace even the most downtrodden.

"Everybody knew him," Marge remembered. "He'd hug them and it'd be like a long lost friend."

The four ambled on, Tom and Stephen in the lead, Marge and Judge trailing. Judge gazed ahead at father and son striding side by side. He told Marge, "You know, I never really knew my dad . . . I'd really like to believe my father would have been like Tom."

Marge grabbed Judge's hand. She told Judge, "Well, you couldn't say anything nicer to me, because Tom is the prince in my life and I really appreciate you recognize that."

As if to confirm Judge's good opinion, Tom paused to give money to a panhandler they encountered. Marge asked Judge what the man would do with it. Judge gave an expanded version of what he had said to Dympna a half century before when he gave a derelict their only coin.

"I don't know. He might get something to eat, he might get a bottle of wine," Judge said. "Whatever it is, Marge, he will be happy for it . . . If everybody would touch another person in that way, look what a beautiful world we'd have."

In Judge's view, a beautiful world also includes sexuality, and he told this to one of the younger friars on West Thirty-first Street who had been so inspired by Judge while an undergraduate at Siena. Brian Carroll was now seeking a way to live within his vows and with the feelings they did nothing to extinguish, feelings only roused by the same exuberance and love and humanity that had made the habit seem such a magical garment on Judge.

Judge assured Carroll that such feelings were part of being human and were therefore both wonderful and important. Carroll later said to a reporter, "He took away the shame. For some people, sexuality is a part of their shame. Or homelessness is a part of their shame. Or addiction is a part of their shame. Mychal helped people embrace all the shame parts of themselves and turn them into something good."

What was important was the love, not the form it took. Whether Judge was in fact gay or straight, his deepest passion was for neither man nor woman, or perhaps both.

"He was more in love with God," Carroll said.

8

That fall, a woman who learned of Steven McDonald's misfortune telephoned and offered the paralyzed officer and his wife a berth on an eighteen-day pilgrimage to shrines in Fátima, Lourdes, and Medjugorje, as well as to Rome. Such a four-nation journey would be too arduous for Steven, and Patti Ann invited Judge to come along in his stead.

Steven arranged through the cardinal for them to see the Pope, and Judge wrote of the event in a 99-cent steno pad whose cover he had inscribed with "Mychal Judge Journal."

Wed. Oct. 19, 1988
    "Audience Day"
    We were up early—Down to breakfast and feeling a bit anxious; Patti was too. Wondering about the day. Where we would sit, would we get close. So many things—

They hopped a cab to the Vatican.

Halfway there, the skies opened but closed again as we got out of the cab. Five big fat German ladies tried to get into it before we even opened the door. Patti dropped some money and—honest to God—one of them picked it up and tried to hold onto it. Patti was stunned.

Patti Ann was stunned all the more when they encountered nuns behaving like rock fans charging into a concert hall.

Then into the Vatican and the push of the nuns. "Wow, what's going on here?" she said. I told her of all that has been written about nuns at the

Vatican and how pushy and brutal they are. [I said] "They will do any-
thing to get near the Holy Father."

The tickets proved the influence of a cardinal who adheres to papal doctrine.

To our seats Wow!—closer and closer—A wave of a papal guard's ("The
Swiss Guards") hand and closer to the throne. Finally, our seats: Row one,
Seats 33 and 34. Stand in awe, look all around. The moment of your
life: St. Peter's Square, the Papal balcony, the statues, the podium, and
there we are—front row center.

A photographer came over to take their names, and Judge realized they
were one of the chosen few. They would actually meet the Pope.

We are in "The Row."

They were just a few feet away when the popemobile rolled up.

We could almost reach out and touch him. Patti kept saying, "I can't be-
lieve it."

An array of priests conveyed the Pope's greetings to the chosen groups in
their native languages.

Then the English and: "We have parishioners from St. Francis of Assisi
Parish in New York City." I cheered and he looked at me.

The Pope started down the Row and Patti Ann broke down as he neared.

Patti told me to speak and tell him why we are here—He came to her. She
showed him the picture of Steven, Conor and herself—[I said] "Holy Fa-
ther . . . her husband is sick."

Patti Ann found her voice.

"Yes," said Patti. "He is a cop and he was shot."

The Pope himself had once been shot. He stared at the photo.

"He is a young man," said the Pope.

Judge pointed to the ring that Patti Ann wore on a neck chain. He said this was Steven's wedding band.

"Please, your Holiness, would you touch his ring?" He did and he signed Patti on the forehead.

Judge then knew just what to ask this Pope who incited rage among those dying back home.

I asked him to bless my AIDS work. He smiled and touched my hand.

Judge then told the Pope they had met a decade before.

"I was on a bus with you in Passaic, N.J.". . . He paused, looked at me as if he did remember.

The Pope signed Judge's forehead and moved on. Judge and Patti Ann embraced. Judge may have once termed the Pope "a great show for the deaf," but the Pope was still the Pope, the Holy Father.

That night, they visited the Trevi Fountain and strolled back to the hotel, window shopping. Judge telephoned Erin. Patti Ann spoke to Steven and learned that two New York City police officers had died in unrelated shootings within hours of each other.

Patti Ann and Judge went to St. Peter's Basilica the next day to pray for Police Officers Chris Hoban and Michael Buczek. The two pilgrims entered the biggest church on earth. The dome conceived by Michelangelo soared above. Directly ahead was the Throne of St. Peter, a huge confection of gold and bronze surrounding a wooden seat said to be from Peter's oaken chair during the earliest Christian services. This chair had been as plain and simple as the man known not for his wisdom or strength or even piety but for his vibrant love of Christ.

I was filled with a great sense of the joy and simplicity of my own faith, of the two churches that I live in—old and new and the great satisfaction that I receive by just being present and speaking to God in my simple way.

What enchanted Judge was not the majestic architecture or the priceless masterpieces, not the gleaming gold or the bronze taken from the roof of the Pantheon, not the statue of Saint Peter in papal robes or the mosaic of Saint Jerome that dwarfed the one back on West Thirty-first Street. The sight he was moved to record was of the faith that shone in the cop's wife beside him.

What a wonderful human being she is.

The two then walked back to the *Pietà,* which Judge had seen at the World's Fair when he was starting out as a priest, when the Mass of the Future was upon them and the old Church was giving way to a new Church that was ultimately an attempt to return to the even older, original Church.

Judge was on the plane home when he ended his journal with three words that stood alone, a declaration of the same love that had made Peter the Rock of the Church when its throne was a simple chair in an unadorned room, the love he embraced at the cost of having no one to embrace him at the airport.

I truly believe!

9

Judge was smiling as he whispered into the ear of the comatose woman known as the Central Park Jogger.

"God loves you."

She was twenty-eight years old and she had been out for a run when she was beaten and raped. The attack had occurred only yards from where Steven McDonald had been shot three years before, and the cop had asked the family if he could visit her. He arrived at Metropolitan Hospital for the first time since he was carried into the emergency room with wounds the first doctor declared fatal. He had Judge with him as he rolled up to the woman's bedside in his wheelchair.

"Tubing lines coming out every place you could imagine," McDonald remembered.

The woman's respirator *whooshed* in syncopation with the portable respirator affixed to the back of McDonald's wheelchair. Judge ever so gently set his hands on her battered head to bless her. He then bent over and whispered.

"She's totally out of it, but he's smiling and having a conversation," McDonald said later.

Judge and McDonald and the woman's family then formed a semicircle around the bed. Everyone joined hands save McDonald, who was unable to because he remained paralyzed from the neck down. The person on either side of him touched his hands as Judge led them in the Our Father and a Hail Mary. He said the same prayer he had uttered during the first Mass in McDonald's room.

"Lord, make me an instrument of Thy peace . . ."

Judge and McDonald departed in the officer's specially equipped van, with which they spread their message of peace and forgiveness in a city that sometimes seemed lost to violence. They took heart in letters such as one a youngster from Far Rockaway sent to McDonald.

"You just changed my life around when you said that you forgived the boy that shot you because I had hate for the person who killed my cousin wife and kids in a fire," the youngster wrote. "What you said touched me so hard that I forgave that person who killed my family. Thanks a lot, Officer McDonald. I will pray for you night and day that some day you will walk again."

When their travels took them near St. John's Cemetery in Queens, they would stop by the Judge family grave.

"He said, 'I've been called "father" most of my life and I can't wait until that day when I am called unto my dad,'" McDonald recalled. "He looked forward to those moments in heaven when he could sit with him and chat. He would have eternity to talk with his dad about what fathers and sons talk about."

The plot was just a few graves in from Woodhaven Boulevard, and once when time was pressing, Judge hopped out to say a few words to Dad through the cemetery fence. "Just saying hello," he explained.

Some nights, Judge and McDonald simply roamed the streets. They would stop into Kennedy's Irish restaurant or the Green Derby Irish restaurant or maybe just get Chinese takeout and park at the tip of Manhattan. They would sit with the Twin Towers rising behind them and gaze out at the Statue of Liberty. Judge proved able to rattle off facts about the statue and other icons of American history just as he could about the Brooklyn Bridge.

The night before he was to travel to a rehabilitation center in Denver, Steven McDonald asked Judge to come see him. Judge went to his fellow friar Julian Deeken, the fire chaplain for Manhattan and the Bronx. Deeken kept a rattletrap FDNY Plymouth in the firehouse across from the friary. He agreed to lend the car to Judge with the stipulation that he would not use the lights and siren.

Judge drove out to see McDonald and returned late that night. He took out the journal he had started and then set aside in the first days of the AIDS ministry. He wrote one more page before setting the journal aside for good.

Steven was in bed—Tonight I felt I was in his body—I felt contained!
It was a very good, a spiritual meeting for both of us. Communion, sac.
of sick and confession. Patti Ann wanted to be up with us but Conor
kept waking up . . . It was one of the best visits. I came home spiritually
high.

On a night when Stephen Smurr was back in the hospital, Judge borrowed the Plymouth again to chauffeur his friend's mother, Marge. He picked her up on Park Avenue and decided she required some cheering up.

"Marge," he said, "watch this!"

Judge dispensed with Deeken's edict and set the lights and siren going in the name of badly needed fun.

"He made a U-turn and this cabbie made a screeching stop, and he's just laughing hysterically," Marge remembered with continued delight.

On the Fourth of July, Judge stood with Marge Smurr at the window of her son's room at Beth Israel Hospital. The window afforded a view of the annual fireworks display on the East River, and Marge watched the detonations in the summer night sky, spectacular bursts of color making only bleaker the fact that her weakening son was struggling to fight off yet another infection. She then glanced over at Judge and saw he was gazing not at the fireworks but at her.

"He was more interested in looking at me and wondering what went through my mind," Marge said later. "He knew I was just so overwhelmed."

As always, Judge walked Marge to the door of the building where she was staying.

"I'd invite him in. He'd say, 'Oh, no, I just wanted to make sure you got back safely. You know our streets over here are unpredictable,'" Marge remembered.

Back at the friary, Judge received a phone call from James Hyams, the man who had held his family at gunpoint in New Jersey. Hyams had been released from prison in 1984. He remained in contact with Judge as he remarried and took a job at a Long Island country club. Hyams was now calling Judge to invite him to a birthday party.

"He was absolutely charming," Judge would recall. "He seemed very happy."

Two weeks later, Judge got another call, from the police, informing him that Hyams had again barricaded himself in his home. Hyams had this time shot his stepdaughter, Lisa, to death and turned the gun on himself. Judge attended the funerals of both.

Judge would be welcomed on his return to the friary by stacks of message slips from callers who urgently needed to speak with Father Mychal. AIDS patients. AA comrades. Former parishioners. Siena alumni. Buddies from England. Far-flung friars. Others he encountered on the street or in the confessional or somewhere else in his travels.

He finally acquired an answering machine, and came home one evening to a message from Stephen Smurr's lover.

"Mychal, this is Michael Mulligan. Stephen's in the hospital. He doesn't want to take any more treatment. I need you to come here as soon as possible."

At the hospital, Smurr slipped in and out of consciousness. Judge tenderly performed the Anointing of the Sick as he had with scores upon scores of others. He had begun mixing scents he bought from street peddlers into his holy oils to add fragrance to the ritual.

In keeping with Smurr's final instructions, Judge presided at two funerals, one in the lower church at St. Francis, the second back home in Columbus. Judge presented Marge and Tom with a copy of *The Steven McDonald Story*, the newly published book by that other Steven and Patti Ann. The inscription read:

To MARGE and TOM,
A beautiful love story like your own about two people I love very much, as I do you.
The depth of faith of the four of you moves me on.
In joy,
MYCHAL

Inside, Judge had tucked a holy card from his first Mass that bore these words, "Priest forever, February 25, 1961."

Judge flew out and back with the heartbroken Mulligan and stayed in close contact with him through the bleakness ahead.

"He'd show up and say, 'Orders from headquarters to take care of Michael Mulligan,'" Mulligan would recall.

Mulligan gave Judge a picture of Stephen Smurr that he kept atop his dresser in the friary.

Meanwhile, Judge's appointment book recorded more hospital visits and more funerals. He noted one of his favorite events as the holidays approached, the annual gathering the Johnson family hosted in a ballroom at the Sheraton Hotel. There were clowns and magicians and face painting and music and dancing and a Santa Claus who arrived with sacks full of presents for the children. There were also politicians and judges and the occasional titan of industry.

The patriarch of the Johnson family was Peter Johnson Sr., a former longshoreman, cop, and marine who had become a prominent civil trial lawyer. His elder son, Chris Johnson, was a police detective whose lungs had been seared while rescuing people from a fire. The younger son, Peter Johnson Jr., was an attorney who had helped write the famous "City on a Hill" speech Mario Cuomo gave at the 1984 Democratic convention in San Francisco. The younger Peter was a cancer survivor, and at Brian Mulheren's urging he had visited Steven McDonald in Bellevue Hospital after the shooting to speak of his own brush with death.

The Johnsons had since become good friends with the McDonalds, and through them Judge. The Johnsons were also close to David Dinkins, who had just narrowly defeated Rudy Giuliani to become the city's first black mayor. Dinkins had won by only 47,080 votes. The deciding factor may well have been support from Steven McDonald, who added credence to Dinkins's claim that he would be tough on crime and still bring the city together.

On New Year's Day, 1990, Judge stood in his sandals among the twelve thousand people squeezed into City Hall Park for David Dinkins's inauguration. Judge always sought to see the best even in politicians, and he found Dinkins less challenging than most with his vision of the city as a "gorgeous mosaic." Two hundred seats had been allocated to the homeless, and the Gay Men's Chorus sang "New York, New York" from the balcony. A small reminder of the difficulty of truly bringing everyone together came at the end, when Cardinal

O'Connor gave the benediction. Several gay activists held up signs reading, JUST SAY NO TO CARDINAL O'CONNOR. Others turned their backs to him.

The inaugural mosaic reassembled afterward at a reception at the Winter Garden at the World Financial Center. Dinkins would not remember seeing there the brown-robed friar who would soon become as dear to him as anyone. Judge, for his part, had no inkling that this new administration would send his life into a direction he had never anticipated, one that would end as nobody could have imagined: in the North Tower, directly across West Street from this glass-domed atrium.

At this moment, Judge was simply delighted by the diversity of the gathering at the foot of the Twin Towers. The vibrant mix of races, nationalities, backgrounds, and circumstance was to him greater proof of his city's magnificence than its highest buildings.

"Just look!" Judge said.

Fate took a turn when Father Julian Deeken fell ill with cancer and asked Judge to fill in as the fire chaplain.

"He said to me, 'Would you cover the fire department job for me?' " Judge recalled. "I said, 'Gee, Jules, I don't know the first thing about it.' 'You just show up,' he says. 'You go to the third alarms and just stand there and bless them. Go to the hospitals occasionally. That's all you have to do. It's a very simple job.' "

Judge was not convinced.

Deeken knew just what to say. "The desk will call you, and when they do, you just go down to the car and put on the lights and sirens."

"Ooooh, I could do that," Judge said.

Over the weeks that followed, Judge would every so often respond to the scene of a fire, getting a kick out of the lights and sirens but not really understanding what he saw when he got there. He would hand out a few blessings to men who just seemed to be doing what they were trained and paid to do.

"I didn't know what I was doing, but I did it," Judge said later. "When they called me, I showed up, and when they asked me, I did what I was supposed to do."

Judge told his friend Tom Ferriter from West Milford of arriving at the scene of a blaze to see a firefighter up on a ladder with a hose, dousing the flames. Judge was inspired to clamber up just as he had years before when Hyams took his family hostage. He held out a bottle of water.

"The fireman's up there with a hose putting out two million gallons, and Mychal's climbing the ladder to give him a drink of water," Ferriter recalled. "They had to post a guy at the bottom of the ladder to keep him off it. He just wanted to help. He didn't know what to do."

As the annual St. Patrick's Day parade neared, a group of handicapped children who had been inspired by Steven McDonald applied to join the procession. They were rejected by the event's overseers, ostensibly because the parade was already too long and there was a waiting list of at least forty other groups. The overseers were also citing a waiting list in barring the Irish Lesbian and Gay Organization. They could not make an exception for the children without its appearing that they were rejecting ILGO out of homophobia, which they almost certainly were.

McDonald announced that he would boycott the parade if the children were barred. Governor Mario Cuomo invited McDonald and the youngsters to march with him and a contingent of state police. Judge joined them in his brown habit. The group drew wild cheers all along the fifty-four blocks of Fifth Avenue.

Dinkins was farther downtown, having initially pledged to become the first mayor in a half century to miss the parade if ILGO was not allowed to march. A midtown Manhattan chapter of the Ancient Order of Hibernians had then followed Cuomo's example and invited the gay group to march with them. Dinkins decided to go along, and Peter Johnson Jr. was with them as they proceeded uptown.

Some of the same onlookers who had just cheered McDonald and the children now jeered Dinkins and ILGO.

"Go back in the closet!"

"Gay sex, no way!"

"You're a disgrace! "

"This is our parade!"

At least two full beer cans were thrown at Dinkins. The mayoral security detail opened up umbrellas to protect him, but Johnson waved them away, reasoning it would be ineffective and look ridiculous.

"It was like marching in Birmingham, Alabama," Dinkins said.

Judge witnessed only the heckling near the end of the route, but that was enough. He uttered words he could never have imagined himself saying.

"I'm embarrassed to be Irish."

Afterward, Judge headed for Cooper Union to hear the Stonewall Choir, named after the Greenwich Village bar that was the scene of the 1969 riot that many consider the start of the gay rights movement. He continued to visit AIDS patients, these now including Steven McDonald's cousin, Michael Ferris.

"His family loved him, but they had a very difficult time accepting his illness," McDonald would say.

On April 19, Judge recorded the latest AIDS death by writing "+ Michael Ferris" at the top of the page. Judge was at Ferris's bedside at the end, whispering words of comfort. Judge held one of Ferris's hands while the other clutched a prayer book that Cardinal O'Connor had given the dying man.

The next day, Judge chanced to encounter the cardinal at an affair where Steven McDonald was presented another of many civic awards. McDonald had heard Judge call the Church's mitered eminences "men with little churches on their heads," but noted he nonetheless knelt when he went over to where the cardinal sat.

"Your Eminence, young Michael died last night," Judge said. "And I want you to know he held on to your prayer book until the moment he slipped away."

Judge may have hoped that in imparting this to the cardinal he could ease the tension between them. Judge was aware the cardinal had become jealous of his closeness to the McDonalds. Judge would joke that he had to walk five paces away from Steven so as not to appear in any news photos.

McDonald suspected the jealousy ran even deeper than Judge imagined, to a part of O'Connor that longed for the days when he was addressed not as "Your Eminence" but "Padre!" O'Connor had spent two years as a navy chaplain with the marines in Vietnam right in the thick of it, just like the famed Father Francis Duffy of New York's "Fighting 69th" in World War I. O'Connor had called this time "as grace-filled and rich and rewarding a life as I could have possibly imagined."

O'Connor had uttered those words after becoming the New York half of

Law and Order, and he seemed to long for those earlier days of flash and action. He went to the scene of an apartment house blaze in 1988 where four people on the upper floors had been killed. Julian Deeken had already climbed the stairs and blessed the bodies. O'Connor nonetheless stopped the firefighters as they carried the dead onto the street and blessed the bodies again. The firefighters did not fail to notice that the news cameras were there to record the cardinal in action.

"I am a priest and I thought I might be needed," O'Connor told the reporters.

O'Connor went back to being a cardinal, an eminence with a cathedral. But Mychal Judge was a real working priest with passion and charm and wit.

"Cardinal O'Connor would have given up his robes to be a Father Mychal," McDonald later said.

Judge was leaving a ten A.M. appointment at his dentist's office near the cathedral on May 14 when he heard sirens converging three blocks away on West Forty-eighth Street. He arrived to see the top floor of a twelve-story building ablaze. Two men were trapped on window ledges at opposite sides of the structure. They were beyond the reach of the tallest ladder, and the fire was raging behind them. The crowd below called out, intuitively understanding the choice people invariably make between being burned alive or plummeting to certain death.

"Don't jump! Don't jump!"

Firefighters from Rescue 1 dashed up the stairs past the fire. Bucca was still a member of the company, but he was off that day. Those working included a lieutenant of modest stature and build whom Judge would learn was Paddy Brown. Judge watched Brown lean over the edge of the roof and shout to one of the men on the windowsills.

"Don't jump!"

The crowd hushed as Firefighter Pat Barr eased himself over the edge, holding on with both hands and then letting go so he dangled high over the street by a nylon rope cinched to a harness about his waist. Barr was being even more courageous than Judge and the other people below could imagine, for there was no place on the roof to tie off the rope. The other end was anchored only by the weight of two fellow firefighters, who slowly fed out more and more at Brown's command until the dangling Barr was even with the man on the windowsill.

The man wrapped his arms and legs around Barr, and several feet of rope ran out faster than before. Judge would have gone into hyperprayer if he had been able to see that the combined weight had lifted the two anchoring firefighters up toward the roof edge. A third firefighter threw himself on the two, holding them down and preventing disaster.

For a few moments, Barr and the man spun in midair, arms and legs entwined in an embrace elemental and profound, a full-body clasp of two total strangers, one unhesitatingly ready to place himself in the direst danger to save the other. Barr broke a pane of glass with a gloved hand, continued to spin and broke a second pane when he came around again. That got the attention of the firefighters on that floor. They pulled Barr and the man to safety and the crowd on the street erupted into cheers and applause. Barr waved.

The fire flared and flames shot out the window where the man had stood. A second man was still on a window ledge and the firefighters pulled the rope back up. Firefighter Kevin Shea affixed the end to his harness and went over the edge just like Barr.

The crowd again witnessed that elemental embrace, no less remarkable, perhaps even more profound, for the repetition showed this was not a lone courageous act but simply what firefighters do. Judge once more watched rescuer and rescued hang high over the street as a single fate, a figure no less stirring than a crucifix, inspiring to those of any faith. Here was a figure divine in the very absence of divine powers, in being so heart-poundingly subject to the indifference of nature's laws.

The sight was suspenseful enough without Judge and the other citizens below knowing the true extent of the danger. Shea had gone over with one less firefighter to anchor him. And department regulations forbade using a rope more than once. This edict had been issued after a rope broke and killed two firefighters eleven years before, one of them Brown's dear friend. But nobody had foreseen that firefighters might find themselves on a roof with no replacement rope and a second man on a windowsill just seconds from jumping.

The same forces that threatened to kill Shea and the second man should the rope break also translated them into a huge, living pendulum. A firefighter who reached out the window was able to pull them to safety by tugging on Shea's booted toe. The crowd again erupted in cheers and applause, but Shea did not wave. He hung back from the news cameras when the fire-fighters returned to the street.

The lieutenant, Paddy Brown, exulted before the lenses that had captured the entire double rescue. He pulled Barr and then Shea to him and therefore to center stage.

"Kevin, baby!" Brown said.

Shea looked uncomfortable, as if the attention were unwarranted, as if he had only done what the circumstances dictated, what any firefighter would.

"I just prayed the man did not panic and jump," Shea told the media mob.

One reporter asked if he had been scared.

"I'm supposed to say no, right?" Shea said.

On June 10, Judge stood on the stretch of Broadway called the Canyon of Heroes and cheered along with a much bigger crowd, a million people who gathered to honor the troops who had served in the Gulf War. The event was called the biggest ticker tape parade in the city's history. Everywhere people were saying that the country was finally shaking off the trauma of Vietnam, the war of Cardinal O'Connor and, it happened, Paddy Brown.

AMERICA'S BACK! a placard announced.

"I didn't know it had gone anywhere," Judge said.

That night, Judge joined Steven McDonald on the deck of the aircraft carrier USS *Nassau*. They watched a fireworks reenactment of a Patriot mis-sile intercepting a SCUD, the aerial pantomime of good rising to meet pure evil that had been this war's most lasting television image.

Judge always concentrated on living only in the day at hand, often saying that there was no use fretting about tomorrow because God had not made it yet. But some of the makings of a September day a decade hence were already in the harbor that night: the celebration of a victory that a Saudi rich kid named Osama bin Laden thought should have been his, the shining Twin Towers.

Another element fell into place thirteen days later, when Fire Chaplain Ju-lian Deeken died of cancer. The funeral was held the following Wednesday in the upper church at St. Francis, and the program bore the fire department logo.

Appointed New York City Fire Department Chaplain December 10, 1981
Returned to the Lord June 23, 1991.

Many of those in attendance were firefighters who had come to know Deeken during his decade as chaplain. Mulheren suggested that Judge was just the man to replace him. But as impressed as Judge was by the firefighters, and however big a kick he got out of the lights and siren, he was already over-burdened with his AIDS ministry. He also had his work with the homeless and his duties as a friar. He told Mulheren he would continue filling in only until a new chaplain was appointed.

Judge had more personal misgivings, which he shared with Ron Pesci, his fellow friar from the West Milford days. Pesci would recall Judge saying of the FDNY, "It's such a macho world. These guys talk about ball games all the time and I don't know the Giants from the Yankees."

Mulheren was not one to take no for an answer. He continued pressing Judge, reminding him that the vast majority of the city's 11,400 firefighters are Catholic.

"I said, 'The fire department is the largest parish there is. They need somebody,'" Mulheren recalled. "I kept saying to him, 'You're the person.'"

Judge recorded in his appointment book what seemed to be his final answer: "Brian Mulheren—No F.D.N.Y."

Judge became even busier when he was asked to head the friary's first fund-raising campaign. The McDonalds helped arrange a dinner with some well-to-do heavy hitters. Judge did not fail to charm them, but their loyalties already lay elsewhere.

"If any money could be raised, it was for the cardinal and the archdio-cese," Steven McDonald later said.

Judge seemed to be making some headway when a very rich family asked him to come to their Park Avenue apartment and pick up a donation. He arrived with expectations proportionate to their wealth. He walked back down the fabled avenue with two coffee cans of pocket change.

Judge remained far short of the six-million-dollar target when the pastor relieved him of his fund-raising duties. But Judge had become close friends with several very successful individuals, including the night mayor's cousin, legendary Wall Street swashbuckler John Mulheren.

The Wall Streeter Mulheren described himself as "a person who has a lot of money," and Judge was "somebody who knows a lot of people who need money." The tycoon was always ready with an anonymous gift whenever Judge encountered someone in a serious and immediate need. He called such arrangements TLOA for "To Love One Another."

Judge was still filling in as chaplain, and he got a first full measure of what the job could entail three days later, after another firefighter named Kevin, thirty-one-year-old Firefighter Kevin Kane, was trapped on the fourth floor of a burning building in Brooklyn.

As his comrades hurried to raise a cherry picker to rescue him, Kane managed to remain in the blazing window and endure the flames when almost anybody else would have jumped. He had burns to 80 percent of his body when the bucket finally reached him and he dove in shouting, "Please don't let me die!"

Kane was rushed to the Burn Center at New York Hospital–Cornell Medical Center in Manhattan. Judge visited him, even though Msgr. Tom Brady was the chaplain for Brooklyn firefighters.

Judge recorded the visit in his book just as he would a visit to an AIDS patient, but he had never witnessed human suffering to match these horrific burns. Kane's father, retired fire chief Edward "Killer" Kane, stood with his son's comrades in the hallway.

"You did your job and I want you to continue doing your job," the elder Kane said.

The son died hours later. Judge learned that the younger Kane had once considered becoming a priest and had attended the Franciscan seminary in Washington, D.C. Judge decided that in signing on to the fire department instead, Kane had answered an even higher calling.

"He knew exactly what could happen to him and he went into that building anyway on the chance he could help somebody he didn't know," Judge said.

Judge had no doubt what he was witnessing when he watched Kane's comrades leave his bedside to risk suffering the same horrific fate.

"The grace of God," Judge said.

Judge had a new answer the next time Mulheren asked him to become the new fire chaplain.

"Yes."

10

The day Kevin Kane was buried, Mychal Judge was away with Steven McDonald on a long-planned trip to Lourdes. Some believe the baths impart miracle cures, but Steven was not counting on one. "I wasn't looking for a quick exit from the wheelchair."

Such ponderings gave way to the more immediate problem of stripping down before the dip. Steven was unable to remove his clothes, and he was a touch uncomfortable as Judge began to assist him.

"As close as Father Mike and I were, I had never been undressed in front of him," Steven would recall.

Judge's relaxed and happy sanctity quickly put Steven at ease.

"It didn't seem to bother me," Steven remembered.

Judge removed his own clothing and asked the attendants to help lift Steven from the chair. They balked, saying it was too dangerous.

"They've seen it all, but I'm me. Not only am I not able to move my arms and legs, but I'm on a ventilator," McDonald recalled. "Father Mychal said, 'No, no, no, he's going.'"

The attendants relented, and Judge got in with Steven. Judge cupped water in his hands and prayed as he ever so carefully trickled it over Steven's forehead and face. Steven felt himself at the serene nexus of the sacred and the marvelous.

McDonald's other spiritual benefactor was back in New York, in the exquisite robes he would have traded to be like the simple friar who could impart perfect serenity even while wearing nothing at all.

John Cardinal O'Connor was known to twitch visibly at the mention of the name Mychal Judge. The prospect of Judge replacing Deeken must have been particularly galling because traditionally fire chaplains are chosen by the cardinal. Fire Commissioner Carlos Rivera made at least a pretense of acknowledging that in a November 13 letter addressed to "John Cardinal O'Connor, Archbishop of New York":

> *With your permission, I would like to offer the appointment of Fire Department Chaplain to the Reverend Michael Judge. Your favorable consideration of my request will indeed be appreciated. May God bless you and keep you with us for many years to come.*

The obsequious tone did not change the fact that O'Connor would have been hard pressed to oppose someone who was so unquestionably well suited for the job, and just as unquestionably well connected. O'Connor followed the news too carefully not to have noticed that Judge was seated up by the pulpit at the October 23 funeral for Mayor Dinkins's father.

And then there was Steven McDonald, who was coming to see Judge more and more as Christ returned to earth in Brooklyn Irish form. The cardinal had little choice but to acquiesce to the appointment, at least overtly. O'Connor might not have been able to stop it, anyway. Mulheren had already started to process the paperwork three weeks before the commissioner wrote the cardinal.

At Mulheren's instruction, Judge acted as if he already had the job, dashing to fires around the clock. Rescue 1, as one of the highly trained elite units based in each borough, also responded to every significant blaze in Manhattan. Judge watched Firefighter Kevin Shea retain the unassuming air of somebody merely doing his job.

As for Paddy Brown, Judge observed that even the biggest and burliest firefighters turned to this bantam-sized lieutenant as if he were a giant by another measure.

"They all looked to him," Judge would later say. "You'd hear them go, 'Paddy! Paddy Brown!' "

Judge learned that with the name came a credo.

"First in, last out."

Brown embraced Judge as if chaplain were the sixth spot on a rig and he was just the one to fill it. Judge could almost have been a regular guy from Brooklyn who learned to play ball from his father and took the fire test and suddenly assumed the grace of God whenever an alarm sounded.

"He's, you know, all right, you know?" Brown said.

• • •

Judge remained a friar, and on November 8 the predawn darkness found him working the breadline outside St. Francis. He attended an AIDS art benefit meeting that morning, after which he said Mass.

At 9:30 P.M., Judge stopped by St. Barnabas Hospital, where he was ministering to several people with AIDS. He drove to a Queens diner with a friend on the staff, who brought along Al Alvarado, a young nurse from the island of Mindanao in the Philippines. The three sat and chatted and at one point Alvarado excused himself. Alvarado was in the men's room when the friend entered.

"I think he's interested in you," the friend said, meaning Judge. "I can tell by the way he looks at you."

Alvarado was not classically handsome in the way of Stephen Smurr or, for that matter, Judge himself. He was slight of build and almost nondescript, but he had an unusual boldness in his eyes and a smile of pure mischief. He had been raised in poverty as dire as Leitrim's of old, making the most destitute of the Bronx seem well off by comparison. He had been sickly as a child, and his parents had sold him for a token amount to another family with the notion that this would get him away from whatever in the household was making him ill.

"To get rid of bad spirits," Alvarado later said.

The other family had been relatively well off, and his health indeed improved, likely more due to food than spirits, the Eucharist not of the next world but of this one. He remained less overtly macho than other young men of his town, though his older brother tried to toughen him up by tying him in a 120-pound rice sack and dumping him in a hollow tree trunk swarming with biting ants whenever he acted effeminate.

"So I had to be a man," Alvarado recalled.

Much of the island's population had been converted by Arab missionaries in the fourteenth and early fifteenth centuries. The majority remained true to Islam despite the often coercive efforts of the Christian colonizers, starting with Ferdinand Magellan. The latter termed the Muslims tribesmen Moros, an allusion to the Moors with whom they warred for seven centuries. The United States elbowed out the Spanish, supposedly as liberators. The Moros of Mindanao introduced the Americans to Muslim suicide attacks, by secular *amoks* (hence the expression "to run amok") and by religious *juramentados* who believed they would be rewarded with a flock of virgins in paradise, a notion shared by the 9/11 hijackers to come.

Alvarado grew up with both Muslim and Christian friends. He was raised what he would term "partly Catholic." He remained a touch mystified by at least one aspect of Catholicism and Christianity in general. He could not understand why any religion would say that the poor were blessed and would inherit the earth.

"Why tell people who are poor they are better off?" Alvarado later asked.

Alvarado had sat down in the diner with his friend and Judge as a devout believer in having enough to eat and getting a practical education and securing a living wage and being gay if that is what you are. He had a keen sense of all that was arrayed against a young gay Filipino man of humble origins, and he took it as a challenge.

"If you're not living on the edge, you're occupying a lot of space," he later told Judge.

This attitude translated to that boldness in his eyes, a glint of *amok* perhaps but bent on life rather than death. Alvarado was the very opposite of a shapeshifter, someone zestfully determined to be who he was no matter what forces tried to mold him otherwise. This apparently roused in Judge everything that longed to break free, to be as liberated as he had been in those moments when he danced in Canterbury, to assume only his own true form, to shake off his longings for what had never been and would never be, to be most literally gay, to escape the unending need of this God who was too much in love with him, to fall into a simple embrace that would satisfy its own demands. And Alvarado was young, as young as Judge's feelings, as young as Judge would have needed to be to go wherever those feelings took him.

For his part, Alvarado returned to the table from the men's room surprised, for Judge was a priest and more than thirty years his senior. The young man who sought the edge would later say that, surprise aside, he was not bothered by the age difference. He found the clergy aspect alluring.

Judge visited St. Barnabas again at eleven P.M. the next night, this time not only to minister to the sick but also to see Alvarado. Judge returned to Manhattan and early the next afternoon walked from St. Francis over the bridge to Prospect Park, as if to collect himself and maybe touch base with

Brooklyn. He was back on West Thirty-first Street in time to say Mass at 5:15 P.M. and again at 6:15 P.M. He spent the next ten days pressing ahead with his AIDS ministry and responding to fires. He delivered unclaimed clothing from Empire Cleaners to a program for people with AIDS called Out of the Closet. He presided at a Memorial Mass for the FDNY Holy Name Society in the upper church at St. Francis. He went to a fire on Dykeman Street and to the opening of an AIDS program on Seventh Avenue. He began November 19 by saying the seven A.M. Mass at St. Francis, had an AIDS meeting, met with Tom Ferriter from the West Milford days, and went to a benefit concert at Carnegie Hall with Patti Ann. He ate at a Chinese restaurant and pasted the slip of paper from his fortune cookie on that day's page in his appointment book: "You are going to have a comfortable old age."

He made no record of another trip to the Bronx, but Alvarado seems to have been prominent in his thoughts and feelings. At the top of that day's page he noted a destination of the heart.

November 19
ALA- Intense
Committed

Judge had long ago declared himself a servant to his God, a groom only to Christ, but Alvarado's boldness engendered a boldness in him that he remembered from his own younger years. He was embarking on what would be the closest he would ever come to a long-term relationship with a man even as he was becoming ever more certain that his place as a priest was with firefighters who would almost certainly be repulsed by such a relationship. He stood before two eager and irresistible embraces that seemed to preclude each other, that seemingly could not be any less like twins.

On the cold, bright morning of December 5, Judge proceeded from the seven A.M. Mass at St. Francis to a four-alarm blaze on West Forty-second Street that surreally juxtaposed the virtues of firefighters and the supposed sins of the flesh. Patrons who had begun the day in peep booths rather than a confessional had fled the blazing Times Square porn palace as Paddy Brown and his comrades dashed under a sign reading, 25CTS XXX VIDEO 25CTS and into the roiling smoke. Judge no doubt offered a prayer for the firefighters who entered this burning house of smut as unhesitatingly as they would an apartment house or office tower or church or anyplace else. The slightest possibility that somebody might need help was enough to send them into the most mortal danger to conduct what they called a "search for life."

" 'Search . . . for . . . life,' " Judge later repeated. "Marvelous."

He was coming to believe that those laughing men in blue workshirts were closer to God than even the very best priests and certainly any of the Church hierarchy he called BFMs, for Big Fat Monsignors. He could formulate no principle more sacred than the one firefighters always practiced but never preached: A life is a life and every life is equally worth saving even at the risk of losing your own.

Along with their tools and hoses, the firefighters brought this visceral sanctity to every blaze, even this one. Judge was only beginning to comprehend the conditions they faced once they disappeared into the blinding smoke. He was learning that the heat forced them to crawl close to the floor, that many of the bravest acts in the city were performed on hands and knees in the most literal and absolute obscurity. The wonderful-sounding search for life was conducted by blindly feeling around with your gloved hands as burning gases roared overhead and you scuttled ever closer to becoming a victim yourself, like Kevin Kane. The initial search was followed by a secondary search to double-check that they had not missed someone, be it a peep-booth pervert or a lap dancer or anyone else.

An engine company got a line going, and an eye more schooled than Judge's would have recognized the whitening smoke as a signal that water had reached the fire. A trained eye would also have seen Brown's fully sooted face when he emerged as an indication that like many aggressive firefighters he had broken with official procedure and dispensed with his air mask at least part of the time. A mask restricted whatever incidental visibility there might be, as well as dampened hearing and generally deadened a firefighter's connection to his surroundings, reducing his ability to combine the fragmentary clues of his senses into a lifesaving sense.

Anybody could see that Brown had undergone what firefighters call "a real beating," for this had not been the relatively benign smoke of a wood frame house but the toxic, acrid, throat-closing stuff that comes from burning plastics and other modern synthetics, in this instance including sex toys and triple-X videos. He had "a big blow," deep breaths of ordinary air turned miraculous in its ability to restore. A news crew recorded him getting a silent pat on the back from Firefighter Gary Geidel as if they had won something they did not have to name. Geidel would die with him at the Twin Towers.

Judge shared the news crew's interest in Brown, later saying he watched this firefighter the way he had once watched his favorite Ralph Branca in old Ebbets Field. Brown bowed his head and removed his helmet and exhaled. He kept sucking in air, his breath white vapor in winter cold that must have been delicious after the heat. He looked about, the marquee of the porno theater behind him billing *Cheeks* and *Rainwoman*.

Brown bowed his head again and put his helmet back on, settling it snug. He was so spent that he went down on one knee in the puddled hose water, his gloved right hand resting atop his short Hallagan tool. He looked almost like he was going to be knighted as he gazed at the last sputtering of the latest fire.

The smoke kept dissipating and the sun poked through, shining on Brown's sooty face as he rose, removed his gloves, and took up a steaming cup of coffee. He smiled as brightly as if he had absolved himself, as brightly as Judge might at the culmination of the Eucharist.

Two days after the porno fire, Judge went to the St. Anthony of Padua church in the Bronx, where he watched Mother Teresa induct two nuns into her order, the Missionaries of Charity. He jotted some of her words on the back of a holy card, words that he would have found no less true if he had known that she was writing privately to a friend, saying she felt an emptiness in her soul untouched by God.

"Holiness is not the liturgy of the few."—M. Tr.

Judge continued to find holiness in the many, including the mayor, who had squeaked into office promising to bring people together but whose approval rating was now plummeting from 58 percent to 33 percent as his critics and supporters increasingly divided along racial lines. Dinkins's critics charged that he had favored his own kind in a boycott by black activists of a Korean grocery in Brooklyn and accused him of anti-Semitism in being slow to quell a riot that erupted in Brooklyn after a Hasidic driver struck and killed a black child. He was also widely blamed for failing to stem violent crime, an opinion trumpeted by a tabloid headline: DAVE—DO SOMETHING!

Judge hand-delivered letters of support on sheets of friary stationery, telling Dinkins he was a good, good man.

"I guess he believed in all people," Dinkins would later say. "He certainly believed in me."

Dinkins seemed to be seeking more than a photo op when he arrived at the friary early on the morning of December 13 to work the breadline. Dinkins afterward joined Judge and two other friars for coffee in the basement dining room with its mural of Saint Francis's life. The mayor felt he needed to look no further than Judge to see a figure in a brown habit who showed by example how everyone should live.

"All I can say is we ought to be more like him," Dinkins said later.

Judge seemed to see something of Jackie Robinson in Dinkins, but mostly what Judge saw in Dinkins was Dinkins, not so much what the mayor did or did not do, but what he intended, what was at his core. Judge said with his smile and with his laugh that he quite simply liked Dinkins, and just being liked can mean the world when almost nothing is going as you hoped.

"I considered him one of my best friends," Dinkins said.

Judge began December 15 by hearing confessions at the Criminal Court of the Catholic Church from people afraid to tell such things to their home pastors. He then crossed West Thirty-first Street for the Engine 1/Ladder 24 Christmas party. The firefighters welcomed him as one of their own, certainly more so than did some of his fellow clergy at the cardinal's Christmas party held the following evening at the Waldorf-Astoria Hotel.

Judge commenced his own Christmas preparations by making his annual visit to a clothing shop at 314 Canal Street in Chinatown with his friend and fellow AIDS worker Pat Kowalski. They once again persuaded the proprietor of Loi Nguyen Fashion to sell them boxes of coats for the homeless at below bargain prices. They crammed the boxes into the car along with themselves and a man of the streets named Eddie Mouson who delighted in helping distribute a bit of holiday warmth.

On Christmas Eve, Judge set off from the friary with a plastic doll and a towel to the Dwelling Place, a shelter in Times Square for homeless and oftentimes mentally ill women.

"He'd walk up Ninth Avenue with his habit and his sandals and he'd have the infant Jesus wrapped in a towel," Sister Nancy of the shelter later recalled. "He said, 'I love walking up the avenue with the Infant in my hand.'"

At the shelter, Judge would lay the doll on the dining table that served as the altar. He would ask in the homily where the baby Jesus might want to be on this night. He would then answer his own question:

"Here with you, celebrating his birthday."

Judge would invite the women to approach the altar.

"If you want to come up and somehow just acknowledge the little baby in your life, if you want to kiss the feet or the hands," he would say. "Whatever you want to do."

The women would do just that, their kisses and cuddles once more making holy the doll that Judge then carried back downtown in its towel.

Near the end of Christmas week, Judge took a few hours with Alvarado to attend the 8:15 showing of *Cape Fear*, and he tucked his ticket stub in his appointment book. The next night was New Year's Eve, but Judge welcomed in 1992 with the Johnsons, who had been so instrumental in propelling his priesthood into the very center of the city's life. Alvarado understood even then that the relationship would never go to where passion might have led.

"He told me going into it," Alvarado later said. "He told me at the beginning he could only see me so much; it could only go so far."

Alvarado found himself unable just to walk away. He continued to see Judge when and where he could.

Alvarado arrived with the dawn at the friary on January 14. They had less than an hour together and then Judge had to head for the sacristy for the seven A.M. Mass. Alvarado took a seat at the back of the church, as solitary in the stillness as the typical morning communicants, who tended to scatter themselves, avoiding any unnecessary proximity to one another. Most of the visitors at this hour were commuters from some outlying realm, stopping on the way to work, perhaps with a particular worry or maybe simply to get a little boost before another day of drudgery, virtually all of them fresh from bed but many looking already weary. The majority were women in their middle to late years, who in winter bundled themselves in coats that were neither pricey nor shabby. Any homeless people seeking refuge from the cold usually huddled in a far corner.

With each new arrival would come the sounds of the street until the door closed again. The hush would return, and as the city outside was commencing its workday bustle, the church was so quiet you could hear people clear their throats and shift their weight in the pews.

A small handheld bell chimed once and Judge appeared in his vestments from the arched doorway to the right of the sanctuary. He was facing the congregants and therefore Alvarado when he bowed to kiss the altar as he had thousands of times before, though perhaps the touch of his lips to starched white cloth was all the more vivid on this particular morning. He began as always.

"Good morning."

Judge raised his right hand and blessed himself as each of the faithful did the same.

"In the name of the Father, and of the Son, and of the Holy Spirit," Judge said.

Judge held out both hands as the ritual dictated a priest do at this moment, a prescribed gesture to accompany a prescribed blessing.

"The grace of our Lord Jesus Christ and the love of God and the fellowship of the Holy Spirit be with you all," he said.

He always added a lilt to "with" and "all," joined by a glint in his eyes and a smile to make the blessing feel like an embrace of each person present, though no more so for anyone in particular, not even Alvarado. The congregants responded by rote, but with Judge it would seem more than that.

"And also with you."

The Mass arrived to where the priest calls for a moment of silence in which each individual ponders his or her sins. Judge would certainly not have considered love between two of the same sex to be such, this including the intense and committed feelings he had for Alvarado. He felt constrained by his vow only because he had made it, not because there was any theological justification. He certainly did not share the Church's official view that homosexuals were "intrinsically disordered"; the only ecclesiastical concern he had in this regard was that he would have to leave the priesthood if he were to enter into an open relationship with a man, or, for that matter, a woman.

He did worry that his view of things sexual was not shared by the great majority of firefighters. He knew that some of them could be loutish homophobes in between the fire alarms that suffused them with such grace. An ever-surprising grace in which he so clearly saw his God of surprises. The very grace he felt to be invoked by the Mass.

He was also acutely aware that the McDonalds as well as the night mayor would be shocked and hurt. He fretted in particular about Steven, who continued to suffer so much physically and who clearly looked to him for spiritual support. Steven had forgiven the kid who shot him and could surely come to forgive whatever Judge might do, but first there would be a painful disillusionment and their relationship might never be the same.

Judge now led the congregants in calling aloud for God to forgive their transgressions, as Steven no doubt would for him. The problem was that Judge did not consider his sexuality to be sinful. The question was how could he be forgiven for something that should need no forgiveness?

"I confess to Almighty God and to you, my brothers and sisters that I have sinned through my own fault, in my thoughts and in my words, in what I have done and in what I have failed to do . . ."

The only serious sin Judge might have felt with regard to Alvarado would have arisen from his views on cheating, as he had once set forth to Jean Willis when she told him she was in love with a man who was engaged to another woman: In situations like that, somebody always gets hurt. But he had warned Alvarado from the very start. And, at this point anyway, Alvarado seemed only enticed by this rivalry with the very Supreme Being whom Judge now invoked.

"May almighty God have mercy on us, forgive us our sins, and bring us to everlasting life."

Here the priest was to call thrice for the Lord to have mercy and each time he was echoed by the congregants. The priest was then to lead them in the Gloria, and the church filled with ritual words of total adoration.

"Glory to God in the highest . . . We worship you, we give you thanks, we praise you for your glory . . . You alone are the Holy One, you alone are our Lord, you alone are the Most High . . ."

Judge held out both hands for a brief prayer and then he sat on the unadorned throne to the right of the altar. The congregants of course sat when he sat, Alvarado following their lead, as if he were just another of the faithful. A layperson gave the first reading, and this being an even-numbered year in the first Tuesday of that period between Christmas and Lent that the Church calls ordinary time, the text at every Mass was 1 Samuel 1:9–20. Here

Hannah asks God to give her a man-child. The responsorial psalm that followed was 1 Samuel 2:1, 4–5, 6–7, 8, which included notions of God and poverty that Alvarado found perplexing, bordering on offensive.

> *The lord makes poor and makes rich . . .*
> *He raises the needy from the dust;*
> *From the ash heap he lifts up the poor,*
> *To seat them with nobles*
> *And make a glorious throne their heritage.*

The congregation responded, "My heart exults in the Lord, my Savior," who in Alvarado's case was the deity he was coming to view as a competitor for Judge's love.

> *He gives to the vower his vow,*
> *And blesses the sleep of the just.*
> *For the pillars of the earth are the Lord's,*
> *And he has set the world upon them.*

The congregation yet again responded, "My heart exults in the Lord, my Savior," and rose as the ritual raised the vower in vestments from his chair. Judge took the Gospel book from the altar and crossed to the pulpit.

"The Lord be with you," Judge said as before.

"And also with you," they answered as before.

"A reading from the Holy Gospel according to Mark."

Judge led them in making small signs of the cross on the forehead, mouth, and heart—a rote liturgical intimacy.

"Glory to you, Lord!"

The Gospel on this day in Catholic churches everywhere was Mark 1:21–28. Judge read from the oldest book in the Gospel of Jesus visiting the synagogue at Capernaum, where "the people were astonished at his teaching, for he taught them as one having authority and not as the scribes."

"In their synagogue was a man with an unclean spirit," Judge read on.

Which was very much how the Church hierarchy would have described Alvarado, or for that matter Judge and all those drawn to their own sex.

"He cried out, 'What have you to do with us, Jesus of Nazareth? Have you come to destroy us? I know who you are—the Holy One of God!' Jesus rebuked him and said, 'Quiet, come out of him!' All were amazed and asked one another, 'What is this? A new teaching with authority. He commands even the unclean spirits and they obey him.'"

Which was very much how the more conservative Catholics imagined homosexuals could be exorcised were they not too recalcitrant to obey.

"The Gospel of the Lord," Judge said.

"Praise to you, Lord Jesus Christ," the people replied.

The congregation sat while Judge remained standing to deliver the homily, as any priest would, except that Judge always stepped from behind the pulpit and out of the sanctuary, which set him apart. He surprised Alvarado and likely any other newcomers, perhaps as Jesus surprised the faithful at the synagogue in Capernaum, speaking not as a man of the pulpit and the scribes, but as a man of God and therefore of the people. Judge did not simply restate what had been drilled into him by a Church hierarchy. He spoke with the authority of personal beliefs and passions and insights and outsights that had bounded into the world along with the rest of him, the authority of seeing clean spirits.

"He was actually a fascinating guy, quite different from the usual priest," Alvarado later said.

The exact content of the homily is long forgotten, but the substance of this and all other homilies Alvarado would hear was what he termed "real life." Alvarado understood that Judge was not showing off for him, that he was giving his all because that is what he did, giving as much of himself to these scattered, solitary commuters as he would to a packed house on Easter. He was at these seemingly routine rituals like a great musician being a great musician even when playing at some airport lounge, still making it his own and doing it because he loved it, because he could not do it any other way, because that simply was who he was. The Mass was that much more extraordinary for this being in ordinary time in a day as ordinary as when Jesus visited the synagogue.

The people in the pews rose and Alvarado rose with them as Judge returned to the sanctuary and the altar servers brought over the bread and the wine. One of the servers came up with water and a bowl, along with an ironed white cloth for the ritual washing of the hands, in Judge's case those big Irish hands.

"Lord, wash away my iniquity; cleanse me from my sin," a priest was to say to himself at this moment.

Those hands held the Host aloft as Judge knelt at the altar, speaking words that Jesus was said to have spoken at the Last Supper, his voice now His voice.

"Take this all of you, and eat it: This is my body, which will be given up for you."

He then raised the chalice.

"Take this, all of you, and drink from it: This is the cup of my blood, the blood of the new and everlasting covenant. It will be shed for you and for all so that sins may be forgiven. Do this in memory of me."

Judge's own voice returned, always as vibrant as that of a groom reciting a wedding vow as he went on with the scripted words and the Our Father. The Mass proceeded to where he called on the faithful to offer each other a sign of peace and the people scattered in the pews turned to each other. A few at this hour usually sidled over to clasp the hand of the nearest person. Most simply raised a right hand in greeting.

Judge himself always shook hands with the altar servers and exchanged the standard "Peace be with you" with those in the pews toward the front. He did not customarily venture to the back, nor did he this time.

He returned to the altar and spoke more scripted words, words he always made sound like what they were for him, a declaration of love.

"Lord Jesus Christ, Son of the Living God, by the will of the Father and the work of the Holy Spirit, Your death brought life to the world. By Your Body and Blood free me from all my sins, and from every evil. Keep me faithful to Your teaching, and never let me be parted from You."

Judge gave Communion to the altar servers and to himself and called the others to receive. The solitary worshippers came together in a line before the sanctuary, proceeding one by one before Judge. Some held out cupped hands, left atop right. Others extended their tongues.

"Body of Christ . . . Body of Christ . . . Body of Christ," Judge said.

At least one figure stayed in the pews, watching, wanting body and blood, but not the body and blood of Christ. Alvarado remained where he was as the communicants turned away from Judge, the Host dissolving in their closed mouths. They invariably returned to the same seat for private prayer until the priest gave the final blessing and said the Mass was ended.

"Go in peace."

Alvarado watched Judge conclude the ritual by again bowing before the

altar and again pressing his lips to that starched white cloth. Alvarado was beginning to understand the depth of Judge's devotion.

"My rival was God," Alvarado later said.

Judge then dashed to Queens to preside at a fire captain's funeral, repeating
the ritual of the Mass once more, now focusing on a family grieving as his
own had at the loss of his father. He returned to Manhattan to visit a cop at
Bellevue Hospital, performed an afternoon funeral and then a memorial, his
fourth Mass of the day. He attended an evening meeting of the friars, answered several dozen phone messages, made his usual announcement, "I have
to say good night to the Boss," as he headed for the chapel and finally retired
to his solitary chamber.

He said Mass again at seven A.M. the following day and hurried to a fire
on upper Broadway, followed by a fire that afternoon on the George Washington Bridge, followed by a fire at a six-story apartment building in Murray
Hill. He stood praying in the street as three firefighters ascended to the floor
above the flames and started down a narrow hallway only to find that the
door to the apartment had been nailed shut.

"Conditions in the hallway were unbearable and the tight quarters made
forcible entry next to impossible," an FDNY history would note. "Suddenly,
the entire ceiling erupted into flames . . . The three were forced to the floor.
The heat mushroomed down and flames moved down the walls around
them."

They were moments from being burned alive when Firefighter Al Gonzalez rose up into the searing heat and flames, suffering intensely painful burns
on his face, neck, and ears as he went to work on the door with a pry bar
known as a Halligan tool. Lieutenant Dan Butler and Firefighter Patrick
McKenna were also burned before he finally managed to force open the door.
They shut it behind them and set to searching for life despite their burns,
continuing until flames ate through the door and chased them to a fire
escape.

"Firefighter McKenna and I are alive today . . . due to the sheer determination and unyielding efforts of Firefighter Gonzalez," Butler would write in
his official report.

The three were rushed to New York Hospital–Cornell Medical Center's burn unit, and Judge stayed with them much longer than was needed to perform his immediate duties as a chaplain. He had been on the go for nineteen hours, and yet he spent three more with these firefighters who had risked all out of that greatest love, three hours that seemed to affirm that Judge's most intense and committed relationship was with Alvarado's rival.

Six days later, Judge was at Jacobi Hospital, visiting four of the nine firefighters who were hurt in a nighttime blaze on 172nd Street in the Bronx. He was just a few minutes' drive from Alvarado, but the Rival's call again proved the stronger and he continued on to visit the five firefighters who were at the Burn Center in Manhattan.

On February 10, Judge was notified that a car had struck Brian Mulheren's long black Lincoln. Judge rushed to Bellevue, where the night mayor was placed in intensive care. The trauma staff again worked their magic.

Perhaps the accident moved the people at fire headquarters to put through the appointment that Mulheren had been pushing for for so long. Judge got a call four days later informing him he was now officially the new chaplain for Manhattan, the Bronx, and Staten Island.

February 14
FDNY

The relationship between God's lover and the New York Fire Department began on St. Valentine's Day. A servant of the Almighty thereupon became a civil servant, and as such was instructed to report to the FDNY personnel office on February 20. He there was presented with a photocopy of Regulation 9.1, "Fire Department Chaplains—Duties and Responsibilities." He was also given a "Civilian Sub-Managerial Time Record." He was told to fill one time sheet out weekly, leaving every box blank save the one for Friday, where he was to indicate that he had put in twenty hours, no matter which day and for how long he had actually worked. The annual salary for doing God's work was set at $15,000, or about $375 every two weeks, which was about $375 more than Judge had ever earned as an adult.

In celebration, he invited a half dozen people to lunch at an East Side restaurant. His guests included Tom Ferriter of West Milford. Judge insisted on paying the full check.

"I said, 'What are you doing this for?'" Ferriter recalled. "He said, 'For the first time in my life I can afford lunch.'"

Nobody was drinking anything stronger than soda, but that did not stop Ferriter from offering a toast.

"To Mary Judge, a mother who got what she wanted in life, a son with a Roman collar and a city job!"

Judge inherited Deeken's rattletrap Plymouth and the radio designation Car 49. He drove that day from St. Vincent's Hospital to St. Luke's Hospital to Lenox Hill Hospital visiting firefighters and AIDS patients. He attended an AA meeting on Seventy-ninth Street and dropped a fellow member downtown. He was on First Avenue, on the way to make his nightly visit to Mulheren at Bellevue when a call came over the radio.

"All of a sudden, I hear, 'Car 49. Manhattan to Car 49,'" Judge would recall. "My God! So, I picked up. They said, 'Are you coming to the hospital? What is your ETA to Bellevue Hospital?'"

Judge had an immediate problem.

"I didn't know what 'ETA' meant," he later said. "I had no idea . . . So, I said, Gee, I better go over there. There must be something going on."

Judge replied, "Ten-four, thank you," and raced to Bellevue. He strode into the emergency room and spoke to a nurse.

"I said, 'I got an emergency! I got an ETA!' She said, 'It must be the two cops.'"

Judge went over to where two cops lay on gurneys after suffering minor injuries in a car crash.

"Hi, guys, I shouldn't be taking care of you. I'm the fire."

The cops got an obvious fright on seeing a priest, and they assured him their injuries were not even remotely life-threatening. Judge told them he would give them a blessing anyway.

"So, I prayed over each," Judge recalled. "'Now, this is an exception,' I said. 'Today is my first day on the job.' 'Oh good luck, padre, good luck.'"

Judge continued upstairs to see Mulheren.

"I've taken care of my ETA," Judge announced.

Only then did Judge learn that the three letters stood for "Estimated Time of Arrival." Mulheren had asked the dispatcher to make the inquiry because he had a room full of people waiting to make a surprise presentation to Judge.

"So there they are, and then all of a sudden, da-da-da-daaaa-da, they bring out a cake and they bring out this badge," Judge recalled. "Brian gets out of bed and they put this badge on me."

Just as they were taking pictures, the phone brought word of a three-alarm fire in Queens.

"You go there! You go there!" Mulheren said.

Judge replied as any Brooklyn boy might.

"Do I have to go to Queens?"

Judge pulled up to the scene in Car 49 just as Fire Lt. Thomas Williams of Rescue 4 was being placed on a stretcher. Williams had just celebrated his thirtieth anniversary on the job, and he could have retired with a full pension a decade before. He kept charging into burning buildings, and on this night he and Firefighter Mike Milner had gone to the second floor in search of tenants who, it turned out, had already escaped. An explosion of superheated gases had driven the firefighters to a large window at the front and Williams had radioed "Mayday! Mayday!" A second explosion had then forced them out the window. Milner managed to cling to the sill. Williams landed in the street, and he was bleeding from grievous head injuries.

"So I start blessing him," Judge later said.

A firefighter whom Judge would later learn was Doug Sloan called out, tears streaking his blackened face.

"Doug says to me, 'Father, Father, go to the hospital with him, go to the hospital! Please go to the hospital,'" Judge remembered. "I said, 'Okay, okay.'"

Judge trailed the ambulance to Elmhurst Hospital, arriving just as the clock ticked past midnight into February 25, the thirty-first anniversary of his priesthood. He walked past the trauma room, where a team of doctors was trying without success to save Williams. Sloan and Milner had gathered with others from Rescue 4 in the back.

"They're all sitting at the table broken, broken," Judge would recall. "No one's saying anything. I'm saying to myself, 'What am I supposed to do?' I said to myself, 'Just be human. That's all you have to do. That's the job.'"

Judge returned to the trauma room, where Thomas Williams had just become the 752nd New York City firefighter to die in the line of duty. Most of the trauma team stepped away, but a few remained. A doctor was mutely staring at his own trembling hands. A nurse gently wiped the blood from the dead firefighter's face with a square of white gauze. Judge anointed Williams, feeling under his fingertips that the skin was already cooling.

"'Lord, bless him . . . Lord, bless the hands that are working on him.' I could see that they wanted to do some more work, so I went outside."

The chief of the department, Bill Feehan, approached. His parents had long ago tried to nudge him toward the priesthood, but he had followed his father into the fire department.

"He says, 'Father, where's the body?'" Judge recalled. "I said, 'It's down in the room down there. Come on, I'll take you.'"

A nurse was coming out. Feehan took Williams's hand.

"'Christ, I knew the guy,' Feehan said. 'Fine, fine, fine firefighter. Good man . . . Good man.'"

Feehan started to cry.

"We'll pray," Judge said.

Feehan was still holding one of Williams's hands. Judge took the other and reached out to Feehan with his free hand.

Judge then followed Feehan to a back room where the firefighters had gathered.

"'Well, what do you want to do?' Feehan asked them. 'It's your call. Whatever you want to do guys, it's your call.'"

The phrase "It's your call" made a deep impression on Judge for reasons he would never be able to verbalize fully; perhaps it was because through his upbringing and his priesthood it was always *their* call. The firefighters said they would go back to the firehouse.

"So they all got up, and they were all so heartbroken and they walked out," Judge recalled.

The chaplain for Queens and Brooklyn arrived. Msgr. Tom Brady is a church traditionalist, and he is one of the few who would later say of Judge, "I never liked the guy." But at that moment all anybody was thinking about was Williams and his family. Brady departed in a police helicopter on the unenviable mission of notifying Williams's wife. Judge went to Rescue 4's quarters and found the firefighters sitting at a table in the back.

Malachy Corrigan, the head of the counseling unit, was there. He asked if the firefighters wished to talk.

"He couldn't get anyone to say anything," Judge would remember. "It was just so . . . It was the wake. It was the real wake."

As Judge drove back to Manhattan, four sets of five tones came over the radio.

"The department regrets to announce the death of Lt. Thomas Williams . . ."

Judge arrived at the friary sometime after four A.M. He managed to fall asleep just before he had to rise and pull on his habit to celebrate the 8:30 A.M. Mass in the lower church. He was stepping away from the altar when he slipped his hand in his pocket. He felt his new badge.

The funeral was held in Williams's hometown of Kings Park, Long Island. Judge stood on the church steps with the other chaplains as the pipe band slowly marched up the street with the ceremonial fire rig bearing the coffin. Judge watched the firefighters who had sat in the back room at the hospital now shoulder their fallen lieutenant.

"They were crying . . . I think Doug's hat got knocked off with the wind," Judge later said. "They went into the church, and then they came out and they did the same thing again. They lifted it up."

Judge joined the procession to the edge of town.

"They got out and they lifted it off the caisson and they put it in the hearse and then, I could see them, they just stood there, they just stood there looking at the hearse. Six of them," Judge recalled. "And then we went to the cemetery and then that was the end of it."

The six pallbearers and the others resumed being firefighters with a truly holy ghost, the same living spirit that Judge had witnessed at the rope rescue and the porno palace, that had sent Williams into the fatal fire.

"It was so powerful," Judge said. "It was nice to be a part of it, if you could say that. I guess. First day on the job."

22

As the new chaplain, Judge was invited to march with the firefighters in the St. Patrick's Day parade. He had been given a dress blue uniform anonymously, though he felt certain it came from the Johnsons. The day took an early twist at the mayor's breakfast at Gracie Mansion.

The gay activists of ILGO had once again applied to march, and the overseers had once again cited the waiting list. The mayor's office imagined it had resolved the situation by offering to pay the incumbent cost of extending the parade for an hour, but the overseers declared that ILGO was still out because it had missed the deadline for applications. Dinkins found himself between what one observer termed "a shamrock and a hard place." He announced to his eighty guests at the breakfast that he would be the first mayor in a half century not to march.

"It hurts that these young men and women are to be rejected and excluded from the greatest celebration of Irishness in the world, just because of whom they love," Dinkins said. "I honestly and truly believe that it is wrong . . ."

As did Mychal Judge, but if he refused to march he would be refusing to join the very firefighters who had been so remarkable at fire after fire, so magnificent on his first day on the job, so stirring at Williams's funeral, who made him feel as if he was born to be their chaplain. The day lurched even deeper into complexity as he proceeded to the annual St. Patrick's Day Mass at the cathedral of the same name.

The cardinal began by saying essentially what he had said after the beer can tossing the year before.

"No one may this day call himself or herself an Irishman, or pretend to be representing the Catholic Church, who treats anyone with contempt or with slander or with violence of any sort, be it mental, emotional, spiritual, or physical," O'Connor said. "Let us see in every person we meet this day the face of the divine Lord."

But he again avoided the question of whether the divine Lord had the right to be in the parade in the form of ILGO. He also did not hesitate to condemn Dinkins for refusing to march as a matter of conscience.

"We will not forget," O'Connor warned.

That could have only made Judge feel like immediately joining the boycott or at least the demonstrators who mounted a protest march along the parade route an hour before the official event, escorted by a phalanx of cops. The prospect of trouble kept many spectators away, and only a quarter of the expected two million people lined the curbs when the parade itself started up Fifth Avenue. The four hundred protestors were gathered on a stretch of sidewalk that had been cordoned off for them just uptown from the reviewing stand. They included not just ILGO, but activists who seemed to view any marchers as bigots. Jeers from the militants drowned out the applause from ILGO as Steven McDonald rolled past with Patti Ann and five-year-old Conor.

"Two-four-six-eight, how do you know your kids are straight?" the militants chanted.

A short while later, the FDNY came up the avenue, Paddy Brown and Kevin Shea and Bill Feehan and row after row after row of others. Just under 40 percent of the firefighters were Irish, but it always seemed much more so, almost as if they became that when they went on the job, no matter what they were before.

"I never knew I was Irish!" said Dennis Mojica of Rescue 1.

Their new chaplain was in the first ranks, wearing his white hat and blue coat with brass buttons and two gold stripes on each sleeve. He must have cringed for both sides as the militants booed and jeered and some firefighters answered in kind. If he knew any of the protesters, or if any recognized him, not a word was said, and he kept marching.

Afterward, he went to the Emerald Society bash and a crowd of firefighters joined him in singing "Steve O'Donnell's Wake" and other Irish songs he had once sent echoing through the seminary.

Judge had been issued a regulation turnout coat to wear at fires and he had it on five days later at the scene of a nighttime crash at La Guardia Airport.

The plane had skidded on takeoff into the bay beyond the runway, killing forty-seven. Judge stood at the edge of the tarmac, watching some of the firefighters he had marched alongside at the parade now charge into the black, freezing waters. He saw none other than Paddy Brown straddle the fuselage.

"Of course," Judge said.

Brown looked like a mythic hero atop some huge downed beast as he made his way up the spine of the half-submerged plane. Brown clambered to the cockpit window and reached inside to where the pilot sat, still strapped in his seat. The pilot was beyond saving and his body was borne sorrowfully to shore, where Judge bestowed a blessing. Judge returned to the friary at three A.M.

The very next night Judge was in the turnout coat again, this time at a fire in an apartment house on Claremont Parkway in the Bronx. Firefighters rescued a three-day-old infant and her mother. Judge went to Jacobi Hospital with the sixteen firefighters who were injured and remained until it was time to hurry directly to the breadline and his morning duties at the friary. He continued the busy, busy, busy life of a true priest, which for him included going to the morgue to identify another of the homeless who had listed him as the next of kin.

He also had such bright moments as when Peter Johnson and his fiancée, Blanche Kwas, came to him for the pre-Cana counseling that is mandatory for Catholics prior to marriage. He boiled down the usual six sessions into a fifteen-minute chat at a jazz joint about not letting anybody or anything get in the way of their love. He made up for the brevity when he was asked to choose the music for the wedding.

"Ten songs," Johnson recalled. "It was probably the longest wedding Mass in American history."

In mid-May, a gay activist named Brendan Fay telephoned to ask if Judge would perform a memorial service for Arthur and Willie Busk, two brothers from Long Island who had died of AIDS within six weeks of each other, feeling so shunned by the Church that they had been cremated without ceremony. The surviving siblings now wanted to hold a memorial at their home but had been unable to find a willing priest.

Judge arrived in his habit seeming to feel only honored to be there. He moved with ease among the mourners as if he were an old friend of the family. The crowd of relatives and friends, young and old, gay and straight, spilled from the den into the laundry room as Judge said Mass. He concluded by placing his hand over his heart and singing "God Bless America." Everybody was startled, but then even those who did not know a hymn were able to sing along.

Two weeks later, Judge was invited to give the benediction at the 1992 FDNY Medal Day. A book detailed each firefighter's deeds, and to Judge these were love stories, the love that his Savior had extolled. Firefighter Joe Angelini was there to receive his tenth medal, this one for rescuing a twenty-five-year-old woman from a blazing building, giving her his air mask to breathe as he carried her to safety through the choking smoke and flames. His full description of the rescue had been, "Yeah, I pulled some babe out."

Most of the other firefighters brought their families, but Angelini had not even mentioned the ceremony to his sons, the younger of whom would later help carry Judge's body from the North Tower. Joe Angelini viewed medals as just something to toss in a drawer.

The department's top medal was awarded to Firefighter Michael Duggan, who had made a rope rescue in Harlem that had not been captured by television as Shea and Barr's had. An outsider might have thought the department was reminding people what Shea himself felt, that firefighters routinely perform heroic acts which receive scant public attention. Department insiders said the most famous rope rescue of all time had in fact been accorded a lesser medal because Shea was wearing an unauthorized T-shirt when he went over the side.

Television had given Shea a kind of celebrity not often accorded firefighters and he was uncomfortable at department functions. Judge recognized his unease at another event and went over to introduce himself. Shea walked away.

"I didn't want anything to do with him," Shea later said.

Shea reconsidered after overhearing Judge conversing "like a real guy" with a group of other firefighters. Shea did not walk away when Judge approached at the next department gathering. Shea eventually came to trust Judge enough to explain why he had walked away from him in the first place.

Shea said he himself had once thought of becoming a priest, and in the eighth grade he had gone to St. Pius X Preparatory Seminary in Uniondale, Long Island.

Some of the priests there seemed to think it was their right to sexually abuse the students. The dean of discipline was Father Alan Placa. He would subsequently become widely known as one of Rudy Giuliani's closest friends. He was also alleged to be a pedophile. He was Priest F in a grand jury report that described him as "cautious, but relentless in his pursuit of victims." The report would further say that Placa employed "deception and intimidation" while he was the Long Island diocese's lead man in the handling of allegations of sex abuse.

"What you see, what's going on, it's insane," Shea later said. "I don't even think they worked for good. Look what they did with that power."

Shea had felt compelled to leave more than the seminary.

"Not only do you not want to be a priest, you don't want to have anything to do with the Catholic Church."

He had left seeing no distinction between homosexuality and pedophilia. He continued to believe "gay" and "child molester" were names for the same thing.

Judge offered no excuses for his fellow priests, saying he understood and shared Shea's anger. Judge suggested that Shea was serving God every time he responded to a call for help, that with both the Church and the fire department the mission was ultimately good no matter what some individuals might do.

"I found my order," Shea announced to Judge. "There's Jesuits and there's Franciscans and there's firemen. And my order has alcohol and sex. I picked the right order. Life is good."

Judge continued to follow his own calling, and Shea decided a Roman collar could be as good as the man wearing it.

"I want to be Catholic as much as the next guy," Shea said. "He healed a lot of wounds, a lot of sore open wounds I never thought would heal."

Judge led Shea to realize that the most celestial bells in the city were those that set a fire company scrambling.

"You're looking for your spirituality and you don't realize your spirituality is in you all the time," Shea said.

• • •

In early August, Judge went to see his married sisters in Ocean Pines, a suburban development on Maryland's Eastern Shore where they had settled. He received an alarming phone call from a fellow fire chaplain. Msgr. Marc Filacchione informed him that rumors were emanating from some of the Catholic societies in the fire department that Judge was a practicing homosexual and had put the moves on someone in a firehouse.

"[Filacchione] said, 'You better get back here,'" Dympna recalled.

Judge understood that such rumors could force him from the department, and he immediately returned to New York. He met that very night with the Johnsons, Peter and Peter Jr. They did not ask if he was gay. The younger Johnson did ask if Judge was anything other than a celibate priest.

"No," Judge said.

The following morning, the Johnsons had breakfast in the hotel at the World Trade Center with the heads of the two fire unions, Richie Brower of the Uniformed Fire Officers Association and Jimmy Boyle of the Uniformed Firefighters Association.

Quite literally in the shadow of the Twin Towers, the Johnsons asked Brower and Boyle to put out the word in the department that anybody who continued to spread these unfounded allegations about Fire Chaplain Mychal Judge would be subject to the most strenuous legal action.

At noon Judge met with the two union leaders. Judge seemed upset and angered. He suspected somebody in the cardinal's office was behind the whispering but had no proof. Brower would recall that Judge did not directly address the question of whether he was gay.

"He said, 'Whether I am or not, I never approached anybody,'" Brower would say. "That was good enough for me."

Judge's last appointment of the day was with Msgr. Edward O'Donnell. O'Donnell was the cardinal's Director of Priest Personnel and as such handled allegations of misconduct involving diocesan priests. The longstanding strategy had been to avoid scandal at all costs and hush up even criminal cases of admitted pedophilia.

Judge arrived at the meeting strongly suspecting that the same archdiocese that sought to quiet allegations against pedophiles was spreading talk of supposed adult indiscretions on his part, scandalous in New York only because he was a priest. Judge kept the meeting a matter between himself and O'Donnell, who after Judge was killed would decline to discuss it.

Whatever its source, the whispering immediately stopped. Judge continued being the chaplain to the fire department as if it were his parish. He visited firehouses. He performed weddings and baptisms for firefighters and their families. He counseled firefighters who were having trouble at home. He held retreats for those with drinking problems.

Paddy Brown invited Judge to his fortieth birthday party at Zinno's, an Italian restaurant in Greenwich Village where a crowd of bachelor firefighters regularly gathered. Lt. Terry Hatton arrived with a young woman who had appeared in the centerfold of a recent *Playboy* magazine.

"I'm allowed to look, right?" Judge joked.

The firefighters forgot even the centerfold as they began talking of their greatest passion. Hatton spoke as the son of a fire chief, as someone who was forever devising new strategies and tools, who would study buildings in the street and in the real-estate section of the Sunday *New York Times*, asking himself how he would attack a fire there. Then Brown began describing a partial collapse in Harlem the week before. Judge seemed less interested in the details of firefighting than in the spirit that propelled these men.

"Marvelous."

Judge noted another birthday three weeks later in his appointment book, on December 4, making a rare use of ALA's full name, *Al Alvarado (24).*

But however intense and committed his feelings may have continued to be, Judge did not see Alvarado that day. He instead visited a firefighter who had been badly burned when a steam pipe burst at a Con Edison plant in Manhattan. Capt. Martin McTigue was from Rescue 4, and Judge had met him at the firehouse the night Lieutenant Williams of the same company was killed. Judge now arrived at New York–Cornell's burn unit to see that the blast of super-heated steam had caused the captain's head to swell more than twice its normal size.

"It is hard to describe the intensity of the pain," McTigue later said.

Many of those who visited this well-liked and highly regarded captain entered his room downcast and uncertain how to act. McTigue felt less like they were approaching his bedside than his coffin. That made Judge's visit all the more remarkable when he breezed in, sunny and smiling.

"Like I sprained my ankle," McTigue said.

Judge recounted incidents from his Brooklyn childhood and his drinking days, making it all seem hilarious. He could have been at the table in Zinno's.

Judge returned to McTigue's bedside day after day, as if each day's page in his appointment book were blank and not filled with other hospital visits and fires and AIDS meetings and weddings and baptisms and counseling, as well as the Masses, confessions, and the breadline at St. Francis. He always ended his visit the same way.

"No matter who was there, he'd have people joining hands and saying a prayer together," McTigue recalled.

On Christmas Eve, Judge visited McTigue, dashed to a fire on Thirty-fourth Street, once more distributed coats to the homeless, and then took the plastic doll to Christmas Eve Mass at the Dwelling Place women's shelter. He afterward headed crosstown with the doll, past the giant Christmas tree at Rockefeller Center and on to St. Patrick's Cathedral. Steven McDonald had suggested it would be nice if Judge joined the priests at the altar during midnight Mass.

Judge arrived with the baby Jesus at the back entrance. He was greeted by Msgr. James McCarthy, a senior adviser to O'Connor and known to the Pope as Jim. McCarthy would in later years become a bishop but resign after admitting a series of affairs with several women.

Judge was now left standing on the doorstep as McCarthy eyed his Franciscan getup and archly inquired if he had brought the proper vestments for the Mass. Judge replied that he had. He might have turned around and left had he not promised the McDonalds he would be there. He later told Peter Johnson Jr., "I don't know why I have to put myself through this with these people. But Steven asked me. It's important to him. But these *bastards* . . ."

On January 14, 1993, Judge returned to the friary to see a call coming in while the switchboard was momentarily unattended. He picked up and a man named Larry Boies said he was trying to contact a priest he had seen at several AIDS funerals, but whose name eluded him.

At eight P.M., Judge arrived at the West Thirty-sixth Street loft that Boies shared with his partner of eighteen years, Ron Dalto. Dalto was a prop designer, and the loft was decorated with life-size artificial palm trees, as well as a poster of Rita Hayworth. A huge square glass coffee table was covered with candles of all sizes that flickered as Dalto sat slumped in a wheelchair, limp and emaciated, nearing the end of a five-year battle with AIDS. Boies had given up his job to care for his lover. They were being assisted by a friend, a former nun who would have made a brilliant priest if the Church had allowed her to become one.

Mary Laney had spent fourteen years cloistered in a four-and-a-half-acre convent in the South Bronx that was self-sufficient until the fruit trees became barren and the well water was condemned as polluted. She and her fellow nuns had for a time sought to support themselves with handiwork such as the fine embroidery on the mitres worn by the Church's eminences. Eventually the nuns were compelled by economic necessity to find outside jobs, and Laney finally left the order for the manifestly secular insurance business. She remained robustly spiritual and had no trouble understanding Dalto's outrage at being shunned by his Church.

"He said, 'My Church rejects me. Is God going to reject me? Nobody is going to make me believe that God will treat me like my Church treats me,'" Laney recalled. "He intuitively believed God made him as he was and God would support him."

Dalto still wanted the comfort of the Last Rites.

"But he didn't think anybody would give them to him."

A smiling Judge now stepped up to Dalto in a fire department jacket, plaid shirt, trousers, and sandals. Judge took Dalto's hand and talked as if to a new friend he was delighted to meet. Judge's words flowed into the Sacrament of Penance, where Dalto asked forgiveness for his sins. Judge then performed the Anointing of the Sick as gently as if he were the one making penance for his whole Church.

This flowed into what Laney would remember as the holiest of Communions.

"Are you able to swallow?" Judge asked.

"Just a little," Dalto said.

Judge broke off a tiny piece of Communion wafer, placing the remainder by the burning candles. He set the fragment on Dalto's tongue.

"The Body of Christ," Judge said.

Then this priest in a fire department jacket and friar's sandals carefully, tenderly, lifted the wracked and ravaged communicant from his wheelchair. Judge cradled Dalto in his arms and crooned to him as if to a child. Dalto's head rested against Judge's chest. Judge crowned him with a kiss.

Five days after what Laney would term "about as close to mystical experience as you could ever have," Judge presided at Dalto's funeral at the nondenominational All Faiths Cemetery in Queens. A winter storm howled as Judge praised Dalto's parents for having passed their values on to their son. Judge said the proof lay in the depth and trueness of their son's love with Boies. Judge added that they should take great pride in their son's grace and faith in the face of such terrible suffering.

"No one ever told them they should be proud of their son," Laney later said.

Boies and his friends stood at the grave and tossed handfuls of theatrical glitter into the storm. Judge led the prayer from atop a snowbank, his feet bare in his sandals, the icy wind whipping at his habit.

"And then he didn't have any money to get back on the subway," Boies remembered.

On February 2, Judge stood among the one hundred firefighters who gathered at Cornell Medical Center to cheer Marty McTigue as he emerged from three months in the burn center. Bagpipes played and McTigue spoke in a voice made raspy by internal burns, saying he just hoped he could go back to full duty someday.

"I'd like to do a little bit more," he told a reporter. "You don't want the fire to win."

Judge returned to the hospital that very evening after five firefighters were injured in a blaze uptown, among them Dennis Mojica of the Zinno's crowd. Judge was back at the burn unit on Ash Wednesday to distribute ashes to firefighters who often had their entire faces blackened with ash they had self-consecrated with their search for life.

"Remember you are dust and back to dust you shall return," he said again and again.

He noted that firefighters certainly needed no reminder of their mortality. The following afternoon, he witnessed anew their care in remembering the fallen when he went to Rescue 4 for a plaque ceremony marking the first anniversary of Lieutenant Williams's death.

The day was also the thirty-second anniversary of Judge's ordination. He was supposed to join Lux Mundi for a reunion, but he was worn down and the flu hit him so hard he did not rise from his bed the next day even after the notification that came over his text pager at 12:15 P.M.

EXPLOSION AT WORLD TRADE CENTER.

When he heard the name of the lone firefighter who was seriously injured at the bombing, Judge forced himself to his feet and made his way to Beekman Downtown Hospital.

Kevin Shea had suffered multiple fractures while attempting to make a garage-level rescue. Shea had come to a doorway on the B-1 level with firefighter Gary Geidel, the Paddy Brown pal who would perish in the second World Trade Center attack. Shea shouted into the smoky blackness beyond, and a victim answered. The two started blindly down what they thought was a long hallway. The floor then angled up and they felt broken concrete underfoot. They saw an orange glow ahead and they felt heat.

Suddenly the floor under them gave way. Shea began sliding into a void. Geidel grabbed the shoulder of Shea's turnout coat but was unable to hold on. Shea fell forty-five feet into what he would later learn was the crater left by the thousand-pound bomb detonated in the underground garage. He landed on a pile of rubble on the B-4 level, close enough to a fire that his shoulder was burned. He saw other fires all around him, as if he had been pitched into hell.

Shea activated his PASS alarm, that high-pitched beeping signal that is supposed to lead firefighters to a fallen comrade. The signal echoed so that it seemed to come from all directions, a confusion compounded by dozens of car alarms. Several cars exploded as the fires reached their gas tanks.

Then, through all the other sounds, Shea heard a cry for help. Shea responded with the spirit of that higher calling.

"I tried to get to him, but my protruding bone got caught on some debris," Shea later reported.

The firefighters up at the crater's edge had no place to secure a rope end, and they used themselves as an anchor, just as in Shea's rooftop rescue. They of course carried out the civilian first.

The mastermind of the attack had hoped to kill 250,000 civilians by toppling both towers. Only six people died. Shea was the lone serious injury among the five rescue companies, eighty-four engine companies, sixty truck companies, twenty-eight battalion chiefs, nine deputy chiefs, and twenty-six special units that responded. The TV news people discovered that Shea was the same guy from the double rope rescue, and that gave them footage to run, a good human angle in a story where there was a monstrous attack but relatively little filmable tragedy.

When Kevin Shea was discharged from the hospital, his tiny home was filled with camera crews. He sensed an unspoken assumption that he was fortunate to be the subject of so much attention. The adulation left him still banged up, still unable to deliver furniture or dig lawn sprinklers or do any of the other second jobs he had always worked. He could not even make a little overtime. The big-shot hero was left with only a hero's salary, which meant he was having trouble paying his bills.

The indifference to the particulars of his life made the adulation seem all the more false and therefore all the more unbearable. The one person who understood from the start was Judge. He remained a steady, calm presence. The firefighter who had hated all priests addressed him as "Father," with familial respect and affection.

"I used to joke with him that I was his unwanted stepchild from his sailor days he doesn't remember and I showed up on his doorstep," Shea later said.

After the second attack on the World Trade Center, Shea would hear the talk that Judge had been gay. He who had once seen no difference between homosexuality and pedophilia would say, "If somebody really convinced me of that, all you could do was tell me I had my first gay friend."

Even if Judge had known that Shea and so many other firefighters would accept him as one of their own, whether he was gay or straight, he still could have been cast out by the Church, whose attitudes were reaffirmed by O'Connor in New York during the annual Mass at the cathedral preceding the 1993 St. Patrick's Day parade. The Irish Lesbian and Gay Organization had suffered a legal defeat in its effort to be included in the line of march, and 228 of its members were being arrested in a protest eight blocks down Fifth Avenue as O'Connor delivered his homily.

"What others call bigotry, we call principle," O'Connor said. "We extend our hearts to them, but we will not retreat one iota from our faith."

O'Connor dedicated the parade to seventeen Irish martyrs of the sixteenth and seventeenth century who perished rather than forsake their Catholicism, suggesting a kinship between these heroes of old and those who strove so hard to bar the gay organization from the parade.

"Sodom and Begorra," somebody later quipped.

Judge delighted in writer Frank McCourt's analysis of his tribe's sexuality: "The lack of the Irish."

Judge chose not to attend this particular Mass, but was among the firefighters as they assembled on East Forty-fourth Street for the parade. They smiled and called out to him as an icy rain fell.

"Padre! Father Mike!"

He got no such smiles and welcomes as the line of march carried him past the cathedral. The cardinal stood there with his minions, enough of a regular guy to be holding his own umbrella, but fixing Judge with a look of imperial disdain. Judge looked straight back at him and smiled as he had been unable to do with the disapproving Father Urban. Judge was right where he belonged.

Judge began Holy Week by spending from one A.M. to five A.M. on Palm Sunday at a fire on West 165th Street, then going with an injured firefighter to Jacobi Hospital. He worked on the breadline at St. Francis early on Good Friday and then crossed the street to the firehouse, where he heard confessions from members of Engine 1/Ladder 24. Judge returned to St. Francis for the Stations of the Cross. Afterward he headed downtown with fellow friar Pat Fitzgerald to what seemed an appropriate place to visit on a holy day of loss.

On arriving at the site of the World Trade Center bombing, Judge flashed his chaplain's badge and they were permitted to walk down the ramp leading to what had come to be called Ground Zero. The two friars stood witness in the crater where Shea had fallen six weeks before. All around was jagged, blasted evidence of evil bent on becoming monumental.

Judge gazed upon the foundation of the Twin Towers as he did at the human core, seeing past the damage to the resilience, the essential integrity.

"Strong," he would later say. "Still standing. Remarkable."

12

Judge was now just a month shy of turning sixty, but in this Easter season of rebirth, he was pursuing his new life as a fire chaplain with the energy of a man decades younger. The growing demands of that work left him with even less time for Alvarado, who embarked on a month-long trip home to the Philippines. Alvarado told Judge to consider whether they should continue seeing each other. Alvarado said that if Judge did not phone when he returned, he would assume the relationship was over.

Judge's beeper and phone and appointment book propelled him on past his sixtieth birthday on May 11. He arrived at a blaze on East 115th Street in East Harlem as firefighters were battling the Red Devil. An excited voice came on the radio.

"I got a baby."

A firefighter passed a tiny form out a window to a comrade atop a ladder. The firefighters below set to work, ignoring that the infant already felt cold, clearing what fluid they could from the airway, going to work with a resuscitator only to find the throat was closed against whatever air they tried to pump in. They had no more luck with a five-year-old girl they carried out. They discovered the children had been murdered, along with four adults, before the killer or killers set the fire, making a cruel mockery of the search for life.

When the smoke in the apartment cleared, the firefighters could see blood spattered everywhere, turning from red to pink where it had mixed with hose water. That brought concern about a disease that was no longer considered to be just a gay plague. Three fifty-foot lengths of hose from Engine 91 were taken for decontamination, along with the gear of firefighters who had slipped and fallen in the water.

Judge stood in the brilliant May morning blessing the bodies as a woman screamed and pointed to a playground, saying the children had played there just the day before. The firefighters climbed back onto their rigs and rolled away having done all they could, the Red Devil in this instance having been joined by a human devil.

God's representative drove off alone in his car.

The paper sign that Alvarado found affixed to his apartment door when he returned to the Bronx read: WELCOME HOME.

Judge subsequently articulated the unwritten message.

"I couldn't not see you," he told Alvarado.

At the chirp of a pager or the trill of a phone, Judge still rushed off to the Rival's instant call. He was notified early on the morning of June 6 that a cargo ship carrying more than three hundred illegal Chinese immigrants had run aground off the Rockaway peninsula in Queens. He sped out to the sandy shore that is home to many firefighters and cops and is sometimes called the Irish Riviera or Civil Servant Beach. Many of the immigrants had leapt from the stricken ship into the chilly waters, and the bodies of the twenty who had perished were still washing ashore.

Judge strode over in his turnout coat to a group of survivors who were huddled under blankets. Many had turned over their life savings to the smugglers. The others had indentured themselves to toil in restaurants and sweatshops. All had endured 122 cramped and miserable days at sea. They now sat soaked and shivering and were very likely to be shipped back to where they had started.

Judge called out for somebody to bring hot coffee. He did not speak a word of Chinese, and none of these poor souls seemed to understand English, but that did not stop Judge from talking away. The most unlikely laughter arose from these hunched figures amid the clatter of the helicopters and the sirens of the emergency vehicles and the shouts of the rescue workers.

The laughter ceased as the immigrants were led away, but they kept looking back at Judge. He made his way across the peninsula and along the low wall that runs beside the bay. The families of the Irish Riviera would stand here on a September morning in 2001, gazing across the expanse of water and the sprawl of Brooklyn to the burning World Trade Center. They would watch one tower and then the other collapse, killing husbands, sons, brothers, sisters, wives, mothers, and a fire chaplain.

On this sunny June morning in 1993, the World Trade Center shone as bright as an immigrant's dream and brighter still in Judge's estimation for having shrugged off the big bomb. The city seemed to have all but forgotten the attack mounted by a group of Middle Eastern extremists who spoke of an epic struggle with "Jews and Crusaders," as if this were the beginning of the millennium rather than the end, as if this were still the time of Saint Francis and the Holy Wars. Whatever continuing danger they presented seemed to pass after a number of those still at liberty were caught mixing explosives for a new plot to bomb the Statue of Liberty, the George Washington Bridge, the Lincoln and Holland Tunnels, the United Nations, the Federal Building, and the Diamond District. The plan seemed too outlandish to be taken completely seriously and not historic enough for Judge to make note of the June 23 arrests in his appointment book.

The jihadists might believe our fate is already written by Allah, but Judge kept to his personal belief that each page to come was blank.

"If you want to hear God laugh," he would often say, "tell him your plans for tomorrow."

Judge's next three tomorrows included a fire, an FDNY promotion ceremony, two funerals, a wedding, a baptism, two hospital visits, and the breadline. The fourth tomorrow had one event important enough that he had made a note in the back of the previous year's appointment book at the risk of God's laughter.

"Keep last Sunday in June open all day for Pride Parade."

The twenty-fourth annual Gay Pride Day Parade kicked off at noon two blocks uptown from St. Patrick's Cathedral, where Cardinal O'Connor had just declared that the Church did not condemn homosexuals, only homosexuality. Some 250,000 people proceeded downtown past the cathedral, the opposite direction of the St. Patrick's Day Parade. Judge was not with Alvarado but with Dinkins. Judge was not marching so much as a gay man but as a priest who had long worked with AIDS victims, who did not have all day for the Pride Parade, who had to proceed down to the World Trade Center for another commitment that same day.

He parked his FDNY car at "Ten and Ten," the quarters of Ladder Co. 10 and Engine Co. 10, the two-story firehouse across from the South Tower that somehow would survive the collapse of the Trade Center even if five fire-fighters assigned there did not. He then crossed West Street to the Winter Garden, the atrium where he had joined the celebration of Dinkins's "gor-geous mosaic." The occasion this time was a concert by the fire department's Emerald Society Pipes and Drums band. He listened to firefighters in kilts skirl the music of his forefathers. Had any of them chanced to see him earlier that day at what they called the Gay Parade they would have assumed he was being a priest among the victims of AIDs the way they were firefighters in the smoke and flame.

For them, he was becoming a fire chaplain unlike any other because he was so much like what a fire chaplain should be. He was their Mychal Judge even at a time many more of them than Kevin Shea were coming to equate gay priest with predatory pedophile. The Church hierarchy had long sought to keep secret such outrages as Shea and thousands of others had suffered at the hands of a criminal few worldwide, but that had only given the predators license, and it was all beginning to come to light.

Yet, even then, the hierarchy failed to directly address a scandal that would grow to alienate some of the most devout followers and threaten to leave entire archdioceses bankrupt, both morally and financially. O'Connor announced "new" guidelines in New York on July 1, saying all allegations of sex abuse would now go to Monsignor O'Donnell, the very man who had been handling them in the first place. O'Connor declared that "so many times I have wanted to cry out to say what I really feel," but he had been largely silent about the pain of the victims because "unfortunately, the archbishop of New York is a legal entity as well as being a moral and spiritual and religious leader."

By "legal," O'Connor was referring not to the law but to lawsuits, which at that time were in the amount of $50 million against the archdiocese and $1 billion against the Church nationally. There was no requirement in the new guidelines to report sex abuse to law enforcement. O'Connor remained remarkably forgiving of even convicted pedophiles, as was evidenced when he sent two representatives to the sentencing of a priest who had sexually abused eleven boys over a ten-year period.

"The cardinal asked me to be here to give support to the father, to give him a personal affirmation," one of the delegates said.

• • •

On July 5, Judge flew off with Dinkins on a four-day trip to Israel and the Holy Land. The thirty-two members of the delegation also included attorney Brian O'Dwyer, son of the late City Council president Paul O'Dwyer, who had run guns to Jewish guerrillas during the British mandate with the notion that their struggle made them comrades with Irish Republicans. The younger O'Dwyer had been raised in city politics and understood the junket had less to do with Israel's continuing struggle for existence than with Dinkins's struggle for reelection.

"We all knew it was a put-up," O'Dwyer later said. "It was a political trip. David was to get his picture taken."

Others in the group were Friar Pat Fitzgerald and Dr. Ruth Westheimer, the diminutive sexologist who declared premarital sex, contraception, abortion, homosexuality, and seemingly everything else to be permissible so long as nobody was victimized. She and the two friars became fast friends.

As the group toured Yad Vashem, the Holocaust memorial, Westheimer told Judge she had been orphaned at ten after the Nazis murdered her family. They strode together past the horrifying photos and such artifacts as a child's battered doll from the Dachau concentration camp.

"We walked hand in hand," Westheimer remembered.

Together, Judge and Westheimer strolled the streets of Jerusalem, where she had been wounded while serving as a sniper with the Haganah underground in 1948.

"I thought to myself, 'Look at this little Jewish lady,'" she said. "Me from an orthodox Jewish background, walking with a Catholic priest on the sacred soil of Israel."

Late at night, long after the day's last staged event, Judge went in his habit with Westheimer to the Western Wall. He donned one of the paper yarmulkes available gratis to visitors and stepped up to the only surviving vestige of the Holy Temple. He followed the Jewish tradition of writing a private supplication on a slip of paper and stuffing it into a crevice between the huge stone blocks.

"I was dying with my particular curiosity of life," Westheimer would say. "I wanted to know what was on his piece of paper, but I did not peek."

No cameras were there to record the visitors from New York as they stood together on the deserted, floodlit plaza. They prayed for peace in the late-night hush.

The next morning, they returned with the news crews to the Western

Wall and the junket was again just that. The wall serves as a bulwark for the Temple Mount, Judaism's most sacred site, as well as the site of Islam's golden Dome of the Rock. The Dome was also on the junket's itinerary.

Judge removed his sandals at the entrance and entered barefoot with the others. The diminutive Westheimer was unable to see over the enclosure surrounding the pitted boulder known as the Rock of Foundation. O'Dwyer joined hands to wrist with Judge to assist her.

"So, Mychal and I made a kind of fireman's carry and put her between us and lifted her up," O'Dwyer recalled.

All three then gazed upon the pitted boulder held by Muslims to be the very center of the earth, where Abraham made ready to sacrifice Isaac and where Mohammad ascended into paradise.

The city's most sacred Christian site was the Church of the Holy Sepulcher, built where Jesus was said to have been crucified and buried. The dim interior had been claimed by a half-dozen fractious sects, Roman Catholic, Greek Orthodox, Coptic, Armenian Orthodox, Ethiopian Orthodox, and Syrian Orthodox, each conducting its own services at its own time in its own way, in a kind of Times Square of liturgy.

"Marvelous," Judge said.

Judge's personal faith remained focused not so much on Jesus' death as his life, a life equally worthy of emulation whether as the son of Joseph or as the son of God. Judge seemed less moved even as he stood at Golgotha—supposedly the very place of Jesus' crucifixion—than he had been at, say, the scene of Paddy Brown's double rope rescue.

One sight in Jerusalem that did deeply stir Judge was on the Via Dolorosa, the Way of Sorrow, the route Jesus was said to have taken to his crucifixion. Judge had just passed the Fourth Station when he came to the wall where Jesus supposedly reached out to steady himself. Judge's fingertips brushed the deep, smooth indentation worn into the stone by the cumulative touch of believers over the many years, a mark that in his estimation would be no less profound if Jesus had never set his hand there at all. It did not matter any more than it mattered what a panhandler really did with a coin.

The junket continued by bus to Bethlehem, which the guide noted was the birthplace of David as well as Jesus. The town was now largely Palestinian, and the Israeli security forces maintained a base next to the Church of the Nativity, complete with watchtower and high wire fence.

Judge hunched over to negotiate his big frame through the church's four-foot-high Door of Humility, whose name was misleading, for the dimensions were intended long ago not to humble those who might enter but to keep out Muslims on horseback. He led the delegation down the aisle between the twin rows of limestone columns to the main altar. They descended a set of narrow stone steps.

In a grotto lined with white marble, two small candles flickered at the place where Mary is said to have given birth to Jesus. Judge asked the delegation to hold hands and he began to sing "Silent Night." The others joined in and their eyes began to well, Jews as well as Christians.

"The most hardboiled, cynical bunch of fucking New Yorkers all crying and singing 'Silent Night,'" Brian O'Dwyer later said.

The grotto suddenly felt as holy as it was supposed to be, no matter what your faith.

"What started out as a run-of-the-mill political trip in Israel ended up being the most intense spiritual experience of my life," O'Dwyer said. "All of us together, Catholics, Protestants, and Jews, in a way I've never seen before or since. I don't think there's one of us who was not transformed . . . And it really was all due to Mychal Judge."

When Judge returned to the city he found most holy, he saw Alvarado for the first time in more than a month. But they had just two hours together before he had to rush off to Bellevue Hospital. He spent five hours with firefighters who had been injured when their rig was in a traffic accident.

Judge was up with the dawn to mark the first anniversary of the death of AIDS activist Tim McGinty by driving with his parents to the Catskill Mountains and scattering his ashes. Judge was back in time to say the eleven A.M. Mass at St. Francis, and he was still going long past midnight, spending from two A.M. to five A.M. with firefighters who had been hurt when a ladder company's aerial bucket overturned.

Judge had scant time to pause and mourn when word came from England that cancer had claimed Peter Daly, the young friar who had helped him explore his true form through dance. Judge grieved privately and on the move as he flew with the McDonalds to Denver the next day. Steven was due for one of his periodic visits to the rehabilitation center in Denver. And Pope John Paul II would be holding a World Youth Day that weekend just outside the city.

Great clouds of dust arose as some 400,000 young people made the fourteen-mile trek from Denver to the Cherry Creek State Park for a Saturday-night vigil followed by a Sunday Mass. They could have been the pilgrims of a millennium past, or rock fans on their way to Woodstock. Some people were calling the gathering Popestock. The youthful faces were nearly as varied and interesting as those of a crowd photo from Woodstock that had so delighted Judge he kept it on the wall of his room at the friary. He was as eager as the McDonalds to attend.

But Steven could not walk with the multitudes, and friends in Denver had failed to come through on a promise to get them credentials. The McDonalds telephoned O'Connor to see if His Eminence could secure the necessary passes.

"He said, 'I can't help you. I can't even help my own niece,'" Steven remembered.

Judge and the McDonalds decided to give it a try anyway. They all boarded a van, Steven and Conor in the back, Patti Ann at the wheel, Judge beside her. They were still miles from the park when they encountered the first checkpoint.

"I was like, 'No, this is not going to work,'" Steven recalled.

Judge told everybody to start saying the rosary, and he hopped out. They prayed and watched through the tinted glass as Judge displayed his fire chaplain's badge to the cops, "showing his tin, talking, schmoozing," as Steven described it.

The cops waved them through, but a little farther on they encountered the next checkpoint. The McDonalds resumed praying as Judge hopped out again, once more flashing his tin, once more persuading the cops to wave them through. So did troopers and national guardsmen at each of the subsequent, ever more heavily guarded checkpoints.

Eventually, they came to a checkpoint whose guardians included several motorcycle cops. A bit of the Mychal magic and the van proceeded through the enormous crowd with a motorcycle escort.

"They literally parted the sea," Patti Ann later said.

People began straining to see into the van as it neared the stage. A visible wave of excitement swept the crowd, and the McDonalds realized everybody thought the Pope was inside.

As the Secret Service approached, Patti Ann remembered that one of the agents working the papal detail was Madeline Conway, a friend of a friend. And who came over but Madeline Conway. She was astonished to discover the McDonalds were in the van and that they had gotten as far as they did.

Conway notified her supervisor, James Heavey, who was Bronx Irish and the head of the New York detail. He escorted them backstage for the Pope's arrival. His Holiness's entourage notably included a familiar eminence, who was stunned to see the McDonalds there along with a beaming Mychal Judge.

"Cardinal O'Connor's like, 'W-w-wha . . . How did you get here?'" Patti Ann recalled.

"It was pretty interesting," Steven said.

The Pope did not remember Judge and Patti Ann, but on hearing how Steven was injured, he granted the foursome a brief private audience. Conor looked puzzled, clearly wondering why his mother was crying. The Pope drew the boy under his cloak for a moment.

Then the Pope stepped onstage. The young people cheered and laughed and hugged each other and bounced up and down. Here was the power that John Paul's eleventh-century predecessor, Pope Urban II, summoned at the Council of Claremont in France when he roused the first Crusaders to action with the cry of *"Deus vult!"* or "God wills it!" The faithful had set off by the thousands to liberate the Holy Land from the "infidels," a conflict the present-day jihadis spoke of as ongoing eight hundred years later in their battle against Crusaders and Jews.

This Pope was more a smiling and charismatic version of the modern Urban who had glowered at Judge during the year at Canterbury. John Paul's crusade was a moral one. His immediate goal was not to send the faithful off to battle but simply to keep them in line. He reiterated the prohibition against contraception even in marriage.

"Conjugal chastity . . . lived according to the truth of the body's nuptial meaning," the Pope said.

However much Judge knew about the importance of condoms in preventing AIDS, he could not have worried that such turgid teaching would have much influence on a crowd so swept up in the spectacle that they seemed barely even to register the message. The Pope then became more succinct.

"Drugs and alcohol abuse, pornography and sexual disorder, violence: these are grave social problems which call for a serious response from the whole of society," the Pope continued.

When he said "sexual disorder," the Pope undoubtedly included what the Church had termed an "intrinsic disorder." His Holiness was placing this particular manifestation of physical love on the same list of ills as physical violence, along with alcoholism, drug addiction, and porn.

Which was only what Judge might have expected. He shrugged at what was on the stage at Popestock and delighted in the faith of the multitude around him.

Back in New York, Judge appeared to take special delight when the FDNY mounted a public display of its techniques at Rockefeller Center, directly across Fifth Avenue from St. Patrick's Cathedral. He seemed more thrilled by the ladder and the high-rise rescue demonstrations than he ever was by the august structure across the street.

"Marvelous! Absolutely marvelous!"

Dinkins was also present, for this was no less a photo opportunity than the daytime visit to the Western Wall in Jerusalem. The polls were indicating that he was still slightly ahead, and no black mayor of a big city had ever lost a bid for reelection, but he needed to secure any vote he could.

At a birthday party for Hell's Kitchen Democratic district leader Jim Mc-Manus on September 10, Judge listened to some of the club's most steadfast members say the city was so out of control they might actually vote for the Republican candidate come November. McManus himself was not prepared to commit heresy, even though he suspected Rudy Giuliani was going to win.

"Crossing party lines would be like . . . like . . ." McManus said, groping for a comparison, "like leaving the Church!"

On Election Eve, Judge raced to a three-alarm fire at the Grace Episcopal Church in the Bronx. He offered his blessing as firefighters staged a four-hour battle to quell the flames in the century-old structure.

When the fire was extinguished, a vestryman retrieved a sodden and singed lectern Bible as well as a blackened angel made of copper that still shone where he scraped away some of the soot with his fingernail. The pastor, the Reverend Glenworth Miles, stood in pajamas and uttered a religious principle that Judge had long held.

"The important thing to remember is that the building is not the Church," Miles said. "The people are the Church."

Judge smelled of burned church, which smells like any other burned building, as he returned to his own St. Francis at four A.M. on election morning. He voted as usual when the polls opened, and went that evening to a meeting of the Gay Men's Health Crisis. He then headed to the Sheraton Hotel with a blue ticket bearing the words:

Dinkins '93 Victory Night
Versailles Ballroom
Sheraton New York

The ballroom was crowded with Dinkins supporters who alternately cheered and hushed as results came over the array of televisions. Judge was one of the select few ushered up to Dinkins's suite on the forty-seventh floor. He stood there in his brown habit as exit polls reported that 85 percent of white Catholics had voted for Giuliani. Dinkins was getting 95 percent of the black vote, and he was managing to keep roughly 60 percent of the Jews and Hispanics.

By midnight, three-quarters of the precincts had reported in, and the candidates were in a virtual dead heat, with Giuliani just a thousand votes in the lead. Dinkins edged ahead eight minutes later by two hundred votes, and the crowd in the ballroom cheered wildly.

Then the votes from that island of America on the other side of the Verrazano Bridge began to pour in, the island that was home to many firefighters. The turnout there was especially heavy because of a referendum calling for Staten Island to secede from the city. Most of these voters also went for Giuliani.

By 12:55 A.M., Giuliani had won by 30,000 votes. This was still the closest mayoral race in the city's history, and some observers would later suggest that the firefighters union had made the difference by mounting a field operation for Giuliani. Firefighters union president Tom Von Essen would later describe Giuliani embracing him on Election Night, saying, "Your guys were unbelievable. They were everywhere!"

An organization of ardent police officers known as the Shields had also been active for Giuliani on Election Day. The polls they had "inspected" for irregularities included several in black neighborhoods and some Dinkins supporters had taken this as an attempt at intimidation. Several top aides in the hotel suite urged Dinkins to challenge the results. Others pressed him to declare that the outcome proved the majority of whites simply would not vote for a black man.

Dinkins said he intended to concede.

"Baby, is it okay with you?" he asked his wife, Joyce.

Joyce hugged him. Dinkins made the call to Giuliani.

"I'm going to make a concession speech and call upon the people of the city to stand with you," Dinkins told him.

Dinkins hung up, having demonstrated to the very end the grace Judge had seen in him from the start. Judge offered to say a prayer before Dinkins went down. Judge asked everyone to join hands, and the howling and grumbling stopped. The white Catholic in his friar's gown then spoke in the hush as if directly to the God of all peoples, asking His blessing.

More howls and grumbles came when Dinkins took the stage in the ballroom. He spoke to all of New York just as Judge had spoken upstairs.

"Now do me a favor and do our city a favor," Dinkins said. "Whether you stand in the room or in the streets of our great city, take the hand of the person nearest you and hold it tight as we hold it and pray for our city, as we pray for our future, as we pray for our next mayor. Now, more than ever, the things that unite us must stand taller and weigh greater than the things that divide us."

The continuing importance of Alvarado in Judge's life was clear in an entry he made atop the page in his appointment book five days later: "November 8 Begin ALA—'91" He drew a double arrow linking a similar anniversary entry atop the next day's page: "November 9 Steven—Patti Ann 8 yrs."

Judge continued to spend what time he could with Alvarado, who was now studying for a master's degree in nursing at Columbia, having originally enrolled at New York University. Alvarado had switched to the more prestigious Ivy League school at his favorite priest's urging. Judge had told him not to worry about the cost and taken him to meet Dympna and her husband, Frank Jessich. Dympna was ready to accept that her twin had a strong bond with his friend, but she would remain certain he was celibate. She and her husband agreed to contribute toward the tuition.

Alvarado continued to work full time at St. Barnabas while undertaking a full course load and as a result was as busy as Judge. Judge would help out by doing Alvarado's laundry. Friars who glanced into Judge's s room would see him folding nursing attire that clearly was not his.

"They would see all the white shirts, white socks," Alvarado would later say. "Can you imagine all that out on his bed?"

Judge was still a new enough fire chaplain that he wrote "NYFD Memorial Mass" instead of "FDNY" in his book on November 21. He added a note to himself to "get nice gong bell to ring after each name," for he had learned the importance the firefighters placed on remembrance. He understood this was their scripture, the memorialization of all that had come before, that rode with them as they lived one alarm at a time, that came with them into the blinding smoke and searing flame, that would continue no matter what befell them, that would honor for all time those who made the ultimate sacrifice.

At the reading aloud of each name, one of the Holy Name Society members rang the bell Judge placed near the altar.

"If you didn't pull hard enough, he'd give you a look," Firefighter Ray Phillips recalled. "He'd walk up to you later and say, 'I guess you didn't like that guy.'"

This was classic firehouse humor, the ever-restorative ballbusting that would fill the hush before the next reading of the names, that made laughter purest prayer, that would keep them charging into fires though they knew that the bell was sure to toll again.

Judge feared he might witness the loss of three more firefighters in the aftermath of a gas explosion at a Queens diner on January 26. A woman's voice was coming from the mound of smoking rubble.

"Pull me out! Pull me out!"

Lt. Terry Hatton and Firefighter Kevin Dowdell stripped off their turnout coats so they could squeeze through a jagged opening that measured maybe eighteen by forty inches. They saw a woman lying on her back, her lower torso pinned in the jumble of wood and concrete. She gripped Dowdell's gloved hand.

"Like you were holding a baseball bat to knock one over the fence," Dowdell later said.

Dowdell slipped away from her determined grip so he could set to freeing her, but she grabbed his hand again.

"Pull me out!"

Dowdell and Hatton put blankets on her upper torso.

"Put your hand in the blanket," Dowdell told her.

The firefighters asked her name.

"Vicky Llenos." She was a waitress and had two children.

"Six and seventeen."

Hatton was still a bachelor, but Dowdell had two boys, aged eleven and thirteen, and nobody was a more devoted father. Dowdell still did not hesitate to join Hatton in beginning the delicate work of extricating someone from a precarious balance of wood and concrete that threatened to crush them all at any moment. They pulled away only those tiny bits that were loose. Anything else might have been the one little piece that was holding up the whole pile. They were playing pickup sticks for their lives.

Bits of rubble trickled down. Dowdell and Hatton then heard shouts from the firefighters above.

"Whoa! Whoa!"

The space was so small that Dowdell and Hatton had to contort themselves to look up. They saw that the big slabs of concrete overhead were shifting.

"Oh my God," Dowdell said.

By then Firefighter Bill Lake had squeezed into another hole, hoping to locate Llenos's lower half. He eased away debris, coming to a bit of blue fabric and then living flesh.

"We've got part of a leg!" Lake shouted.

Lake kept on, shoring up as he went, sweating in the chill, staying careful, careful, careful. He kept in mind one of those essential laws of physics against which firefighters test their spirit.

"For every action you take, there's a chance there could be a reaction," Lake said afterward.

They discovered the explosion had wrapped a copper coil around part of Llenos's right leg. There was no room for a saw, and Lake ended up cutting the metal with the serrated blade of a pocketknife. The concrete slabs over-head shifted again.

"You stop, and for that second you hope nothing comes down on you," Lake later told his comrades, including Judge.

At the other end, Dowdell slipped a deflated airbag under one of two concrete slabs that were keeping Llenos trapped. He raised a thumb to signal the firefighters above. The bag began to inflate ever so slightly until Dowdell made a cutting gesture at his throat for them to stop. He and Hatton repeated the process eight times before the slab had risen an inch. They then did the same with the second slab, going not a tenth of an inch past what they absolutely needed.

The last major obstacle was a two-by-four that Dowdell and Hatton feared cutting. They decided to use a sling to ease it aside two inches. They announced to Lake that the moment had come.

"You ready?"

"Yeah . . . Let's do it."

A supervisor called down for Lake to ascend to safety. He ignored the order and stayed in the hole, pulling a piece of wood back from Llenos's ankle. Hatton and Dowdell took her under the arms and eased her ever so gently from the rubble, then Lake climbed out himself.

Llenos was fine. All three firefighters would die at the Trade Center along with the chaplain who recognized grace most actual and sanctifying in Hatton's matter-of-fact recounting of the most perilous moment in the rubble.

"We use our bodies to shield her. It hits us before it hits her."

23

The day after Palm Sunday and all those green fronds destined to become ashes, there came the start of a story Judge would call as biblical as the Bible.

At 6:25 P.M., a tenant on the first floor at 62 Watts Street in Greenwich Village left a pizza box atop a gas stove and headed out for the evening. The pilot light ignited the box, and the fire spread to the wooden floor, but was dampened by a dwindling supply of oxygen. The eighteenth-century building had recently been caulked, sealed, and insulated and otherwise made more energy efficient. The doors and windows were new, and in this particular room they were closed. The only ventilation was the fireplace.

As a result, the fire was kept to little more than a smolder. The rising smoke and combustible fumes meanwhile built up until they banked down to the level of the open flue. Sparks began escaping from the chimney along with thick smoke. A passerby called 911 at 7:36 P.M.

Within minutes, Ladder Co. 5 and Engine Co. 24 rolled out of their firehouse at Sixth Avenue and West Houston Street. Paddy Brown happened to have stopped in the firehouse to say hello to the captain, John Drennan, while on his way to an eight P.M. AA meeting. He followed the truck and engine on foot the four blocks to Watts Street.

For once, Brown was just an observer, and he found himself impressed by the precision of a routine he himself had so often performed. The firefighters of Ladder 5 moved with a speed and sureness that marked Drennan a great commander. Here was courage as precise as ballet.

"I was kind of like proud," Brown later said. "I was like going, 'These guys are doing a good operation.'"

Drennan charged into the three-story structure with Firefighters James

Vina collected herself and addressed Giuliani. She was a compact woman who had what she sometimes called "good Norwegian legs" along with the blue eyes of the fjord, eyes that stayed steady in the midst of her terror. She was direct, as if she were in the classroom where she taught third grade.

"I didn't vote for you," Vina said. "But my husband loves you, and we used to fight about you all the time."

Safir had also come in. He turned to Giuliani.

"Oh, we knew there were ten people on Staten Island that didn't vote for you," Safir said. "Now we only have to find the other nine."

The clearest memory Judge would have of the encounter was of the smile Vina managed, as brave as her husband's. A surprising effect, given that Vina was in the grip of absolute terror.

Judge escorted Vina into the trauma bay where her husband lay. Brown pulled the sheet up to hide the burns as best he could and stepped back. She stroked John Drennan's hair just as Brown had.

"John Drennan, I loved you from the first day I saw you," she said.

She had first glimpsed him almost four decades before at Tottenville High School, and she had practiced saying his name aloud before their first date. The pain now caused his hands to appear from under the sheet and rise in the way of a startled infant.

Brown covered the hands again, but they came back out.

"He's moving and he's shaking," Brown later said. "It was horrible. It was a tough scene."

Brown was a former Marine who had seen extensive combat in Vietnam. These wounds were as bad as any he had ever witnessed in war, but Vina did not seem to recoil, even inwardly.

"She saw how bad he was and she hung in there," Brown remembered. "She just hung in there and focused on John."

A medical person poured more Betadine on her husband's burns. Even the smell of the disinfectant was preternaturally vivid to Vina, yet she remained unflinchingly attentive.

"Oh, John Drennan, you're wonderful and I love you and you're big and you're strong and you're going to make it," Vina said.

She paused.

"You're a tough guy," she said.

"I know," he said.

Judge watched and listened and he would later say that he felt as if he were the one receiving spiritual guidance. He would recall being momentarily puzzled by one thing Vina told her husband.

"And I said that Hail Mary you taught me all the way here," Vina told him.

Judge would remember telling himself, "That was a strange statement." He could not immediately fathom how a firefighter's wife could not have already known the prayer. Vina then squeezed Judge's hand and said, "I'm Lutheran."

Vina turned back to her husband and kissed him lightly on the forehead as he slipped from consciousness.

Siedenburg's father and mother arrived.

"A firefighter told us, 'Chris was in a fire and got hurt,'" the father recalled. "We didn't think it was that serious."

The head doctor, Michael Madden, came over. Madden said their son had been badly burned and might require surgery.

"I just said, 'Whatever you have to do,'" the father remembered.

The Siedenburgs were then taken in to see Chris. He was unconscious and covered by a sheet, save for his face. His eyebrows and mustache were gone. His mouth was bleeding around the breathing tube in his throat. A nurse said he would probably hear his parents but would not be able to respond.

Judge was at their side. He led them in a prayer, his tone as always so intimate he seemed to have no doubt God could hear him.

When the budget director Lackman arrived, Drennan was also in the burn unit. Lackman was taken to where the two firefighters lay in agony, and he was visibly shaken by the injuries. Giuliani said he wanted Lackman to speak immediately with someone who could brief him on the full human cost of not having bunker gear.

Lackman sat down with a man in an FDNY jacket who spoke to him passionately about the enormous risks firefighters routinely face. Lackman returned to the mayor and promised to find $12 million somewhere in the budget. He did not realize until after the Twin Towers had fallen that the man in the FDNY jacket had been Fire Chaplain Mychal Judge.

• • •

After midnight, Judge went with Giuliani and Safir to Drennan's firehouse. They entered to find the apparatus floor deserted. A toy fire engine sat atop the riding board, on which the names of those working the current shift were written.

6 to 9 tour
March 28
Ladder Co. 5
Capt. Drennan
Waugh
Young
Monahan
Siedenburg

Another board hung inside the deserted kitchen. A hurried hand had chalked a message.

Be strong. Be you. Be firefighters.

Dishes sat in the sink. The alarm had come in just after dinner.

The three men climbed the stairs to an area lined with lockers. Many were open and had pinups taped inside. Giuliani hurried to close the lockers, as would any good Catholic boy with a priest present.

"It's all right," Judge said. "It keeps them relaxed."

They continued into a room where the firefighters sat as stunned and heartbroken as the men had been after Thomas Williams of Rescue 4 died on Judge's first day on the job two years before. Judge had been unsure how to respond back then. He now knew exactly what to say.

"This firehouse is a holy place," Judge said. "It will always be holy ground for you."

Judge reminded them that James Young, Chris Siedenburg, and John Drennan, along with the rest, had dashed from this house to place themselves in harm's way for the sake of others. Judge said this made them dear to God and only more so when one of them laid down his life.

Nobody listened to Judge more intently than Craig Monahan, the firefighter who called Drennan "Uncle John." The usual rotation should have put Monahan inside the building with Drennan. Young was to have been on the roof. Drennan had switched the assignments moments before the alarm came in to give the less experienced Monahan an added opportunity to vent a roof. Monahan could not help feeling that he should have been the one who was incinerated. Judge was telling him that this was not just a twist of indifferent fate.

"He just made it seem like everything has a reason and we'll all be back together later on," Monahan said. "He made it have a purpose."

At the hospital, Brown secured permission to watch over Drennan's family as well as his company. He spoke his first words to Vina.

"I don't talk much, but I've been assigned to you."

Brown rode with her up to the seventh-floor burn unit. He had been there as a patient twice for seared lungs, and he felt himself go faint as they stepped off the elevator.

"That's something you don't want to do as a captain, faint," Brown later said.

Brown steadied himself and watched with Vina as Drennan was wheeled into intensive care. Drennan called out to them.

"Okay, I'll see you in a while."

At two A.M., two firefighter friends drove Vina home.

"I have never been so scared in my life," she remembered.

Brown stayed a while longer. He watched two doctors work on Drennan. The burned hand rose again and another thumbs-up sent Brown off to Ladder Co. 5 just as Judge was arriving back at the hospital.

The next morning, Vina returned to the burn unit with her four children. They all joined Judge in putting on surgical gowns and masks, for the slightest infection can turn deadly for a burn victim.

The family was given a sort of hotel room in an adjacent building, just on the other side of the sloping driveway that leads to the emergency entrance, a dimly lit dip Vina would dub the Valley of the Shadow of Death. She sought to steady herself through the long hours by beginning a journal in a school composition book such as her students used at P.S. 42. Judge would come to call this "The Book of Vina."

"John is bandaged and heavily sedated, but he knows we are there," Vina wrote. "His hand moves. The children cry large silent tears. I wonder if I will ever get another hug."

Giuliani and Safir came by.

"The Fire Commissioner says the Mayor forced [Lackman] to look at John and Chris. The $12 million will be found for Bunker suits. John's injury will prevent another from having to go through this because of lack of equipment."

Vina went into a waiting room where Judge sat with Siedenburg's parents and their other son, Chris's twin, Charlie.

"The father shakes and the mother sits quietly," Vina wrote. "Their fear is felt by all in the room."

At 8:10 P.M., a doctor came in and said that Chris had gone into cardiac arrest. The Siedenburgs went into the room, where Chris lay in a bed beside John Drennan's, beyond all earthly help.

"Chris, I want to see your eyes, open your eyes," the brother, Charlie, said. "I want to see your blue eyes, Chris."

As Charlie broke down, Judge quietly sought to calm him. The crying father stepped into the hall and embraced the first firefighter he saw. He chanced to clutch Timothy Stackpole, who had come after recognizing John Drennan in a late-night news flash as one of the firefighters being carried from the Watts Street fire.

Stackpole was a firefighter who loved going to fires so much that some called him "Jobs." He lived for a good rescue and was shaken by not being able to help Siedenburg's grief-stricken father. Stackpole could think of nothing to do but hug him.

Ladder Co. 5 and Engine Co. 24 were just going back into service when a phone call brought the news that Chris was dead. The engine that had stood ready for the next alarm rolled out of the firehouse to make room for the van that arrived with Judge and the Siedenburg family. Judge led everyone in prayer. He again spoke of holiness and sacrifice, though even he seemed to falter when he was shown a trio of goldfish that had been found at the scene of the fire on Watts Street.

The goldfish had been discovered alive in their tank just on the other side of the door that the trapped firefighters had pounded upon with all their might in a vain attempt to escape the fireball. The priest who always spoke so confidently about God and His plans stood silently watching these three tiny fish that had survived whereas two firefighters had died and a third was now in hellish agony.

After midnight, Brown went into the small captain's office and lay down on the bed where Drennan would have slept. Judge departed for the friary and ended the night as he always did, in the small, snug chapel down the hall from his room, talking to God, Lord Almighty of firefighters and goldfish.

In the morning, Judge spoke to Him again from the usual spot at the right front pew in the lower church. Judge afterward spent an hour and a half returning calls that had piled up on his answering machine.

Judge then headed for the burn unit. Vina had been there since before dawn, having been roused at two A.M. when her fourteen-year-old son, Johnny Joe, climbed into her bed at the guest suite across the street from the hospital.

"I held him and I feel his warmth and I am so afraid," she later wrote.

At 4:30 A.M., she had gotten dressed and gone to the burn unit. Her husband was now alone in the room.

"We talked about heroes only a week ago," she wrote. "His hands are bloodied and raw. I can't find a spot to touch him. I am helpless to help."

John Drennan was then wheeled off for five hours of surgery in which his legs were grafted with cadaver skin. The doctor told her that her husband was strong, but the burns were worse than initially thought, all third and fourth degree.

"Such a man can't die—pray God," Vina wrote. "I come back to this room and sob the tears of heaven."

As if those prayers might be answered, Dr. Madden took Vina aside later that same day and said her husband had been doing remarkably well in the hours after the surgery. Madden went so far as to say he was guardedly optimistic John Drennan would pull through.

"He adds he does not ever just say it," Vina wrote. "Oh the joy I felt again to hold onto some hope."

Judge was there and he blessed John Drennan as he had blessed so many others. Judge's voice was sure and steady and confident in the face of the captain's injuries, the sight of which made even experienced nurses wince.

"You're a good man, John. God loves you."

Drennan repeatedly raised his right arm, almost as if he were reaching for something. Only Judge imagined what that might be.

The next day was Holy Thursday. Judge stopped by the firehouse. Vina had been over at the scene of the fire and discovered that passersby had left floral tributes.

"Flowers are placed in the charred ruins," she wrote.

A lieutenant had escorted her inside.

"I see the blackness, the smell and the tiny staircase, I see where John tried to break the heavy metal door. I see his power bent it, but there was nowhere to go."

She looked up.

"The melted glass hangs like an icicle from the skylight . . . I am proud of these men who can walk into the unknown to help people. I am proud that John has spent his life this way."

Many more flowers had been left outside the firehouse, a sight that would become common throughout the city after the Twin Towers collapsed. A man stopped at the firehouse to leave a check for five hundred dollars and walked off. A woman left a single white lily and hugged Vina.

"People stand and cry," Vina later wrote. "I talk with a young man. It is Matthew Broderick."

Vina went inside and sat with Judge and the firefighters hurried to get her coffee. Neighborhood people had also brought food that filled the big table in the kitchen on this day of the Last Supper.

"Marvelous," Judge said.

At 5:30 P.M., Judge was back at St. Francis of Assisi on West Thirty-first Street for Mass in the upper church, the first and only on Holy Thursday. Judge stood with his fellow friars as the main celebrant washed the feet of twelve parishioners, just as Jesus had with the disciples, much as Judge had rubbed the feet of AIDS sufferers.

Following Communion, the main celebrant clutched the Blessed Sacrament in the folds of a white cloak that looked to be of humble cloth until the light caught the added threads of glitter as he led the Procession of the Eucharist. He ended by setting the Eucharist in the tabernacle at the side altar, at which burned fifteen candles arrayed in a triangular candelabra known as a hearse. The main altar was stripped bare and the candles were extinguished. The crucifix was covered with a white linen cloth.

The priests retired to the dining room, Holy Thursday being the Feast of the Priesthood, when the friars traditionally gather for a fraternal meal to commemorate the Last Supper.

Judge missed the meal, attending instead Jimmy Young's wake. He stayed until eleven P.M., then stopped by the burn unit. Marty McTigue and his wife had been by and they had spoken to Vina of their own experiences there. Vina had now gone off to lie down, if not sleep. Judge stood by her husband, speaking softly as the wall clock ticked past the midnight hour.

On the afternoon of Good Friday, Judge was back at the burn unit. The local head of Vina's church, Bishop James Sudbrock, also visited the burn unit that day. Sudbrock was Cardinal O'Connor's rough equivalent in official rank, but the Lutheran hierarchy has a very different relationship with its followers.

One fundamental difference is that a Lutheran pastor is hired by the particular parish, not appointed by a central authority. The pastor is essentially an employee, less answerable to the Lutheran hierarchy than to his parish council, which is governed by a majority vote.

All of which Vina well knew from her days as president of the Eltingville Lutheran Church on Staten Island. She felt not the least bit cowed by any person of the cloth, be he her bishop or a Catholic fire chaplain. Sudbrock only expected this, and arrived without the pomp and pretense demonstrated by many Catholic clergy considerably below his rank.

At three P.M., traditionally the hour of the Crucifixion, Judge stood with Vina and Sudbrock at John Drennan's bedside, holding a bottle of water that a well-wisher had sent from Lourdes.

"The priest blessed John," Vina later wrote. "He has such comfort in his hands and his words truly bring peace."

The hands seemed to Vina to be what made the water holy. Her indifference to the persona of the priesthood enabled her to see Judge as a true priest, just as the very absence of dogma and doctrine allowed a purer, more actual, and vital faith.

Vina, Judge, and Sudbrock joined together in reciting the Twenty-third Psalm. Vina had learned the words as a youngster, but only now grasped the full meaning.

"It's amazing how something you learn as a child can bring such comfort and is stored inside you forever," she wrote. "I remember Sunday school and not knowing how surely goodness and mercy could overflow in a cup. Now I know."

God seemed to have come right into the room. And Dr. Madden said something that gave Vina cause for more hope.

"Dr. Madden said 'slight improvement' and it's such a good sound," Vina wrote. "The power of words—and hugs and prayer."

Vina returned to her hotel room. She numbered the days since the fire on a calendar and was optimistic enough to number the days ahead. She stopped at the fortieth day for no reason she could explain.

Judge dashed downtown, for he was due at four P.M. for the Stations of the Cross in the lower church at St. Francis. He departed immediately afterward for Siedenburg's wake on Staten Island. The priest with the secret shamrock tattoo saw a big shamrock hung over the coffin of the firefighter whose own shamrock had been burned off his shoulder, whose first station had been his fire station, who had been able to say nothing more after he declared it the greatest job in the world.

As the FDNY repeated its white-gloved funeral ritual twice in one day, John Drennan underwent ten hours of surgery in an operating room heated to a hundred degrees because his ability to regulate his body temperature was compromised. He remained semiconscious and in critical condition, but life was still strong in him as Judge stopped by the burn unit.

"In five days, we might be able to breathe easier," Dr. Madden said.

Madden figured everyone was already breathing a little easier thanks to Judge. The doctor spoke of the priest just as others had during the AIDS epidemic, noting Judge's "singular ability" to impart peace in the most extreme circumstances by intuitively adjusting his approach and demeanor to exactly what they needed.

"He would go off on one direction, then reverse, depending on what he was getting back," Madden would later say. "Doing whatever it took to put that person at ease."

The Jesuit psychotherapist John McNeill had once spoken of Judge climbing down into someone's private hell and embracing their pain and rage and sorrow. Madden now watched Judge do precisely this with the Drennans and the firefighters.

"He would absorb the pain the family was feeling," Madden later said. "As he took it on himself, he was really lightening their burden as much as he could."

The very act of sharing brought a grace to the pain, a presence that felt divine, whether or not you believed in any particular divinity, a sudden sense amid senselessness. Judge became what people needed, and that helped make his words what they needed to hear.

"He had that ability to explain the inexplicable," Madden later said.

Madden was unversed in the ancient tradition of shapeshifters. He would only learn of it almost a decade later, and he would be startled by the similarities between those figures of Celtic myth and the priest he had watched in the Burn Center.

"That's it," he said. "Exactly."

The modern shapeshifter returned to St. Francis for the Saturday night vigil, arriving just as the lights in the crowded upper church were doused for a ritual rooted in pre-Christian Ireland. The ancient Celts greeted the approach of springtime and rebirth by lighting nighttime bonfires atop the highest hills. In a bit of his own shapeshifting, Saint Patrick spurred the conversion of fifth-century Ireland to Christianity by lighting fires outside churches on the eve of Easter. Pagan fire became the paschal fire, which evolved into the bowl of flammable liquid that was now set alight midway up the center aisle in the darkened upper church.

The sanctuary and side altars were as stocked with flowers as the front of

Ladder 5 had been. Their heady scent suffused the vaulted chamber. The flame flickered with its primal power, capable of unleashing the Red Devil, but was here the symbol of life amid death, the sole light in the darkness through which the head priest and his procession approached.

The fire was used to light an eight-foot paschal candle. The procession then started down the center aisle. Everyone in the packed church had been given a votive candle when they entered. Those in the procession now lit the candle held by a person at an aisle seat. The flame was used to light each candle along the pew.

When every candle along the pews to the left and to the right was alight, the procession continued to the next row, the tiny flames from that pagan paschal fire illuminating face after face as with faith. A warm and gorgeous glow filled the church as the paschal candle was set beside the main altar. This was all holy fire, but a parishioner was posted in the back pew with a bottle of water just in case a candle should ignite somebody's clothing or hair.

At the end of the service, all the candles were extinguished with the breath of life, save for the big one on the altar, which flickered on into Easter morning as Judge concelebrated three Masses among the flowers, at eight A.M., nine-thirty, and eleven.

Judge then departed for the burn unit, where fire had no splendor, where John Drennan continued his agonizing struggle to remain in this life. Judge prayed over John Drennan as he might have over his own father.

"God, he's a brave, strong man. He's a good, good father. He loves his family and they love him . . ."

John was heavily sedated and the tube in his throat prevented him from speaking, but he seemed to register what was said. The proof came as his eyes welled with tears.

After a while, Judge left the room and went down the hall to join the firefighters in the waiting area. The firefighters had been bringing in food for those keeping the vigil and his experience at firehouses led him to expect a meal of lamb and turkey or maybe ham for Easter. He discovered instead a stack of pies from Ray's Famous Pizza.

Then Giuliani arrived with a box of cookies baked by his aunt. He and Judge and the firefighters all sat and talked and passed around the cookies, and when the double doors to the waiting area opened, laughter rang down the burn unit hallway. John Drennan might almost have felt he was back in the firehouse.

• • •

All the Burn Center's precautions did not prevent Drennan's legs from becoming infected toward the end of the second week. Judge urged Vina to keep writing.

My John is on morphine and can't talk. I see tears in his eyes when I talk to him. There must have been six surgeries so far, hours and hours. How much can he take? If he dies, this time would have been so cruel. Just hoping so much makes losing him so much harder . . . Pity scares me more than pain.

On the fourteenth day, John had yet another operation. Vina went with Paddy Brown to Battery Park at the foot of the World Trade Center that night. The Twin Towers rose shining behind them as they stood at the edge of the Hudson River. Brown thought to throw in a coin, but that did not seem enough, so he threw a whole pocketful of change into the dark water.

The infection spread to John's bloodstream and his entire body began to swell. Dr. Madden operated for eleven hours and leaned exhausted against a wall, saying they could only hope for a miracle now. Judge could not promise one and he administered the last rites, proceeding from the eyes through to the feet with the oil that had been sanctified at the cathedral and laced by him with the scents from street vendors.

"Through this holy unction and His own most tender mercy may the Lord pardon thee whatever sins or faults thou hast committed by sight . . . by hearing . . . by smell . . . by taste . . . by touch . . . by walking."

These were the same senses that guide a firefighter into harm's way for the sake of others, and Judge would have been the first to say that by so doing John Drennan had already placed himself in a state of total grace. Vina stepped up to the husband who had suffered so much more than anyone ever should. She spoke through her surgical mask.

"John, you can go," Vina said. "We love you, John. You can go."

The burn unit nurses were crying as Vina went into the hallway and removed her surgical garb. Judge walked her across the Valley of the Shadow of Death. The mayor arrived and joined her at the hotel room, along with a crowd of firefighters, including Capt. Mike Currid of the Uniformed Fire

Officers Union. They were all on their best behavior in the presence of this fire chaplain most of them had not yet come to know.

"We tried not to curse," Currid recalled.

Currid watched Judge sit down on the bed to call his answering machine and write down his messages on a pad. Currid himself received a seemingly endless number of calls from members needing something, but he could see that this was of a whole different order.

"Writing and writing and writing," Currid recalled. "I said, 'Wow, you get more messages than I do.' He said, 'Oh yeah, some they just say hello, some ask me for money, some tell me to go fuck myself.'"

The room full of good Catholic boys went silent. They then exploded into laughter that Vina could not help but join.

"I said, 'Holy cow, this is going to be a great priest for us,'" Currid recalled.

Judge went back across the Valley of the Shadow of Death to keep a vigil. Vina stayed in the hotel room, and as midnight neared she was still waiting in dread for the phone call from Judge that the end had come. She took out the Book of Vina.

"I let him go," she wrote. "I want the suffering to end."

Judge remained at the captain's bedside into the early morning. John Drennan's life was still flickering when Vina returned with Brown after dawn. The swelling was down and it seemed a miracle just might come to pass.

"Oh, you never listened to me anyway."

Vina rode with Paddy Brown through a rainy morning to Staten Island so she could see the kids. She tried to catch up on the laundry and saw that her son had written something in small letters on one of his socks.

"Dad."

At 12:30 P.M. the phone rang. Vina picked up, dreading the worst, but heard burn nurse Chris Casey say that her husband was improving.

"*Yes!*" she wrote.

In the evening, Vina returned to the Burn Center with the kids. Her youngest daughter, nineteen-year-old Justine, wandered off from the hospital just before it was time to head back to Staten Island. Vina waited a half hour and then went outside with her son and stood on the corner of East Seventieth Street and York Avenue.

"Johnny Joe and I just looked all over for her. I started to cry," she later wrote.

The tears were streaming down Vina's face when a car pulled up. Out stepped Mychal Judge.

> It was really pretty funny 'cause he said I had been so strong and all that and here an annoying teenager could get to me. Ha! He should have a 19 year-old. Anyway, he kept talking to me and lo and behold she comes strolling along at 12:30. Of course, she saw us—priest and all—and thought John died.

Judge calmed them and gave his blessings. He went up to see the elder John Drennan as the rest of the family returned to Staten Island.

In the morning, Vina headed back to the hospital with the kids. The elder John was again in surgery.

"I luckily got them out of here before they brought him down," she later wrote. "His head looked like chopped meat . . . The kids did not have to have that image in their mind all week."

She had brought a bag of mail from home, and she lugged it to the hotel room.

> It took 11 hours to open it. Yet it was wonderful reading good stories people remember. He did a lot of nice things that he never told anyone about.

More letters arrived directly at the hospital. Judge stood with Paddy Brown, marveling at the sacks upon sacks of good wishes. Vina took out her composition book, and the Book of Vina made scripture of Judge's God of Surprises.

> Everyday in the midst of this shit, good things happen. Looking back on all these days, I can't believe how a good thing happens each day. There are some men in the coffee shop who sell us coffee each day for

half price . . . They must come from someplace like Pakistan and they nod and say, "Good morn-ning, Vina" . . . The hot dog vendor gives us free hot dogs . . . People stop and say they're praying for us. I'm always surprised.

For all the goodness she encountered and for all Judge's soothing words and for all the peace his hands imparted, Vina found she could not even listen to her in-laws' talk about God's will.

I told them I didn't want any part of a God that would will this kind of shit . . . Praise the Lord and dump on the holy water.

An unending stream of firefighters visited the burn unit, but infection remained the direst threat to John Drennan and they had to remain at the end of the hallway, beyond the double doors that opened automatically like some TV spaceship airlock.

"Push the button on the wall, the doors would be open, and outside there would be two or three or four firefighters, a lieutenant, a captain, a chief, maybe a policeman or two," Judge would recall.

Brown would serve as emissary, going in his gown and mask to report to Drennan who had come to visit.

"I'd go in every day and tell him which firemen were out there," Brown recalled.

Drennan was still able to move his hand and he would press it against the tracheotomy tube in his throat.

"He'd grab his trache and he'd try to speak," Brown remembered. "And he'd say, 'Help me, Paddy. Help me.' I'd say, 'Look, John, your kids are going to be taken care of. Your wife's going to be taken care of. The fire department's going to look after them, John. I know you want to struggle. I know you want to live.'"

Drennan would nod. Brown would repeat what Vina had said.

"I'd say, 'Look, John if you want to go, it's okay. John, you can go. We'll take care of your family.'"

John Drennan held on. Among the steady visitors to the burn unit was Firefighter Peter McLaughlin, the youngest of the Zinno's crowd. Brown loved him like he was a kid brother. He was big and gentle and, in the words of Vina, "decent to the depths of his sparkly soul."

On his first visit, McLaughlin and Vina fell into conversation for an hour and parted feeling as if they were close friends already. His charm and openness made him seem heaven-sent in much the same way as Judge.

"Goodness just seeped out of him," Vina later said. "You couldn't help but be touched by it. He filled a room with sunshine. If there was one word for him, that was it: sunshine."

He kept bringing the sunshine, sitting on one side of Vina while Brown sat on the other. They were often joined by Terry Hatton and Firefighter Tim Brown.

"They wrapped me up in a love most people don't get to feel," Vina recalled.

Vina never ceased to marvel when McLaughlin and the others would excuse themselves to head off to the firehouse.

"Peter would come to the hospital and he'd sit and he knew how badly hurt John was and he went and did his job," Vina later said.

The firefighters kept trooping up to the burn unit and on the nineteenth day they began keeping a record in an oversized hardbound ledger.

> *4/15/94*
> *John,*
> *Your strength and courage have given new meaning for my life.*
> *Capt. Pat Brown*

Then came entry after entry by firefighters sounding as devout as friars. They included the young firefighter who had become one of Vina's favorites.

> *4/18/94*
> *Capt.,*
> *My prayers and all firemen's prayers are for you. Your strength and*
> *courage is something I will keep with me. God speed.*
> *—Peter McLaughlin (Rescue 4)*

Another entry was by the firefighter who had been the first to reach Drennan, Siedenburg, and Young. This firefighter from Rescue 1 would perish along with his firefighter brother at the World Trade Center.

> *4/18/94*
> *I worked the night of the fire on Watts St. It broke my heart to see John like that. I felt almost helpless, yet I had a job to do. I had an obligation to a friend and fellow firefighter. I did the best I could to make John and Chris as comfortable as I could. God Bless you all.*
> *Harvey L. Harrell*
> *Rescue Co #1*

There was also:

> *4/20/94*
> *John, I've gone back to praying and getting religious. I guess I can blame you for that. At least my mother is happy about that. The whole family is thinking and praying for you. The grandkids have you in their prayers every night. God bless you and get well soon.*
> *Fitz*

The vigil continued through to the dawn and on to the next and the next. The nurses monitored John Drennan's vital signs and the firefighters filled more pages of the Book of Visitation with prayers that he be restored to the life he once lived.

> *When I told my wife what I was doing tonight she pressed my shirt and said as always, "Be careful." She also says she prays for you. Another day, another victory.*

And there was one from a firefighter who was just starting out:

> *Hi Capt*
> *I'm a probationary firefighter . . . before my first tour I found myself going to 2 fellow firefighters' funerals. I found myself praying for their souls. Hoping I wouldn't be praying for yours. Well here I am on watch and my hopes are still alive. You're doing as well as*

can be and so far our prayers have been answered. I hope to see you
on your feet one day. So until then, I'll keep praying. Hang in there
and keep the faith.

FF. Andrew Herbert

John Drennan continued to stave off the infection, but his liver began to falter. Madden told Vina that something called the bilirubin count stood at eighteen. A count of one was normal. Twenty could be fatal.

"I never prayed or cursed so much," she wrote in her book.

As if in answer to all the prayers, the number dropped to sixteen over the week ahead. The count stood at eleven on the thirty-first day, but that was still hardly normal. John Drennan was far from on the mend. His wife kept writing in the Book of Vina.

"I looked at his good leg today and it's a fucking mess . . . There's no flesh left. Shit, and that's his good leg."

She was standing by his bed when his teeth clenched.

"Are you in pain, John?" she asked.

John nodded. Vina told him that he would be home soon. She added that he might finally get their yard in shape.

"But you've been saying that for twenty years," she said.

John's teeth unclenched and Vina was sure that he smiled. Her face was covered by a surgical mask, but her own smile shone in her eyes. John's teeth then clenched again and her eyes dimmed. She could do no more than touch his forearm with her hand tucked inside the sleeve of her surgical gown.

The morning of Day 32 saw Vina back at the hospital. The bilirubin was going toward eight, and the doctor was again saying that John Drennan might survive. He proved able to raise his arm in a toast when Vina sang the Irish anthem, "A Nation Once Again."

"[The doctor] said, 'If he makes it through next week I might even raise the chances from fifty-fifty,'" Vina told Judge when he arrived. "There is magic. I think we call it love."

At 4:30 P.M. that day, Judge dashed from the burn unit to a four-alarm fire on Jerome Avenue in the Bronx. He returned accompanying a firefighter with burns serious enough to require hospitalization, but not life-threatening. He then went back down the hall to John Drennan and he stayed until after midnight.

At seven A.M. the following morning, Judge was working the breadline at St. Francis. His appointment book shows that he was as busy as always, his FDNY duties including the blessing at a street-naming ceremony for fallen firefighter Al Ronaldson of Rescue 3, who had been killed in a fire in 1991. He proceeded directly to the bedside of the captain, who was fighting so hard not to become the department's 756th fatality.

Vina went home to check on her children, and Brown went off to see a girlfriend who was not quite The One. Judge stayed for a time and then returned to the friary and answered calls.

On Day 35, Drennan underwent yet another surgery. Brown tried to give Vina a psychic break by taking her and Judge to Zinno's for dinner. She was becoming as much a legend in the department as Brown and Judge and the others. The Zinno's crowd had come to consider her one of their own.

"I had earned my spot at the table," Vina later said. "Most forty-nine-year-old women don't get to be one of the guys."

After dinner, Brown and Judge went with Vina to the hospital. Her husband was wheeled away for still more surgery, the second time in one day. He seemed to be resting comfortably afterward, and he remained so the next day. Vina headed off to see her kids, but Judge and Brown lingered at the captain's bedside, agreeing that he appeared to be doing well.

"He seemed to be talking to us," Judge recalled. "His lips were going and he wanted to speak."

Drennan's hands rose as if reaching, as they had during all the time in the hospital. He then drifted off and Judge and Brown later called Vina to say that her husband was stable, maybe even on the mend.

On the fortieth day, Vina went with Brown to the burn unit and Madden told them her husband had taken a sudden turn for the worse.

"We heard fear in Dr. Madden's voice . . . ," she later wrote. "John's blood pressure dropped to 90. Surgery postponed until it's determined what's causing the crisis. They let me look in on him and there was fear in his eyes. God how I hate that look . . . This is the worst part, to see those frightened eyes."

Drennan was wheeled off for a CAT scan that might help to explain the crisis. Paddy Brown was with Vina when they brought John back from the tests and into the room past the two probationary firefighters who stood honor guard at the door. A nurse was squeezing an Ambu bag, and there was a *whoosh, whoosh, whoosh* as she forced air into John's chest.

Vina entered the room and Brown came with her. She again saw the terror in her husband's eyes. Brown also saw it.

"John was wide awake and I could see his eyes looking around and he knew," Brown recalled. "He knew he was going to die. I put my arm around Vina. She says, 'I love you, John.' I said, 'Good luck, John.'"

The sound of the Ambu bag followed the two as they returned to the hallway so as not to interfere with the medical team. They stood listening to that *whoosh, whoosh, whoosh.*

After an hour, the whooshing stopped. Madden emerged from the room and told Vina that her husband's straining heart had finally given out. She sought what little comfort she could in knowing that his agony was over.

"He suffered enough," she said.

Brown went with Vina back into the room.

"We cried over his body and stuff. It was kind of beautiful, you know," Brown remembered.

After twenty minutes, they emerged. Vina paused to speak with the two probationary firefighters still standing guard at the door.

"My husband went to work every day and he was happy. He loved this job. It's the greatest job in the world," she said.

Vina went off to call her children. Brown brought the two probies into the room. He told them to put their hands on the fallen captain.

"This is a great man," Brown said. "You might never meet a man this great again."

The probies stood there, each with a hand on Drennan, as if standing over an ancient chieftain.

"Do you pray?" Brown asked.

"We do now, captain," one of them said.

Brown said a Hail Mary. He touched Drennan's face and left, telling the probies, "Nobody goes into this room."

Brown strode off to page Judge and do what he could for Vina. One of the probies, who would later coproduce the documentary shot in the lobby of the North Tower, made an entry in the Book of Visitation.

My name is James Hanlon . . . The doctor has just come down the
corridor and informed your wife of your passing on. I had the honor
to meet your wife, Vina. She is an incredible woman. Anyone can
see why you chose her for your wife. God bless you, captain.
May God hold you gently in his palm.

Firefighter James Hanlon

Directly below that was an entry by Dr. Michael Madden.

Capt—
I'm sorry. I tried.
MM

Word reached fire headquarters and First Deputy Commissioner Feehan arrived at the burn center. He was about to enter the room when the probies barred the way.

"I'm sorry, but Paddy Brown says nobody goes in the room," Hanlon said.

Feehan stood amazed.

"Do you know who I am?" he asked.

"Yes, sir," Hanlon said. "Paddy Brown still says nobody goes in the room."

The probies managed to get Brown on the phone. They only then told Feehan he could enter.

"Paddy Brown says you can go in," Hanlon said.

Judge stepped off the elevator. Giuliani arrived soon after. Judge and Feehan went with him to the hotel room to see Vina. She had already spoken to her kids.

"There are worse things than having your children remember you as a hero," she was saying to a reporter friend when Judge walked in with Giuliani and Feehan.

"We've already planned the funeral twice," Vina said. "But I really thought we had turned the corner."

Giuliani stood with his arms crossed. He looked in amazement at this woman who seemed to know only how to be brave.

"He's at peace," Vina said.

"He looked peaceful," Giuliani said.

Giuliani and Vina embraced.

"He had a good run," Vina said.

Vina again sought what comfort she could, remarking that at least John would never know that two of his firefighters had died.

"That would have hurt him worse than the pain," she said.

Her eyes reddened and her grief suddenly seemed about to crush her.

"I guess by now, he does know," she said.

Vina imagined aloud that John was sitting in heaven with his two fellow firefighters. She turned to Judge.

"There is beer in heaven, right, Father?" she said.

Those reddened eyes were gazing directly at Judge. She was joking, but not. She was still ready to believe.

Brown and Judge took Vina back to Staten Island. They pulled up outside the house and walked in past a magnolia tree that had been barely a sapling when Vina and her husband were first starting a family. They had taken a picture of the kids in front of it each Easter, and it had grown with them.

Vina had told Judge of this, and he saw that the tree was now a good twenty feet tall. He also saw that the last of the Easter petals had fallen. He entered the house and stayed until dawn was breaking.

Vina's first full day as a widow was Mother's Day. She was awakened by one of her full-grown daughters crawling into her bed. Then another daughter joined them, and then her son. After Justine rose, she made an entry in the Book of Visitation, which had come home with them.

> 5/8/94
>
> *Your pain is over and this will be just the beginning of ours. Our lives have changed and that piece of the puzzle will forever be missing. You have touched a lot of lives. You have always been a hero to me though. I was always so proud to say my father's a fireman. I wonder what you're doing right now? Are you with grandpa Andersen and all your relatives? Tell everyone I said hello. We all know you tried so hard to live for us. I'm selfish in some ways because I wanted you to so badly, but then I think about how miserable life*

would've been for you. This next week will be the hardest week of
my life. There was so much more I wanted to do. I had this plan for
a while now that when I had a job I was going to send you to Ire-
land. That was going to be my gift to you for all you have done for
me. You did so much and I will forever admire you. I wish I could
just give you a great big hug and tell you how much I love you. I
feel we were coming to an understanding of each other these past
two years or so. There won't be a day that goes by that I do not think
of you. Please always know that I loved you dearly, even if I didn't
always show it and that your soul will always be with me, dad.
 I love you always,

Justine

Justine was nineteen years old, not an age to discuss "the whole spiritual thing" with your friends. She could with Judge, who seemed to know exactly what she meant when she said her father was still with her and would remain with her no matter what was to come.

"Like God," Justine said.

And Judge represented for her what priests had for him after his loss.

"He was the only person I could call father," Justine would later say.

The phone rang and one of the firefighters who had come to the Drennan house picked up. He told Vina that a monsignor from the archdiocese was on the line, saying the cardinal was offering the Drennan family St. Patrick's Cathedral for the funeral.

Vina sat down in the living room and took a moment to ponder the offer. She had been thinking maybe the funeral should be at tiny Eltingville Lutheran Church on Staten Island, where she and John were married. But she realized that was impossible.

"We can't even handle Christmas Eve," she told herself.

Her husband had officially converted to Lutheran when they were wed, but he had remained enough of a Catholic to teach her the Hail Mary. She closed her eyes and had a single definite thought.

"As long as Mychal Judge can do it."

Judge had, after all, been with the family through all the horrors of the forty days. He was at this very moment upstairs talking with the Drennan kids, who had found him so incandescent during the darkest days of their young lives, who would be looking for him on the altar no matter what the church.

She picked up the phone and His Eminence himself came on the line. She thanked O'Connor for the offer of the cathedral.

"And Father Judge can say the Mass!" she said.

Vina got off the phone with no inkling that O'Connor might be choking down a fury, that in offering the cathedral he had also been offering himself, that in providing a stage for the end of this drama he expected to be at its center. O'Connor could hardly tell a newly bereaved widow who had won the city's heart that she could not have the priest she wanted at her hero hus-band's funeral. The cardinal did let it be known in other quarters that he was not pleased, and word reached Giuliani.

"There was a little problem," Giuliani recalled. "The cardinal didn't want [Judge] to say the Mass."

Giuliani called O'Connor and, by his recollection, "appealed to our rela-tionship," which likely meant that after some flattery the mayor offered the cardinal an opportunity to appear magnanimous, a true eminence. Giuliani would not have had to say that O'Connor risked looking like a real schmuck if he did not.

Giuliani then relayed the great news to Vina.

"Father Judge can say the Mass!"

She took it as being simply the way it should be. She still did not imagine that the cardinal would be anything but pleased to have a priest who had done so much for her family.

"What did I know?" she would later say.

In his phone log, Judge usually made no more than a one-word summary of the message, often using just PCB for "please call back" or HAY for "how are you." He returned from the Drennans and wrote out two full messages. The first was from a former fire official with close connections with the cardinal:

"Make O'C look good—I work for him—I am just [a] little guy but want him to look very good."

The second was from Giuliani:

"Media has excld O'C—Need you to help include O'C more in this process—only you can help."

• • •

The drama became national when President Bill Clinton made a previously scheduled trip to the city two days after Drennan's death and decided to visit the firehouse. Judge was notified and he was standing outside the quarters of Engine 24/Ladder 5 in his habit when the presidential limousine pulled up. Clinton stepped out and shook hands with Giuliani all in one motion.

Giuliani introduced Judge. They shook hands, Clinton making the clasp more personal by setting his free hand on Judge's upper arm. The event paused as the two chatted, arms loose at their sides, two fatherless and charismatic self-creations, instantly at ease in each other's company.

President and priest examined the flowers and notes that had been left outside the firehouse. They then strode inside with Giuliani and Sen. Daniel Patrick Moynihan, passing beneath the black and purple bunting hung over the door for the three dead firefighters and continuing by the three goldfish that swam around and around. Clinton addressed the surviving firefighters.

"I thank you so much for your service," Clinton said. "I'm sorry for your loss."

The president shook hands with at least a half-dozen men who would perish at the World Trade Center, as well as a firefighter who would help carry Mychal Judge's body from the North Tower.

Vina Drennan had been stepping from the shower and reaching for a towel when a voice called through the bathroom door that the president was going to be at the firehouse. She got dressed and hurried the kids out the door, but they were still running late. They caught up with Clinton at the New York Hilton and waited in a hallway until he finished giving a speech about health care. He stepped directly up to Vina and took both her hands.

"I'm so glad to see you," Clinton said.

Clinton offered his condolences. Vina told him her husband had died doing what he loved.

"He went to work happy every day," Vina said.

Clinton turned to young John, the son.

"You look like your father," Clinton said. "I saw his picture in the firehouse."

Clinton could have been saying just what you would expect a politician to say, but then he reached out a hand to touch the boy's face.

"Same face. Same square jaw."

Clinton was exactly right, and a smile came to the square-jawed face that was so much like his father's. Clinton no doubt had a fatherless son's sensitivity to father-son similarities, but, even so, he had seen that firehouse photo of Captain Drennan for only an instant. Clinton at this moment was much like Judge, and not just in taking Vina's hands and gazing into her eyes and making her feel what he felt. Both men paid attention.

The Drennans then returned to Staten Island for the first night of the wake at what seemed the only place for it even if the captain had technically converted to his wife's faith.

The wake was held at the new Roman Catholic Church of St. Joachim and St. Anne, the old one having burned down after achieving a kind of prominence as the scene of the christening in *The Godfather*. John Drennan had grown up just across a grassy field, and Paddy Brown arrived with a framed sketch his fallen friend had made in his boyhood of the old church.

Brown set the charcoal sketch beside the coffin. It was an improbably meticulous and deeply felt rendering by a famously rowdy boy of a church that burned down after he had become a firefighter. His mortal remains now lay in the new church that had risen from the ashes and anyone who looked at the drawing of burnt wood on paper could not feel he belonged anywhere but here.

"Marvelous," Judge said.

Hundreds of firefighters began to file in for the wake, so many they waited in line outside for an hour or more. Brown had also brought the Book of Visitation, and they signed it as they had at the burn unit. They were now joined by women such as Louise O'Connor, who had driven with her kids to pick up her husband at his Brooklyn firehouse on a summer day in 1978 so they could go to the beach. She had arrived just as the rig was pulling out and she followed it to a supermarket fire in Sheepshead Bay. Firefighter William O'Connor had been atop the building, waving to his family, when the roof suddenly caved in. He and five other firefighters were killed.

•   •   •

5/9/94

Dear Vina,

I share in your loss. My number is on the card. If you need help, call.

Louise O'Connor
Waldbaum's Fire.

And then there was an entry by the wife of one of the seemingly lucky ones, Firefighter John Santore, surviving member of Ladder 5. His luck would run out at the World Trade Center.

Dear Vina,

We are proud of our men but we always worry about them. Only we can understand that. They are what they are and we love them more each day for what they do and what they stand for. I am so proud of L 5 and E 24 and all the firefighters who risk their lives each day. I can never look at the Job the same way.

   I will think of you always.

Frances Santore L-5

Brown stepped outside, and he was standing in the driveway when he saw Timmy Stackpole and his wife, Tara, approach. Tara would remember watching her husband and Brown embrace, one to be killed by the collapse of the South Tower, the other by the North.

"Timmy, he's better off," Brown said of Drennan.

The Stackpoles joined the line of those waiting to pay their respects. The Drennans had been at their wedding and this was Timmy's first personal loss as a firefighter. Tara took his hand. She could feel him trembling.

The Stackpoles knelt together before the coffin and prayed, Tara pregnant with their fifth child, a baby they would name Terence John, the middle name for John Drennan. At least seventy-eight other firefighters who would perish at the World Trade Center were now crowding in for a wake where the death of even one firefighter seemed almost too much to bear.

14

A half-dozen police motorcycles led the way down the broad, fabled avenue. The members of the fire department pipes and drums band began a slow march to a muffled beat in their red coats and plaid kilts and bearskin hats. Right behind them rolled Ladder 5's truck, the roof lights flashing as when Drennan, Young, and Siedenburg rode it to their deaths, but now the siren was silent. Two small American flags fluttered atop the cab.

Then came seven fire officers striding in formation, and after them was the ceremonial fire rig that served as the caisson, the eight pallbearers aboard, six flanking the coffin, two on the back step. The limousine bearing Vina, Brown, and the kids trailed. Young John Drennan began to cry.

"Let's do it with dignity one more time," Vina said.

Young John stemmed his tears as the caisson and then the limo stopped before the cathedral. He was struggling to mirror his father's strength as well as jawline as he stepped into the sunlight with his mother and three sisters. The middle daughter, Adrienne, put her right arm around him.

The band fell silent and the Drennans stood with Brown under a perfect blue sky on a Midtown street suddenly gone so still they could hear the birds chirping. The moment could have been scripted, right down to the faint breeze just strong enough to ripple the flags flying outside the cathedral.

In the hush, the pallbearers took the coffin down and turned slowly clockwise. They shouldered it and a voice called out.

"Detail . . . hand salute."

Ten thousand white gloves responded. The band began a mournful "Going Home," as the pallbearers started across the wide pavement. A line of firefighters stood on either side of the entrance to the cathedral. The huge brass doors were open.

"Stand to!" the voice called.

The white gloves lowered as the pallbearers reached the final three steps. This is the same ritual that is repeated for any firefighter who dies in the line of duty in the City of New York.

"You try to be so brave, and you see all these firemen crying," the oldest daughter, Jessica, would later say.

The difference was that these tears were shared by much of the city. This captain's heroic struggle had been recounted and detailed in newspapers and on television, and it had touched what is tender and caring in a town that is thought to be tough. Vina felt as if New York itself accompanied the reassuring touch of Brown's gloved hand as she entered the cathedral. She gazed up into the vaulted vastness and she momentarily lost all sense of time and place.

Then her gaze fell on the coffin. Beside the coffin she saw the fire department's Catholic chaplain who had been with the family through it all. Judge was wearing a golden chasuble, white alb, and stole over his simple brown robe. His familiar sandals peeked from under the hem. He had an open copy of the official *Order of Christian Funerals* in his left hand. He began to intone the prescribed prayer, but his voice was as heartfelt and intimate as when he had stood with Vina at her husband's bedside.

"May the Father of Mercies, the God of all consolation be with you . . ."

Judge had learned about the grace of firefighters with his first line-of-duty death. What he had learned in the forty days with the Drennans was the grace of a firefighter's family. And the City of New York had learned it with him.

He was always anxious before he spoke in public, even before his daily Masses. And this would be, as he told Dympna when he called to ask his sisters to attend, a "very big funeral." He took this measure of the rite not just because it was at the cathedral or because the scowling cardinal was so manifestly displeased or because this happened to be his sixty-first birthday. This funeral, this family, this fire department, this Church had brought together so many of the forces at work within Judge.

Yet as he sprinkled the coffin with holy water and the time now came to begin the Mass of his priesthood, he moved sure and steady down the aisle. The pallbearers brought the coffin before the altar and Judge gazed over to the front pew, where Brown was helping the Drennans to file in.

Judge bade the packed cathedral good morning, acknowledging the cardinal, as well as the two customary personages at a line-of-duty fire department funeral, the mayor and the fire commissioner.

"But, most of all, Vina and Jessica, Justine and Adrienne and John," he went on. "We welcome you to this magnificent cathedral at the heart of the center of the world."

He did not seem to feel he was speaking even slightly in hyperbole.

"Last Saturday evening about five o'clock, the mayor and Vina and myself were in the hotel talking about John and the last hours and Vina turned and she said to both of us, 'The city has suffered long enough and has mourned enough. And now I want the city to celebrate John's life and to know what a great hero, what a great husband and father he was.'"

Judge smiled.

"And so, in a sense, she has invited you to come here this morning to celebrate the life and the new life in God of John Joseph Drennan Jr."

The rite proceeded exactly as set forth in *The Order of Christian Funerals*, and came to the reading of the Gospel, in this instance a story from Matthew, where a woman who has been hemorrhaging for twenty years sees Jesus and declares she need only touch his cloak and she shall be cured. She does so, and Jesus tells her, "Courage, daughter! Your faith has saved you," and she is cured.

The reading is supposed to inform the homily and Judge casually tucked the gilded Gospel under his arm as he stepped over to the Drennans. He spoke their names again, Vina through to young John.

". . . I think from the very beginning when we were going into the room to visit Dad . . ."

Judge spoke that word *Dad* as he would of his own.

". . . to visit John . . ."

Judge had spoken in the next breath as of a friend.

"I think this Gospel came to my mind. Remember how he was always trying to put his hands up to his face? His hands were always going up in the air. There was one night we were there and he put his hand up, and the nurse said he had just pulled out his tube and you said, 'That's all right, put it back.'"

The "you" was Vina. She smiled.

"That was well over, I guess it's about forty-five days now, since we had the terrible tragedy. A big fire in a little house."

That described the Watts Street fire exactly.

"So many men gone to fight the fire and now the last of the heroes of the fire gone home to God."

Judge took the tome from under his arm and gazed down at it.

"It was a terrible night. Do you remember, Vina? It really was."

He turned and casually set the book on the white marble sanctuary rail. He began another biblical story that was at the heart of his homily, a story of living gospel from Mychal. He told of the emergency room and how gently Brown cradled John Drennan's head and how Jimmy Young was already dead and how terribly injured Chris Siedenburg had been and how Vina arrived. He leaned over as if over a gurney and recalled aloud her very words as she leaned over her husband and kissed him on the forehead and called to him by his full name and told him he was wonderful and she loved him and he was big and strong and he was going to make it.

Judge straightened.

"Beautiful," he said. "Absolutely beautiful."

Judge raised his hand, indicating he was now talking to the whole assemblage.

"And we began the days . . ."

He continued. Chris died the next day. John Drennan went into "the deep sleep," but surely heard Vina call his name, felt her kiss.

"Then we had the good days and the bad days and we waited and we hoped and there were moments we thought, 'Ah, he's going to make it.'"

He addressed the middle daughter.

"Remember, Adrienne, the night you and John came and we put on the masks and you went up and you stood by Daddy and I stood back and you kept talking to him and he heard you. He heard everything you said . . ."

Daddy, what Judge called the father he so wished he had been able to visit at the hospital. Judge moved closer to the front pew.

"And then we prayed."

His hands went out.

"We held hands and we prayed together and we asked God to give him a gentle night's rest and a good day tomorrow."

The eyes fell again, for one, two, maybe three heartbeats.

"And He did."

Judge began to step away but turned back.

"He gave him forty days. Forty days of preparation. That's what Christ had before he began his public life. He went out to the desert for forty days . . ."

Judge repeated that biblical number.

"Forty."

Judge spoke of the bond that formed in those forty days between Vina and the firefighters who kept a constant vigil.

"Some wonderful things happened. Some beautiful relationships were started during his suffering and trials."

And he spoke of the Easter dinner at the burn unit, when they ate pizza and passed around the mayor's cookies.

"It was the joy that the Lord had sent us in our faith so that we could be together and support each other and love each other."

And he spoke particularly about Paddy Brown, who was also there through it all. Judge addressed him as a comrade, telling him how wonderful he was, how he had never left Vina's side.

"And then, if I were to ask all the people who probied under John, all the people who played football in high school and were coached by John, all the people that worked with him in the different houses, and if I were to ask them to stand, about half the cathedral would stand."

Judge had moved over beside the coffin, his gaze sweeping the assemblage, his tone intimate.

"And if I were to say all those who prayed for John, then everybody in the church. In your own way—you heard his name, you didn't know him but you asked God to bless him if it be His will, to give him life, one way or another to take care of Vina and the kids."

He had called the cathedral a church, and rightly so. He was making this cavernous place feel like a little Irish country church.

"And we hoped and we prayed and we waited . . ."

The "we" seemed to encompass everyone present, along with those who had sent the letters that filled sacks and sacks, along with everyone everywhere who had paused even a moment to think of the valiant fire captain.

"And last Friday night he was so good. He seemed to be talking to us. His lips were going and he wanted to speak. That last surge of good life and God's grace and the hands went up again . . ."

Judge's hands rose.

"Then on the fortieth day, the Lord knew it was time. And we mourned. The whole city mourned."

He now addressed Drennan's mother and father, telling them what he

had said to the parents of Young and Siedenburg, that it was against the laws
of nature for your children to predecease you.

"But when we come into the fire department we know that the laws of nature can change so easily."

He was speaking to the assembly, his voice almost preaching, but soften-
ing with the very next phrase.

"At least the laws of nature that we know . . ."

He was including himself as a member of the department, which was fine
with the firefighters, who had through these forty days come to consider him
one of their own.

"And we accept what comes our way . . . for the Lord . . . is our God of
Surprises."

Judge stood silent, his hands clasped before him, his face now slackening
with sadness. He spoke directly to the young son.

"You're a fine young man, John. And you stay close to your father and
you pray to him every day . . . I've done that for my own father for fifty-five
years and he's never left my side once."

Dympna had not until this moment realized how deeply her brother still
felt the loss of their father. Michael Judge's only son turned from John Drennan's only son, emitting an audible sigh.

"Well, here we are," he said.

Judge seemed suddenly weary as he stepped to the center aisle, to the coffin.

"We come to the end of the forty days and mourning and viewing and the
prayers and the faith. And come together to say good-bye . . . To be reminded
of the greatness of the man and to be reminded of today. Just today."

The weariness began to fall away. A kind of power was beginning to light
his eyes, rise in his voice.

"By this time next week or next month someone in this church, in this
beautiful cathedral will have been called by God. And all that we know for sure
is that God gives us today. And he gives us the grace that we need today to love
each other and to be at peace with each other and to forgive each other."

The power was belief—not scripture or dogma, but what he felt most
true, most vital, what he had known intuitively on that day a half century before when he placed a coin in a drunk's hand and told Dympna, "It doesn't
matter," what he had held on to through the abuse in school and at the

seminary, what he saw confirmed at the bedside of AIDS patients, what he witnessed in the courage of firefighters and their families.

"And to accept each other. It's all we have."

Judge had stated his full creed in four sentences. He raised both hands, the palms up, a ceremonial pose that seemed just right.

"And with this beautiful tribute to John Drennan in this magnificent cathedral we know that John knew exactly what that meant."

He clasped his hands before him, glowing with faith confirmed. His voice was at once passionate and calm.

"Life will go on now, and Ladder 5/Engine 24, the great men there will carry on his spirit."

He walked back over toward the Drennans.

"So I think what happened on Friday night, the Lord came down from heaven and he saw John's hands moving . . ."

Judge raised his hands again, as the captain had in the burn unit.

"And He said, 'John, touch me. Touch me, John.' And John reached out and when he did, Jesus took his beautiful cloak and wrapped it around him and the two of them just winged to heaven."

Judge swept his chasuble as if it was his cloak.

"His faith had saved him."

Judge then spoke the words of Julian of Norwich, the fourteenth-century mystic whose *Revelations of Divine Love* he had found in a London trash bin.

"And all is well."

He said this by the coffin of a man who had suffered horribly for forty days.

"He's at peace. And we have known his love. Amen."

He took the gilded Gospel off the sanctuary rail and went back up the steps, Mychal of the newest testament carrying Matthew, Mark, Luke, and a long-ago John. He bowed to the altar and then to the cardinal, who had been loudly sighing and pouting and generally making his displeasure so apparent during the homily that the Drennan daughters were shocked.

"God, this is so disrespectful," Adrienne would remember thinking.

The Mass proceeded to the Offertory, where the family was to bring up the gifts, the wafers, wine, and water. Vina, not being Catholic even by blood, was going to remain in the pew as her daughters and son went up, but an usher who assumed she must be part of the fold presented her with a silver bowl, or ciborium, of Communion wafers.

Judge kissed the daughters on the cheek and the son on the forehead and passed their offerings to an attending priest. He turned back to see Vina standing alone before him, the ciborium in both hands. She still seemed small as Judge placed his right arm around her and pulled her to him. Her right hand remained on the ciborium as he accepted it with his left and they both held it as they embraced.

"I love you," Judge said.

Judge kissed Vina's cheek.

"Thanks," she said.

Judge kissed her again. He did not pass off this offering but rather kept it in his left hand as he escorted her down the steps, his right hand on her upper arm. He climbed back to the altar with Vina's offering.

After the Lord's Prayer and the Sign of Peace, Judge followed the ritual and gave Communion to the cardinal. Judge kept his gaze lowered as he set the bit of Host in O'Connor's palm, seemingly not so much out of reverence as simply to avoid eye contact.

The cardinal started down the steps with a ciborium and veered right when he saw the Lutheran widow take a place in the Communion line to his left. He gave Communion to Giuliani as Judge gave Communion to Vina.

The great Irish tenor Frank Patterson had offered to sing, and the Drennans had requested "Danny Boy," but the cathedral's music director deemed the song insufficiently religious. Unbeknownst to Vina, one of the firefighters had suggested Patterson instead sing "How Great Thou Art." The God of Surprises seemed to be at work as Vina heard the cathedral fill with the song that had been played at her wedding.

As at all such funerals, the fire commissioner and the mayor spoke. Giuliani made what sounded like a solemn pledge to Vina.

"The entire city of New York is there to help you and to support you and to help and support the children and not just today but forever."

Judge then descended the sanctuary steps with the cardinal, who had donned a white miter with the help of an attending priest. The cardinal was to conduct the conclusion of the service, the Final Commendation, which is also the point at which the uniformed members of the department are traditionally asked to file out so they can have time to fall into formation in the street.

That would have meant they were departing just as His Eminence had a moment at center stage. The order was not given, and everyone remained in the pews as O'Connor commenced the Signs of Farewell.

"Trusting in God . . ."

His Eminence proved almost melodiously at ease with the scripted prayer.

". . . we have prayed together for John and now we come to the last farewell."

Judge stood with his hands pressed together like an altar boy's as O'Connor sprinkled the holy water on the coffin with a deliberate mien and circled it with the incense. He paused for the attending priest to remove his miter. He was not done yet.

O'Connor began to speak, his tone becoming stilted with his own words.

". . . Father Judge because of his closeness to you—I know what he did throughout all the course of the suffering—those words had to be particularly meaningful to you and to all here."

The words were lagged by a stiff, two-handed gesture of inclusion, as if O'Connor suffered a disconnect between speech and gesticulation.

"For more than ten years, I have had countless funerals in this cathedral," the cardinal continued. "Mrs. Drennan, I have never seen more people at this cathedral under any circumstances."

Judge gave Vina a wink.

"Midnight Mass at Christmas when you have to have tickets to get in. Utterly astonishing and magnificent tribute."

O'Connor said he would not try to add to what Judge had said.

"These words were too meaningful."

The cardinal's voice was wooden, his face nearly blank, but the displeasure still unmistakable in his eyes.

"I simply want to thank you for your graciousness to me when I called you."

O'Connor was speaking to Vina.

"Very foolishly I called to [offer] support, my consolation, compassion. I hung up the phone feeling supported, comforted by you, by the depth of your faith, by your almost unbelievable courage."

Judge well knew that was not all the cardinal had felt. Judge tilted his head back slightly and breathed in, seeming to sense something was coming.

"But there is one thing I want to do before the final prayers and blessing, which are very brief . . ."

Whatever it was, it was coming now.

"John, you're the youngest here. You've heard magnificent things said about your father. You have undoubtedly read what has been said in the newspapers . . ."

Judge kept his eyes on the cardinal.

"But I want you to hear a sound that you'll never be able to forget. Could you come up here a moment, please?"

Judge's eyes went to young John, who rose from beside his mother in his black suit and white shirt, his thin black tie askew. The boy had entered the cathedral a tiny downcast figure, his face still in that stunned first stage of everlasting heartbreak, but there had come a moment in Judge's homily when his chin rose and his shoulders straightened.

Now, as he stepped from the pews, he once again looked hunched, quite nearly bewildered. Judge seemed to do his very best to give the boy a reassuring smile. The microphone caught Judge saying under his breath, "Christ."

"Here," the Cardinal said to young John, pointing to a spot no more than six feet from Judge yet completely beyond his protection.

"I want you to know what all these people and all the people outside and all of New York think of you," O'Connor went on. "You want to tell him?"

The cardinal began to clap his hands together and the entire congregation joined him and now the cathedral filled with what O'Connor always seemed to crave for himself, what he must have imagined the boy needed. Judge could only join the applause, and when he started, he seemed to be struggling to contain his anger. As the sound grew louder and kept on, Judge's eyes began to well and he was fighting back tears. He looked toward the boy, then away.

The applause ebbed.

"But you know why they think that of you?" O'Connor went on. "Because that's what they think of your father and they are hoping it will be like father, like son. God bless you."

His Eminence looked eminently satisfied as the applause started up again. Young John returned to his mother and sister, who were now doubly shocked.

"I remember thinking, 'That dumb man, he doesn't have a family. He doesn't know,' " Jessica would recall.

The only son of big, strapping John Drennan was so small that he had started a rumor at school that he was really an eleven-year-old genius. The one thing that had struck him in the newspapers were the reports that he was in fact fourteen, blowing his cover. He was never going to be a big ladder company hero like his dad, which is not what the fallen captain desired anyway.

Nobody in the Drennan family had ever wanted young John to grow up and be like anybody but himself. And here was this cardinal, calling the boy up before thousands, announcing that the entire world expected him to be what he never could become, to be exactly like the father who lay in a coffin before him.

"So wrong," Jessica later said. "It's like, 'What's wrong with you?'"

Judge took a deep breath and gazed heavenward until O'Connor addressed the Almighty.

"Into your hands, Father of Mercies, we have committed our brother, John . . ."

Judge dropped his eyes, then bowed his head, though not necessarily in prayer. His head stayed down until the end of the Prayer of Commendation, item 231, page 244, in *The Order*.

Judge then raised his head. He was the grim one as he watched a minion place the white miter back on O'Connor's head. The FDNY Holy Name Society was in attendance, and Firefighter Joe Angelini handed O'Connor the crosier that the Vatican had sent to the cardinal upon his appointment.

"If my brother priests will join me please," O'Connor said.

O'Connor commenced the Prayer over the People, item 233, page 246. His voice once more seemed to luxuriate in orthodoxy.

"Eternal rest grant unto him, O Lord."

Judge uttered the next line along with the other priests.

"And let perpetual light shine upon him."

Judge sounded hoarse, spent. He was just another faint mumble as he joined in the final amen.

Later, at Oceanview Cemetery on Staten Island, Judge regained his voice. The grave had been dug in a sunny patch of grass that otherwise might have made a good spot for a family picnic. He led the mourners in the Our Father, and as he was coming to the last words, "deliver us from evil," a monarch butterfly fluttered down out of the sunlight. Vina smiled to see it alight on the flowers set beside the coffin.

"Amen."

Judge and the others stood in silence, watching his God of Surprises at work as the monarch slowly folded and unfolded its delicate wings. The butterfly then lifted from the flowers and fluttered away.

Judge turned and followed it with his eyes until it disappeared among the other tombstones, ending the story, or so it would seem.

Seven years hence, on another sunny day, hundreds of monarchs would flutter through the smoldering ruins where Judge and Brown and Hatton and Stackpole and Feehan and Harrell and Hannifin and so many now standing at this Staten Island graveside would themselves be killed.

15

Judge had never met John Drennan before the fire, but he had been stirred to his very core by the forty days with the captain's family, by the intimate love between husband and wife, between father and children in hope and in despair. He had at moments experienced a psychic tumble back to when he lost his father. He had also taken a new look at all that had passed since then and at what might be to come.

A lifetime of longing was compounded by a corollary yearning when Judge met Jean Willis from his Siena College days for what she expected would be just another of their periodic chats in a coffee shop near the friary. He had asked her as well as his sisters to be at the Drennan funeral, but as moving as that was, she only now began to understand how profoundly those forty days had moved him. They soon were having what she would call "a major life conversation." He who had so often said, "If only I had a dad," was now saying to Willis, "If only I were a dad."

He spoke to her about marriage and family and all he felt he did not have in his life. She asked him why he chose to stay in the priesthood. His answer was stark and simple.

"Jean, I don't know anything else. They got me so young."

As she sat talking with this man she so greatly admired, the most gifted priest she ever encountered, she had an epiphany: "I think he was afraid to be anything else."

She also began to suspect why he had asked her to the funeral. He suggested that in a life where he could marry somebody and start a family he would want that somebody to be her. The notion seemed less an if-only than an only-if and too impossible to require an answer. The conversation left Willis convinced that he was a man longing for love in this world, a complex emotion made all the more so by his love of God and his great calling to be a priest. She had no inkling he was gay and she would remain convinced he was not someone who could be easily labeled.

"That's why I have a tough time with that gay thing," Willis would subsequently say.

Judge had spent his life shapeshifting into what others needed. The Judge in the coffee shop seemed to assume the shape of what he himself needed, or of what he imagined he might have been if only, only if.

The firefighters across the street decided that what their padre needed was to get away from it all, and they convinced him to join them on a sailing trip. He spent three days at sea, removed from the city and its demands, away from the ever-ringing phone, beyond the beeper's range.

"Did you have fun? Did you have a good trip?" Lt. Mickey Kross asked when he returned.

"I couldn't wait to get off that boat," Judge said, and of course laughed.

He was back on shore not twelve hours when he was notified that Lt. George Lener of Ladder 6 had been critically injured. Ladder 6 had filled in for Ladder 5 the day of the double funeral and Lener was the officer who had told them not to worry, he would take care of cleaning up after the gathering at the firehouse. He had been back at his own firehouse in Chinatown on June 8 when an alarm dispatched the company to an arson fire in a warehouse on Worth Street. He had somehow become separated from his men as he searched the basement for the source of the blaze and possible victims. He was overcome by smoke and was found facedown in a puddle of water, his air tank empty. His heart had stopped, and he was not breathing when he was carried to the street.

The firefighters and paramedics managed to resuscitate him, but he had breathed only toxic smoke for too long. He remained in a coma at Jacobi Hospital in the Bronx for week after week. The firefighters began another Book of Visitation. Ladder 5 stood vigil for Lener the way Ladder 6 had stood vigil for Drennan. This latest injured fire officer lived on Staten Island not far from the Drennans and had a devoted wife and three young children.

Judge remained as attentive as he had been with the Drennans, coming at all hours as this new horror stretched past the biblical forty days.

"He was just the closest thing you could find to God on earth," the wife, Maura Lener, later said.

Judge was still helping the Drennans however he could, and now that he was intimately involved with a second family, his friary room could only have felt more solitary when he returned. The little red light on the answering machine would be blinking with messages and there would be more phone calls with the dawn and the beeper could go off at any time.

On the forty-fifth day, the pager alerted Judge that George Lener had died. Judge joined Maura at the hospital. Her most immediate worry was that the children would learn from the media what had happened before she had a chance to tell them.

A police helicopter was summoned, and Judge said he would fly with her to Staten Island. The standard altitude for such a flight is a thousand feet above sea level, nearly level with the Twin Towers, which stood off in the distance, one 1,062 feet, the other four feet taller. This height afforded a view of the entire city and yet the individual people directly below remained distinct enough for Judge to discern what they were doing. He could gaze off to the right and see the Manhattan skyline, the great bridges, the harbor, and the Statue of Liberty in a single vista. He could also peer straight down to see someone crossing a street or emerging from a store or shooting a basketball.

The individual details of these tiny figures were not distinguishable, any more than those of individuals Judge would see seven years later as they leapt from this same height. The seeming insignificance of these details might lead someone of lesser faith to doubt any holiness beyond the hive. But Judge had only to look at the woman beside him to be reminded of the enormity of the loss of even one of these figures.

The helicopter touched down in Clover Lake Park and a waiting police car took them to the Leners' modest home. The younger son, Brian, was outside with his sister, and he came running up with the question he had asked his mother every day for forty-five days.

"How's Daddy? Did he wake up?"

The cop sat stricken at the wheel. Judge touched Maura's arm and said, "I'll help you, I'll help you."

Lt. George Lener had struggled for five more days than that other daddy, Capt. John Drennan, but perhaps because there was no real hope from the start and because he was not suffering the agony of burns and maybe even because a second protracted horror so close to the first was too much to bear, the drama did not grab New York in the same way. The city had always gone through cycles. A great tragedy would briefly bring the bravery of firefighters to the public consciousness, as Drennan had done for weeks, but people had their own lives to lead and their own hardships and trials. The city was returning to viewing firefighters as essentially just doing their job, however dangerous that job might be.

The pipe band slow-marched up Manor Road on Staten Island just as it had on Fifth Avenue in Midtown. If Judge had made a cathedral feel like a church then, now he made a church feel like a cathedral. Maura Lener's most vivid memory of the funeral was of Judge speaking to her children about the helicopter ride he took with her from the hospital. He told them that was how their father now saw the world, from on high yet right beside them.

As the coffin was carried to the street at the end of the Mass, the children stood transfixed as a police helicopter made the traditional flyover and clattered off into the distance. They would continue to attach a particular significance to helicopters for years to come.

"There's Daddy!" they would exclaim.

Just as many firefighters snapped a white glove salute outside Blessed Sacrament Church as outside St. Patrick's Cathedral, and Judge was at the widow's side at St. Peter's Cemetery. He saw no butterfly there. What Judge did see was Maura slumped sobbing over the coffin, her hair spilling as if on a pillow as she pressed her cheek against the polished wood. Judge stepped from beside the older son and set a white-gloved hand on Maura's heaving back. He stood silent and still and grim, looking as if he were, for just a moment, forlorn in his love of God.

Maura finally rose and stared with reddened eyes down at the coffin, as tenderly as she must have looked at her husband before the altar on her wedding day. She seemed to have a moment of her own, a moment when she felt love so much stronger than loss.

"You could see it," Judge later said.

What Judge also saw was firefighters again turning from a grave to risk the same fate on behalf of strangers. The populace may have gone back to its own worries and even many of the firefighters with families would resume fretting over mortgage payments and arranging "mutuals," swapping tours of duty so they could keep up their second job. To Judge the resumption of the everyday made their true grace only more extraordinary. He told them so, and they loved him for it.

Many firefighters were coming to feel he was the only priest for them in all aspects of their lives—baptisms and weddings and illnesses and family troubles. Judge saw it all as part of what they routinely risked losing. He welcomed the baptism of a new baby as a firefighter's ultimate reward but knew the child could end up fatherless.

Judge and the firefighters also had great fun together and there were many more good times than bad. He continued to embrace the ministry with seemingly inexhaustible passion as its demands extended to firefighters of all faiths, even to fire buffs such as a Jewish hardware store owner from Yonkers named Mort Greenbaum.

Greenbaum had never shaken a boyhood fascination with fire engines and firefighters. He was a member of all three major buff organizations associated with the FDNY. He died of natural causes, leaving a request to have his ashes scattered from a fireboat in New York Harbor.

A family video shows Judge standing on the bow of the Fireboat *John D. McKean* off the tip of Manhattan, the sky as blue and cloudless as it would be on that other September 11, in 2001.

"World Trade Center . . ." a mourner said aloud. "Brooklyn Bridge."

The Twin Towers shone in the sun directly behind Judge on this September 11 in 1994. He wore a short fire department jacket, zippered to the neck, as if it were a formal vestment.

"And then when our time is finished, the Lord calls us back to Himself in His way and our own particular beliefs," Judge now said.

Judge was saying God receives us in accordance with however each of us believes He does. The family stepped up to the rail with what looked like a silver gallon-sized paint can and one of Greenbaum's sons poured the contents overboard. The heavier grit cascaded audibly into the water, but the wind caught the lighter ash and created a small gray puff the very color of the huge clouds that would billow out across these same waters seven years hence.

In his own particular faith, Judge knew of no truer Catholic than the living paragon of faith and forgiveness, Steven McDonald. The two retained a deep connection and returned to Lourdes on September 18, this time with Conor, who was now seven. Steven had no thoughts about Judge's sexuality to dispel the serenity as the priest again helped him undress. The boy joined them in the baths and made straight for the figure of the Blessed Mother statue at the end of the tub. He gave the Virgin a big hug.

Near the pilgrimage's end, Judge wrote a letter to fellow friar Brian Carroll back at Thirty-first Street.

> *Almost midnight, September 26, 1994.*
>
> *The Mass was beautiful. I got a spot to stand right under the feet of Mary so I could keep looking up at her and tell her of all my New York people and their needs, and I knew she heard me. Like all other people in the world, Mary knows that New Yorkers are a very special people, and that we need to be looked over in a very special way. For sure, I march to a different drummer . . . Looking around at all the clerics in the Church, they are great men, probably good to the core—but I often think I'm in a different church than them . . . and that's okay.*

The next day, Judge returned to what he considered the center of the world, where he was increasingly a figure in a particular stratum of New York public life. He was no longer just a cleric who appeared in the background on the cathedral steps on St. Patricks's Day. He was invited along with Steven McDonald to an event at the Plaza Hotel honoring the latest sensation to come to town, Gerry Adams.

The leader of the IRA's political wing was in America on his first extended visa, which had been allowed by the White House as part of an ongoing effort to further the peace process in Northern Ireland. The IRA was still shooting policemen and British soldiers there and Adams was still reviled in Britain as a terrorist mastermind, but he was received in New York like a kind of pop star.

Nobody appeared more surprised than Adams himself as Mayor Giuliani awarded him a crystal apple and other politicians lined up to present him with three city proclamations. He was swarmed everywhere he went, but among the faces that would remain distinct in his memory was the smiling priest who came to the hotel ballroom with Steven McDonald.

McDonald watched Judge and Adams chat amid the tumult, first jesting and laughing, then turning serious. Judge was not some diddlydee Irish American who sang the old rebel songs and romanced the modern Troubles as if it was the terrible beauty of 1916. He also was not starstruck as so many others at the gathering seemed to be. He was for all his merriment as serious about Ireland as he ultimately was about his faith. He focused on what he saw as good in Adams just as he did with everybody he encountered. He saw Adams as a true rebel, one who could finally bring a just peace to the North.

"You could see the expression on their faces and their eyes, they were locked in on something important to both," McDonald remembered.

For his part, Adams understood Judge to be a true priest.

"A holy man," Adams would later say.

In his new life and ministry, Judge never forgot his friends from the dark and dreadful days before doctors learned how to prevent and somewhat manage AIDS and before the public terror abated.

Judge had come into a bit of cash from one of his benefactors, and for once he did not simply give it away.

"Come on, come on, I got some money! I'm taking you to dinner!" he told Michael Mulligan.

Judge chose Ottomanelli's, a restaurant a dozen blocks up York Avenue from the burn unit. A gay artist also came along, and Judge was as funny and warm as he was at Zinno's. He would have been singular in either group as someone delighted to be the one getting the check.

"He was even more excited because he was paying," Mulligan recalled.

Judge had not invited Alvarado, for at this dinner he was a priest, just as he was a priest at Zinno's. With Alvarado, he was a man, though his appointment book contained only a dozen "ALA" entries over the eight months since the Watts Street fire. On one of these days, Judge brought Alvarado to get fitted for sandals at the small leather shop run by a friar named Sebastian under the friary's front stoop. Judge noted a moment of domestic life at Alvarado's apartment as "ALA Dinner. Home Made." But Alvarado more than once prepared dinner for two only to have Judge call and say he had to rush to the scene of a fire and then go on to the hospital to minister to an injured firefighter.

● ● ●

The Judge children.
Left to right: Erin, Emmett (Mychal), and Dympna.

Young Judge in Washington, D.C., shortly before his ordination, 1961.

Father Mychal Judge and Henry, one of the street people in his holy city, 1991.

Mychal Judge and Patti Ann McDonald meet Pope John Paul II in Rome, October 1988.

Mychal Judge and Steven McDonald in a procession in Lourdes, 1991.

Fire Chaplain Mychal Judge.

Capt. Patrick J. Brown leans over a parapet to direct as Firefighter Kevin Shea is lowered for a rope rescue, May 1991.

The Drennans before the fire, 1994.
Left to right: Jessica, Adrienne, John, young John (Johnny Joe), Vina, and Justine.

Capt. John Drennan's coffin is carried from St. Patrick's Cathedral at
the conclusion of his funeral on May 11, 1994. Behind is Vina Drennan,
with Mychal Judge on her left, Paddy Brown on her right. The children follow.

Mychal Judge and President Bill Clinton outside John Drennan's firehouse,
May 1994.

FDNY Holy Name Society Man of the Year, 1995.
Left to right: Mychal Judge, Paddy Brown, Vina Drennan,
Tom Von Essen, Peter McLaughlin.

Mychal Judge with Pipe Major Tim Grant (left) and Drum Major
Liam Flaherty (right) of the FDNY Emerald Society Pipes and Drums.

Mychal Judge and Rudolph Giuliani, January 1997.

Mychal Judge in the lobby of the North Tower of the World Trade Center
during the last minutes of his life, September 11, 2001.

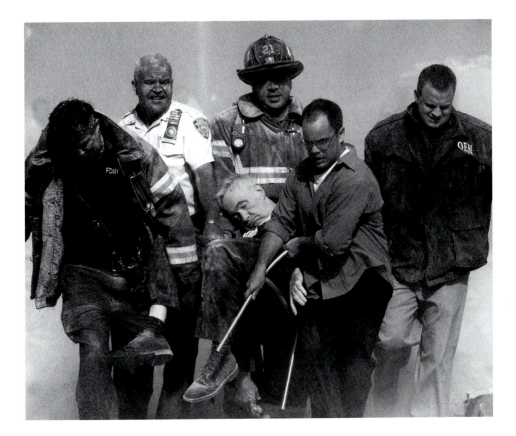

Survivors carry out the body of Fire Chaplain Mychal Judge from the North Tower,
September 11, 2001.

Al Alvarado (in suit and sunglasses) with new Fire Chaplain Chris Keenan (in habit) outside the firehouse across from the friary, joining in the final blessing at Mychal Judge's funeral, 2001.

There was to be one more fire death in 1994. Wayne Smith had once been a baseball player of such promise he was recruited by the Detroit Tigers, but his father had told him to get a real job, meaning a city job, meaning the fire department. He was one of the firefighters who had convinced Judge that he should sign on as an FDNY chaplain three years before, after Judge watched them matter-of-factly head off from the bedside of a horribly burned firefighter to risk the same fate.

At a subsequent fire, Judge had seen a huge figure seem to fall out of the smoke-filled sky and land at his feet. Six-foot-five Wayne Smith had tumbled from a third-floor window, prompting Judge later to say, "The giant falling out of the beanstalk. The earth shook."

Smith had risen with only an injured ankle, so he just taped it up and returned to the fire. He went on to become the youngest captain in the FDNY, and he was given command of Ladder 136 in Queens. His men signaled their devotion to him by wearing T-shirts announcing the firehouse's new nickname, "Wayne's World."

He had married Connie, a dancer with the Martha Graham Company who had never known a firefighter until she met Wayne at Jones Beach. Their friends dubbed them "Tarzan and Jane." They had two children. The younger, Dylan, was six months old when his father was engulfed by flames at a restaurant fire in Queens.

The city had begun to distribute bunker gear a week after Drennan's funeral, but Smith still had the old equipment. His coat disintegrated in the heat; his face mask melted away. He arrived at the hospital with burns even more serious than those suffered by Drennan. The doctor, Madden, termed them "incompatible with existence."

The once promising southpaw's left hand was so badly charred the doctors had to amputate. Connie was given the wedding band that she had slipped onto his ring finger at their wedding. The band had been a touch too big and suntan oil had caused it to slip off at the beach during their honeymoon in Jamaica. Wayne had searched for the ring into the night, renting scuba gear and setting up lights, digging and sifting the sand for hours until he found it.

She had declared that a miracle, but she held no hope for another, much bigger one after she saw her husband's injuries. She bristled when her Catholic in-laws said he would pull through, as if the unseen hand of God was going to reach down. She was beginning to feel she must be a terrible person for not being in denial, for believing what her eyes saw. A priest appeared.

"Of all the thousands and thousands of people I met at that point in my life I always remember Father Mychal Judge. I would never forget the name or the face," Connie later said. "He just had the kindest face and the most beautiful eyes and he made you feel good just being around him."

She is Jewish, but she listened to this priest tell her just to listen to herself.

"You do what you do and don't worry about it," he said. "You know you're a good person. I know you're a good person."

And he told everyone else to let her be.

"Let her just do what she wants to do."

She figured he kept her from losing her mind, and she knew how close she came to losing it. She realized they made an unlikely pair.

"Let's face it, there aren't too many little Jewish women running around the fire department, and who did she choose to feel more comfortable running around with? A Catholic priest," Connie said. "What was a day in intensive care without Father Judge?"

She would joke that if he was what Catholicism is all about, she wanted to convert.

"If you don't, that's okay, too," Judge said.

From this, the first priest she ever knew, she realized something about the first firefighter she ever knew. She suddenly understood why Wayne had kept running into burning buildings.

"He was doing what he felt was his calling," Connie decided.

After fifty-four days, Wayne Smith died. His four-year-old daughter, Ashley, had just lost her first baby tooth and Judge told the girl her daddy was surely a pal of the Tooth Fairy. After all, he said, her father was a good giant who had once fallen out of a beanstalk, right at Judge's feet.

Wayne's body was so disfigured that the coffin was closed when Judge arrived with Connie for the wake. She decided that her husband could not possibly be contained in so small a box; his shoulders were much too wide. She announced that she had to look inside. The funeral director joined the in-laws in trying to dissuade her. Judge stepped up and took her hand. He told the funeral director, "It's okay. If she wants to see, everyone else can leave the room and I'll stay with her."

The funeral director raised the lid and there lay Wayne in the dress uniform that Connie had taken to the dry cleaners before all those other funerals. His burns looked only more terrible in death and the contrast with the pressed uniform made his face seem a mask of absolute suffering.

Connie had brought the wedding ring that Wayne had lost and then found in Jamaica as if by a miracle. She placed it on Wayne's right hand. She put Ashley's first baby tooth wrapped in a tissue on his chest, above his heart.

That same evening, Judge attended a surprise fiftieth birthday party for Vina at Chumley's, an old Greenwich Village bar whose owner had been friends with John Drennan. Chumley's had been a speakeasy a half century before, and the police of Prohibition times always made sure to call ahead before a raid there, even indicating which of the two unmarked entrances they would be storming, 54 Barrow Street or 86 Bedford Street around the corner. A tip that they would be coming in via Barrow Street would elicit a cry from the bartender.

"Eighty-six!"

Afterward, patrons would say they had "eighty-sixed" themselves. The expression evolved over time and being "eighty-sixed" came to mean being ejected. One entire category of people was preemptively eighty-sixed from Chumley's in 1965 as being just too wild and boisterous even for the writers and artists of the Village. Firefighters were still banned from the place in 1993 when a lieutenant from Ladder 5 called to request a special dispensation.

Ladder 5 was receiving a medal for its efforts after the first bombing of the World Trade Center, which included rescuing seventeen trapped people and recovering two bodies. The lieutenant wondered if the company could hold a gathering at Chumley's after the ceremony. The new owner, a merchant seaman turned actor turned MBA named Steve Shlopak, ended twenty-eight years of exile with a single sentence.

"Sure, come on in."

At the gathering, Shlopak became instant buddies with the company's new captain, John Drennan. The friendship came in handy when some of Chumley's newer, more affluent neighbors sought to have it closed as a nightly nuisance, no matter how historic. The neighbors lobbied the local community board, and the eventual result was that Ladder 5 was dispatched to check for fire code violations.

"How many horses?" Drennan supposedly inquired.

The certificate of occupancy dated back to before Chumley's was a speakeasy, to its earlier incarnation as a stable. The place was authorized to be occupied by no more than nine horses.

"None," one of the firefighters replied.

Drennan turned to Shlopak.

"Okay, you pass."

Drennan was back in the bar on what Vina would term his "High Holy Day," St. Patrick's Day. Drennan and Shlopak talked about Irish music and spoke of attending a Chieftans concert a few weeks hence.

Eleven days later, Drennan was caught in the flashover on Watts Street along with Young and Siedenburg. Shlopak in essence moved Chumley's to the firehouse, taking it upon himself to ensure there was food aplenty during the long days of wakes and funerals.

When he learned of Vina's query to Judge as to whether there is beer in heaven, Shlopak recalled that the fallen captain had been especially fond of a particular draft beer.

"If I ever could have a beer named after me, this would be my beer," Drennan had said to Shlopak of the Irish Red Amber.

Shlopak rechristened the beer Captain Drennan's No. 5 Red Amber and a big picture of him that had been in the firehouse window after the fatal fire now went up behind the bar, an honor not accorded Eugene O'Neill and Dylan Thomas and the other literary lights whose photos filled the walls. Shlopak decided to add a collage of shoulder patches that Drennan had worn at various times, and Chris Waugh of Ladder 5 brought some from the Emerald Society and from a softball team. The firefighter who would be among those to carry Judge from the North Tower had just come in when the jukebox turned itself on, as it sometimes was wont to do, only on this occasion with the Irish tune "Celtic Symphony."

"Here we go again, we're on the road again, we're on the road again, and we're on the way to paradise."

Judge cheered along with Paddy Brown and Terry Hatton and Peter McLaughlin when Vina entered, their voices ringing off the walls where their pictures would eventually hang with John Drennan's. She would later say she was glad the party was a surprise.

"Otherwise, I wouldn't have gone," she added.

• • •

Six days later, on October 12, Judge stood with Vina and Connie, as well as Maura and the Siedenburgs and the Youngs at the annual memorial at the simple stone Firefighters Memorial Monument on a steep hillside in Riverside Park in Upper Manhattan. The families of the five firefighters killed that year then sat in a row of reserved seats.

The seats were in the shadow of the hill and Connie adjusted her youngest child's blanket as he sat in his stroller. The baby did not startle as the bagpipes started up with "America the Beautiful." This was followed by a moment of silence that filled with the twitter of birds, the hum of traffic, and an older child's cry.

As the ceremony progressed, the mounting sun began to cut the shadow, its rays falling first on Maura Lener and then on her hushed children. Another moment and the rays reached the Drennans.

The families were called up one after another. Young John Drennan accepted two medals for his father, and he had them in his pants pocket as thousands of firefighters marched past the families in mute tribute.

After the last of the polished dress shoes had shuffled past, the firefighters returned to the very dangers that had killed five of their own that year. The families and their nine fatherless children departed with their medals to a luncheon at Tavern on the Green hosted by the FDNY, escorted by Judge.

Paddy Brown came along.

"Did you cry?" Johnny Joe asked him.

"Yeah," Brown said.

"You did?"

"You bet. Did you cry?"

"No," Johnny Joe said.

Johnny Joe then mumbled an addendum.

"I did on the stage," he said.

Young John reached in his pocket and took out the two medals, the pair glinting in the sunshine. The Medal of Valor had a red ribbon. Vina stared at the one with the blue ribbon, the Medal of Supreme Sacrifice.

"This is one medal I hope you never get, Patrick," Vina said.

"Me too," Brown said.

Nobody thought to say this to Judge, for no New York fire chaplain had ever been killed in the line of duty. The boy stuck the medals back in his pocket as he went with Judge and Vina and Brown and the others into the restaurant.

Afterward, the families returned home to lives that continued to include the active presence of Mychal Judge. He maintained a particularly close friendship with Vina. He would try to talk to her every day, often telephoning just before bedtime, and she would stay up for his call.

"Did I wake you up? How are you? Are you all right? What did you do today?"

The two would talk for hours, warm, comfortable conversations like some ideal married couple rather than a widow in her grief and a priest in his friary. Vina later said, "I think we really needed each other."

She was able to laugh when she told him about putting young John's pants in the laundry without checking all the pockets. She had taken the clothes from the dryer to discover she had run the Medal of Supreme Sacrifice through the wash. The medal was fine, but the ribbon was ruined.

She was also able to tell Judge of a dream in which her husband had suddenly appeared at the edge of their bed, his face free of pain, his charred legs miraculously healed.

"Oh, John, your legs are fine," she had told him in the dream.

Judge continued to urge her to keep writing, telling her just to trust herself, asking her to read aloud, a lone request from a priest who gave so much. Even when she felt too heartsore to pick up a pen she would do so anyway.

I hope more than ever there is a heaven and someday John will be waiting for me and he'll hold me and say, "Rest now, Vina. You did a good job."... But if he's in heaven he can see us, [and] if he sees us, he knows we're suffering. So, much as it would be nice to think he's watching over us, he doesn't need to know how much we hurt. It's easier to just be grateful that he's out of pain, that he's no longer suffering. It's easier to think there's nothing; after all this, nothing sounds very good.

Vina was wondering if there was only Wilderness. Judge simply kept her company, sure she would find her own way out. He did not speak up on behalf of God, and she wondered if he harbored some doubts of his own. He never voiced any. He just continued to listen.

She kept telling Judge, "You're Jesus," and he always replied "Stop that!"

and she would say, "You are. You're Jesus!" and he would say again, "Stop that!"

Vina did not consider until later the psychic stamina required for him to be still buoyant and giving night after night despite the onerous demands of his days.

"It must have been so hard to be everybody's Jesus," Vina later told a friend.

16

"One day at a time" was the guiding principle at the AA meetings that Judge continued to attend, often at the noontime gathering in the bookshop adjoining St. Francis. One of the regulars, Jeanne Fonseca Brennan, noticed he often wore a fire department windbreaker. She complimented him on it.

"Oh yeah, the guys take care of me," Judge said.

In AA, Judge found people who wrestled with intense doubts and urges just as he did. He felt kinship with them even if he seldom talked about himself.

Perhaps his fear was less of falling off the wagon than of falling from grace, though the struggle was essentially the same.

"A very human being," Brennan later said.

The noon meeting was attended largely by working people on their lunch breaks, many from the nearby garment district, some from computer firms that had begun to spring up in the surrounding blocks. A number of the Catholic regulars also attended Mass at this same church, and when they saw Judge step from the sacristy, they knew they were going to get a homily that had the familiar ring of a meeting.

Not that Judge's theosophy sprang from AA. He was simply in concordance with it, and the resulting resonance made him a more powerful presence in both venues, imparting actuality to the Mass and dignity to the meetings. The effect at the secular gathering was apparent even to the Jewish participants.

"That was their first real contact with a priest," Brennan noted after Judge's death. "Even today you'll hear someone say, 'Father Mike told me . . . ,' and that's right up with God."

Judge saw the stuff of Scripture, the struggle of goodness itself, in these souls who sought to follow the serenity prayer to change what they could and accept what they could not. He felt this effort must necessarily originate in an essential decency that underlay all the shame and sorrow. His recognition of this quality in them made them feel as if he were touching their very core.

"He had a way of getting to people through the layers," Brennan said.

That year, AA's intergroup office asked Brennan to find an appropriate cleric to deliver the invocation and benediction at the annual Bill W. dinner. The Marriott Marquis was one of only three Manhattan hotels with a ballroom big enough to hold the two thousand recovering alcoholics who attended. Judge came in his friar's outfit and afterward described the event as another kind of Communion.

"Only this time it's wine into water," he said.

In early November, a series of events honoring the fallen firefighters began with the annual Fire Foundation Benefit aboard the *Intrepid,* a World War II aircraft carrier turned museum moored at the end of West Forty-second Street. The families of the five who died that year were invited as honored guests to the $300-a-plate black-tie gala. Four of the families attended. Vina described the scene in her book:

> *Not a detail was overlooked. The vegetables were arranged like works of art, flowers were arranged in elaborate containers . . . We were being honored for the sacrifice of our firefighters—the Youngs, the Siedenburgs, Mrs. Lener and me. But they put us at our own table.*

And horribly, there were four unoccupied places at the table.

Four empty chairs.

The lights went down and a huge screen filled with a video of firefighters in action. The face of Jimmy Young then appeared, and his mother began to sob. The next face was Chris Siedenburg's and then John Drennan's and George Lener's and then Wayne Smith's.

Soon, the whole six of us were crying in the darkness.

When the lights finally came up, Judge appeared at the table.

Two weeks later, on the night of November 16, Vina Drennan and Maura Lener were seated together at the Police and Fire Widows' and Children's Benefit at the Hilton Hotel with other women who had been widowed for as long as four decades. The two fell into conversation. Vina recorded it in her book:

> *I had come to think that sex was like water—if you are thirsty you go to the faucet and get a drink. I realize it was shortsighted for me to take something so special for granted. Since March, my body sure has been thirsty. And this is one hellova desert.*
>
> *I read that widows often feel very horny and I was really surprised. It's got something to do with wanting to reaffirm life in the face of death and sex is the most powerful way to say yes to life. It'd be a way to affirm you're not dying yourself even though your soul is in agony. Women my age don't usually talk about such things, but I've been doing some research—like, "Hey, Maura, are you horny?"*

The two fire widows who had sobbed at the dinner aboard the *Intrepid* now giggled like schoolgirls. Later, Vina read the passage to Judge. She felt not at all awkward speaking to him about these yearnings that were as strong and surprising as when she had first felt them in her teens.

"I remember being so scared with all these feelings," she would say. "It was a shock to me. Jeez, if you're married for twenty-seven years you forget what it was like to be horny. It was a shock to me . . . It's scary to be an adolescent at fifty."

Judge assured her that these feelings were only wonderful. He viewed them as the force of life itself and therefore holy and all the more so for being spoken of without embarrassment or shame.

"He applauded the honesty," Vina recalled. "He just thought it was remarkable women were so open and honest."

Judge offered his ultimate approbation.

"Marvelous!"

If Vina had not been a Lutheran, Judge surely would have put her at the top of the list when he recruited a group of Eucharistic ministers to assist him with his fire chaplain duties. Among the eight he invited to a training session at St. Francis was Capt. Marty McTigue, who had been about as badly burned as someone can be without dying. There was also the ever-smiling Capt. Joe Bryant of the Holy Name Society, along with his wife, Mary Eva. Firefighter Jackie Dowling and his wife, Marie, attended, as did Firefighters Jackie Boyle and John Driscoll. The eighth was Dottie Rogers, wife of Capt. Jim Rogers of Rescue 1.

Judge sat them down in a front pew and said what they already knew, that the ranks of Catholic priests had dwindled to the point of crisis. The fire department, meanwhile, was suffering tragedy after tragedy, adding to an already demanding schedule of funerals, memorial Masses, plaque dedications, and other such rituals. He figured with these new ministers he would always have help on hand.

"He felt that whatever came up he could call us up from the audience," Mary Eva Bryant would recall.

Beyond the practical benefit of having extra hands to distribute the Host, Judge saw something else in these ministers-to-be who sat before him like a pew full of overgrown parochial school kids. He viewed Eucharistic ministers as a step toward a church that would thrive even as the clergy dwindled, a church that would have no need for monsignors, bishops, or cardinals, or, for that matter, a Pope. These particular candidates were doubly inspiring because they hailed from what Judge had come to consider the one religious order higher than the friars.

"He wanted the firemen involved in the Mass," Joe Bryant later said. "And he felt the women were very important to the husbands and to the Church."

Judge announced this particular training would be somewhat different from the customary extended instruction.

"He goes, 'Now this is our secret. This is a very deep secret. This is not going to be eighteen classes or eight months. This is going to be a quickie,'" Bryant recalled. "Little did we know how quick."

Judge gave a demonstration that took but a moment.

"This is what you have to do," Judge said. "Look the person in the eye and say, 'Body of Christ.' That's all there is to it."

Judge described the sacrament with a single word.

"Simple."

He called them up to the altar and had them practice this simplicity with the unconsecrated Host.

"Now, don't forget to look them in the eye, but make sure you put it in the hand," Judge instructed.

He suggested they add the person's name if they knew it. "You could say, 'Body of Christ, Mary.' It makes that person feel more special."

Dottie Rogers told Judge she did not feel worthy to be doing this at all.

"None of us feel worthy," Judge said.

Rogers felt her fear fall away. She told herself, "If this saintly man feels the same way, I can do this."

After twenty minutes, Judge declared their instruction complete.

"It was like an accelerated course," Bryant later said.

Judge invited them to join him in the friary's dining room for homemade chocolate chip cookies, as well as beer for those who were drinking. He talked and laughed with them for more than an hour in this refectory, where the aging regulars seemed to be the last of their kind, living a centuries-old way of life that threatened to end with their deaths.

On another day, Dympna had worried aloud to her twin that the priests might dwindle to none. He had told her not to fret. Who, she had asked, was going to run the Church?

"The people," Judge said.

People such as these new ministers. They were knights and ladies of the New York Fire Department, perhaps not courtly like those of whom the French troubadours sang, but in their own distinctly outer-borough way no less gallant and honor bound. They joked and laughed amid the polished wood paneling and the wraparound mural depicting the life of the saint who had written that God's true servants were "but minstrels" who "must inspire the hearts of men and stir them to spiritual joy."

At the outbreak of AIDS, the panel of the mural that had seemed most applicable to Judge was the one depicting Saint Francis kissing the leper on the road. The applicable panel on this night was the one where a voice from the crucifix in San Damiano commands the saint to rebuild a church falling into ruin.

The church as manifested at this gathering was never more vibrant. Judge did still have the hierarchy to fret about.

"He said, 'If anybody asks you, you had classes. You had many classes,'" Bryant would recall.

Judge called several of the new Eucharistic ministers to duty at the annual FDNY Memorial Mass on November 20. They took positions on either side of him, he in his vestments, they in their dress uniforms. Firefighters in the same uniform lined up in front of each of these comrades who had been trained in the essence of the Eucharist.

With the sight of firefighters stepping up to receive the Host from another firefighter came the feeling that the FDNY truly was a religious order, spiritual as well as spirited, vibrant in an age of doubt. There might no longer be many boys in the city who dreamed of someday becoming a "peest" to take the place of Judge, but there were legions who wanted to become firefighters. The seminary where Judge trained had long since closed, and the priesthood itself seemed to be slouching toward an end, but thousands were on the waiting list to join the FDNY, and there would always be these men and women in blue as long as there was the Red Devil to fight.

The new ministers of course looked each of their fellow firefighters in the eye.

"Body of Christ, Timmy."

"Body of Christ, Brian."

"Body of Christ, Peter."

"Body of Christ, Terry."

"Body of Christ, Paddy."

Five days before Christmas, Judge took part in an event a group of firefighters staged each year at the pediatric wards at New York–Cornell Medical Center, which is also home to the burn unit. The festivities began as usual with Ladder Co. 13 from the local firehouse driving up to the hospital's main entrance with Santa standing in the bucket.

"Everybody stops and they're looking," Firefighter Andy Bainton said. "This is New York City. This is supposed to be so sophisticated, but all their jaws dropped."

The ladder extended its full seventy-five feet with Santa waving to the pediatric patients staring out the windows. A troupe of firefighter musicians played Christmas songs, the guitar players this year including young John Moran of Rescue 1, who would become a chief in special operations only to die at the World Trade Center. Among the singers was Mychal Judge wearing a Santa's helper hat.

"The man loved to sing Christmas songs," Bainton said.

The Santa in the bucket was Ray Phillips of Rescue 3 and the Holy Name Society. Phillips, Judge, Moran, and the others headed inside while a second Santa slipped into the hospital via its underground passages. He was Firefighter Doug Hantusch of Rescue 3, who had just the month before participated in a daring rescue from atop a twenty-story housing project. He and the other Santa now set off in different directions with a laundry cart of toys. They maintained radio contact to make sure no child would see two Santas bump into each other. They went from bed to bed, from burns to oncology.

"We got a four-year-old boy. We got an eight-year-old girl . . . What do we got that's good for this kid?' " Judge said.

Up at St. Barnabas Hospital in the Bronx, Alvarado was deciding to yield to the Rival. Judge still noted the anniversary of the day he met Alvarado and he jotted down Alvarado's twenty-fifth birthday on December 6. But Judge's crammed appointment book records him as seeing Alvarado fewer than a dozen times through the fall. Judge could not have been stunned when Alvarado announced he was taking a nursing job in faraway Kuwait.

Three days before Christmas, Judge and Alvarado met for what was to be their final farewell before he flew away. Judge tried to be supportive, telling him that this was a good thing, that he was finding himself. As Alvarado tells the story, "Then he started crying. We were both crying."

Judge then had to hurry off to a wake and comfort his Eucharistic minister, Dottie Rogers, whose fire captain husband Jim Rogers had died of cancer while awaiting a liver transplant.

However intense his private pain may have been, Judge had to continue on in his world, where almost nobody knew of Alvarado. He almost certainly did not discuss Alvarado at the AA meeting he attended the following day. His beeper sent him from there to a blaze at a Mexican restaurant on East Thirty-fourth Street. Several fire companies had been inside when a gas explosion tore through the place. Sixteen firefighters were taken to Bellevue Hospital, but their burns proved to be minor, thanks to the newly issued bunker gear that was John Drennan's legacy.

"All of a sudden I heard a noise, like a pop and then I saw the fireball come rushing toward us," Firefighter Sean O'Brien said. "Because of the bunker gear, I couldn't feel anything, I couldn't feel the heat."

"My bunker gear last night was worth ten million by itself for what it did for me," said Firefighter Tom Yuneman.

"The floor opened up right where we were standing and we were thrown into the air by the heat," said Firefighter Larry Montross. "But we didn't get hurt because of the added protection. The bunker gear did the job."

Mayor Giuliani summed it up: "Everybody was wearing bunker gear. This would have been a very different situation if they weren't."

One of the grimmest years in the 130-year history of the FDNY, 1994, was ending with the hope the new equipment would break the unprecedented series of tragedies. But burns are only one of the ways a fire can kill, and all these perils mounted moment by moment after a candle was knocked over in a basement Chinatown gambling den in the predawn hours of December 29.

The resulting flames ignited the kerosene in an illegal heater, and someone called 911 but gave the wrong address. Multiple fire companies still managed to arrive in time to rescue an infant from the five-story tenement where dozens of immigrants lived packed into warrens of cubicles.

Among those who continued into the blinding smoke was Probationary Firefighter Thomas Wylie of Ladder 18. He had taken the fire exam and waited for seven years, working as a butcher in a supermarket, until he was finally called. He took a big pay cut when he joined, and his wife went to work at the Gap to help support their three children, two of whom were still in diapers. She asked only that he promise he would not go back into a fire once he had gone in and come out.

"If somebody's in there, I'm going back in," he told her.

Now, in his new bunker gear, and with an air tank and mask such as all firefighters now wore, Wylie followed his lieutenant into his first real fire. They were still searching the cubicles when the Virbra-alerts on their air tanks signaled they were running low. They had difficulty getting out, and the lieutenant radioed a mayday before he was overcome. Their fellow firefighters rushed to their aid and found the lieutenant in time, but Wylie was near death from carbon monoxide poisoning when he was carried to the street. He was rushed to Jacobi Hospital where there is a hyperbaric chamber, which is filled with 100 percent oxygen at more than double normal atmospheric pressure, translating into a ten- to fifteenfold increase in oxygen in the blood.

His wife, Randi, called to him to squeeze her hand if he heard her say she loved him and he did, but a CAT scan indicated he was essentially brain dead. Judge, as always, was there. He finally returned to the friary having slept only a few minutes in two days.

Judge was roused by his phone ringing with what threatened to be another emergency. Judge picked up, was surprised to hear Alvarado's voice, and figured he must already be in Kuwait. A much bigger surprise came when Alvarado announced he had decided that leaving would have been even worse than staying.

However touched Judge must have been, his first duties remained those of a priest, most particularly a chaplain who had yet another critically injured firefighter in a hospital. Judge returned to Jacobi, where Wylie was still clinging to life as 1994 ticked its final minutes. Judge remained at Wylie's bedside until one A.M.

O n the second day of the New Year, the doctors decided that Firefighter Thomas Wylie was unlikely to survive to the third. Randi Wylie is Jewish and not well versed in her husband's religion, but she figured she would go right to the top. She asked Giuliani when he arrived at the hospital if he could get the Pope to pray for her husband's recovery. As Giuliani wrote in one of his weekly columns, "I somewhat impulsively agreed, then realized I had no idea how I could deliver on my promise."

Giuliani then had an idea that could also help smooth some still-ruffled plumage.

"I thought, 'I'll call Cardinal O'Connor.'"

O'Connor was on retreat but arrived at the hospital an hour later. Judge yielded to O'Connor the way the senior man in a firehouse might to a headquarters chief, acknowledging rank but not forgetting who was the real firefighter.

O'Connor said a healing prayer over Tommy and assured Randi he would call the Pope. She told Giuliani, "I don't think the cardinal would lie."

Randi also asked the cardinal if perhaps there might be a special Mass for Tommy at the cathedral. The miracle Mass took place the next morning, the cardinal presiding.

"No matter what the doctors say, I believe in miracles," Randi told reporters. "And if everyone says one prayer for Tommy, maybe he'll pull through."

Three hours after the Mass, Firefighter Thomas Wylie died. Randi now told the press, "All those prayers from everyone, even the cardinal and the mayor, helped send Tommy to a better place. And that's helping me get through all this."

• • •

The funeral Mass was at St. Luke's in Queens, Cardinal O'Connor officiating. The pipe and drum band played the Scottish "Will Ye No Come Back Again?" as the coffin was carried out. Five-year-old Joey Wylie saluted and then rode with his mother to the cemetery.

"If Daddy's in heaven, what's in that box we keep following?" he asked.

His mother's reply confirmed that she and Judge were of the same persuasion, if not religion.

"Memories," Randi said. "The box is full of memories of Daddy."

Though Judge was the one who continued consoling her, Randi remained grateful for the cardinal's kindnesses. When she heard that O'Connor was having a birthday, she went to a Catholic supply store and said she needed a present for a cardinal. She decided on a pict, a small silver container used to carry the Host for Communion outside church. Randi had it engraved, "In Loving Memory of Tommy Wylie."

"Do you think he's actually going to get this?" the clerk asked.

Randi might as well have been buying a gift for the president of the United States as far as the clerk was concerned. But Randi and her three kids were ushered right in when they arrived at the cardinal's residence. Randi recalled, "He couldn't believe I could pick a gift like this."

The cardinal was appreciative, warm, and amiable, benevolence in a red skullcap. He gave no sign of displeasure when Randi explained that she and Tommy had decided to raise their children in both faiths, that the children had been given Hebrew names as well as being baptized.

Randi was stunned by the letter from the cardinal that arrived at her home shortly afterward.

"He said, 'I am perplexed to hear you would change your mind about raising the children Catholic. You should do as your husband would do,'" Randi recalls.

She was both hurt and angry that the cardinal would seek to make her feel she was somehow betraying her husband's memory.

"It was not a positive feeling," Randi later noted.

The cardinal was still the cardinal the way the president was the president. She sought Judge's counsel. He told her, "Don't let them tell you what to do.' " He pointed to his chest as he added, "It's here. It's what's in your heart that's going to get you through this."

Judge and Vina attended a cocktail party for the New York Firefighters Burn Center Foundation at the Water Club, a barge turned trendy restaurant on the East River. They then went to dinner at Zinno's with Paddy Brown.

Both men had found a sense of family with the Drennans that they sorely missed in their own lives. But between Brown and Vina a sexual tension began to disturb their relationship. Vina was still the widow of his friend and comrade and therefore inviolate. Brown stopped calling Vina over the days that followed.

"It's kinda intense, you know?" he explained.

Three weeks later, Lt. Raymond Schiebel, a father of three, collapsed and died at a Brooklyn fire. Brooklyn was the jurisdiction of that borough's fire chaplain, who presided at the funeral. Vina asked Paddy Brown to go with her. She wrote:

> I called Engine 69 and got my favorite captain. "Hey, cutie, you got a date for the funeral?" "Vina, is that you?" And we laughed and fell back into our closeness.

The two went from the funeral to the collation afterward.

> It's over for the thousands and we walk back to the cars. Hundreds of fire-fighters loosening their ties, looking for a beer. I used to get furious at John. "I don't mind you go to funerals, but why do you have to come home so late and so drunk?" And I never understood. But somehow that's where life is reasserted. Their talk, their laughter and stories as they stand shoulder to shoulder with their beer. They're getting brave again. You can't fight a fire alone. You've got to love and trust the guy next to you. So they act like college boys these brave men who challenge fate and conquer fear and fire . . . We're standing in a big grassy field and I am the only woman in this sea of blue uniforms. I feel their respect. I have earned my spot. I am comfortable with them as I hear the stories and tell jokes and reaffirm that life is good . . . Paddy and I are as close as any sister and brother.

Over the next three days, Judge maintained his own equilibrium by walking the Brooklyn Bridge and attending two AA meetings as well as a meeting at the Gay Men's Health Crisis; AIDS was still killing some twenty New Yorkers a day. He also met with Gerry Whelan from the old neighborhood and with Gerry Adams from Sinn Fein. The IRA had just declared a cease-fire in Northern Ireland, and Judge parted with Adams almost giddy with hope there might finally be peace in his heart's homeland.

The prospects for peace notwithstanding, St. Patrick's Day was dark and misty. Judge was at a Mass in the cathedral officiated by the cardinal while eighty-eight gay activists were arrested for blocking Fifth Avenue in a pre-parade protest that was almost becoming part of the tradition.

WE'RE IRISH. WE'RE QUEER. WE'LL BE HERE EVERY YEAR, a banner read.

One difference this year was that O'Connor had agreed to march as the grand marshal, having repeatedly declined the honor in the past. Some activists contended he had accepted this year to reward the parade's organizers for winning a court fight to bar the Irish Lesbian and Gay Organization from the event.

Judge was of the opinion that O'Connor's primary intent was to appear energetic. He noted that the cardinal had turned seventy-five in January, the age when all bishops and above are required to submit a letter to the Pope offering to retire. The Pope was himself turning seventy-five that year, and he had been known to let favored eminences stay on indefinitely so long as their health held up and they remained true to Vatican edicts.

As on every St. Pat's Day for three decades, the FDNY Emerald Society Pipes and Drums started up Fifth Avenue, sounding only more spirited for having played those slow, mournful processions. To make the day complete, the band was headed by Big Jim Corcoran with his tall bearskin hat and gleaming drum major's staff and outlandish mustache.

"He came strutting as he always does," Judge said. "He put up his hand to salute, and under the salute he gave me the wink."

At the parade's end, Corcoran and the band continued down into the 86th Street subway station to catch a local two stops to East Sixty-eighth Street and the armory, where the band traditionally gathered to have a few postparade beers and induct new members. Inductees were given a list of instructions that Judge stuck into his appointment book at the March 17 page as a keepsake.

NEW MEMBERS

• Bring a bottle of Whiskey (Good Stuff).

• Don't wear a bathing suit under your kilt no matter what your mother says.

• Be on time.

A drumstick would be employed to lift the inductee's kilt and ensure that he was indeed wearing nothing underneath.

"Regimental," a piper called it.

Judge was on his way to the armory anticipating great *craic*—a rousing good time—when he was notified that bandleader Corcoran had suffered a fatal heart attack on the downtown subway platform. To have a figure such as Corcoran, so central to the rituals of the FDNY, drop dead at the end of the St. Patrick's Day parade seemed a cruel twist in a continuing series of tragedies that was beginning to feel like a curse.

The green stripe up the middle of Fifth Avenue was still visible when the leaderless band slow-marched Big Jim Corcoran's coffin down to the cathedral for the funeral. Giuliani must have understood the importance of this moment, for he had ruffled the cardinal again by insisting the department and the band in particular needed its chaplain to say the Mass.

The Gospel was from the book of John and recounted Jesus' first encounter with Nathaniel, the Israelite who had no guile. Judge began the homily by saying how proud he was to be chaplain of not just the department but the FDNY Emerald Society Pipes and Drums. He spoke of how important pipers were through all Celtic history and how Big Jim Corcoran had understood its importance to the fire department and to the parade and to all of the city of New York.

"What'd he tell you, Elaine?" Judge asked the bandleader's widow in the front pew. "On St. Patrick's Day, Fifth Avenue belonged to him."

Judge raised his hand.

"Except this year, I've heard it tell, that he said it belonged to him only after the grand marshal, His Eminence, was to lead the parade."

Judge turned to O'Connor, speaking respectfully but with something else in his tone.

"To march behind you . . . What a great moment it was for him and for you, Eminence."

O'Connor was the eminence, but Judge was the storyteller, which the ancient Irish recognized as a figure of great power, the one who could tell the king what it meant to be king, who was now telling the cardinal what the moment had been for the cardinal.

"There are stories. There are so many stories . . . Some could be told in this cathedral. Some better left unsaid."

Laughter rose from the mourners but stopped at the sanctuary rail. The cardinal's face was blank.

"But he was good, this man of faith," Judge went on, meaning Corcoran. "He led the band on Paddy's Day. Never, never, could he have realized the great way that God had for him to enter into a new life."

Judge raised both hands.

"This is the most extraordinary thing that has happened in this city in an age. Unbelievable! No matter where you go, people say, 'Oh, wasn't it wonderful the way he was called to go home.'"

His eyes were alight. He smiled as if it were all simply remarkable.

"A man of faith and family and the job. What a way to live! What a way to die! Having it all together. Walking up Fifth Avenue, passing this cathedral, giving the salute."

Judge gave a salute.

"And the joy that you gave him all these many years you'll never know," he told the band. "For all the band members in the city, it's a big day because today you've given the best you've had and you've given him back to the Lord. You're generous men. You're kind and good and loving."

He paused and addressed the entire congregation.

"Let me tell you what I think happened last Friday. He made the turn on Eighty-sixth Street, and he gave us the salute and the wink and in earthly terms he went down into the subway to go down to Sixty-eighth Street to have a few. But in heavenly terms he kept marching right through the clouds and he walked up on to the throne, the baton back and forth, and as he came, the Lord stood up. 'Ah, Jim, you're here. I've called you.' Then He turned around and looked at everyone in heaven, the Lord did, and He simply said, 'Behold the New Yorker in whom there is no guile.'

"The party began and all is well. Amen."

• • •

A lone piper played "Amazing Grace" during Communion. Jim Ginty, who had cofounded the band with Corcoran three decades before, gave the first eulogy. He thanked those who had tried to revive Corcoran on the subway platform.

"And, last but not least, I want to thank Father Mychal Judge," Ginty said. "I never met a man . . ."

Ginty's voice caught.

". . . that could bring out . . ."

He choked up and stopped for a moment as he collected himself. He started again, his chin trembling.

"I never met a man that could bring out the faith in people like Father Mychal Judge."

Judge sat with lowered eyes as Ginty stepped down. O'Connor looked as if he had become one of the cathedral's stone figures. Fire Commissioner Safir was next and read from a citation for valor that described Corcoran crawling into a blazing apartment to rescue a three-year-old child. Giuliani gave the final eulogy, first thanking O'Connor, then Judge.

"Father Judge, who is able to convey an ability to transcend where we are to someplace else better than anyone I know," Giuliani said.

This was not likely to help matters with O'Connor, and Judge delayed the call for the firefighters to fall in outside so as not to interrupt O'Connor's opportunity to say something at the end.

O'Connor praised Giuliani for his dedication and the Corcoran family for its faith. He joked that he always dreaded shaking hands with Big Jim.

"The ring that our Holy Father gave me as archbishop of New York has very sharp edges, and each time in a very big bear grasp he would crush my hand and it would be bleeding for weeks after," O'Connor said. "So much has been said about his gentleness, I thought that might be added."

O'Connor got some titters, but his humor was too deliberate and a little off. He adjusted that gold ring on his finger as he continued a custom he had begun at Drennan's funeral.

"It remains particularly for the sake of the family to applaud but one, Jim Corcoran."

O'Connor did not lead the applause; rather he waited until everyone else was clapping before he joined, then with royal dispassion. He read another prayer and seemed done when Judge decided the moment had come to issue the delayed call.

"Will the uniformed members of the department please—" Judge began.

O'Connor raised his left hand to silence Judge.

"May we have the final blessing first, please. Excuse me."

Judge stood stunned.

"May I ask that my brother priests join me in a final blessing," O'Connor said.

Judge seemed not so much unwilling as unable to respond immediately.

O'Connor proceeded with the blessing and was preparing to make the Sign of the Cross when he suddenly paused.

"If you'll join me."

O'Connor was addressing Judge, loud enough for all to hear, seeking to make the final blessing of Big Jim Corcoran's mortal remains double as a public humiliation for this upstart fire chaplain. Nobody seemed to pay much attention, for Judge's homily had indeed transported them to a better place, to where the bandleader's death itself seemed almost a blessing, at the very least an inspiration. They had to hurry to fall into formation, but they did so affirmed in feeling they themselves were so much closer to blessed than cursed for wearing the uniform of the FDNY, no matter what the future might bring.

Judge afterward spoke to his twin of the cardinal's anger and shrugged.

"I think he was at a stage in life where he kind of came home to himself," Dympna later said. "He was at the center of his own life. He had this very personal relationship with God."

He was no longer rattled as he had been by Urban during those days in England. He now seemed almost to seek conflict with the cardinal.

"Stay away from there," Dympna would warn her twin. "You're going to get bounced out of the diocese."

"Okay, okay," he would say.

There were only two possibilities. One being that there was indeed a God, in which case He and Judge were on the most intimate terms. The other being there was no God, in which case His Eminence and His Holiness were just a couple of guys with outlandish headgear.

The prospect of recriminations from the cardinal's office did not prevent Judge from offering general absolution to any firefighter who wanted it before the firehouse Mass marking the first anniversary of the Watts Street fire. The instant takers included Liam Flaherty of the band.

"I definitely partook of that," Flaherty said. " 'All right, I'm going to get general absolution!' He took all those stuffy church traditions and brought them into the twenty-first century for us. Made it a lot more palatable for the regular guy."

The men of Engine 24/Ladder 5 had rolled out their rigs to clear the apparatus floor for the ceremony. The three goldfish swam in their tank as the firefighters set up three plaques draped in black. Vina had the consolation of seeing bunker gear hanging from the hooks along the wall. Young John Drennan had come wearing his mother's slippers because they were comfortable. He ate jelly beans out of a Styrofoam cup as his family sat in the first row of folding chairs and waited for the ceremony to begin.

"Marvelous," Judge said.

Judge of course gave Communion to the Lutheran widow along with all the firefighters he had absolved moments earlier by making the Sign of the Cross. Liam Flaherty and the others from the band played "Amazing Grace" at the unveiling of the three memorial plaques, each bearing the name of one of the fallen.

As Judge had predicted at Drennan's funeral, life had indeed gone on for Engine 24/Ladder 5, with a new captain and two new firefighters. Judge saw them in action the following afternoon when he responded to a fire at the Fulton Fish Market.

Vina happened to be nearby and came down to the scene after smelling the smoke. The job was nearly done by then and a young firefighter called out, "Hi, Mrs. Drennan!" He came over, sooty-faced and smiling.

"I just thought I'd come down and see if everybody was okay," Vina said.

"Somebody got dizzy, but everybody's okay," the firefighter said.

"That's good," Vina said.

"I've got to take up this line now," the firefighter said.

He started rolling up the hose to make ready for the next job.

Nobody outside the family seemed to take John Drennan's death harder than the doctor who fought day after day to save him. And nobody was happier than Judge when Michael Madden became engaged to a woman so wonderful as to seem a heaven-sent reward for his heroic and ultimately heartbreaking effort.

Judge took it as a compliment when Madden and his fiancée, Susan, came to him for pre-Cana counseling. Susan told him she was Jewish but was willing to convert.

"You'd be going backward," Judge replied.

"What are you talking about?" Susan asked.

"Jesus was Jewish," Judge said. "We came from you. If anybody should convert it should be Michael."

Judge married them as Catholic and Jew at St. Stephen's Roman Catholic Church on the Upper East Side of Manhattan. The tireless burn doctor who had written simply "I tried" on the last page of the Drennan visitor's log began a new life by uttering "I do."

The reception was to be held at the swank Carlyle Hotel. Madden's mother had just stepped from the limo at the main entrance when she collapsed with what would prove to be a fatal heart attack. Madden went with his mother to the hospital and asked Judge to stay by Susan's side as the reception went ahead.

"He held my hand from the moment that happened, and I don't think he let go for four hours," she recalled. "There were more wedding pictures of Father Mychal and me than of Michael and me. There's Father Mychal and me by the cake. There's Father Mychal and me by the dance floor. It's like I married the priest."

He was even given the seat next to the bride that would have been the groom's. The place card had "Father Judge" in elegant calligraphy and he pasted it into his appointment book. He no doubt was happy to have been able to help Madden and his new bride make the best of the situation, and he might have even felt the reception was a little like some dream arising from his own longings for a family. But more than anything, he was angry this good doctor should have that happen on his wedding day.

Judge had ministered to people such as a man in his Siena days who had cancer and then meningitis and then lost his assistant to a serial killer. He had tended to AIDS patients at their final moments. He had been with burned firefighters in their agonies and the families in their grief. He told Susan that he still did not usually feel God needed any forgiveness.

But each new tragedy hit him hard and maybe left him with a residual and cumulative feeling that possibly his God was not so much one of surprises as of indifference. The death of Madden's mother seemed to be one irony too many. He arrived at Holy Week telling Susan that at this point he felt God owed him an explanation.

On the Friday before the one called Good, Judge responded to a fire on East Fifth Street, and it seemed there might be more proof of divine indifference when a fire officer radioed "Mayday! Mayday!" and appeared at a top-floor window, trapped by the raging flames. A firefighter from Lener's Ladder 6 was lowered down from the roof by rope and embraced the officer. The sudden weight caused the rope to skitter across the roof edge and the two suddenly dropped a half story. The rope held and they were lowered to safety. Judge joined the cheers.

Another bit of brightness came on Easter, when the fire commissioner approached Vina at a gathering at Gracie Mansion. Safir asked her to address the annual legislative conference of the International Association for Firefighters in Washington a few days hence. She accepted, and Judge cheered from afar when she read to him afterward of standing all of five feet tall before a crowd of two thousand, hoping they could see her behind the podium as she told them her husband's death certificate read "cause of death: multiple burns," but the real cause was carelessness.

I went back to my seat and someone said to me, "Are you glad it's over?" and I said, "No, it's just beginning."

The next page of the Book of Vina recalled a lesson to the third-grade class she had resumed teaching. It was a lesson she taught each spring and she called it a "$19.95 miracle," the price of a kit that began with some dark goo in a jar. The goo was larvae, and the children watched it become four or five cocoons. Then: *Mrs. Drennan, look!* The metamorphosis began. "Soon, boys and girls, soon." And sure enough, the miracle happened.

Beautiful orange and black painted ladies on legs no thicker than an eyelash. We watch them wobble and fly.

On one perfect spring day, the class trooped outside.

The child who carried the box held it high with great honor. And we let them go one by one and watch them flutter weakly and then soar and we felt such pride, such joy in being part of the wonder.

The last one had just begun its flight when a bird swooped out of nowhere and

swallowed our miracle in one gulp . . . And we learned the feeling of powerlessness. We could only stand by and watch.

It's a harsh reality—whether it's a bird or hot flames that gobble up your dream, that steal what you love. Yet from the moment the cocoon shakes or the labor begins we know the fragility of life. We know the vulnerability once we allow ourselves to love. And isn't life great because in spite of it all—in spite of losing and pain—it's worth loving and we would have done it no other way. Yep, I'd get a new Butterfly Garden for $19.95 every year. Let's take our chances. Loving is worth it. Miracles happen even if we can only treasure them for a little while. There's no other way to do it.

No priest could have offered a better homily on the importance of embracing the totality of life. Judge's faith was doubly steadied by Vina and by the grace he repeatedly witnessed at fires such as she was now determined to prevent.

Judge continued representing God at those fires, blessing firefighters and ministering to the burned and injured. The firefighters felled by natural causes included Anthony Ferrera, brother of Carol Safir, the wife of Fire Commissioner Howard Safir. She chanced to see Judge climbing into his battered old Plymouth after the burial.

"*That's* the kind of car you give Father Judge?" she asked her husband.

Judge was summoned to headquarters on what was not coincidentally his sixty-second birthday.

"Well, Father Judge, you finally did it," Safir would recall saying.

"Did what?" Judge asked. He clearly feared he might be in some kind of trouble.

"You finally convinced me you need a new car," Safir said.

Along with a shiny Crown Victoria, the headquarters staff then surprised Judge with a birthday cake on a day he had planned to spend with Alvarado. He soon after was racing in his new car to a fire on West 135th Street. He visited an injured firefighter at St. Luke's Hospital and then headed to the firehouse across the street from the friary for a second birthday cake.

The next month, Judge was back at Zinno's with Brown and Vina as well as Terry Hatton. The talk at the table was of Hatton's journey to Oklahoma City after the bombing of the Federal Building in April. He had gone with a team led by Ray Downey, the FDNY's chief of rescue operations, nicknamed "God" in recognition of his singular expertise and acumen. Brown and Vina and Judge sat rapt as Terry recounted the seven days of searching vainly for survivors, then just for the dead. The team found ten bodies during the first twelve-hour shift. They had seen just the hand of a young woman extending from the rubble, an engagement ring glinting on her finger. The second day, they had coaxed a reluctant crane operator to help them clear some of the wreckage where nine floors had pancaked. They had found another two dozen bodies, including that of a Marine.

Terry told of how on their return they had been met at the airport by a crowd of city officials, including several who had balked at funding the team in the first place. These same "suits" had crowded around to have their pictures taken with the Downey team. Downey was now warning that the same sort of attack or even worse could happen right here in New York.

Vina spoke of her fire safety research, citing facts and figures. The firefighters at the table hushed. She might as well have been telling Knights of the Round Table that she was studying ways to prevent jousts before they happened.

"Vina's kinda, I don't know," Brown said afterward. "You know?"

Judge admired Vina's self-appointed mission to make her husband's death save others from the same. He also understood what Brown did not say, likely even to himself: Brown needed to view fire as the manifestation of a more epic evil than simple carelessness. He had to see this incredibly dangerous job as a heroic battle with the Red Devil.

And perhaps part of the reason Brown embraced Judge was that he cast the job in those terms. Brown listened to Judge do so again the following month, when giving the blessing at a street renaming in honor of two firefighters who died in 1980. Judge again invoked the pure heroism of charging into a fire of whatever cause.

That was better than saying Firefighter Lawrence Fitzpatrick had died while rescuing Firefighter Gerard Frisby from a seventh-floor window with a rope that had been left in service despite being doubly inadequate. The fire department brass were found to have been both "misleading" and "unprofessional" during the subsequent investigation, at first trying to say that the rope had been cut by the edge of the roof. Investigators determined that the rope was already frayed and of a type that had been deemed deficient in laboratory strength tests five months before.

"How do you tell yourself your friend died because of a shitty rope?" Brown said after the street renaming.

The entire pipe band had played at the Fitzpatrick and Frisby funerals, a first, as if to say the firefighters' spirit and nobility were undiminished by the betrayal. That was the start of a tradition of having the whole band at all line-of-duty funerals. Judge had since made it complete by putting into words the human godliness in the face of ungodly events that the pipes and drums made everybody feel.

Judge remained ever attentive to the widow who kept talking of preventing fires before anybody had to be heroic, before any rope was needed, shitty or no. He set an entire day aside for her, but unlike with Alvarado, no other demands materialized.

On what he recorded as "Vina Day" in his appointment book, Judge took her for a drive through his native borough and then swung up through Manhattan. They were both hungry when they happened past Elaine's, the celebrity hangout favored by stars of the literary and movie persuasion.

"Did you ever eat in Elaine's?" Judge asked.

The hour was still early, so they had little trouble getting a table. The place was not known for the food, but it seemed to Vina that nobody could have delighted in a meal more than Judge did.

"Everything he did, he did it with such joy," she recalled. "I can still see him picking up the fork and smiling into it. You wouldn't think he had a care in the world, and here he is stuck with some widow."

Elaine herself came in and of course Judge went over and chatted with her.

"If they only knew how special he was," Vina later said.

• • •

Judge had become such a special spiritual figure in the FDNY that firefighters would call out "Padre! Padre!" at fires and come over for his blessing. The pregnant wife of Capt. Joseph Kennedy from the firehouse across from the friary called him when the doctors had said her baby might be hydrocephalic. Judge said he would meet her at the firehouse.

"When I got there, he took my hand, and he took us into the back of the firehouse, behind the truck and blessed us all," the wife, Christine Kennedy, would recall. "It was nothing fancy, but very real . . . He put his hands first on my belly, and then one hand on my head and one on Joe's, pulled us close until our heads touched—and prayed. I remember vividly how large his hands were. I really mean it, this man had the most enormous hands I had ever seen. Large hands that to me were a sign of comfort and strength. What a sense of security. He kissed us both and said, 'I gotta run!' And he was gone."

The baby girl was born in perfect health. The priest whom Christine Kennedy would say "had a hand in it" presided at the July 22 baptism of Jacqueline Kennedy. The mother said she chose the name because their daughter was surely destined for greatness.

Around that time, Firefighter Mickey Kross of the same firehouse chanced to mention that his girlfriend's mother was critically ill with brain cancer in Norwalk, Connecticut. Judge hopped in his car.

"She's in her bed dying and all of a sudden the [FDNY] chaplain comes in to see her," Kross said.

On other days, Judge and Kross would walk to a diner up the street. Judge would give a folded dollar bill to any homeless people they encountered, addressing those he knew by name, learning the names of those he did not. Kross remembered one day when Judge sat down to have his usual grilled cheese, only to make a discovery when it came time to pay the check. "He gives me this almost naughty-schoolboy look and said, 'I don't have any money.' He'd given away all his money and he couldn't pay for the lunch."

Kross is someone who looks at the person rather than the position, in Judge's case the guy rather than the priest. Kross was one firefighter who would drop by Judge's room at the friary expecting him to be nobody other than himself. Judge responded by confiding his fears that he could not keep being what he felt ever more people expected of him.

"He said, 'I can't do this anymore,'" Kross recalled.

Kross added, "He would always feel he had to be perfect. He was always afraid he would let people down. He always thought he would disappoint people. But he never did."

Capt. Brian O'Flaherty of the fire officers union also sensed that it was not easy being Mychal Judge. He arranged for Judge to get away and accompany Vina to a convention in San Francisco on August 25. She delivered her "carelessness kills" speech to the International Association of Firefighters and she started with a bad case of nerves until she saw Mychal Judge sitting in the front row, giving her a thumbs-up.

"Somebody like Mychal Judge starts to say you're wonderful, you start to think, 'Maybe my parents were wrong. Maybe all those schoolteachers didn't have it right,'" Vina later said.

The overall reception was positive enough, but Paddy Brown was hardly the only one in the world who felt the way he did regarding her notions about firefighters and fire.

"I've never been invited back," Vina noted.

Young John Drennan went along to San Francisco, and Vina took him sightseeing. They returned to see a commotion outside the hotel. A cabbie had been run over after a dispute arising from a fender bender, and he now lay bleeding on the street. A familiar figure was crouched beside him.

"We leave New York with all the dead firemen and widows and here's Mychal kneeling in the street," Vina recalled. "This holy, holy man in the street."

Judge remained with the cabbie until the paramedics arrived, but he was beyond saving. Judge finally rose with blood on his one pair of pants, wrote the man's address on a piece of hotel stationery, and trekked across town to his home. Inside the small house was a Buddhist shrine, and only the man's brother spoke English. Judge was still able to ease their grief somewhat by letting them know the man had not just died alone in the street.

Young John wrote of the San Francisco trip in a journal of his own that he had begun keeping.

[Father Judge] is remarkably calm as we walk into the hotel with offi-cers unfurling a police tape behind our backs as we walk into the lobby. He is not high strung at all. He is the last person that man will ever see and he speaks so calmly, not disrespectfully in any way, just calm. He talks about how sad it is to see someone die so senselessly, at such a young age . . . He is remarkable how he always knows how to say the right thing at the right time. I guess it comes from years and years of helping people through every different kind of problem a human can have . . . Father Judge is an equal opportunity lender of his time and prayers. He doesn't care what social background, what race, what you believe in, what your sexual orientation is, what your bank account looks like. He probably doesn't even care if you are a nice person. He will try to help you in any way that he can . . . an angel walking around, reading peo-ple their last rites, helping people through grief, amusing everyone with his jokes and sense of humor. It is hard to put a finger on what he does to make him so special, hard to explain it to others who have not had the good fortune of meeting him. You just have to meet him. That is all you can tell anyone who wants to know what he is like. You just have to meet him.

The answering machine was full when Judge returned to New York, and he had a funeral his first morning back. He had a wedding in upstate New York the next day and a five-alarm fire in Midtown the next and a baptism on Long Island the next. He was back at the friary when he got a call that sent him racing out to Steven McDonald's home.

The teenage gunman whom Steven publicly forgave for shooting him had been killed in a motorcycle accident three days after being released from prison. Shavod Jones had telephoned Steven before his release to express his remorse and there had been talk of the two visiting schools together to tell their respective stories after he got out of prison. Steven had seen this as an opportunity for something truly remarkable to come out of his continuing ordeal.

Judge arrived to see that even nine-year-old Conor was shaken by the unexpected turn. Patti Ann had screamed on hearing the news. Steven was stunned, and Judge found himself comforting the cop over the death of someone who had left him a quadriplegic.

Judge stayed until 12:30 A.M. He then raced off to a three-alarm fire on West Seventy-first Street and remained at the scene until 2:30 A.M. He was up in Harlem later that morning as an emissary, conveying the McDonalds' condolences to the Jones family and asking if Steven could attend the funeral. He had to tell Steven they refused.

That afternoon, Judge was at the FDNY quartermaster, thanks to the legacy of John Drennan. Judge was among the very last issued the new protective bunker gear and nobody on this particular September 11 imagined a chaplain could ever really be in danger. The back was stenciled with F.D.N.Y. CHAPLAIN M. JUDGE in keeping with his official place among those who perpetually confirmed his faith and thereby made it all the more impossible to forsake his priesthood, even if he felt at times forsaken by the hierarchy of his Church.

Judge would never have chosen to see Alvarado at the expense of not visiting a burned firefighter. But when fate and his schedule allowed, he took a rare out-of-town trip with his friend to Boston, telling him, "I'll take you to Faneuil Hall!" Alvarado saw no magic in the building where the cry of liberty arose in the aftermath of the Boston Massacre, saying only, "I like the smell of New York." They cut the visit short and caught the next train back. They had to ride standing because the car was packed with the faithful on their way to see Pope John Paul II in Central Park.

Judge stood on the Great Lawn as the Pope said Mass at a hundred-foot-long altar, the towers of Midtown rising behind him. The Pope told the huge crowd to embrace the poor and the sick, but also to "stand up for purity!"

Judge afterward went with the McDonalds to the cathedral. The Pope remembered Steven from Colorado and came over, another man who had been shot and then forgiven his assailant. His Holiness then spoke from the altar, calling O'Connor "my dear friend" and extolling the "dauntless leadership you all know."

In the evening, the Pope retired to the cardinal's residence for meetings with religious leaders. Judge dined with Vina, who had suffered a crisis of faith after she burned her finger on a coffeepot and the pain of even a tiny burn made her think of how much her husband must have suffered. She was ready to mark God absent.

"Just maybe we're alone and we're afraid to believe there is no magic," she had written in her journal.

But now here was Mychal Judge, who saw as much magic in her as she did in him. He would also be just as shaken by what transpired early the next afternoon.

October 8 happened to be the first day of Fire Prevention Week, and if the city was not yet serious about preventing fires, there was at least a nice ceremony at the South Street Seaport at the very moment the youngest of the Zinno's bachelors was responding to an arson fire in Queens. Thirty-one-year-old Firefighter Peter McLaughlin had just transferred to Rescue 4. He was right in the thick of it when a fireball suddenly engulfed him with such ferocity not even bunker gear could save him. A fleeing civilian heard him cry out, "Oh my God! Help me! I'm burning!"

Judge raced to the hospital and began another journey with the family. McLaughlin had been like a kid brother to Paddy Brown, who took this death hard, his grief intensified by unreasoning guilt for having arranged for McLaughlin to get into the elite rescue unit. Peter's younger brother, Keith, told Brown not to blame himself. Judge did the same, but Brown could not be consoled. He set up a kind of altar by his bed in his apartment, a low table on which he placed holy cards from the wakes for John Drennan and Peter McLaughlin, along with religious objects from various faiths, including a Buddha that Judge gave him. He posed questions to Judge that joined with the answers to constitute a kind of catechism.

> Q: *How can you be sure there's a God?*
> A: *You still go to fires.*

> Q: *Who is God, anyway?*
> A: *God is what still sends you in.*

> Q: *What if I don't go in?*
> A: *You will.*

> Q: *Because of God?*
> A: *Because of you.*

Brown kept charging into danger along with the rest of the FDNY, knowing that luck runs in streaks, almost always at least one loss a year, sometimes as many as eighteen, most often somewhere in between. The four years leading up to Drennan had been good ones, with no fatalities in 1990, two in 1991, and just one each in 1992 and 1993. Now the bad luck was back, and there seemed no end to it as they suffered three more losses. Fire Lt. John Clancy was killed on the morning of December 31 while venturing into a blazing crack house. He left a pregnant wife who tucked her hand inside her gray tweed coat during the funeral and felt their first child kick.

The next day, January 5, 1996, Firefighter James Williams was killed, also at a fire in Queens, also leaving a pregnant wife, as well as two children, aged four and two. His funeral paused when the younger one called out, "Daddy! Daddy!" The widow, Jean Williams, still managed not to cry until Judge's homily. Judge noted that Williams was the brother of two firefighters and that the father was a retired fire lieutenant who had assembled the family the previous Christmas Eve, instructing them "to look at each other because they might never be together again." Judge then spoke the words that brought the widow's tears.

"You won't see him and you won't hear him, but you'll feel his love and presence," Judge said.

Then, on February 5, Firefighter Louis Valentino of Rescue 2 was killed at a fire in Brooklyn. Judge passed under a bleak full moon to notify the parents. The firefighters who arrived at the family's home included Al Fuentes, who had been with Hatton in Oklahoma City after the bombing. Fuentes also had been particularly close to Valentino, and he told Judge he needed to speak with him. Judge went with him into the bathroom.

"I said, 'Father, I can't take it anymore. So much death. When is this going to end?'" Fuentes recalled. "He put his hands on me. He had a way of talking to you. It would just melt away."

The mother, Philomena Valentino, was so grief-stricken she would not remember speaking with Judge until the wake two days later.

"Father, I want to tell you I've been saying the rosary for thirty years and I never asked God for anything except to protect the kids," she then said. "I would just ask the Blessed Mother, 'Protect my Louis while he does these dangerous things. Especially when he goes into these burning buildings.'"

She figured her Louis should have been under some sort of divine protection without her even having to ask. He was an usher at the parish church.

He taught swimming to retarded people. He gave clothing to the homeless. And he routinely risked his life to save others.

"I'm so mad at God," the mother said.

"So, tonight when you pray, tell him how mad you are," Judge said.

He added, "I don't blame you. You *should* be mad."

On Ash Wednesday at fire headquarters, Judge applied a smudged cross of mortality on the brows of those who needed no reminding. The deaths at the FDNY were weighing on Judge when he made a brief pilgrimage in his department car over the Verrazano Bridge to Staten Island. He was coming at Vina's urging to meet her quilting group, saying they had a profound and hard-won understanding of life. All but one was a widow, and Vina was the youngest.

"Each of them had their sorrows," Vina said. "You don't live to be old if you haven't had sorrow. They had been through everything."

Judge watched them cut and stitch, creating beauty with scraps of fabric.

"Making something from nothing," Vina said.

The wisdom lay not in anything any of the quilters said but in their spirit as manifested and preserved moment by moment, stitch by stitch, in shape and color and texture. Here in these quilts Judge saw not just perseverance and resilience, such as he had witnessed in his widowed mother, but transcendence.

"That was where he saw God," Vina later said.

And for these quilters Judge had reverence such as no miter inspired.

"Those were his holy people," Vina said.

18

Judge kept traversing the city from fire to fire. He had just come from a multiple-alarm blaze in the Bronx as he sat in his FDNY jacket in the front row at the ten P.M. AA meeting on East Seventy-ninth Street. The patch caught the eye of a young newcomer whose stepbrother was a firefighter.

Michael Walker was an ex-Marine from Poughkeepsie who found himself in the big city with thirty dollars in his pocket and a serious alcohol problem. He was the product of a broken home and was broken himself. While most people his age are starting their lives, he was asking himself, Where did it all go wrong? He figured the way to start making it right was to stop drinking, but he was wary of what he later termed "kind of a motley crew" at this late-hour meeting. He decided the safest person to approach was the silver-haired man he assumed to be a retired firefighter. He introduced himself and was thrilled when Judge produced a business card saying he was an FDNY chaplain.

"Thank God, because I really need to talk to a priest," Walker said.

"I'll tell you what, Michael, all you have to do is not drink tonight, wake up tomorrow, go to a meeting, and give me a call," Judge replied.

Walker did not drink, and in the morning he called Judge, who drove him over to the Gracie Mews Diner on the Upper East Side. Judge had no trouble parking his department car thanks to the official placard he put in the windshield.

"He goes on and on about how he can park anywhere he wants and isn't God good and isn't New York great," Walker recalled.

Walker was starved as the two sat down, but he had little money and ordered only a burger.

"He sees me eating the cole slaw and pickle, too," Walker remembered.

Judge said he was paying, and added, "You better get dessert."

Before the meal was done, Judge had learned that Walker also knew what it was to grow up without a father, having lost his when he was just two. They were both amazed to discover that his father, Bill Walker, had been in Judge's freshman class at St. Francis Prep.

Judge drove Walker down to the Brooklyn Bridge. The two stood at midspan, high over the harbor, the Twin Towers and all the spires of Manhattan glittering before them.

"You see that, Michael? That's the greatest city in the world," Judge said. "You're sober. You're here. And if you don't drink one day at a time, who knows what God has in store for you."

Judge spoke as if Walker were on the verge of a great adventure.

"It's the God of Surprises!"

Walker's father had gone on to become a cop before his untimely death. His mother had cleaned houses until she fell ill with cancer that was now proving terminal. He himself figured on finding construction work, but Judge had another notion that seemed at first as if it might draw a pretty good chuckle from the Almighty.

Judge began by summoning Walker to the friary and presenting him with a suit and tie from the donated clothes. Judge had arranged for Walker to get a job interview at a Wall Street firm through Mickey Brennan, a bond trader whose wedding he had officiated earlier that year.

"If anybody asks, you're Mychal Judge's nephew," Judge said. "That's how we know each other."

The firm hired Walker as a trainee and paid for him to attend New York University at night so he could obtain his trading license. Walker was a lad transformed. Judge began driving him to see his dying mother in Poughkeepsie every Wednesday.

"We'd say the rosary on the way up and we'd talk and talk and talk," Walker recalled.

Judge would say Mass in the mother's living room, a bit of peace at the end of a difficult life.

"She loved him," Walker said. "In her mind he saved her only son."

The way a son will follow the example of the father, Walker himself became a sponsor in AA of another former Marine named Eddie Quayle, who had been in the barracks in Beirut in 1983 when a suicide bomber struck, killing 241. Quayle had been buried alive for two and a half days, a survivor such as everyone would hope to find after the Twin Towers collapsed. Trapped in total darkness, unsure of which way was up or down, he banged a tin coffee cup seemingly endlessly until his rescuers found him. He recovered physically, but his psychic wounds left him an alcoholic living with his family in a trailer park in Poughkeepsie. He sought refuge in AA for a time, and Walker did his best to help, but sobriety was a constant struggle. Demon rum joined Qualye's own demons in chasing him out into traffic, where he was struck and killed. Walker got a late-night call and he in turn called Judge.

Early the next morning Judge picked up Walker in his department car. Judge was on the phone with the Marine Corps as he drove north. An honor guard appeared in time for the funeral at what Walker would describe as "this little church in Poughkeepsie, basically the family from the trailer park and a couple of people from the meeting up there and this Marine Corps color guard."

Judge delivered the homily for this victim of a terrorist bombing that had already faded from public consciousness. Judge of course gave it his all, once again making a little church feel as spiritually grand as a cathedral.

Back in New York, Judge gave the prayer at the dedication of a new memorial to the victims of Ireland's Great Famine. The memorial was by the harbor's edge at the Battery, where immigrants landed before Ellis Island was opened. Either the importance of the event or the frenetic pace of his schedule prompted him to write down his prayer beforehand, for the first time anyone could remember. He delivered it in the freezing wind with the Twin Towers soaring behind him.

> *God, Father of our City, of our Nation, we stand here today a people well fed, warmly clothed and securely sheltered—We come to bless this spot where 150 years ago our ancestors came with only the strips of cloth on their backs, no house to sleep in and no potato—their staff of life—to fill their bellies. Nothing but faith, deep faith in you, faith in this blessed land you brought them to and faith in each other. And so, with faith, they built the churches, they paved the streets and dug the subways. To them today we erect and dedicate this monument, for all to see—their immigrant faith—*

and to renew our spirit of faith in you and each other on our immigrant
journey to your heavenly kingdom.
Amen.

In his marvelous metropolis, Judge found the Irish spirit most alive among the members of the FDNY Emerald Society Pipes and Drums. He regularly attended band meetings, including one that became particularly contentious. The language was rough enough that Firefighter Liam Flaherty felt compelled to point out that unbeknownst to most of them, their chaplain was sitting in the back of the hall. The language cleaned up, but a half hour later they were back at it.

Judge did not scold them when he stepped up to give a concluding prayer. He began by invoking the band's glories, saying, "Good, great mysterious Lord, lay your blessings down on this band. The skirl of the pipes and the beating of the drums bring a tear to the eye and a smile to the face. When the band marches up the streets, you look so majestic to those before you. You do such a great job to inspire the members of the fire department."

Judge paused.

"And, just to put it in your words, you're so fucking good."

They were indeed, but they still did not have a new leader. The tryouts for drum major were held on February 26 at the Elks Hall on Queens Boulevard. Flaherty had been practicing hard at Judge's urging, mastering a precise code that had evolved over the centuries since Celtic musicians adopted the bagpipes from instruments Muslim armies once played to rouse their troops against the Crusaders. Strict rules dictated exactly how the drum major should stand at various moments and how his grip should shift as he brandished and twirled his staff. The rules even extended to the drum major's eyes.

"Looking up at the mace when it is above the head and about to be brought down should be shunned," one authoritative guide noted. "The law of gravity will ensure that the mace will come down when released."

Flaherty's eyes stayed level as he let the staff he held overhead slide down through his fingers. He reasserted his grip at just the right moment and completed a nuanced routine as if out of Judge's vision of him. He was erect but not stiff, his every motion exact yet fluid. The firefighters in the balcony roared their approval and held up signs reading "10." The band had a new leader.

· · ·

Three nights after the drum major election, Judge suffered what seemed to be a heart attack in his friary room. An ambulance was summoned. The paramedics wanted to take him to St. Vincent's Hospital, a Catholic facility just down Seventh Avenue, where Judge had ministered to many AIDS patients. He insisted on going to New York Hospital–Cornell Medical Center because this was home of the burn unit and therefore in his mind a spiritual extension of his other religious order, the FDNY.

At the same emergency room where John Drennan had first been treated, the doctors determined that Judge's problem was not his heart but his gall bladder. Judge underwent what was supposed to be routine and relatively minor surgery by one of the hospital's most prominent surgeons. This illustrious doctor managed to perforate Judge's intestine. Peritonitis developed and threatened to be fatal.

As word spread that Judge was in the hospital, visitors began arriving at all hours, shocked by his condition. He kept trying to comfort them. His sisters finally posted a sign on the door reading ISOLATION.

When Alvarado came, he immediately put his nursing skills to work in one form of physical intimacy that not even the Pope would have found sinful.

"I changed his dressings, of course," Alvarado said.

Another regular visitor was Paddy Brown, who was visibly shaken by even the thought that Judge might die. Brown could not accept that fate might take so mundane a turn, that this magical priest might meet his end this way.

"This kind of, you know, sucks," Brown said.

The crisis passed, but Judge was still too sick to march on St. Patrick's Day that year. He also missed the formal induction of Liam Flaherty as the new drum major the following day. Flaherty and band chairman Joe Murphy arrived afterward at the hospital.

Judge forced himself from the bed and told the six-foot-five Liam to kneel. The considerably smaller Murphy also knelt. Judge placed a "big mitt" on each of their heads and blessed them, speaking of the great traditions that have been passed down from father to son through the ages.

"In the name of the ancient Celtic gods of Ireland, may you carry the mace for many years and make us proud."

The brief ceremony gave Flaherty goose bumps, and when he rose, he saw Judge was in tears.

After twenty-four days, Judge was released from the hospital. Most people assumed he would file a malpractice suit against the surgeon. He told the lawyer Peter Johnson he was not interested, even though it would almost certainly have resulted in a huge settlement.

"Ah, the poor doctor," Judge said of the surgeon who almost killed him.

In an example of what some called the Bad Rudy, Giuliani pushed out Police Commissioner William Bratton for hogging too much of the limelight over a dramatic reduction in crime. Howard Safir moved from the FDNY to become the new police commissioner. The new fire commissioner was a big surprise.

Tom Von Essen had been the head of the firefighters' union, and many firefighters grumbled that he sold his soul in making the leap to management. Judge was not of the opinion a soul could be sold, however willing the owner might be to do so. He became as close to the new commissioner as he had been to the old one. And the new commissioner became just as close to Judge.

"You keep your hands off Father Judge," Von Essen said when Safir tried to lure him to the police department. "You're not getting Father Judge. No way."

Judge remained with the fire department and proceeded just as before, from fires to weddings to baptisms to hospitals to wakes to funerals. He was there when Louis Valentino's brother got married and when First Deputy Commissioner Bill Feehan's wife was buried.

29

The phone rang after midnight on July 18, 1996. Steven McDonald was calling.

"Father Mike, did you hear about the airplane crash?"

Steven had heard on the news that TWA Flight 800 from New York to Paris had crashed off Long Island. That was outside the jurisdiction of the FDNY and Judge had not been paged. But the news also reported that the families were gathering where the flight had taken off, Kennedy Airport in Queens.

"So I got in the car," Judge later recalled. "I went out. I went there as a chaplain, as a priest."

At one A.M. Judge arrived at the Ramada Inn, near the airport, where some of the passengers' families awaited word of their loved ones. Giuliani was already there, moving from table to table with a partial passenger list from the airline, trying to match families with those on the manifest.

When a name matched, Judge would linger with the family for a few minutes. He caught up with Giuliani at a table where the mayor was having difficulty finding the passengers' names on the sheet.

"This is terrible. We don't know who's on there and who's not on there," Giuliani exclaimed. "This is terrible! TWA doesn't know what it's doing!"

Judge watched as Giuliani strode out to tell the press the same thing.

Judge kept being Judge. He stayed until just before dawn, caught a few hours of sleep at the friary, and returned to the hotel at eleven A.M.

As it became clear there had been no survivors, the initial shock was giving way to grief and anger. Giuliani had also returned. He watched as Judge was confronted by a man whose child had been one of twenty-one high-school students and chaperones from Montoursville, Pennsylvania, aboard.

"What are you doing here? What the hell are you doing here?" the man demanded when he saw Judge's clerical garb. "All these people died. You represent God. How can there be a God? How can you believe in God? What God would let all those kids die? It's all a big lie!"

Giuliani moved to intervene, but then saw Judge take the man's hand.

"He just grabbed the man's hand and encouraged him to keep going," Giuliani remembered.

The man railed on for a few moments more, then suddenly broke down in tears and hugged Judge.

"God lets evil happen and I don't understand why," Judge told him.

The man recovered himself, and Giuliani watched as Judge moved on, facing such anger again and again. Giuliani began to discern a basic principle in dealing with people in these circumstances.

"A lot of it is just listening," Giuliani would later say. "People are going to get angry. Let them get angry. Let them get it out."

This principle went against Giuliani's nature and was hardly his usual impulse, but Judge would serve as his model in the aftermath of the much bigger tragedy the mayor would face in five years' time.

"There is no way to exaggerate his ability to understand people and get into their minds and hearts," Giuliani said later. "Flight 800, that was like a marathon. It was in many ways a prelude to the World Trade Center."

On the second day after the crash, Frank Carven arrived at the hotel along with his mother and brothers. His sister, Paula Carven, was an off-duty flight attendant who had been flying to Paris with her nine-year-old son, Jay. Frank Carven found the ballroom where the families waited to be "a madhouse. Everybody was in charge and nobody was in charge." He sat down at a table amid the chaos.

"A few minutes later, Mychal Judge came up," Carven recalled. "We just started talking right then. He was very unassuming. I don't know how to explain it. You felt very comfortable, very safe in his presence. It was just an amazing thing with all this commotion and confusion going on around you. You felt things were going to be okay."

Carven told Judge he was a lapsed Catholic. Judge assured him, as he had others, "It's all in your heart. Your faith is in your heart."

Carven's mother, Ann, was in no mood to chat with a priest. Her daughter had married her first husband in the Church but divorced him, saying he was taking drugs. She then married an airline pilot outside the Church, only to leave him, telling her family he was a wife beater. She died believing she had been automatically excommunicated.

Ann Carven's sons were certain their mother would benefit from talking to this particular priest, but she kept refusing. Finally she told them, "I'll make a deal with you. The day they find my daughter's body is the day I'll speak to him."

The plane had exploded off the south shore of Long Island, the wreckage scattering over twenty-three square miles of ocean. The murky water ran cold and 120 feet deep. Only a few bodies had been recovered in the immediate aftermath.

"We sat there and we waited for sixteen days for bodies to be found, and all kinds of things happened," Judge later said.

On the fourth day, Giuliani asked Judge to organize a prayer service for all faiths to be held at Hangar 208 at the western edge of Kennedy Airport. More than two thousand attended. Each was handed a white rose by a white-gloved police officer as they entered. The names of the dead were read aloud and anguished cries echoed through the cavernous structure. Some of the grieving relatives collapsed to the concrete floor, convulsed in tears. Priests, ministers, and rabbis offered prayers in five languages.

By then 101 bodies had been recovered, and only forty-six had been identified. The families began to complain angrily about the pace of the search and identification. Governor George Pataki instructed the medical examiner to meet with them. Judge was there.

"It's about death, shock, and separation, not knowing if the bodies will be found, not knowing if they'll be able to see them, to touch them," he later said in an interview. "The medical examiner's report was quite graphic. People cried out loud. I found myself crying a number of times. I was feeling such pain with them. They told me stories about their daughter or son or husband or wife, and these people seemed so real to me that I couldn't believe they were dead. Someone's talking about a beautiful face that is now so broken, marred, and scarred."

On the fifth day, there was a memorial service at Smith's Point, the stretch of beach closest to the crash site. An ancient, universal impulse prompted the families to fashion a makeshift shrine in the sand with candles and photos and notes. Judge stood with them at the water's edge as they tossed in bouquets of flowers.

"The water is sacred to them," Judge later said.

The mourners could see the boats and helicopters of the continuing search offshore. The divers were from the U.S. Navy, the NYPD, and Long Island police departments, as well as an FDNY team supervised by Ray Downey, who had organized the recovery effort in Oklahoma. The fire department boats that responded included the *Kevin Kane,* named after the young firefighter who was Judge's first line-of-duty death. Among the divers was Paul Hashagan, who was quoted as saying of the arduous dives, "Just reminded me of the difficulties we face in a high-rise fire, where often you have to walk twenty or thirty stories and then go to work there."

Also on the team was Terry Hatton, who had dinner with Judge just hours before the crash. They were supposed to get together again on July 23, along with a woman Hatton had met while drinking Captain Drennan's No. 5 Amber at Chumley's bar. Beth Patrone also happened to be Giuliani's longtime personal assistant.

Instead, Judge was with the grieving families and Hatton was on a dive boat. Hatton would call Judge from a cell phone between descents into an underwater zone of sharp metal and literally miles of entangling wire where the visibility was as limited as in a fire. The dead would suddenly appear, their necks invariably snapped, the initial rigor mortis lapsed, the arms floating. The hands sometimes seemed to reach for the diver as he wrapped his arms around a victim. The two would then begin a long and intimate ascent, the diver gradually adjusting to the lessening pressure by rising no faster than the bubbles from his scuba gear.

At the hotel that evening, Judge offered a prayer service at 8:47 P.M., the exact time of the crash. He told the families that another kind of recovery had taken place at the very moment the plane exploded and plunged into the ocean.

"God is present, loving, smiling, having recovered our loved ones," he said. "They are in His presence illuminated by His smile, and warmed by His love. His kingdom is enriched this day, so enriched by so many beautiful souls. So much beauty. Our world is so empty without them. Our hearts are broken, our sadness immense, our tears so abundant."

He spoke as one of them, and nobody doubted it.

"We live our sorrow together."

Whenever a body was identified, the family would be summoned to a room on the sixth floor of the hotel. Among the recoveries was a flight attendant who had been on her maiden international flight, Jill Ann Ziemkiewicz. Her family met Cardinal O'Connor when he visited the hotel. They asked if the funeral could be held at the cathedral. As there were no Lutherans involved to confuse matters, O'Connor officiated at the flight attendant's funeral Mass. Judge was just one of several priests in attendance.

"Ah, Father Judge," O'Connor said on seeing him. "How good of you to come."

Judge continued to say a seven o'clock Mass each evening at a makeshift altar in a small courtyard at the back of the hotel, welcoming those of all faiths as the remaining families continued their vigil. He would remain at the Ramada late into the night.

"He would be walking around, sitting in the ballroom with family members," Frank Carven would recall. "Many of my talks with him were at one o'clock in the morning when I couldn't sleep. He'd still be there for anybody who wanted to talk to him. I thought he lived there."

In their early-morning chats, Judge would tell Carven about his Brooklyn childhood, about the city he loved, about his struggle with alcohol, and even about his shamrock tattoo.

"I'm not sure how it got there," Judge said. "But I'm sure it was a good idea at the time."

Carven had been away from the Church for thirty years, and in the midst of a horror that was enough to make anyone question God, this smiling priest with a shamrock on his butt proved to have more spiritual power than that entire august institution.

"Since I met that guy, I'm thinking, 'There's something to this,'" Carven would later say. "He was like no other Catholic priest I'd ever met."

• • •

Judge would return to the friary and find an answering machine full of messages from other people who needed him. He would grab a few hours' sleep,
attend to any pressing emergencies, and head back to the Ramada.

"There was so much confusion and pain and suffering and fear and finding bodies and not finding them and hopes and dreams and then going out to
the memorial services and throwing the flowers in and trying to pray and trying to hold hands and trying maybe to find something to say," Judge later
said.

On July 31, two weeks after the crash, a woman appeared at the seven P.M..
Mass and uttered her first words to Judge.

"Father, I'm Ann Carven."

"I know who you are."

"I just want you to know at one twenty-six today they did find my daughter's body."

"Isn't that wonderful!"

The two later talked of Paula and of her split with the Church.

"Somebody told her she was excommunicated," Carven said.

"We don't even use that word anymore," Judge replied.

Carven described Paula's troubles with her first husband, saying her daughter would have known not to marry him if they had lived together before.

"He said, 'That's right, she would have,'" Carven recalled. "I said, 'Here's
a priest saying she should have lived with a man.'"

Carven recounted her daughter coming to her after the second wedding,
saying her new husband had struck her. The mother had said if he hit her
once he would hit her twice. The only course to take was divorce.

"She said, 'How can I? It's a sin.' I said, 'I don't think God wanted that,'"
Carven remembered.

Judge was clear as to his views regarding Paula's relationship with God.

"He said, 'She's in heaven,'" Carven recalled. "I said, 'If you go before I
do, tell her to give me a phone call. I know *you're* going to heaven.'"

The next morning, Judge drove to La Guardia Airport to pick up Alvarado,
who had been visiting family back home in Mindanao. Alvarado settled beside him in the new official FDNY car.

"Come on, let's see your influence," Alvarado said half-jokingly. "I want to see your power."

"You want to see?" Judge asked.

He hit the lights and siren and off they roared through traffic.

"You know," he told Alvarado, "I could actually get into trouble for this."

Judge dropped Alvarado at his Bronx apartment and headed straight back to Kennedy Airport to see the TWA Flight 800 families.

A "Month's Mind" Mass was held at St. Patrick's Cathedral for the victims of the TWA crash. A Month's Mind is an Irish tradition in which people gather in remembrance a month after a death.

Afterward, the families were invited behind the altar and given flowers. O'Connor had mentioned Paula Carven and her young son during the Mass. Ann Carven now presented the cardinal with a photo of her daughter and Jay. Ann then gestured toward Judge, who stood a few feet away.

"I said, 'I'd like you to meet my friend Father Mychal Judge,'" Ann recalled. "[O'Connor] said, 'Uuugh.'"

The cardinal looked at Judge, needing to say nothing more.

"I said, 'Why don't you like my friend Father Judge?'" Ann recalled. "I told the cardinal he was wrong, Father Judge is very nice. My son, Sean, said, 'He's a great guy. He tells it like it is.'"

Ann looked over at Judge, who was looking at her.

"His hair was almost red he was so red."

Later, Ann chided Judge for not coming over.

"I said to Mychal, 'Why didn't you come over and meet your boss?'" Ann recalled. "He said, 'He really isn't my boss.'"

Judge added, "You should never have mentioned my name. We don't get along."

Ann replied, "I thought you got along with everybody."

Judge was technically correct in saying O'Connor was not his boss; the Order of Friars Minor was a separate entity ultimately answerable only to the Vatican. But a friar was only able to act as a priest within the the archdiocese with the cardinal's permission, which O'Connor would surely have loved to revoke in Judge's case if this exasperating Franciscan were not so well connected.

Judge had not forgotten that those connections all began with Steven Mc-Donald, who had become such an icon that he was invited to address the Republican National Convention that month in San Diego. McDonald asked Judge to come along.

Steven was instructed to submit his speech for review, and when the time came for him to rehearse speaking from a teleprompter, the screen scrolled Lincoln's Gettysburg Address. When his own speech was returned, he saw that it had been heavily edited. Virtually everything he had wanted to say was gone except some praise for Bob Dole.

"I said, 'Father Mike, did you see what they did to this?'" Steven recalled.

Judge here seemed to reach the limit of his ability to focus on only the good. He took the edited speech and stormed off to Haley Barbour, the Republican national chairman. His Franciscan robes greatly heightened the effect of his invective.

"He came up to me after and said, 'You know, Steven, I haven't used language like that in thirty years,'" Steven recalled.

The speech's sentiments about human life were restored, but the section about Northern Ireland stayed out. So did the bit about gun violence, perhaps because Steven was to be followed by the president of the National Rifle Association. This was one circumstance where Judge did not feel all was well, particularly when the Republicans indicated they would only pay part of Steven's hotel bill.

"Father Mike said to them, 'Listen, you invited him here. What are you doing, trying to leave him with the bill?'" Steven recalled.

The bill was paid.

After his return, Judge received a call from Frank Carvill, who had been an altar boy during Judge's first tenure at St. Joseph's in East Rutherford. Carvill's father had died, and he was turning to Judge for consolation. Judge immediately drove to New Jersey. As night gathered, they sat together talking, two men whose fates would be strangely linked by two towers that shone in the distance.

Carvill was now a paralegal. On that September morning five years later he would leave his office in the North Tower just before the plane hit. Judge would perish in that same tower.

Carvill would end up going to Iraq with his New Jersey National Guard unit, and he would be killed in a bomb and grenade attack after giving up his regular home leave for a young soldier who had a death in the family. Carvill's funeral would be held in the same church where he had served Judge as an altar boy. The street where Carvill lived would be renamed Frank T. Carvill Way, just as the block where Judge lived would be renamed Father Mychal F. Judge Street.

Over a dozen firefighters who would later die at the World Trade Center gathered at the quarters of Rescue 4 for the plaque dedication marking the first anniversary of Peter McLaughlin's death. Among them was young Tom Foley, perhaps the only rodeo star in the FDNY and one of *People* magazine's sexiest men alive. He had been broken in as a probie by McLaughlin, just as McLaughlin had been broken in by Brown.

"You knew when [McLaughlin] was there you would never get hurt," Foley said. "Some people, they never notice if it's a sunny day out. Me, I go out there, take a deep breath, thank God I'm alive. What I believe is, I'm only here for a short time."

Paddy Brown stood nearby, still unable to shake the feeling he was responsible for McLaughlin's death. Judge said the Mass at a makeshift altar. He was looking at Brown as he reminded the assembled firefighters of the holiness of their calling.

"You go where God wants you to go," Judge said.

Brown and Foley and the others knew it was just a question of time before the next loss, though there was a beautiful silence after Valentino's name was read at the annual FDNY Memorial gathering the next day. The department had suffered eleven deaths in the two years following the Watts Street fire, but now it had gone eight wonderful months without a fatality.

Vina felt sure that if God was sending her anywhere, it was to continue advocating fire prevention as the way to keep another firefighter from joining the list at the next memorial. She saw it as her big chance when she was invited to speak at the annual Fire Safety Foundation benefit on the *Intrepid*. Tables were going for ten thousand dollars, and five hundred of the city's top business leaders were expected. She sat on her bed surrounded by scribbled thoughts that boiled out of her. How dare we make fire safety a charity? How do we bury one dead firefighter after another and not change the system? How dare you rich insurance moguls give out fire safety coloring books when you collect your premiums from such agony and not change this? How dare you fire chiefs permit all these medals glorifying this failure of prevention? How do we ignore the nineteen New York City babies that died in fires already this year?

She decided if she were that blunt, she would only offend. She submitted a draft in advance that was meant to persuade, but apparently this was still too strong. She waited and waited in her seat beside Judge long past the point in the program where she was supposed to speak. She was called dead last, as people were getting up to leave.

The more unwelcome she felt, the more determined she had become, and she gave her "Carelessness Kills" speech with all she had. Her hands were trembling when she sat down. She was exhausted.

"You die after you give it your all, every time," Judge told her. "You do. It drains everything out of you."

Absent from the audience of big shots was the person Vina most wanted to persuade, the firefighter who had become her best friend, Paddy Brown. Vina's greatest hope, continual and unreasoning, was that she might somehow manage to convince him to join her quest.

She knew he was righteous at heart. He often had cuts and bruises from spending his off-hours teaching karate to the blind. He made sure to patronize the last surviving mom-and-pop coffee shop in his neighborhood. He always tipped delivery boys five dollars no matter how small the order.

And he seemed immune to peer pressure. He would bicycle to work in Spandex shorts and bring his purple yoga mat to the firehouse and try to get his men to join him, once convincing a mountain of a firefighter named Mike Moran to attempt a "downward facing dog" position on the apparatus floor. He would ask for the no-fat balsamic dressing on his salad. He had a Mickey Mouse phone in his apartment, and he was just now taking up the piano. The teacher arrived the first day asking for "little Patrick" and he answered, "That's me!"

And he certainly did not worry about the bosses, who more than once said they were unsure whether to give him a medal or bring charges for his listening only to his own keen and fearless sense at a fire. He was bounced from Rescue 1 after he went on TV and asked the mayor to come down to the firehouse to listen to the men's grievances.

But, at heart, Paddy Brown was a warrior who had come back from Vietnam shocked by the violence of combat. He never forgot the hurt of being called a babykiller when he got home. He had become a paragon among baby savers.

To him, firefighters who died fighting fires died confronting an element of creation turned to roaring destruction, a symbol of life gone deadly. Those who battled it were champions of human life in whatever manifestation, quick to risk all on even the chance somebody needed to be rescued, be that person a dope fiend or a dignitary. They were not holy men, but their actions were holy, and it was what a firefighter did at a fire that mattered, not what sparked the fire.

Brown bristled on hearing that Vina was saying that firefighters needed to be protected from their own courage and that the Drennan medal should be given for prevention rather than valor.

"Vina's getting kind of, you know, nuts," Brown told a friend.

Brown did not say this to Judge, who was in attendance at the City Hall ceremony where the Hundred Year Association of New York bestowed on Brown a public service award, honoring him as the most decorated member of the FDNY. Brown stood resplendent in his dress uniform with a Marine Corps pin on his chest next to the rows of medal ribbons for saving lives. Judge marked the October 30 event as "Pat Brown Day" in his appointment book.

On the early morning of November 25, Judge's pager sent him to a five-alarm blaze at a hotel turned homeless shelter in Upper Manhattan. The fire had apparently been started by a blind tenant who was burning incense on a dresser. A grandfather clause in the city law had exempted the building owners from having to install sprinklers. Trapped residents were at the sixth-floor windows when the firefighters arrived.

"I'm not going to burn!" a woman screamed.

"Don't jump! Don't jump!" voices screamed from below.

Flames shot out past her and she jumped.

"I'm burning!"

She hit the concrete six floors below with a sickening hollow sound. Paramedics fought in vain to revive her as firefighters rushed to save the others. Their effort would be documented in a department history written by Firefighter Paul Hashagen. A firefighter from Ladder 28 ascended a hundred-foot aerial ladder, whose top rung just reached the sill of a window where another woman and a man were poised to jump. A child safety gate blocked the lower half of the window, and the firefighter straddled it, one boot on the top rung of the ladder, the other on the windowsill as he helped the pair to safety. They informed the firefighter that two other people were trapped inside. He was about to go in after them when he saw two different people pop their heads out of windows of the neighboring apartment.

The firefighter knew that these two might very well end up jumping before he made the other rescue. He called for the ladder to be shifted over and he helped the people in the window to safety. He then dove into this apartment rather than wait for the ladder to be returned to the first window.

Other companies inside the blazing building made numerous rescues and prevented at least a half-dozen more from jumping. Rescue 3 saved five civilians, three of them unconscious. They then encountered John Duddy, the firefighter from Ladder 28 who had pitched himself in from atop the aerial ladder. They helped Duddy pull yet another unconscious victim to safety.

By the time the blaze was out, three of the two hundred residents had perished, but very likely dozens more would have died had the firefighters just fought the blaze from the safety of the street. Judge left having witnessed both the results of carelessness such as Vina decried and courage such as Brown exemplified.

"Firefighters ask me to bless them," Judge said. "But I feel blessed by them."

20

Giuliani had been scheduled to attend the gathering at the *Intrepid* where Vina spoke, but the Yankees had a championship game that night. Giuliani was the team's self-appointed number-one fan, telling people he had worn a Yankees uniform during his early years in Brooklyn, when rooting for anybody but the Dodgers was viewed as sacrilege. He often told of a day some of the local kids supposedly tried to hang him.

"Is that all?" asked Judge, ever the Brooklyn boy.

This year, the Yankees went on to win the 1996 World Series and Giuliani arranged for a big ticker-tape parade up the stretch of Broadway known as the Canyon of Heroes. Judge remained a true Brooklyn Dodgers fan, but there was no denying the Yankees knew how to play ball and a ticker-tape parade was a ticker-tape parade. He went with Alvarado, one of only a dozen "ALA" entries in Judge's 1996 appointment book. The 1997 book shows he did start the New Year by helping Alvarado move into a new apartment on Grambling Avenue in the Bronx, but he had ever more demands on his time. People left so many messages, he wore out another answering machine.

The two had a quarrel—"ALA—WALK OUT"—though Alvarado seemed to reconcile himself again to a situation that held no promise of changing—"ALA—OK." Judge worried aloud to Alvarado how the McDonalds would respond if they knew he was gay, in particular the truly sainted Steven, who seemed to need his faith almost as much as his ventilator to continue. And Judge was beginning to consider his AA sponsee, Michael Walker, as the son he never had. Judge feared that any hint of gayness would prompt Walker to think he had some other agenda. He was no less concerned about how the firefighters would take it.

"I would say, 'Isn't that difficult?'" Alvarado remembered. "He would say, 'Yes, it is.'"

Judge also had other worries, and when his anxiety was more than he could relieve with the priestly resort to prayer, he sometimes sought out his fellow Franciscan Brian Carroll in the friary. Carroll later recalled nights when there would come a knock at his door. Judge would enter in a state such as Carroll had never seen him at Siena.

"I just did a rosary, but I'm feeling anxious," Judge would say. "I'm just full of anxiety."

The cause was sometimes personal, other times a bit of friction with some other friar, or as Carroll recalls Judge saying, "That fucking fuck downstairs." More often it was an impending talk before a gathering of one sort or another.

"Who am I to do this? I can't do this," Judge would say. "I'm not a good speaker. I'm not that smart."

The two friars would set out on long walks through the city and the anxiety would begin to fall away. The next day, Carroll would ask how the talk had gone.

"They loved it," Judge would invariably report.

But at the approach of the next talk, there would again come a knock at Carroll's door and the two friars would again set out walking. They often ambled up Fifth Avenue, past the New York Public Library and the two stone lions. Judge told Carroll that Mayor La Guardia had dubbed the uptown lion Patience, the downtown one Fortitude, two qualities he thought would guide New Yorkers through the Great Depression.

Those were two qualities Judge relied upon in his dealings with O'Connor, whose cathedral the two friars would approach as they walked on.

"It'd be the easiest job in the world being cardinal," Judge said to Carroll as they paused outside St. Patrick's Cathedral late one night. "Just go out and be with the people. Can you imagine what you could do with that kind of power? You could turn the city around!"

As exasperated as Judge became, however intolerant and intolerable the cardinal and the those Big Fat Monsignors, the BFMs, might be, Carroll knew what Alvarado knew: Judge could never leave the priesthood.

"The Church to him was flesh and blood," Carroll said.

• • •

The Brooklyn fire chaplain, Monsignor Brady, was of the Church the way an old-time Brooklyn desk sergeant was of the department, and he considered Judge to be a showboater suffused with vanity and sorely lacking in respect for the institution he was supposed to represent and serve. He made clear he had little use for his Manhattan counterpart whom he called "the Franciscan."

Judge nevertheless attended the farewell party at the Knights of Columbus Hall on Nostrand Avenue after Brady decided the death of Louis Valentino had been one too many fire tragedies and resolved to step down. Judge of an earlier time would have been rattled by Brady's scowl. Instead, Judge seemed simply to accept Brady's disapproval for what it was.

"He can't stand me," Judge later said. "But I am sure he is a very good man."

Brady seemed so different from him that Judge did not seem to consider that he, too, might come to the point where he could bear no more heartbreak.

Three days later, Judge accompanied the Flight 800 families on a visit to the hangar where fifty thousand bits of the jetliner that had been retrieved from the ocean were being pieced together. Judge was excused from having to sign the waiver presented to the 160 other visitors pledging not to file suit for any mental anguish that might result. He had not personally suffered a loss, and as a chaplain he was presumed to be unperturbed by such things.

Inside the huge structure, the family members filed past what remained of the center fuel tank and the engines and such surreal bits of wreckage as a steel toilet bowl made convex by whatever triggered the blast. Most maintained their composure until they came to the reconstructed passenger cabin. The seats had been set in rows on a black felt carpet like pews in a starkly grim cathedral.

Some of the seats were shockingly intact. Others were burned and twisted and torn. Most still had armrests bearing the seat numbers, and relatives were able to determine exactly where their loved one had been sitting. These included a woman whose tissue and bone fragments had just been identified the day before through DNA gleaned from hairs the family found on a pair of socks in a clothes hamper.

The relatives gazed at these empty seats, their sobs echoing in the hangar as they placed the white roses where their loved ones had been. The seats seemed to fill with all that the families missed so desperately, all they still could not believe was gone forever. To Judge it seemed a congregation of souls.

The only refuge from the unbelievable was in belief, and Judge comforted Catholics and Protestants and Jews alike. The one concrete question nobody could answer with confidence was what had brought down the airplane. Investigators had determined that an explosion had taken place around aisle 23, directly over the center fuel tank. They had also noted that the surrounding metal did not have the type of tearing and pitting that could be expected from a bomb. The damage was more consistent with a gaseous explosion.

Boeing was insisting that such an accident was impossible, and the FBI had all but decided early on that the crash was the result of terrorism. The victims included the wife of a well-liked FBI agent, and his colleagues had responded as law enforcement people usually do. They looked for a bad guy.

The only actual connection to terrorism turned out to be that the plane was delayed while airport security personnel traced an unaccounted-for piece of luggage as a precaution against a bomb. The result was that the plane sat on the hot runway, the heat causing vapors to build up in the almost empty center tank. An arcing spark from the corroded wires of a fuel pump then apparently caused the vapors to explode.

The final determination was still months away and some would later say that the TWA case distracted the FBI from investigations that otherwise might have prevented the attack on the World Trade Center, where the use of DNA to identify a bit of bone or flesh would become routine.

Judge continued to move between the twin towers of his own existence, between two lives lived as one. He went with Michael Mulligan for brunch at the very gay Food Bar and later went with firefighters to Connolly's bar to hear the Irish band Black 47. Another day, he proceeded from a memorial Mass for the victims of AIDS to a lunch for firefighters in AA. His immediately apparent conflicts were only ones of scheduling, as on the night he had planned to go from a meeting of the Gay Men's Health Crisis to an Elks Lodge on Staten Island for an annual FDNY event organized by one of the city's first women firefighters, a mother of three named Judy Beyer.

On other years, Judge had always managed to make it to the Staten Island event and give a benediction, but he was unable to extricate himself from the GMHC event in time. He telephoned Beyer the next day with an apology.

In March, Judge attended two fortieth-birthday parties, one for Steven McDonald, the other for Michael Mulligan. The party for McDonald was at his suburban house, and the invitation featured a photo of him when he was not yet in kindergarten. The party for Mulligan was at Vong, a French-Thai fusion restaurant.

The following evening Judge went to the Park Avenue Christian Church for the Oiche Aerach III, the third annual Lavender and Green dinner, a "celebration of Irish and Gay Life." He was not among the thirty-five gay activists who were arrested two mornings later, once again protesting their group's exclusion from the St. Patrick's Day parade.

Judge marched in his chaplain's uniform with the FDNY. At noon the parade went still and observed a minute of silence in honor of the 1.5 million who perished during the famine 150 years before. The moment passed, and Liam Flaherty called for the pipes and drums to strike up "Gary Owen," the tune they played after a fallen brother was borne away.

Judge joined the band at a postparade gathering in the basement of Loyola Ignatius Church. He laughed and sang Irish songs, and all that seemed to set him apart from the guys was the absence of a beer in his hand.

On Palm Sunday, Judge and Alvarado flew to England for their first vacation together. They spent Holy Week walking the London streets in sandals and returned to New York with a poster from the National Portrait Gallery.

Judge headed off to a memorial Mass marking the third anniversary of the Watts Street fire. Vina had been unsure she wanted to attend, but several firefighters had told her that her absence would be taken as a sign of disrespect.

After the Mass at St. Anthony's Church on Sullivan Street, Vina was not anxious to join the firefighters at the firehouse for food, so Judge whisked her off to a little Greenwich Village spot called Triplets. She wrote:

"He gives me permission to never go again and we laugh at how simple it all really is. We talk seriously about guilt and fear. It's a conversation we have often. Mychal lets me go on and on. He knows I feel so alienated from God and he doesn't try to change my mind."

The forty days following the anniversary of the Watts Street fire brought the full bloom of spring. Judge took an evening walk with Paddy Brown up into Central Park. The two men paused at the top of the Great Lawn, gazing beyond the broad expanse of grass and the trees to the spires of Midtown Manhattan.

Brown had come here often, jogging or on a bicycle, and he had marked the spot with a small X on a map of the park. Here was where he wanted his ashes scattered should anything happen to him.

"There's a beautiful view of the Manhattan skyline which looks really cool at night," Brown wrote in a letter to his brother that was to be opened only in the event of his death.

Brown did not have to say that Judge would officiate. That was a given.

On the anniversary of Drennan's death, Judge was attending the annual "safety conference" of the fire officers' union at the Villa Roma resort outside Callicoon. He was the life of the hospitality room even if he did not imbibe in what one fire captain termed "free beer, free booze, and everything."

"He was one of the guys," union trustee Mike Currid recalled. "We loved having him there. At least I know one guy who was definitely getting into heaven."

Judge went along on the inner-tube float down the Delaware River, gazing up to see the imposing stone tower still standing atop the hill in Callicoon.

He had heard that the seminary had been shut in 1972 for a lack of seminarians. The building and grounds had been sold to the federal government for a Job Corps facility, and the statue of Saint Joseph holding the Christ Child had been carted away to a nunnery in the Bronx, which subsequently shut as well. The chapel had become a game room where disadvantaged urban youths shot pool.

Where the altar had stood a giant TV screen now flickered with images not even graven, that had become the modern idols, actors who were worshipped like the shapeshifting gods of distant times.

• • •

The first Captain John J. Drennan Memorial Medal was to be awarded on June 4. Judge offered a prayer from the steps of City Hall at the annual FDNY Medal Day ceremony. Firefighter Vernon Cherry led the singing of the national anthem with a pure and soaring voice, a moment many would recall after he was killed at the Twin Towers.

Vina was sitting among the officials on the dais, and when the time came she rose to present the new medal named after her husband. The first recipient was Firefighter Kevin Sherod of Engine Co. 225, who had been off duty when he saw smoke coming from a home in Queens. He had charged into the house and crawled without any firefighting gear through what the citation described as "punishing conditions." He had emerged with an elderly woman who had been trapped in the rear.

The crowd applauded and cheered this firefighter whose actions had been just what John Drennan would have most admired. Vina still wished the medal could have been stamped not with VALOR but with PREVENTION or simply COMMON SENSE.

Her ire had only increased when she learned three years after the fire that there had been no smoke detectors at 62 Watts Street, where her husband and the two other firefighters were roasted alive.

"There was an occupant at home on the second floor," she wrote in her book. "She would have heard the alarm. The fire would never have had time to smolder for so long, building in its intensity.

> *A $10.00 smoke detector and Jimmy Young would be eating Sunday dinner with his family, Christopher would be fixing up that car he had in his yard. I wouldn't be a widow . . . We have to stop reacting to fires only after they start . . . It's time FDNY to stop your crying over dead firefighters. Tears are hollow when each could have been prevented with just common sense.*
>
> *Had Ladder 5/Engine 24 gone out doing these mundane boring jobs we might have saved our tears and heartache. "Knock, knock, Mr. Landlord of Watts Street, does your building have smoke detectors?" Knock on those doors. Do those boring, unglamorous jobs where there is no recognition and no medal.*

Judge took Vina's anger at the fire department much as he did the anger of so many other grieving souls over the years. He seemed just as sure there would be a reconciliation, that ultimately all would be well, even though Vina seemed to be growing only more angry, even though more firefighters than Paddy Brown were wondering despite themselves if she was becoming a kind of heretic, if she were indeed "getting a little nuts."

21

Judge had an opportunity to demonstrate his own bravery and bring together manifestations of goodness from all the facets of his life at an upcoming dinner dance at Antun's catering hall in Queens, marking the thirty-fifth anniversary of the FDNY Pipes and Drums band. He was to be one of three Irishmen of the Year, and as an honoree he was allowed to fill a table with guests of his choosing. Vina was off giving her fire safety speech, but he invited his sisters and Steven and Patti Ann McDonald, the friars Michael Duffy and Jude Murphy as well as Tom and Noreen Ferriter from New Jersey, and Michael Walker, "MW" on the list in his appointment book right next to "ALA." There was also "Mulligan" and "Brendan—Tom."

ALA was, as always, Al Alvarado. Mulligan was Michael Mulligan. Brendan was Irish-born gay activist Brendan Fay. Tom was Brendan's live-in partner, pediatrician Tom Moulton. Brendan was stunned when Judge telephoned to invite them.

"I remember he called me and I said, 'No, this can't be right. This guy can't be mixing these two worlds. He's making a mistake,'" Fay recalled.

Judge acted as unperturbed as Paddy Brown facing a four-alarm blaze, but the underlying apprehension could only have added to the physical stress of his unrelenting schedule. He had still not completely recovered his strength from the botched surgery the year before, and he suffered a physical collapse five days after Medal Day and five days before the June 13 pipe band dinner. He went this time to St. Vincent's Medical Center.

Judge would have needed only to stay in his hospital bed to bow out of the event, but when the day arrived he discharged himself and returned to the friary with enough time to take a quick rest and don the kilt the band had given him for Christmas. He was still feeling so weak he asked Michael

Walker to drive the department car despite prohibitions against civilians taking the wheel. They set off with Erin and the fellow friar Jude in the backseat. They were nearing the toll to the Midtown Tunnel when a car cut them off. Judge reached over and hit the siren in a rare spasm of road rage.

Judge was uncharacteristically curt, as close to ill-tempered as Walker had seen him. "He was anxious about something," Walker later said. "I'm not sure exactly what it was."

The hall at Antun's was packed with a sellout crowd of eight hundred. The table for Judge's guests was at the center of it all, with Erin and Alvarado and Walker and the McDonalds and the friars and the friends from Jersey as well as a pair of Wall Street financiers from AA, along with Mulligan and Fay and Moulton. Fay looked around at the hundreds of firefighters and their wives.

"I said, 'This crowd would hate me. I'm their enemy,' " Fay recalled.

Judge himself was seated on the dais with the two other honorees and nine assorted dignitaries. The first presentation of the evening was to him: a large clock fitted with a cord so he could hang it around his neck. Everyone who knew him, family and friends, straight and gay, firefighter and no, laughed as one, for he was famously tardy in all the realms he traveled. He was also known by all to be intensely proud of his Irishness, and they understood how deeply he was stirred when the honorees were called to the floor for the Circle of Honor. A ring of pipes and drums formed around them as if in ancient ritual and sent up a rousing set.

"That would raise the hair on the back of your neck," fellow honoree Bill Whelan of the Emerald Society would recall. "It's indescribable. I couldn't have words to tell you how it feels."

After the pipe band was done and the last of the speeches ended and dinner was over, a dance band began to play. Judge stepped down from the dais and voices called to him from every direction. He was swarmed by people wanting his attention.

"He never had a minute to enjoy himself," Whelan recalled. "Every time I turned around he was surrounded."

Judge eventually reached his table of guests. Paddy Brown and Terry Hatton came over and seemed only delighted to meet everybody. Fay was still amazed to find himself and Moulton and Mulligan in a hall full of firefighters who seemed to feel that anybody who was good enough for their beloved padre was good enough for them.

"I said, 'This is a frigging miracle,'" Fay recalled. "And then Mychal said, 'Get up and dance!' And we did."

Fay, Moulton, and Mulligan got to their feet along with Walker and most of the others and formed a circle of fun, moving together but each in his or her own particular way to the music, the dance floor the equivalent of Judge's theology. Steven McDonald surely would have joined if he was able to.

"Steven always *loved* to dance," Patti Ann said later. "And he could really move."

Judge just as surely would have declined to dance even if he was not still feeling ill. He had no Peter Daly to urge him on, and he had long since fallen back into a trepidation of assuming physical shapes in response to his own impulses. He had told Walker that dancing was the one thing that terrified him, that somebody had once made fun of him and he had never gotten over it.

Perhaps his deeper fear was not of being mocked but of being really seen, of becoming fully himself, in front of all these people as he had in the dance class at Canterbury, when he had danced beyond self-consciousness and constraint. He was not ready to move here as freely as the others in the happy and diverse circle, giving exercise not just to limbs but to urge, wish, inclination, yen, desire, whim, fancy.

The shapeshifter could be simultaneously one thing to the McDonalds and another to Mulligan and maybe anybody else, all of whom were sure they knew him to the core, but he could not assume the shapes dictated solely by his own prompting beat by beat. He was not ready to reveal his full self even to Walker.

Even so, Judge was undeniably brave not only to include Alvarado, Fay, Moulton, and Mulligan at his table but to rouse them to be all the more visible. Fay, who was by temperament an in-your-face activist, decided that Judge was accomplishing something that militants could never do.

"[The militants] never built a bridge," Fay later said. "Mychal Judge did probably the most amazing thing of all: opening doors and bringing all of the people together."

The priest who so loved the Brooklyn Bridge seemed to feel he was at least beginning to build a span between the shores of his own life. The anxiety appeared to leave him as his friends danced and laughed with the others.

"At the end of the night, he was fine," Walker recalled.

Walker assumed the gays were connected to Judge's AIDS work and attributed his inclusion of them at this event to an Irish streak that runs much deeper than Catholicism.

"He had that kind of rebel in him," Walker said.

Two nights after the gathering, on June 15, 1997, Judge responded to a five-alarm fire at the century-old St. Philip Neri Church on the Grand Concourse in the Bronx. More than thirty companies responded as the stained glass in the front shattered and flames exploded from the interior. The supervising chief at the scene ordered the firefighters back out when the structure was deemed in danger of collapse.

Commissioner Von Essen was there, technically the boss but by tradition and practice expected to cede to the chief. Von Essen nevertheless went ahead and asked men from Rescue 3 to help him lug statues of the Blessed Mother, St. Anthony, and St. Philip Neri from within the collapse zone. The chief chastised Von Essen for putting men in harm's way for the sake of some plaster. Judge would later say he could not help but admire the faith that drove the commissioner, the God that was in his heart, however crowded it and all human hearts might be with other impulses.

But this happened to be Father's Day, and Judge could well imagine the horrible impact on the families if these men had been killed. He knew that any unresolved family issues would leave a legacy of hurt.

Judge had heard rumors that one of Von Essen's sons was gay and that the commissioner had been having considerable difficulty accepting his son's sexuality. Judge paid a visit to Von Essen's office at fire headquarters, entering as a chaplain who was revered and respected by the firefighters as none other in the department's history, who was accepted in firehouses as if he were one of their own.

"What would you say if I told you I was gay?" Judge asked.

Von Essen would later say he was not shocked; he had heard talk. He had also noted that sexual orientation did not keep Judge from being the priest all priests should be, not to mention a regular guy.

"It doesn't bother me," Von Essen said.

"I just wanted you to know," Judge said.

Maybe, as Von Essen believes, Judge was simply trying to address gossip that had been going around since he became chaplain, "just to alert me about his sexual orientation."

More likely, the unspoken message Judge was trying to impart was *If a guy like me who is welcome in any firehouse is gay . . .* Von Essen confided in him about his son and about his initial difficulties of accepting what he had thought was a sickness.

"Coming from the macho world of firefighters," Von Essen would say of his mind-set. "'How did it happen to me?' It's a disease."

Von Essen was on the way to acceptance and "beginning to feel better about my son." Judge furthered this when women would gush over this handsome priest while he was in the commissioner's company. Judge would speak under his breath to the commissioner.

"If they only knew."

Von Essen would laugh, Judge having magically converted gayness into the kind of running inside joke a firefighter could love.

Those who did not know included virtually all of FDNY and Vina and the other fire families, as well as the McDonalds and Brian Mulheren, parishioners in New Jersey, and so many of the others who also considered Judge to be one of their own. He seemed to them to be as close as any mortal could be to Christ on earth, and they did not even think of him as a sexual being, much less as gay.

The very fact he could inspire them to believe caused him to fear that if he broke that spell they would feel betrayed and lose their faith. That they did not suspect, even after seeing his spectrum of guests get up and dance at the Emerald Society dinner, suggested how determinedly they believed their shapeshifting priest to be who they needed him to be.

Judge appeared to elicit nary a raised eyebrow as he and Alvarado ate at their favorite Korean restaurant and went to the movies together. They seemed able to do just about anything with little worry about scandal as long as nobody came out and said they were having sex.

An extremely public demonstration of what can transpire following public allegations of sex came in August, when *Vanity Fair* magazine published an article alleging that Mayor Giuliani was having an extramarital affair with his closest aide.

Cristyne Lategano had been an assistant manager at a running-shoe store when she volunteered for Giuliani's mayoral campaign. She rose quickly, becoming press secretary and then director of communications. She was constantly at his side, and Judge often encountered her in emergency rooms when Giuliani arrived to see an injured firefighter.

"I would be so happy to see [Judge] and then it would hit me: If he's here, it must be bad," she later said.

Rumors had abounded. There had been a news report that Giuliani had escorted Lategano when she went shopping for a skirt. But until the *Vanity Fair* article nobody had publicly said that Giuliani's relationship with Lategano was sexual. The ensuing uproar persisted even after there proved to be factual errors in the magazine's account of exactly when the supposed affair began. Nobody seemed to pay much attention to the denials from Giuliani and Lategano, or to an aide who suggested theirs was "an affair of the spirit."

Judge apparently felt that Giuliani could fend for himself, but he worried for Lategano and hand-delivered a note urging her to be strong and to know that people loved her. He seemed to take the matter personally.

"He said, 'Don't let them get you down. It'll make you stronger,'" Lategano recalled.

The very next page in the appointment book shows that Judge devoted most of a day to what truly was an "affair of the spirit." He and Alvarado did nothing memorable, which is to say they did what Judge seemed to want more than anything.

The next month, on September 11 to be exact, they went to Vermont and stayed at a bed-and-breakfast that allowed Alvarado to bring his new dog. Judge for once actually seemed to enjoy being away from the city. Alvarado was in earthly heaven, but he restrained himself from asking Judge to go off with him somewhere for the rest of their lives. Alvarado knew part of Judge might want to say yes, but he would be compelled to say no,

"I think he spent most of his life in purgatory," Alvarado later said.

They were back in New York by the morning of September 13. Judge had to attend a ceremony in which a fledgling friar formally took the vows of poverty, obedience, and chastity. The day had long passed since the order would induct forty or more new priests at a time. The last sizable group had been fourteen in 1971. Ten had been ordained over the next two years, but then the numbers dropped to single digits.

The sight of a lone inductee into their graying ranks was less worrisome to some witnesses than seeing that many of the friars appeared ground down by the daily challenge of maintaining reverence in the face of indifference. The friary sometimes felt less like a religious community than an extremely tidy but forlorn boardinghouse such as Judge's mother had run. Only, these boarders were not going to move on when they met the right girl or got a better job.

Judge still had that other, vibrant religious order. Firefighters from the firehouse across the street were in the friary, expressing their devotion to him by painting his room even as he witnessed the taking of solemn vows in the upper church. Vina came by with a box of Christmas lights as the holidays neared, and they went out to buy a tree that twinkled in his window over the last days of the year.

In the last hours of 1997, Judge made his way down to an area at the South Street Seaport that had been reserved that night for the FDNY. He stood at the harbor's edge, gazing heavenward as the people around him counted down the final seconds of a year when there had been not a single line-of-duty death.

22

The New Year began with Giuliani's inauguration for a second term. Judge was surprised to see that Vina was not among the guests. She had been at the center of Giuliani's first line-of-duty tragedy, and he had pledged at her husband's funeral to watch over her through all the days to come. She had made a campaign commercial for him. Judge felt sure if she had not been invited it must have been an oversight.

In March, Judge was not at all surprised when Vina did not attend the Mass marking the fourth anniversary of the Watts Street fire. But some of the firefighters grumbled. One asked her, "The church was full. Where were you?" They did not understand, as she told Judge, "Every day is March 28 for me."

Vina did attend a fire safety press conference at which the FDNY announced it was distributing 23,000 smoke detector batteries and otherwise greatly expanding its fire safety program. The department was responding to an audit by City Comptroller Alan Hevesi, which found that while crime was way down under Giuliani, fire deaths remained higher than in most major cities. Hevesi credited Vina Drennan with prompting the audit. She had opened his eyes about fire safety during a lunch he had with her and Mychal Judge. She now said much the same things at the press conference.

"If each month in our country an airplane, a 747, fell into the sea, we would spend millions of dollars finding out why," she was quoted as saying. "Well, each month in our country, that many people die because of fire. And we do nothing."

Her remarks were in the next morning's *New York Times* when Judge met Brown for brunch at Zinno's. Brown still did not tell Judge that he thought Vina was becoming "a little nuts." Both men knew why she had not gone to the Watts Street memorial. Both also keenly felt the absence of a family life as they sat among the brunching couples.

Judge was coming to his sixty-fifth birthday on May 11, a milestone celebrated with a party arranged by Brian Mulheren, the former night mayor. The gathering was at Il Campanello, across from the friary. Judge was told to invite whomever he wanted, and the diversity outdid his table at the pipe band dinner, now including fellow priests and homeless people and Wall Street bigs and Siena alumni and AA pals along with buddies from his Brooklyn childhood. Many of his favorite firefighters were there, as were Vina and Jean Willis and, of course, Dympna and Erin.

When the cake came out, they all sang "Happy Birthday" in one voice and cheered when Judge blew out the candles. He was asked if he had made a wish and he gazed smiling about at so many of his favorite faces, seeming at that moment, anyway, like someone who yearned for nothing at all.

"I couldn't think of anything more than this," he said.

At eleven A.M. on June 3, Judge once again represented the Almighty at the Medal Day ceremony on the steps of City Hall. He failed to note that several high-ranking city officials moved their assigned seats away from Vina when she took a seat on the dais. Vina was puzzled but said nothing. She watched as the Drennan Medal and fifty-one other decorations were awarded for acts of valor that truly were remarkable. Giuliani declared the firefighters were "greater heroes than the Yankees!"

Two dozen firefighters proceeded uptown from Medal Day to an outdoor café in a park behind the public library and its twin lions, Patience and Fortitude. They there became the personification of Drunk and Disorderly. They passed lewd remarks. They chased women into the ladies' room. They exposed themselves. They urinated in the park. A bloody brawl erupted, and the police had to break it up.

"Like nothing I've ever seen before in my life," a patron said of the firefighters.

Judge could not just excuse such a rampage by citing medal-worthy acts.

He knew it would lend credence to the view among some that firefighters were at best a collection of overgrown kids and at worst a bunch of racist, sexist, and homophobic louts. He could imagine what such men might say about their beloved padre if they knew he was gay.

Judge felt the shame still hanging over the entire department two days later, as he headed for Ladder 6 to preside at a memorial Mass marking the anniversary of Lener's death. But the two dozen rowdies were momentarily forgotten as everyone remembered Lener and the ten others of the FDNY who died in a terrible twenty-four-month period that ended with Valentino's death in 1996. The department had now gone twenty-eight months without a firefighter being killed in a blaze. Everyone on the job knew that the lucky run had to end.

"We're in that type of business," said special operations chief Ray Downey.

That evening, at 8:40 P.M., Judge was notified that the FDNY's luck had turned bad in a horrific moment on Atlantic Avenue in Brooklyn.

An alarm had come in for a fire in one of a row of wood-frame houses. The first responding units were informed over the radio that they were racing toward a 10-75, a confirmed fire.

"We knew we were going to work," Lt. Timmy Stackpole later said.

The firefighters arrived to see a family standing in the street, screaming that the elderly grandmother was trapped on the blazing second floor. Stackpole was among those who charged inside.

"We went straight for the woman on the second floor," he recounted. "We crawled through the smoke, knocking down the visible fire with the hose, pushing farther into the apartment."

The firefighters were unaware that fire in the adjoining building was breaching the common wall on the first floor. The flames burst through directly below Stackpole and the others, flaring with the sudden supply of oxygen. A load-bearing wall had been illegally removed during renovations, and the floor suddenly gave way.

"We fell ten feet into a crackling orange furnace," Stackpole recounted. "Everyone was screaming. I could hear prayers. One of them was my own. I thought of my kids, my wife, my family. Then *boom!* I landed. I could hear guys shouting around me. Then the debris just fell on top of us: radiators, refrigerators, timbers, walls, flooring, furniture. Buried. I had on my Scott Air-Pak mask so I could breathe. But I thought no one would ever find us."

He found himself pinned by burning debris.

"Most of my legs were melted off," he would say. "The pain was excruciating. The building was still coming down on top of us and we were all burning and we were praying."

Above the trapped firefighters, four dozen of their comrades were doing all they could to answer those prayers, at the same time praying a further collapse would not bury them as well.

"When each rescuer's still got a chance of being killed and they're still digging us out," Stackpole said, "it was the most beautiful thing I ever saw."

The rescuers were unable to reach Lt. James Blackmore in time to save the forty-eight-year-old father of four. Another officer was carried out still alive, but burned beyond recognition. He had been filling in at Ladder 176, and in their shock the firefighters at first could not remember his name when reporting to the command post.

"It's not LaPiedra, is it?" Chief Downey asked.

Downey had been speaking to Capt. Scott LaPiedra on the phone just the day before about a transfer. The officer was indeed LaPiedra, and he was suffering from severe carbon monoxide poisoning along with the burns. He was helicoptered to Jacobi Hospital in the Bronx, which has a burn unit as well as a hyperbaric chamber.

After thirty-five minutes of daredevil digging, the rescuers freed Stackpole and brought him out in a wire Stokes basket. He was still conscious but he had been trapped in the burning timbers so long that even bunker gear had not prevented his legs from being burned to the bone.

Stackpole was rushed to Brookdale Hospital and Judge arrived there around the same time. Judge blessed Blackmore's body, then saw that Stackpole was being loaded into an ambulance for transfer to New York Hospital–Cornell Medical Center's burn unit in Manhattan. Judge jumped in along with Stackpole's friend and fellow firefighter Mike Brady. They rode through the potholed Brooklyn streets and Judge was shocked by how badly they were bounced around inside the ambulance. Judge began to pray aloud, but Stackpole stopped him.

"Excuse me, but I have to pray in my own way."

Judge went silent and listened as Stackpole offered a prayer of a pure firefighter in his agony.

"God, take care of the others, take care of the others."

Brady had a set of rosary beads in his pocket. He handed them to Stackpole.

"That was a case of, 'Here, take these. This might help,'" Brady recalled. "I really didn't know what to do. I didn't know what to say."

Stackpole was holding the rosary beads when he grabbed Judge's hand in a spasm of pain. The lieutenant continued praying for the others, and his grip stayed tight until the ambulance reached the hospital. Stackpole was wheeled in as Judge stood gazing down at his hand. The imprint of the rosary beads had formed the shape of a cross.

Bits of glass clinging to his hair, his face blackened, Stackpole lay in a trauma bay and asked for a telephone to call home. His oldest son, fifteen-year-old Kevin, answered. Stackpole's wife, Tara, was out.

"Tell Mommy I got hurt, but I'm okay," Stackpole said.

He could hear the television in the background, and he did not want his children to learn about the the fire and his injuries on the news.

"Do you have homework?" Stackpole said. "Turn off the TV."

Word reached Tara at a restaurant. She arrived at the hospital soon after, as did Stackpole's mother, followed by the mayor. Stackpole lay in searing pain, telling Giuliani not to condemn all firefighters for what a few knuckle-heads had done in Bryant Park after Medal Day. Stackpole said that the real firefighters were firefighters like the ones who risked death to rescue him. Everyone around the gurney hushed as Stackpole recounted moment by moment what had happened, saying he had been left in awe of his comrades. He ended by looking over at his mother.

"And, Ma, I wore clean underwear."

Judge laughed with everybody else and then turned serious, telling Stackpole's mother that her son had restored his faith. Anybody who overheard that could only have been surprised. Judge was one priest whose faith seemed to need no restoring. He may have meant his faith in firefighters or perhaps his faith in God. Maybe the two were becoming one and the same.

For Judge, faith was the continuing effort to see the good and fight off the feeling he was being sentimentally naive, that he was just making louts into lords, jerks into giants. His faith in the Church as an institution had been sorely tested by the hierarchy and by some of his fellow priests. He had since embraced the FDNY and even told its new cardinal, Fire Commissioner Tom Von Essen, he was gay. Then had come the vulgar, drunken violence in Bryant Park. Now, here was Timmy Stackpole.

Judge continued on to Jacobi Hospital in the Bronx to see the gravely injured Scott LaPiedra. The captain's wife arrived, and together they went in to see him. He was burned over 70 percent of his body. His head was charred, nearly beyond human form. Addie LaPiedra ran out of the room. Judge hurried down the hall after her, trailed by Giuliani and Von Essen. They all kept following her after she yanked open what she thought was the door to a conference room.

"It was the broom closet," she later recalled. "Now we're all in the broom closet. Mayor Giuliani said, 'Is there a room we can put her in?'"

A bigger room did not make Addie any more ready to hear the doctors say that her husband's injuries were "incompatible with existence," that there was no hope of saving him.

"They're talking to me and I'm not listening because I thought he was going to be okay," Addie later said. "I felt he was going to be all right. I just thought there's no way he's going to die. I just didn't feel that in me."

Then the priest she had just met began to speak. She would remember the effect if not the words.

"He had this soft-spoken voice and he just calmed me down," she recalled.

He seemed ready to listen to whatever she had to say.

"I was telling him how scared I was," she said. "He said, 'You don't have to be afraid. I'm here. Everybody's here.'"

Judge gently asked her about their four kids, two boys, twelve and thirteen, and twin ten-year-old girls.

"He just brought me back to reality," she recalled.

She said Scott had spent the day with his family, getting the two boys to paint the fence. He had left for work a happy man.

"He felt good," she told Judge. "He had such a good day . . . He's got to live. We had so many plans."

Judge kept talking to her in that soft voice, calming her, making her feel safe. She was ready to go back and see her husband.

"He had no face," she later said. "No lips. No ears. No [eye]lids."

But he was still alive. She asked Judge, "There is hope, right?"

"There's always hope," he told her. "Just go with it."

She said she was not ready to just leave it in God's hands.

"I can't, because He won't give me what I want, and I don't want Scott to die," Addie said.

Judge did not even try to persuade her otherwise.

Judge left Jacobi in the early morning darkness. A firefighter dropped him in Brooklyn so he could retrieve his car, and on the way back to the friary he swung by Atlantic Avenue. The fire was still smoldering long after midnight. Judge and a newspaper columnist stood with Downey as he directed men on a tower ladder to extinguish some small but hungry flames that were licking up the exterior wall of the building where the blaze had started.

Water hit the fire and white smoke rose up, momentarily obscuring a nearly full moon. The sky then cleared, and the moon shone bright for a moment, until the water hit another pocket of fire.

Judge continued on to the friary smelling of smoke. He caught a few hours' sleep and returned to Jacobi. Scott LaPiedra was fighting on, but the doctors continued to tell his wife that nobody had ever survived burns this severe, that there was no real hope.

"He'll die when he's going to die," Addie replied. "We have to let him know we're giving our all because Scott's giving his all."

She asked Judge if he knew anybody who had survived severe burns. He brought Marty McTigue, who told Addie how he could hear his family talking to him when he lay comatose in the burn unit.

"Marty McTigue said, 'Always talk to him, always give him hope,'" Addie recalled. "That's what I did."

She sang to Scott and spoke only in positive tones even after the doctors were forced to amputate his hands. The doctors had to use flaps of bone to protect his lidless eyes.

"You're still a cute skeleton," Addie told her husband. "You still have your dimples."

Scott would move his mouth and she was sure he was trying to tell her something, but everybody save Judge insisted this was impossible.

Three days after the fire, Judge enlisted the help of the person whose perseverance he considered living gospel. He picked Vina up and drove her to

New York Hospital–Cornell Medical Center. She knew, of course, about the Atlantic Avenue fire and that one of the firefighters had died and another was not expected to survive. A third, Timmy Stackpole, was fighting for his life, and she had been told he only had a chance because of bunker gear. Stackpole had worked with her husband at Ladder 147. She remembered John Drennan saying, "Vina, this Tim is the greatest guy." She also remembered Stackpole had been at her husband's wake. She now stepped off the elevator with Judge to see this firefighter she knew her husband had loved.

She saw that the burn unit had been remodeled in the four years since she had been there. Gone were the gray, boxlike rooms, replaced by well-lit, open areas. But, as Vina observed, the pain was the same.

They donned the gowns and masks just as before and went to where Stackpole lay. He was on a respirator, having taken a turn for the worse. His wife, Tara, was there. The rosary beads that made the impression on Judge's hand hung from the bedpost.

Stackpole's legs were wrapped in gauze, yellow-brown fluids oozing through the bandages in places. Vina did not dare ask how deeply he had been burned, but she knew it would have been even worse without bunker gear. Tara told her that Timmy carried John's picture in his wallet, and as the tale took an added twist, Vina was certain what the outcome just had to be.

"Oh, Timmy Stackpole, it's going to hurt like hell, but you'll live to see those five children of yours grow and go off to college and marry," she told herself. "Your sons will have sons like you and John sang about, and they will toddle over to you and call you Grandpa."

She stood a figure of resolute and determined faith in the ward where her own hopes had ended in grief. She left the hospital with the thought that firefighters usually die for strangers, but her husband had died for a friend and comrade. She was right to figure this was just the effect Judge must have hoped her visit would have on her as well as the Stackpoles. She was wrong to figure her mission was done and he would drive her straight home. He announced he was taking her to Paddy Brown's firehouse for dinner.

"Patrick's expecting us," Judge said. "It's One Hundred Thirty-third and Amsterdam."

Soon Judge was muttering, "Now, where is it? I know it's here, but the park is in the way."

They came to a police stationhouse. Judge went in to ask directions to the quarters of Engine 80/Ladder 23 while Vina waited in the car.

"Now, when Mychal Judge goes off to do the simplest of things, time is variable," Vina would recall. "People see the priest collar and the goodness in his face and he stops and listens and prays and blesses."

He was laughing when he returned, saying, "It's One Hundred Thirty-ninth Street, and look, I had written it down, too. But, oh well . . ."

In another twist, the firehouse happened to be where Scott LaPiedra worked before being promoted. The shock of the latest horror made the tensions between Vina and Brown fall away, for this night anyway. They felt only the bond between them as they sat in the kitchen with the other firefighters and Judge. No alarm came in, and no mechanical voice started chanting, "Ladder. Engine." Vina decided it was the best spaghetti dinner she had enjoyed in a long, long time.

Judge casually said he had to stop by Jacobi Hospital. Vina understood he wanted her to meet Addie LaPiedra. The two women talked for three hours before Judge finally took Vina home, arriving after two A.M.

As her husband fought on, Addie periodically needed to escape the smell of the burn unit. The hospital's chief executive gave her his office to sleep in. Judge began saying Mass there, granting general absolution to any visiting firefighters.

"All the guys would go hurrying into the room. 'Father Judge is saying Mass! Father Judge is saying Mass!'" Addie recalled. "He would forgive all."

Word of Judge's laxity reached the archdiocese and he received a scolding letter from a young chancery official that began, "Are you the Father Judge who says Mass without proper vestments? Are you the Father Judge who gives general absolution?" Judge immediately telephoned the official and angrily declared he had never brought disrespect or embarrassment to the Church he had loved and served nearly his entire life.

"If I have, you can take me out and crucify me in front of St. Patrick's Cathedral," Judge said, as fellow friar Brian Carroll tells it.

"Well, don't let it happen again," the official sputtered, stunned by the force of Judge's response.

Judge hung up and laughed.

"Madness," he later said of the incident. "Sheer madness."

• • •

Addie had come to dread the squeak of the medical staff's shoes on the hospital floor as much as she welcomed the clap of Judge's sandals. She wished aloud that she could visit Scott without being interrupted by doctors and nurses who had no hope in their eyes. Judge suggested he stand guard outside the room and accord her some privacy.

He knelt in front of the doorway in prayer, and when Addie finally emerged, he was still there, kneeling on the hard floor as if lost in a trance. Addie did not think he even saw her.

She went away and returned in an hour.

"He was still praying," she recalled. "He didn't see anything around him."

That Sunday, Judge took the time to attend a gathering for a new FDNY couple, Terry Hatton and Beth Patrone, who had been married at Gracie Mansion by her boss, Rudy Giuliani. Judge made another of his daily visits to Stackpole and returned to stand with Addie at her husband's bedside.

On Father's Day, LaPiedra was in no condition for his kids to visit him, so Judge went to see them. LaPiedra and his oldest boy, thirteen-year-old Scott, had planned to run together in a five-kilometer Father's Day race named in memory of a fallen firefighter. Young Scott ran it alone in twenty-eight minutes and fifty seconds, with Judge among those cheering. The boy credited his time with the kind of advice a dad gives.

"Smaller steps on the hills," the boy explained. "Land on the heel first."

LaPiedra was still alive at the end of the week and the FDNY decided it might be good for Addie and the kids as well as the Stackpoles if they went for a ride on one of the fireboats that operate from the department's crumbling pier on the Hudson River.

"I said, 'A boat ride? What are you, crazy?'" Tara recalled.

Firefighter Kevin Dowdell told Tara he would go with her. And Judge agreed to say a special children's Mass on the pier beforehand. He donned proper vestments for the occasion, including a shamrock stole. The LaPiedras and the Stackpoles arranged themselves on the buckled concrete and wooden beams.

Just as Judge was about to begin, he noticed graffiti scrawled on the top of the oversized wooden wire spool that was going to serve as the altar. He quickly removed his alb to use it as an altar cloth covering JOSE SUCKS. He was no longer in regulation gear when a helicopter happened to clatter over-head and he quipped, "It's probably the cardinal."

During Mass, Judge spoke directly to the children, saying, "Let's pray for your daddies. Our daddies need our prayers right now." Tara was struck by the thought that she had not had a minute to take full account of how hard this was on them.

Three-year-old Terence John Stackpole, the middle name in honor of John Drennan, gazed into the river.

"Are there alligators in that water?" he asked softly.

"Only crocodiles," Judge said.

The following week, Judge again marched in the Gay Pride Parade. At the hospitals, he often told stories of his AIDS ministry to the firefighters who were visiting LaPiedra and Stackpole. Tara remembers in particular his re-counting how he picked up a dying man from his wheelchair and he sang to him and kissed his forehead after giving him Communion. She was amazed he would talk of such things in front of macho men she figured would never even say the word *gay*. She remembers thinking, "Ain't he great?"

He was exactly what she had always hoped the Church would be.

"With him you really felt you were part of something bigger," she later said.

Addie continued to believe that when Scott moved his lipless mouth, he was trying to speak to her. The moment came. He turned his head and suddenly his voice was so clear even a nurse could hear.

"Ad . . . Ad," he said.

"What, Scott?" Addie said.

"I love you," Scott said. "I love you. . . . I love you."

After this, Addie arrived where Judge had hoped she would, a place she could have only reached on her own.

"Now it's in God's hands," she said.

On July 4, twenty-nine days after the fire, the doctors told Addie that her husband's heart was racing and his condition was deteriorating, that she should go up to his room quickly. She remained downstairs, saying, "No, he's going to die when I go up there."

She finally rode the elevator up. Giuliani was visiting, and he approached Scott's bedside with her. The beeping of the heart monitor slowed.

"Scott, tell God no! I can't tell God no. It's up to you to tell Him no," Addie said.

"Scott, tell Him no!" Giuliani called out.

But Scott died moments later, at 9:30 P.M. The long struggle ended with Addie kissing his charred face.

"I wanted my miracle," she said afterward. "I guess I got it. It gave me the strength to say good-bye to him."

She added that she owed this other kind of miracle to Mychal Judge.

"He gave me the strength to just stick to what I wanted and what I needed for Scott," she said. "Father Judge loved everyone. He judged no one. He let us speak."

Judge had been sent to a Franciscan gathering in Vienna that week and a stand-in chaplain arrived at the LaPiedra house. The stand-in began walking around, peering at this and that, as if on inspection. He told Addie the song she wanted for the funeral, "The Wind Beneath My Wings," was not on the approved list for Catholic Masses.

"He's in heaven. I don't need a funeral," Addie said. "And if I can't have my song, I'm not having one."

A group of firefighters had just arrived.

"We just want you to know if there's anything we can do," they told Addie.

"Get rid of the priest," she said.

"What?"

"Get rid of the priest. Father Judge isn't here, and he isn't Father Judge. Get rid of him, please."

The firefighters did as asked.

Addie got the song she wanted at the funeral and she later credited Judge with giving her the gumption to insist. The precedent was set at LaPiedra's funeral and "Wind Beneath My Wings" would become an anthem during the hundreds of FDNY funerals and memorials held after the towers came crashing down.

On August 10, two months after the Atlantic Avenue fire, and a month after Scott LaPiedra's death, Timothy Stackpole was released from the Burn

Center. His family came to bring him home, and six-year-old Brendan told the doctors and nurses, "Leave my daddy alone now."

A line of firefighters outside the hospital cheered when Stackpole emerged in a wheelchair. He rose, wobbly on his scarred legs, and asked them to pray for the two firefighters who had not been so lucky. A police escort led the way to his modest Brooklyn house in Good Shepherd Parish in Marine Park and the pipe band was there to welcome him home with the music he loved. The kids had hung a sign on the front door.

WE LOVE YOU DADDY.

Stackpole pronounced himself "the luckiest guy in the world," saying, "I'm George Bailey in *It's a Wonderful Life*. In tragedy I've learned just how amazingly beautiful people and life truly are."

Stackpole's legs were still far from fully functional, and he could have simply retired with a tax-free disability pension. He instead announced his intention to return to full duty, however long it took him, however hard it was to get there.

23

On August 15, 1998, word came from Ireland that extremists opposed to the peace process had detonated a bomb in the town of Omagh, killing twenty-six and injuring two hundred others. Judge and young Conor were at Steven McDonald's side when he held a press conference three days later to announce he was taking his message of forgiveness to Ireland in "Project Reconciliation."

"First I will listen to their pain and feeling, then I will share my story," Steven told the reporters. "God has His design and He wants me to be His legs . . . It's worth it all if I can help one person . . . If I could change the heart and mind of one person."

He and Judge then led the others in the Prayer of Saint Francis.

"Lord, make me an instrument of thy peace . . ."

The McDonalds and Judge departed the next day. They went from Omagh to Belfast. Steven and Judge visited IRA hero Joe Doherty in prison, but they also visited a Protestant church in a part of East Belfast where Catholics feared to tread. Judge witnessed what he took to be living scripture when a quartet of homeless people put together what change they had and bought Steven a chocolate bar along with a card wishing him a speedy recovery. One of them, a woman, bowed to kiss Steven's hand.

Judge discovered one hazard of pushing the wheelchair in his habit when his rope belt caught in the spokes. He had to scrub away the resulting grease, undoing the three knots symbolizing his vows. He hastened the drying by swinging the rope over his head like a cowboy with a lasso. He then reknotted it and undertook a bit of peacemaking of his own by taking a stroll in his Franciscan habit along a virulently anti-Catholic street.

"We don't like your kind here," a man told him.

Someone else inquired if his habit was bulletproof.

"No," Judge said.

In the hard looks in East Belfast as well as the grieving faces in Omagh and all the visages of irretrievable loss, Judge saw firsthand the importance of President Clinton's ongoing effort to bring peace to Northern Ireland. Judge was asked by Catholics and Protestants alike how Americans could be so fixated on Clinton's consensual dalliance with Monica Lewinsky when much graver matters hung in the balance. The Irish seemed mystified that America could not appreciate the man they had come to call "Our Billy."

"When the Irish start calling Americans prudes . . ." Judge remarked after his return.

On September 11, 1998, Independent Counsel Starr released his report on the Clinton shenanigans. The country was buzzing about blowjobs in the Oval Office and semen on a dress as Judge joined a delegation to the White House to honor Clinton for his efforts as a peacemaker. Brian O'Dwyer was to present Clinton with a dove of Waterford crystal, the first annual Paul O'Dwyer Peace and Justice Award.

The delegation was ushered under a big white tent on the South Lawn. The crowd gave the beleaguered president and First Lady a six-minute standing ovation when they emerged from the Oval Office. Clinton set aside a prepared speech and spoke from what seemed truly the heart.

"Hillary and I will never forget what you've done for us today. And I suspect you know . . ." Clinton said.

The Marine Band played "Wearing of the Green."

On December 1, World AIDS Day, a small group of activists gathered in City Hall Park to read aloud the names of the seventy thousand New Yorkers who had died of the disease. They included Stephen Smurr and so many others Judge had assisted through their final hours.

On orders from Giuliani, the Department of Environmental Protection sent a team with a noise meter, and instructed them to shut the rally down if the level exceeded the 75 decibels allowed by the permit. The level only reached 74.1 decibels, and the reading of the names continued.

The activists had mounted a prolonged court battle to gain access to the steps of City Hall, this traditional place for civil dissent having been closed off in August as part of a Giuliani effort to tighten security against a possible terrorist attack. Police sharpshooters watched from the roof as demonstrators were admitted under a court order. The demonstrators took the seemingly excessive security as an attempt to intimidate them.

"Shame! Shame!" they cried out.

The sharpshooters and the decibel meters were seen by Giuliani's many detractors as more manifestations of the Bad Rudy. Vina was by then coming to suspect that she was also a victim of the Bad Rudy, that she had been shunned for having inspired Hevesi to conduct the fire safety audit. She had done so completely unaware that Hevesi was viewed as a possible political rival and that it was considered treason to suggest something was not better under Giuliani. The mayor would later insist that he never turned against her, but she was led to believe otherwise by a sympathetic fire official.

"I hate what they are doing to you, Vina," he said.

The official told her it had been no accident that the seats had been moved away from her on Medal Day and that she had not been invited to the inauguration or to several events where the other widows were included.

She did not say anything to Judge when he called her the day after a Widows and Orphans event.

"Where were you last night?" he asked.

Judge continued to focus on the Good Rudy even as Brown became alarmed by the mayor's attitude toward dissent of any kind.

"What are you doing with this guy?" Brown asked Judge about his relationship to Giuliani. "He's *really* nuts."

"No, no, no, you have to understand," Judge replied. "He's really a good man."

Judge spoke of the Good Rudy he had seen during all the fire deaths as well as the aftermath of Flight 800.

"And in times of loss there is nobody better."

Neither Judge nor anybody else was hoping Giuliani would get another opportunity to demonstrate that quality anytime soon. Six months had passed since the Atlantic Avenue fire and Judge's life quieted to a continual bustle. Alvarado was turning thirty this year, and Judge set all else aside and actually saw him on his birthday on December 6.

Then, the week before Christmas, three firefighters from Ladder 170 were killed in a Brooklyn fire started by an elderly woman who had been smoking in bed. Judge set off to notify Lt. Joseph Cavalieri's wife while others broke the terrible news to the families of Christopher Bopp and James Bohan. Deborah Cavalieri had put out some clothes on the porch for donation to the poor. She assumed Judge had come to collect them.

"Oh, Father, the clothes are right there," she said.

After he had done what he could, Judge proceeded on to see Bopp's wife, who was three months' pregnant with her first child. He visited the quarters of Ladder 170 and learned that Timmy Stackpole had come by with coffee and bagels.

The funerals for Bohan and Bopp were held on the same day. Judge picked up Brown at his apartment on the East River and they went together to both. The sight that stayed with them was of Timmy Stackpole standing in salute, his eyes welling, one of his legs still bandaged. The three dead firefighters had been among those who had joined the vigil for him in the burn unit.

At the start of the New Year, Stackpole returned to the hospital for even more surgery. Tara was feeling bleakly alone as she walked into the recovery room. She pulled the bedside curtains aside and saw Judge already there, giving a big smile upon seeing her.

"I didn't know this person before June and it's January and how did we ever live without him?" Tara later said.

When a big snowstorm struck the city, many friends were unable to come to the hospital, but in strolled Judge with his collar up and a ski hat.

"Let's go for a walk," he told Tara.

The two trudged together through the hushed streets, arm in arm in the snow.

They were circling back to the hospital when Judge checked his messages. He told Tara he had an urgent call from someone in AA and he had to go. He paused to give a homeless man a neatly folded dollar and set off.

Tara returned to her husband, who was no less determined to resume full duty. He underwent grueling physical therapy, pushing himself to where he fainted from the pain, then going right back at it.

24

On March 13 of that year, Judge had dinner with a gay friend from the East Village AA meeting. The friend urged him to begin keeping a journal that could become an autobiography in which he "came out" as a gay man. Judge bought a spiral notebook like the one he had used as a diary of his pilgrimage with Patti Ann. But this was to be more like the Book of Vina, more personal, deeper, revealing. He inscribed the inside of the front cover:

Some Mother's Son. 230 Dean St. Irish, Catholic, Democrat, priest, gay and more . . . No one (ever) asked me!

As if he were still at St. Paul's Grammar School, he put a cross at the top of the page and began what promised to be the Book of Mychal.

March 15, '99

The best days are the ones filled with talking to people—all kinds everywhere. So I am very happy as I find my way to chapel to thank God for the wonderful day, for the man that I am and the people I met—face to face and on the phone. At 65, I ask how much should I do each day— God seems to show me exactly and I am amazed when I feel like I am not doing anything, a wave of things will happen.

Oh Lord—you know me so well—I can't hide from you—I have nothing, nothing to fear—All I have to do is your will and all will be well—Make it known to me—

His next entry was on St. Patrick's Day. He met the pipe band at the end of the parade at a church hall.

March 17, '99

I arrived at St. Ignatius to greet the band—Wow! They treat me like a long lost brother—hugs, kisses, laughs, digs, jabs and "I'm home!" And I ask myself again, "But, if?" And I can't stop and wait for the answer. I blessed many.

He turned reflective in a March 24 entry:

Callicoon days keep coming back lately—over and over. Some St. Paul's stuff a bit of St. Francis Prep and many Callicoon memories and feelings.

He wrote of thinking he was the only one who was gay, but not being exactly sure what that was. He had known he would be sent back to Brooklyn in shame if he had tried anything sexual, and yet he would have been willing if the opportunity had arisen. He marveled that despite that reckless streak he had been able to remain celibate for year after year after year. The entry ended as they all did, with words to his truest and longest love.

Oh well, Lord, here I am today—You, you alone brought me here—I have nothing to fear today—thank you, thank you.

During Easter week, the McDonalds invited Judge to join them on a vacation to Miami Beach.

He had to scramble to leave New York, presiding at a funeral on Long Island, rushing back to the friary in traffic, hearing an urgent confession from a fellow friar, hurrying to the airport, and missing his flight.

I wound up in first class on the next flight. It was nice. Fell a little bit infatuated with the person next to me—But it passed, thank God!

He sought to soothe himself just as he had so many others.

Mychal Judge, there is nothing to fear, everything will work out just fine. You will see everyone, you will have time for them . . . All I have to do is get up and show up each day, try to get to a [AA] meeting, stay in constant contact with God—and not worry or fear.

As he relaxed into his holiday, he wrote.

A thousand thoughts and desires run through my mind at everybody I see. But only for a moment—Drives, desires, passions, energy, excitement, yearning and all the rest. I see the beauty, how God created it and how, in a sense, the Church scorns your dwelling on it—Sexual, sinful—Hand in hand—But they are not connected at all. I love, I applaud the beauty of God's handiwork.

Back in New York, Judge was so swept up by all the demands on him that weeks flashed by. He did not make another entry until the day after the fifth anniversary of John Drennan's death. He had spoken on the phone to Alvarado, who had also been beyond busy, newly promoted to supervisor of nursing at the St. Barnabas nursing home.

Wednesday 5/8
 Just had a quick conversation with Al. He has a terrible headache— He is overworked—no doubt about it—but he is RUNNING up the ladder at work—Great!

He made another entry the day after his sixty-sixth birthday, while in St. Louis at a workshop run by Patch Adams, doctor-activist-clown extraordinaire made famous by the movie of the same name.

As Patch spoke of freedom and being completely oneself I thought of my gay self and how the people I meet never get to know me fully—and why? Because it is not acceptable.

He seemed poised to delve into the depths, but his day-to-day existence was too buoyant.

No one, absolutely no one lives two fuller separate lives as I do. Little wonder I am so tired at day's end. Time—time—time! Well, I am so blessed and my life is so good . . . Thank you Lord for all that you have given me, for all you have taken away and for all that is left. 12 midnight. Amen.

He was on the flight home when he took out a book, *Gay Lives,* that his friend from the East Village group had given him as an inspiration for his own.

I truly get into it and I relate and I hear what these men say and feel and write and I feel so close to them and then distant . . . Well, I feel so much better off, or should I say, more at ease. They have, how would you put it? A sense of rage in their lives and I don't feel that . . . I am so blessed despite my two or three lives.

He felt all the more so upon his return.

Back from St. Louis about 4 o'clock and I felt good, real good. Plenty of birthday cards and white slips with phone messages. It was so heartwarming.

There were two beautiful cards from Al in the mail. Very sweet and telling. The word sweetheart was used and that moved me. We have never used that sort of vocabulary before—but—everything is changing. He sent a great card that really made me laugh.

What did I feel with all the cards? Remembered! And it was so nice. Everyone tells me how much I am loved—and I know it—But I doubt it or I don't dwell on it and or maybe I don't own it. It comes to me now— Is it because I am afraid it will all change or I will lose it if my true self were known to everyone—I don't know.

Sexually, I am alive as I can be. The thoughts, the drives, the desires are there always. Can't see enough on the street . . . and I am grateful for it . . . And you, Lord, are always there and you so nicely remind me to call on you and you show me your presence. I love you.

He wrote in the next entry of bringing God's presence to the funeral for a firefighter from Ladder 7 who had died of natural causes. He had trouble easing the firefighter's little girl away from her father's body so the casket could be closed.

Just hugged and hugged her daddy and we could not get her free.

The girl clutched Judge as the casket was loaded onto the hearse.

It must have been the way she hugged her daddy when she was frightened.

Judge no sooner returned from the funeral than he got a call from the wife of a firefighter from Ladder 133 who was critically ill. The doctors were advising her to take her husband off life support, and he went to the hospital to be with her.

It was a beautiful ending and I was just present.

He returned to the friary exhausted.

I am dead tired, but here is a feeling of accomplishment—the day was so funereal and deathly but I feel that God used me to help his people . . . I thank you Lord for a very special great day . . . moving closer to you.

At an annual meeting of the friars known as Chapter of the Mats, so named because in the earliest days of their order the brothers would sleep on mats when Saint Francis summoned them to a gathering, Judge was standing in a room with another friar when a bird swooped in an open window. His hands surprised him with a speed and sureness he never imagined he possessed.

I will never believe it that he actually flew into my hands and that I was not afraid and carried him out so easily and gently released him.

A bird is a Christian symbol of the Holy Spirit, but the magic of the moment was not in the tiny creature. The big Irish hands that had always surprised people now astonished Judge.

I never caught a great ball in my life, never mind a line drive, and then to be ready and have the hands open and at the exact level and to be able to close them so quickly—baffles me!

He was emboldened. He was beginning to think that writing a book was actually possible.

Every group can have an advocate—good, bad or indifferent. Maybe, maybe a chapter in a book by Mychal Judge—well respected, loved by many, faithful to his profession, loyal to his community and friends, compassionate beyond bounds—you would like to be in his company, to be his friend— well if he is gay there must be something okay about "them"—you could talk so freely, explain so much, release fears, explain the pain, show the joy and give peace to so many . . . I keep thinking my fear is lessening but there is still so much there . . . Lord, be with all of us here, especially keep your eye on me right now—hold me tight. Don't let me do anything foolish . . .

He made another entry two days later.

I am told how many, many people really love me—how I fill their needs, how I am always there. Now, if I come out in "this book" why will all this love change? Why will they have such a hard time being close to me still? I will have been with them 66 years—so present—why, why will they have to change? Fear, fear, fear, societal pressures, unknown reasons— What is there about the whole gay question, situation? What is the driving force of homophobia?—How to change it? Can it be changed? Where did it come from (the fear)? How did it start? What was the moment? The situation? The person or persons who found it out? How did they re- act? How did they get the homophobic movement started? . . . Could it ever be answered, does anyone have a clue?

Well, here I am . . . I'm somehow started, I think, on this new journey—not sure where it is taking me, how I am to go, etc. etc. But I keep praying and asking for guidance and leadership. It is a real test of my faith and belief and that God is there.

He needed to convince himself anew he was worth a book.

If I keep thinking about it and working on myself, and taking seriously what people say about loving me—if I go back and see all the goodness done over the years and never an unkind word said or a pain inflicted I can begin to see that I can write a book about me.

God of all creation—you have made me for all sorts of reasons. If this new idea be one of them, then simply show me. Amen.

His daily ministry continued at an unrelenting pace.

"I can't keep doing this," he told his Lutheran counterpart, Fire Chaplain Everett Wabst. "I don't know how to tell them no. I can't keep up this pace. I have to keep praying about it."

He wore out a third answering machine, and when the firefighters bought him a fourth, he recorded a new greeting:

This is Mychal Judge. It's so good to get your call. But if you're calling
about a wedding or a baptism or funeral, I am so sorry, but I will not be able to
do it, because my primary commitment is to the Fire Department.

He had always made everyone feel so special that callers told themselves
he could not possibly mean them, and the requests came in unabated, along
with calls of seemingly every kind. The machine was often filled to the limit
when he arrived back at his room at night. He would write the messages
down, then run a line through each after he had returned the call. Hardly a
message went unlined for page after page after page.

He did not write in his journal again for more than a month, when he was far
from the ringing phone and on another trip to Lourdes, this time without the
McDonalds. He found that the remove from the exciting swirl of the city
also accorded a respite of another kind.

I am so pleased that the sexual drives are so diminished here and I can
breathe easy—Not completely at rest, but better than at home . . .

He wrote of revisting the grotto.

I kneel there—and I feel so uplifted and good—no guilt, no fears, no
anxieties—just peace.

He prayed for everyone he could summon to mind, a single roster from
one priestly life.

I try to remember all the names and I do quite well but there must be
thousands left unmentioned, but God is a great bookkeeper and he takes
care of them.

He was accorded a priestly joy such as would likely be denied an openly
gay priest.

I felt so very special this morning to be the principal at the grotto's English
Mass. I was very nervous about the homily but I "turned it over" and then

the words of the angel, "Do not be afraid, Mary" struck me. FEAR, FEARS.

He once again proved he had no cause to fear, about a homily anyway. He afterward visited a hospital with a fellow priest.

There is in his life like so many other religious loneliness—an aloneness. We had a nice visit in the emergency rooms. We exchanged Cardinal O'Connor stories—WOW!

Judge must have felt that if he were forced to leave the priesthood, he would be yet another Catholic cleric out the door, deserting already lonely comrades such as this one and leaving the Church in the hands of those such as O'Connor. The evening concluded with a happy surprise.

Irish night in the pub (hotel) tonight. The fellow was playing but no one singing, so I picked up the mike.

This fifty-seven-page Book of Mychal and the notion of becoming an advocate at the risk of no longer being the priest adored by so many ended here, with Mychal Judge being his singular self.

A good time was had by all.

25

At summer's end, Judge received a call from Brian O'Dwyer, who had presented Clinton with the peace award the previous September 11, the day *The Starr Report* was released. The White House had contacted O'Dwyer hoping to find the right cleric to sit next to the First Lady; a preacher who was not going to preach to her or a minister who was not going to start ministering or a priest who was not going to do either. O'Dwyer told them he knew just the one.

"It wasn't that hard a call to make," O'Dwyer later said.

Judge arrived at the White House on September 28 knowing only that he was to be one of the 129 guests. He did not shy from going up to President Clinton at the welcoming reception, asking him to sign an autograph for an admiring Irish kitchen worker at the friary.

"I told him how to spell 'Hugh,'" Judge later reported.

Only when he went to his assigned table did Judge realize he would be sitting next to the First Lady. He proved indeed to be just the one after the president spoke in his opening remarks of how difficult a year it had been and how he had learned "the pure power of grace, unmerited forgiveness through grace."

The Clinton people were worried that the cleric next to the First Lady would also start speaking to her about what a difficult year it had been and about forgiveness and grace. What happened was Judge began marveling at how wonderful it was to be in the White House.

"He took more joy in it than a child," Hillary recalled. "I had to tell him about everything he saw."

By making manifest how lucky he felt to be there, he was also telling her how lucky she was to be there, scandal or no. He was ministering to her after all, but in his own way, relying on the same intuitive sense with the First Lady as with a firefighter's wife. He spoke of other houses—firehouses and the friary and of those with no house at all. He told her of his work with the homeless and with AIDS victims.

"People overlooked, left out," Hillary later said.

The very fact he was speaking of these matters was acknowledging they were more important than her husband's reversion to adolescence at the sight of an intern's thong. These were questions of life and health, questions as big as peace.

"We just started talking and it didn't stop," Hillary said.

He was already going to take his menu as a souvenir and he could think of any number of people who would love to have it. He asked if he could have hers as well and she signed it for him. He was amazed to see she was so well briefed he did not need to tell her how to spell Mychal.

One sound nobody in the White House expected was Hillary's laughing like a schoolgirl in delight at Judge's little-boy enthusiasm.

"It was so much fun," she said.

The breakfast done, the president opened a discussion about juvenile violence and hate crime. He then said there was time for just one more response before he had to leave for a meeting with the prime minister of Turkey. Judge raised a hand and spoke in praise of Alcoholics Anonymous.

"Bill Wilson and Dr. Bob, its founders, have done as much good in this century or even more good than Mother Teresa—forgive the comparison," Judge said. "Why? Because AA is a spiritual program, not a religious program . . ."

Judge meant that AA was not a creed but an undertaking, one open to those of all beliefs. He then said as an aside something that would be remembered on another September day.

"Religions often cause wars . . ."

Before leaving, Judge visited a White House men's room and discovered a stack of disposable hand towels bearing the presidential seal. He took a good number home with him and distributed them to everybody from firefighters to friars to the homeless in the city that would be learning firsthand about religion and war.

26

On New Year's Eve, the New York Fire Department was on high alert, having been notified that Islamic terrorists might mark the start of 2000 and the new millennium with an attack on the city. Chief Ray Downey fielded teams equipped with hazardous-materials protective gear in the event of a chemical, biological, or radiological incident. Squads were beefed up and brought in from the boroughs. A command post was established in Central Park, and Judge stopped by as the year neared a close. He then went down to Times Square, where two million celebrants were gathered.

Judge walked in his FDNY jacket past manhole covers that had been welded shut as a precaution against bombs. When he reached the police barricades, he produced his FDNY badge, in the shape of a Maltese cross dating back to the Crusades. A cop admitted him into the frozen zone, where he stood with fire and police officials, as well as federal agents. These included John O'Neill, the FBI's lead man on terrorism. A would-be bomber had been caught at the Canadian border out west with 130 pounds of explosives apparently meant for either Seattle's Space Needle or Los Angeles Airport. That had led to other arrests, but O'Neill worried that Al Qaeda might still strike in New York, and as he watched the ball drop, he figured that if it came it would be right here, right now.

Three!

Two !

One!

Happy New Year!

Nothing happened. In the morning sanitation crews swept up tons of confetti. Everybody save O'Neill and a few others forgot about a threat that he feared would culminate in what he called "The Big One." Elsewhere men who arrived at the new millennium imagining themselves at the start of a war with Crusaders and Jews were even then taking flight lessons. They had little interest in learning how to land.

The days of so many innocents were being numbered even as Judge continued living one day at a time in the AA way. His faith remained centered in the present instant as he went about in the habit of a religious order that had been accorded custodial care of the Holy Land at the time of those same Crusades.

He marched in this medieval garb along with Hillary Clinton at the first inclusive St. Patrick's Day Parade, organized in Queens by Brendan Fay. Judge continued to receive funds from the better-off to distribute as he saw fit, and he contributed an envelope of cash to the event, all two-dollars bills, almost as queer as a three.

He went to Ireland twice that year, once to little Keshcarrigan with Michael Walker after arranging for his surrogate son to get an interview with a financial firm in London. Judge stood where his father had been raised and gazed out at the tranquil water and the ancient hills beyond, among them the one where some believed Fionn of myth was buried. He tried to imagine how his father must have felt looking at this, knowing he was never coming back.

The fruit trees where the fairies were supposed to have played were gone. Only one wall of the old house remained, now part of a cowshed. Judge picked up a small stone, or stoneen, and held it in his palm for a time before slipping it into his pocket.

Judge later made another trip to Northern Ireland with Steven McDonald, along with Rev. Fanny Erickson, a Protestant minister from Riverside Church in Upper Manhattan who had some knowledge of Celtic mysticism. She would later write to McDonald that Judge made her think of the ancient shapeshifters. The virulently anti-Catholic crowd outside a Protestant church in Drumcree saw only the priest's habit. They brandished weapons and uttered threats as Judge smiled and entered to hear a Kids for Peace Choir. He afterward spoke at an ecumenical service, echoing something he had said at the White House. His words would equally apply after a September morning now little more than a year away.

"People want to rule over other people and have God on their side, and if you are not on their side, then God's not on your side and all these sides.

When you think about it, it is a tremendous waste of time and energy and all it does is cause wars and people get killed and families get divided and everything goes wrong."

He allowed that the situation was complex.

"I know it's real and I know it's here and it's centuries old and it's very, very complicated. As simple as I see it, it's very complicated."

The simplicity was in his viewpoint, his theology, his belief that prayer and love and goodness will ultimately prevail.

"There will always be people who want to destroy what God builds up through good people, but God will overcome. And God someday—I don't know how He is going to do it—but He's going to make the headlines rather than the devil. He will in the end, so don't give up. We pray together, we believe together, we love together, and God reigns. Amen."

Judge arrived back in New York imagining he had left behind centuries-old grudges and killing in the name of God. His New York was one to which people brought their hopes. He took Alvarado past the house on Dean Street where his mother had planted her sprig of green. The ivy had long since spread to backyards up and down the block.

Judge had not forgotten his childhood lesson about the value of having a house in the event of a calamity. He urged Alvarado to put the salary increase accompanying his promotion toward building a house back in the Philippines.

Alvarado said he would first have to get an architect. Judge's theology regarding plans for tomorrow proved to extend even to home construction.

"He said, 'You don't need a plan! Just build a matchbox. Walls and a roof,'" Alvarado recalled.

Alvarado did as Judge said. A construction crew down in Mindanao began building without so much as a sketch, while men as fanatical as the amoks of old patiently prepared for an attack on New York, already years in the planning.

In the meantime, calamity as measured one individual at a time had visited two significant figures in Judge's life as a priest and a chaplain. Mayor Giuliani was diagnosed with prostate cancer, but it had been caught early and the prognosis was good. Cardinal O'Connor underwent surgery for a brain tumor and announced that the doctors were very hopeful. He began to weaken as the cancer returned, and he succumbed on May 3.

Jean Willis of Siena days was now working as a television producer. She asked Judge to go on the WCBS morning show and speak about O'Connor. Judge observed the old Irish adage to always tell the truth, but don't always be telling it. He said what good he was able to say. The anchors remarked off-air afterward that Judge must have been very close to His Eminence.

"Please! He couldn't stand me," Judge said.

Almost four thousand mourners attended the cardinal's funeral, many of whom genuinely respected and admired O'Connor. As O'Connor had requested, the homily was delivered by the other half of Law & Order, Cardinal Law of Boston, who was on his way to scandal for shuffling pedophile priests to unsuspecting parishes.

The rite concluded with O'Connor becoming the eighth archbishop laid to rest in a crypt under the main altar.

Judge made sure he was the first to descend into the crypt after the entombment and he brought a little Brooklyn with him. He offered the cardinal some of the words that had filled him when O'Connor pulled the stunt with young John Drennan at the captain's funeral.

The dignitaries at the cardinal's funeral included the Clintons. Giuliani came without his wife, Donna Hanover. He announced four days later at a press conference outside Bryant Park that he and his wife were separating. A shaken, hurt, and angry Hanover had a press conference of her own outside Gracie Mansion.

"For several years it had become increasingly difficult to participate in Rudy's public life because of his relationship with one staff member," she said. "Beginning last May, I made a major effort to get us back together, and Rudy and I reestablished some of our personal intimacies through the fall."

She paused.

"At that point, he chose another path."

Everyone, including Judge, knew the staff member she meant. Whatever may or may not have transpired between Lategano and Giuliani in the past, she had certainly not precipitated the present split. Giuliani had indeed taken up with another woman, a former medical supply saleswoman named Judith Nathan.

When he announced to the world that Rudy really, really loves Judi, Giuliani passed from an icon to a public embarrassment. He left his wife and kids in Gracie Mansion and took temporary residence in the spare bedroom offered by a wealthy gay car dealer who lived with a longtime partner just as Alvarado dreamed of living with Judge.

In the solitude of his friary room, Judge had late-night phone chats with a mayor in a mess such as might make a priest almost grateful for celibacy.

"Pray for me," Giuliani said.

"No, no, I pray all the time. He probably gets tired of it," Judge told him. "But God would love to hear from a real sinner. If *you* do it, just think . . ."

Judge offered counsel he felt held true in all matters.

"Life is complicated," Judge said. "Remember the good things you do. Keep thinking about that. Keep building on that and you'll come to an answer."

Judge kept practicing his theology moment by moment, person by person, at fire scenes and in the street. His many phone calls included one from the police saying that his number had been found in the pocket of a man arrested for jumping a subway turnstile.

The man was Everald Brathwaite, and Judge confirmed to the cop that he indeed knew him well. Brathwaite was an immigrant from Trinidad who had been periodically undomiciled for two decades. Brathwaite had noted that Judge did not hesitate to embrace and comfort even those who had gone months without a bath or a change of clothes.

"He didn't care," Brathwaite recalled. "He'd touch anybody."

Brathwaite saw Judge routinely give money to panhandlers who were only looking for a drink or drugs. Brathwaite became the latest person to ask Judge the question Dympna had posed to him more than a half century before. Judge articulated only a step or two beyond simply saying it did not matter.

"Whatever he does, he does," Judge replied. "One day, he's going to come to God or God is going to come to him."

. . .

Judge also understood what people who are down on their luck can need as much as or even more than a handout: someone willing to listen untiringly not just to the troubles common to all in their plight, but to their individual and most intimate torments.

"I could confide with him anything," Brathwaite said. "We keep talking and talking. I saw him as a person of the heart."

Judge listened and responded just as he would with a firefighter or an AIDS victim or a mayor.

"Whatever he saw in me, I got potential," Brathwaite later said.

Brathwaite responded as Judge hoped, helping others as he had been helped. One bitterly cold night Brathwaite happened upon a homeless man named David who was sleeping a few doorways up from the friary.

"I had a good coat and a sweater," Brathwaite said. "I took the sweater off. Like a spirit come over me."

On another day, Brathwaite learned that a female drug addict's baby had died. He went to Judge, who immediately sought out the grieving mother at a crack spot.

"He had no fear," Brathwaite said.

Brathwaite's own health began to fail, and he once again fell on hard times. He ended up at Bellevue Hospital suffering from kidney troubles as well as despair. He took a sudden plummet into absolute hopelessness.

"Something hit me like a brick," Brathwaite later said. "After that I decided to stop eating."

Judge had been visiting almost daily, often bringing pizza to Brathwaite and of course the nurses. Judge now arrived to hear Brathwaite make an announcement.

"I don't feel like living no more."

Judge summoned all his priestly powers on visit after visit, but he could not persuade Brathwaite to take more than a few ice cubes.

"No breakfast, no lunch, no dinner," Brathwaite recalled later.

The hospital tried a feeding tube, but Brathwaite retained enough strength to resist. He seemed near the end as his hunger strike against the state of his existence reached a biblical marker that had assumed added meaning for Judge.

"I remember him coming by late that night on the fortieth day and giving me the last rites, giving me the sacraments and he prayed over me," Brath-waite said.

The medical staff warned Judge as he departed that on his next visit he would likely find Brathwaite dead. Brathwaite drifted off to what threatened to be his final sleep.

He awoke the next day to discover his spirits had rebounded as suddenly as they had fallen forty-one days before. "I said. 'I'm feeling good! I need some Chinese food, ginger ale, cranberry juice, and whatever snack.'"

Brathwaite was out of the hospital on September 6, 2000, his fiftieth birthday. Judge bought him breakfast.

"Coffee, toast, eggs scrambled soft," Brathwaite recalled.

Judge then took him shopping on Fifth Avenue.

"Dozen pairs of socks, a pair of jeans, shirt, sneakers," Brathwaite re-counted.

Brathwaite was living in a single-room-occupancy hotel on Thirty-eighth Street that was loud and plagued by drugs and crime. Judge found him better accommodations up in the Bronx but knew the room could be snapped up if he did not act right away. And he had an important meeting with the mayor in just half an hour.

"He said, 'Put everything in the car and we're going to go,'" Brathwaite recalled. "He said, 'I'm going to do this, but I can't let my boss know.'"

Brathwaite did not understand what the boss was not supposed to know until Judge hit the lights and siren.

"It was a great experience!" Brathwaite said. "He was a good driver, too. He moved in and out."

Judge reached the Bronx in record time for a priest.

"He came back the following day to make sure everything was okay, make sure I had everything I need," Brathwaite said. "That was Father My-chal."

27

With the other holiday rituals came the Johnsons' Christmas party. Judge was off somewhere else in the hotel ballroom as Vina stood with Paddy Brown, who was still hurting over Peter McLaughlin's death. Brown started in on Vina about her views regarding firefighting and prevention as the band struck up some Irish music and a group of step dancers began to perform. Brown told her that she just did not understand. She assured him that she was seeking only to help, not to detract.

"So we lose three or four guys a year," Brown said. "That's too bad. That's the cost."

Vina knew she should just walk away and maybe she would have had it not been for the music her husband loved, for the insistent rhythm of the dancers' feet.

"John's dead because he was stupid, too stupid to value his life, to think about how to do his job more safely," she would recall saying. "Every day my kids wake up without a father. That's the cost. That's the price of your glory, Patrick. Every night I lie in bed alone, Patrick. That's the cost of your damn traditions. How many widows, how many children, how many mothers and fathers have to grieve for your Medal Day? John's dead for this macho crap. There should be no glory in fighting a fire that can be prevented."

She had no way of knowing that what she then said would be the last words she would ever utter to him.

"You should take those damn medals and shove them."

Brown spoke what would be his very last words to her.

"You used to be my best friend."

The music still playing, the dancers still dancing, Brown strode from the ballroom. Vina encountered Judge by the buffet line.

"Who does he think he is?" she asked.

On into the New Year, Judge and Brown continued to speak nearly every day. Judge did not come out and say he also felt Brown sometimes went beyond brave. Judge only quietly inquired if perhaps Brown could take a little more care. Brown laughed, but he seemed to take the very suggestion as a betrayal.

"I thought you said that God sends me where he wants me to go," Brown said.

Brown kept being a firefighter. Judge kept being a priest. On February 25 he reached the anniversary he would always record in his appointment books by writing only the number of years. He no doubt wrote "40 years" at the top of this day's page. He further marked the occasion by sending out a letter to those he had touched and who also had touched him.

> It is midnight and the day is almost done. Today is the 40th anniversary of my priesthood—1961—and the cold rainy day is an exact replica of the day in Washington when Archbishop Vagnozzi, the Apostolic Delegate, laid his hands firmly on my head and gifted me with the priesthood. Glorious!
>
> Someone asked me today if I had any idea, at all, what lay ahead for me that day. I knew I would say Mass and preach, that I would baptize, bury the dead and perform weddings. The rest was all in the hands of God. I could never have dreamt of all the parish years I would enjoy; the lively days at Siena College; the extraordinary challenging year at Canterbury; the filling and the emptying of the clothes closet for the homeless; the blessed ministry to the sick and dying with the AIDS virus; and now the joyful challenge as Chaplain of the New York City Fire Department.

His duties as a chaplain sent him to the scene of a fire on East Thirteenth Street early on the morning of March 15. He arrived to see Paddy Brown and Firefighter Jeff Giordano carry out a twenty-one-year-old woman named Jessica Rubinstein. She was naked and blackened by soot. She was not breathing.

Brown and Giordano had quite literally walked through fire to get to her, and they were not about to give up now. They tried to resuscitate her. No luck. They tried again. No luck again. The moment seemed to arrive when Judge would have to step up to offer a last blessing. Brown and Giordano tried once more.

Then, they saw it, that most beautiful sight: the light of life coming back into her blue eyes. Judge later wrote Brown a note.

> *You are right, Patrick, God puts you where He needs you when He needs you and as often as He needs you and you always respond.*
>
> *Love, M*

A message from Brown was the sixteenth of fifty-seven messages that Judge wrote down in his phone log for May 20 going into May 21.

> *Pat Brown—Love you*

Judge and Brown met that month at the annual FDNY Holy Name Society Communion breakfast honoring Joe Angelini, firefighter for forty years and bearer of the crosier at Drennan's funeral. Judge and Brown went down the steps of St. Patrick's Cathedral together.

"It's nice to be here when nobody died," Brown said,

In June, the Franciscans held another Chapter of the Mats meeting in upstate New York. Judge returned to the city and took two friars from out of town for a stroll over the Brooklyn Bridge.

The bridge was still the structure he held most sacred, and he was still unable to articulate exactly why; he would just say there was something about the Brooklyn Bridge. One part of its magic surely was the view from midspan, a panorama of the whole harbor. The Statue of Liberty. The steeples of Brooklyn. The much taller spires of Manhattan.

The Twin Towers remained the tallest of all, but Judge never found height to be any more of a true distinction than wealth. He seldom mentioned them on these walks and likely did on this night only because the friars were visitors. The bridge spanned from one realm to another, connecting the brawn of Brooklyn with the magic of Manhattan.

In his bleaker moments, Judge felt that however full his life had been, it still stretched from one absence to another, from the early death of his father to the finality of having no family of his own, a lonely span from what was lost to what would never be. He was unable to be open about his needs without the risk of being driven from the work he loved, his chaplaincy and his Church. He sometimes felt not so much connected to the next world as unconnected to any world at all.

In his moments of glory, Judge felt at one with both realms. His priesthood spanned the gay and the straight, the rich and the poor, the Catholic and the Jew. His denomination was to be the common denominator between the death of Stephen Smurr and the death of John Drennan, between the struggle of Michael Mulligan and the struggle of Vina Drennan, to bear working witness to what bound everybody together, to what was the very best in them and therefore God.

Nowhere on earth did Judge feel closer to his God than on the wooden walkway of this suspended structure of stone and steel. He was sometimes solitary but never alone, separate and yet at one with the borough of his childhood and the capital of his priesthood, high above the harbor that had welcomed his parents from Ireland.

Judge loved that New York was not a Jerusalem arising around a holy rock. New York became New York because of the harbor that brought not pilgrims but refugees who were driven by the material more than the spiritual, who aspired not to save their souls but to fill their bellies and to give their kids a better life. Judge's great delight in the Holy Land had been to see the everyday amid the sacred shrines. His great delight in New York was to see the sacred amid the everyday. The bridge was the spiritual altar of that joining to his God of Surprises.

He had been known to fall into prayer in church and to become so lost in God that he would be shocked to find several hours had passed. Here on the Brooklyn Bridge he could connect to the Almighty but also remain intensely aware of himself, seemingly of his every bracing breath.

Back on West Thirty-first Street, the Italian restaurant across from the friary took to clearing the floor for ballroom dancing on Tuesday nights. Judge would watch from the sidewalk as the couples moved to muted music on the other side of the plate glass. He spoke of taking dancing lessons right after he had mastered Rollerblading.

Such things were forgotten when an explosion involving gasoline and a pilot light at a Queens hardware store killed three firefighters, leaving eight children suddenly fatherless on Father's Day. The thwarted rescuers included Liam Flaherty, who had been playing a wedding with the band and raced to the scene, still in his kilt. The first funeral was for Firefighter Harry Ford, who worked with Flaherty at Rescue 4, the "heartbreak house," having already lost Peter McLaughlin as well as Lt. Thomas Williams, Judge's first line-of-duty death. Ford's wife asked that Judge say the Mass.

A new chaplain for Brooklyn and Queens had replaced Monsignor Brady and he insisted on officiating. Judge stood as a concelebrant outside St. Ignatius Martyr Church in Long Beach as Liam and the band slow-marched through the sunshine. The caisson bore Ford's coffin past the ten thousand firefighters lined up six deep. Paddy Brown snapped to attention beside Terry Hatton, who had returned from a European trip for the funeral. They gave a white-gloved salute.

As at the funerals for Williams and for McLaughlin, Judge watched Rescue 4's rig roll up, the siren mute but the lights flashing. The ritual became wrenchingly particular when Denise Ford and her three young sons stepped from the black limousine. Piper Billy Murphy joined the band's pipe major, Timmy Grant, in playing "Amazing Grace." Murphy faltered slightly when his eyes fell on the children.

"I try not to look at the kids," Murphy said later. "I look at the ground."

Judge said that faltering sometimes makes the whole effort more human and therefore more perfect.

Some firefighters given to discerning the Almighty at work noted that the sunny sky clouded over two hours later, as Liam again called the band into formation just down from St. Raymond's Church in East Rockaway. Rain began to fall in tear-sized drops, as if doing this a second time in a single day was too much for even the sky to bear.

The next day saw the funeral of Brian Downing of Ladder 163, who was to have flown off to Ireland with his wife and two young children after working on Father's Day. Judge retained a special connection with Rescue 4, and in the days that followed he noted in his phone log calls from Capt. Brian Hickey and Lt. Kevin Dowdell, both of whom would die with him on 9/11.

• • •

In the aftermath of the Father's Day fire, Judge took particular delight in a department ritual he saw as proof that the spirit of the fallen does indeed live on. The graduation of the latest Fire Academy class was held on July 23 at the Tribeca Performing Arts Center, four blocks uptown from the World Trade Center. Judge was there to bless the 150 new probationary firefighters, or "probies." They were fresh and impossibly young and so lit by a common spirit that Judge had difficulty remembering particular faces a month and five days later, when a probie named Michael Gorumba suffered a fatal heart attack at a fire. His wife was four months' pregnant.

Judge listened to fire officials ask the dead probie's mother what she wanted the department to say in her son's memory.

"Just tell them how much he loved his job," she said.

Judge noted that her words were so much like Chris Siedenburg's last words at the Watts Street fire. Judge wondered aloud after young Gorumba's funeral on the first of September if there was a limit to how long he could continue his own job if such losses kept coming one after another. He would at least be spared ever knowing that fifteen probies would be among those to die at the Twin Towers just ten days from then.

September 6 was Everald Brathwaite's birthday. Judge had promised to take him out this year as on the year before, but Brathwaite had fallen ill again. Judge visited him at Bronx Lebanon Hospital.

"He come in and he blessed me and he blessed the other guys," Brathwaite would remember. "I said, 'Don't forget my birthday.' He said, 'This time, we're going to have steak.'"

Judge proposed a date when Brathwaite should be back on his feet.

"We were going to celebrate September 11," Brathwaite recalled.

On September 9, Judge attended the Great Irish Fair in Coney Island, just up Surf Avenue from the big Seagate houses where his father had "chanced" to encounter Mary Ann of the stones. Timmy Stackpole was there, resplendent in the honor of being the fair's Irish Man of the Year. He was newly promoted to captain and back to full duty after nearly three years of determined rehabilitation.

"Nobody thought I was going to be back," Stackpole had said on his return. "But I'm a fireman, and all firemen have faith. I couldn't come back here if I didn't have faith."

He had told his wife, "The only thing I can't do is run."

He and Tara's first date had been to the 1984 Irish Fair.

"We thought that was this big twist of fate," Tara later said. "I believed and he believed God gave him to me. There was no question."

And now here they were.

"We were on top of the world," Tara said. "He'd come all the way back from the dead. We came through so much. No one was gonna beat us now."

She would remember how completely happy he looked.

"He said, 'I told you everything was going to be okay. I told you,'" Tara recalled. "He gave me a big kiss and he told me he loved me."

She watched Timmy standing with Judge. Later she would try to remember every detail.

"You try to relive the day in your heart," she said. "Father Judge looked like he was so proud of him, and Timmy with that big beautiful smile on his face."

She would also remember what Judge said when she told him her oldest son, Kevin, was going into the navy.

"This is a good thing," Judge said.

"I know, but I'm a mother," she said.

"You have to think of it differently," he said. "We're in a new millennium. God has great things planned for us. We're on the verge of a generation that's going to find patriotism again. You're going to be so proud of him."

Judge returned to West Thirty-first Street that night and encountered Firefighter Craig Monahan standing in front of the firehouse. Monahan was the one who had survived the Watts Street fire because Drennan had ordered him to switch places with Jimmy Young as they were climbing onto the rig. Monahan had learned that Judge knew exactly what to do in the face of a terrible loss, just as Paddy Brown did amid a raging fire. Monahan had concluded

Judge possessed a divine gift for seeing the heart of things, for peering directly into your soul even as he remained so human as to have always addressed him by the wrong name, the name of one of the dead firefighters.

Monahan had been detailed to Ladder 24 for the night. He expected Judge to once more mistakenly call him Chris.

"Hi, Craig," Judge said. "How are you?"

Craig Monahan was not so surprised that he failed to ask Judge to quickly bless his helmet.

The next morning, September 10, Judge drove to the Bronx and presided at the annual memorial Mass at Engine 73/Ladder 42, followed by a rededication of their renovated quarters. The fallen to be remembered included Capt. James McDonnell, who was killed in 1985, having pushed two firefighters to safety just as he was engulfed in an exploding fireball.

"I wouldn't be here if it wasn't for Jim McDonnell," one of the two firefighters, Peter Bielfeld, now said. "I'm blessed."

Judge was wearing his proper vestments as he stood behind a folding table that had been covered by a white cloth. He gave a homily that was inspired less by Gospel than by a fire on Wales Avenue two days before, during which firefighters from this house had made two rescues.

"You do what God has called you to do," he said. "You show up, you put one foot in front of the other, and you do your job, which is a mystery and a surprise. You have no idea, when you get on that rig, what God is calling you to. But He needs you . . . so keep going."

At least a dozen among the crowd that spilled out onto the street would be killed the next morning, including the blessed Bielfeld, who would end up at the Twin Towers only because he had switched an appointment in order to attend this ceremony.

"Love each other. Work together," Judge continued. "You love the job. We all do. What a blessing that is."

Judge then placed his hand over his heart and began to sing just as he had at the AIDS memorial for those two shunned brothers.

"God bless America . . ."

28

Judge was lying down on his foldout sofa, catching some rest after early prayers, when Brian Carroll burst in. The time was 8:50 A.M. The date, September 11, 2001.

"Mychal, you gotta get up," Carroll said. "A jet just hit the World Trade Center."

"What? Oh my God, oh my God," Judge said.

Carroll had been out on Sixth Avenue. He had seen the jetliner as it flew so shockingly low, and he had watched it strike the North Tower. He knew that if the firefighters ever needed a chaplain, it would be on this day.

Judge's beeper went off and his phone started ringing as he changed from his habit to a pair of black slacks and a clerical collar. Carroll noted that Judge reflexively took a moment to smooth his hair. A painting titled "The Last Call" was propped in his rocking chair. Firefighters had presented it to him just that week. It showed men in FDNY dress uniform bearing a flag-covered coffin down the steps of St. Francis.

Judge now dashed to the firehouse across the street to get his car. An off-duty captain named Danny Brethel was there and he offered to drive. They were joined by off-duty Firefighter Michael Weinberg, whose sister worked in the World Trade Center. They roared away, lights flashing, the siren wailing in what seemed like a city of sirens.

As they sped downtown, they could see smoke and flames coming from a huge hole in the North Tower where the hijacked Boeing 767 had hit. The FDNY radio crackled with calls from units racing toward the direst danger the department had ever faced. Among the voices on the radio was Paddy Brown.

"Truck three to Manhattan," Brown said.

"Three Truck go," the dispatcher said.

"Civilian reports from up here a plane just crashed into the World Trade Center for your information."

"Ten-four, K."

"Truck is available."

Brown and Ladder 3 may have already been out on a run. Or they may have simply started downtown. The voice came again, determined but edgy.

"Three Truck to Manhattan."

"Three Truck go."

"We're at Houston and West Broadway. We could see this from here. We've been directed by numerous civilians. You want us to take this in or do you want us to stand fast?"

There was a pause.

"Take that in, K," the dispatcher said.

"Three Truck res—"

The rest of *responding* was cut off, as if Brown was in too much of a hurry to get there to say it. The five on-duty members of Ladder 3 were on the way with seven off-duty members in the first wave of what would soon total one thousand firefighters. Ladder 3's rig pulled onto West Street, which could have almost been designed as a staging area for such a disaster, six lanes stretching alongside the lobby entrance to the stricken tower.

Judge's car arrived moments afterward. Brethel and Weinberg hurried off, later to be found crushed to death under a fire rig, where they had sought shelter from the collapsing towers.

Judge donned his white helmet and pulled on the turnout coat that had F.D.N.Y. CHAPLAIN M. JUDGE stenciled on the back as he strode toward the burning tower. A firefighter from the firehouse across from the friary, seeing Judge, would remember the look of pure sorrow on the priest's face as he watched the people pitching themselves from hell on high. Judge was praying. The firefighter began saying an Our Father as yet another person jumped, plummeting for nine seconds through "Thy will be done" and "as we forgive those who trespass against us" and exploding onto the pavement at the "deliver us from evil" as if to mock the "amen."

Another firefighter asked aloud a question many would remember thinking.

"How could anybody jump from up there?"

An answer came from Timmy Stackpole.

"They're choosing their own fate. Nobody wants to burn."

Giuliani had arrived from City Hall a half-dozen blocks away. He called out to Judge.

"Pray for us," Giuliani said.

Not *me. Us.* Giuliani was still the mayor, and he was speaking of the whole city.

Judge managed a smile. "I always do," he said.

Giuliani followed with his eyes for a moment as Judge continued toward the tower. Judge surprised no one who knew him when he joined the firefighters dashing into the lobby.

He entered looking almost his sixty-eight years. His usually vigorous stride slowed and shortened as he crossed the broad expanse of white marble, his hands slightly raised, as if ready to do something if he only knew what. Sunshine was pouring in windows shaped like the gothic arches of a cathedral. The jet fuel fumes had exploded down the elevator shafts and cracked some marble sheeting on the walls. At least one window was shattered, but otherwise the lobby was unscathed. All ninety-nine elevators were out, and three of the four stairways ended a floor above the mezzanine that extended over one side of the lobby like a choir loft or balcony. That was the way the great majority of the office workers were fleeing from the floors below the impact. Few were exiting through the lobby, where most of the firefighters trooped in.

Judge exchanged not a word with a ladder company that brushed past him, their hands so much like his own, hefting firefighting tools. He stood solitary as firefighters kept arriving, most of them silent and somber, making none of the banter usually heard at fire scenes. His lips moved in silent prayer as he again peered from under his helmet brim at the pristine white ceiling. The fiery inferno was eighty stories directly above, as unseeable as heaven.

The unseen became actual when the especially loud sound of a jumper hitting the canopy over the tower's entrance boomed through the lobby. Even the most experienced of the white-helmeted chiefs turned along with Judge in the direction of the sound.

The chiefs then resumed their huddle by the building's fire safety station, an area fronted by a high marble counter. Communication consoles there should have enabled the firefighters to boost their radio signals as well as to communicate to the whole building through a public-address system, but nothing was working except the intercoms to some of the elevators.

Battalion Chief Joe Pfeifer had been the first supervisor on the scene. Then the more senior Deputy Chief Pete Hayden had taken over, and he was summarizing the strategy to Commissioner Von Essen as ever more ladder, engine, and rescue companies arrived.

"As they come in, we're sending them up," Hayden said.

Hayden was religious enough to have carried a cross when he retraced Jesus' final steps on a trip to Jerusalem, but neither he nor the other chiefs seemed to be counting on much immediate assistance from a greater power. Hayden knew they would not be able to extinguish a fire of this magnitude. Their mission was to rescue as many people as they could. And this was a department whose firefighters routinely faced the most mortal danger on just the chance a single person was in peril.

Brown was already climbing, having headed directly to the one stairway that reached the lobby.

"Don't go up there, Paddy!" a firefighter called out.

"Are you nuts? We've got a job to do," Brown yelled back.

Too many other firefighters were also going straight up without checking in at the command post, making it impossible for Hayden to keep track of exactly who they were and where they were headed. He was a commander whose troops were almost too brave. He was unable to reach them by radio, and he was no more able than Judge to see the inferno overhead. He had to operate knowing less about the fire's immediate extent and progress than the millions around the world who were watching the news coverage on television.

But no viewer could have fully imagined the sound of jumpers that continued to boom through the lobby, singly, then in a flurry, then singly again.

"We got body parts all over the place," an arriving firefighter said to Chief Pfeifer.

In a small twist, a firefighter who had stood guard at John Drennan's door on that fortieth day was now coproducing a documentary on the FDNY with two French brothers. One of the brothers was in the lobby with a video camera and filmed Terry Hatton leading Rescue 1 in through a shattered twenty-five-foot window next to the command post. Hatton set his chin on the high counter as he waited for his assignment, looking for a moment like an overgrown little boy. He then embraced fellow firefighter Tim Brown, who was posted in the lobby as a liaison with the other emergency agencies.

"I love you like a brother," Hatton said. "I may never see you again."

Another ill-fated Rescue 1 firefighter, Gerry Nevins, the father of two young sons, said, "We're going to be lucky if we survive this."

Firefighter Chris Waugh stood in front of the lobby's fire safety station and moved a half-inch white metal rectangle marked *R1* on a metallic board used to record each company's deployment. The board was on the inside of an aluminum suitcase that rested on four scissored legs. The top was propped vertically, the outside bearing the words COMMAND POST and a battered fire department logo.

Another half-inch rectangle marked *L5* recorded that Ladder 5 was there, having arrived on the same rig that John Drennan and the others had ridden to the Watts Street fire. Waugh had been a member of the company that night, and he had helped carry out James Young while their comrades filled the blackened windows, removing their helmets and blessing themselves.

As Judge had said at Drennan's funeral, the captain's spirit was living on, now ascending with Ladder 5 and all the other companies up a stairway only wide enough for a single file of firefighters going up and a single file of office workers coming down. The firefighters were doing exactly what Drennan would have done, what any firefighter would do, what even Vina knew they had to do.

The office workers marveled at this spirit as Judge so often had. The same spirit seemed to fill the office workers, who remained heroically calm amid this sudden horror, helping those who were burned and injured, calling out encouragement to the firefighters. The word Captain Jay Jonas of Ladder 6 would use to describe the prevailing emotion fit those going up and those going down: "Altruism."

Some of the usual banter began, and a civilian who was descending with a golf club later reported one of the firefighters called out, "I saw your ball three floors down." The office workers saw that the firefighters were struggling under the weight of their equipment, the bunker gear, helmet and boots weighing twenty-nine pounds, the oxygen tank and mask another twenty-seven, or a total of fifty-six pounds even without tools or a length of hose. Some firefighters became winded and had to pause.

Others pushed themselves to keep going. Paddy Brown was thirty-five floors above Judge when he found a working phone. He reached the dispatcher he had been unable to contact on his radio.

"Dispatch, Captain Brown, Ladder Three . . . I'm at the World Trade Center."

"Yeah," the dispatcher said.

"I'm on the thirty-fifth floor, okay?"

"Okay."

"Just relay to the command post, we're trying to get up, you know. There's numerous civilians in all stairwells. Numerous burn injuries are coming down. I'm trying to send them down first. Apparently, it's above the seventy-fifth floor. I don't know if they got there yet, okay?"

"Okay," the dispatcher said.

"Three Truck, and we're still headed up, all right?"

"Okay."

"Thank you."

Brown hung up, and the dispatcher relayed the message to the command post, the words crackling over the radios in the lobby.

"Also Ladder Three is reporting on the thirty-fifth floor up on the stairwell they've got numerous injuries. They're treating numerous injuries from burns."

The relayed message confirmed what Judge had imagined, an explanation of the continuing sound of the jumpers landing outside. A particularly loud boom came as Judge turned away from the command center. He was one figure in turnout gear whose arrival did not need to be recorded on the board. He walked off.

Still more engine, ladder, and rescue companies arrived. Judge's friend Lt. Mickey Kross led in Engine 16 and stopped at the command station, a button pinned on the back of his helmet.

DON'T PANIC! it read.

Kross looked across the lobby at Judge.

"He was kind of like praying, and he looked very troubled," Kross recalled. "That scared me. I got a chill."

A magnetic rectangle marked E16 went on the board as Kross led his firefighters up toward their assignment on the twenty-third floor.

Judge stood alone in the sunny expanse of marble that extended around the elevator banks and stairwells at the building's structural core. He set his hands on his hips and took two steps backward for no apparent reason. The lucky office workers kept trooping toward safety on the mezzanine overhead. The unlucky ones, the jumpers, kept landing one after another after another. Pfeifer at one point picked up the microphone to the building's public-address system on the off chance it had not been knocked out. It had, and his words went no farther than those around him.

"Please don't jump. We're coming to get you."

At 9:02 A.M., the lobby was then shaken by a boom magnitudes bigger than the sound of jumpers. Burning debris began cascading down outside and somebody shouted out that the South Tower had been hit.

Firefighters began heading for the South Tower. The most senior of them was Chief Donald Burns, who had been present at the 1993 World Trade Center bombing.

"I'll go over and see what's there," Burns told Hayden.

Judge remained in the North Tower, his supplications to the Almighty having been met by a doubling of the horror. He stepped closer to the huddled white helmets, then backed off as if he was afraid of being in the way, then eased in again.

"There could be another fucking plane out there," said Albert Turi, the chief in charge of safety.

"We know that," Hayden said.

"Get as many people out of the building and let it burn up," Turi said.

"We got a lot of people in the building," Hayden said. "We got to get these people out."

"That's the priority," Turi said.

Hayden turned to a firefighter.

"There's a report of people trapped in the twenty-first floor and the seventy-first floor," he said.

"Which tower?" the firefighter asked.

"This tower," Hayden said.

Richie Sheirer, commissioner of the Mayor's Office of Emergency Management, the man in charge of coordinating the city's response to calamities, had received a report of a third hijacked jetliner. His liaison with the FDNY, Tim Brown, took it upon himself to get on a phone, dial 411, then call the main number for the Air Force.

"Who do I speak to about getting some air cover?" he inquired.

The prospect of another plane prompted Chief Joseph Callan to get on the radio.

"All units in Tower 1. Down to the lobby."

Callan got no response. He radioed again.

"Any unit in upper floor, Tower 1."

Cell phones were still working, and Von Essen answered his. "The mayor wants to talk to you. He wants to know what's going on."

The mayor liked to have his commissioners around him in times of crisis, the standard joke being that the emergency services were run by Police Commissioner Rudolph Giuliani and Fire Commissioner Rudolph Giuliani and OEM Commissioner Rudolph Giuliani. Von Essen exited the tower as a jumper's body exploded a few feet away. He continued to the mayor's emergency command center that Giuliani had built on the twenty-seventh floor of the building at 7 World Trade Center despite numerous warnings about establishing a bunker in the sky at a complex proven to be a prime terrorist target.

The mayor had already evacuated. Von Essen eventually caught up with Giuliani and suggested they go a dozen blocks uptown to Drennan's old firehouse, Ladder 5/Engine 24, because it had telephones and a television. They arrived, but both companies were down at the towers and the door was locked. The mayor's party had to break in.

Judge could have just walked out the same way as Von Essen, but he stayed in the lobby.

"You should go, Padre," a firefighter urged him.

"I'm not finished," Judge replied.

He stayed where he was, talking to God as the sound of yet another jumper resounded through the lobby. He paused, once more tilting his head to eavesdrop on the chiefs who were trying to reach the firefighters.

"See if we can get Stairway B . . . ," Hayden was saying.

Hayden's words were drowned out by another boom and then yet another and still another. Judge returned to the area between the balustrade and the elevators. The French filmmaker in the lobby zoomed in on Judge as he joined the firefighters who were seeking at least the illusion of protection under the mezzanine's overhang. Judge stood by a large potted plant, his face appearing from behind the fronds in the close-up. His mouth was half open, his lips pursed, his eyes peering up from under his helmet brim, his expression mirroring the fear and edgy grimness of the firefighters around him. He was heaven's official representative on a day when all you could see was hell.

Not a syllable could be heard that was not directly and urgently related to the actual rescue effort. The chiefs continued to radio and confer. A Port Authority official chanted a starkly secular phrase into an intercom as he punched a keypad that connected him to one after another of the building's elevators.

"Anyone in this car? There anyone in this car?"

Suddenly, somebody answered him from an elevator that had been stuck on the first floor since the first plane hit. The P.A. official working the intercom called to firefighters, who forced open the elevator. Five men and three women filed almost blithely out. One of the men turned and looked up but then walked on. There were none of the exclamations, none of the excited chatter that might be expected.

The priest who always seemed to notice everything did not appear even to see the people who filed miraculously out of an elevator directly in front of him.

He absently turned back toward the command center, where a dapper figure in a dark suit with a white three-corner pocket square was on the phone. This was John O'Neill. He had just retired as the FBI's lead man against terrorism, the man who had worried that Al Qaeda would strike as the ball dropped in Times Square, who had told friends he sensed "a big one" coming. Bureaucratic inanity had driven him to take a job as director of security of the World Trade Center. His voice remained calm as he spoke into a command center phone, a smudge of concrete dust across the back of his suit jacket.

"Sounds like they got the Pentagon," he said.

O'Neill hung up and strode past Judge on the way to his death.

Chief Pfeifer picked up the phone with the hope of reaching the dispatcher he had been unable to contact on the radio.

"Do you have to dial nine to get out?" Pfeifer asked.

From his post at the magnetic board, Chris Waugh saw a firefighter with a 21 on his helmet's front approaching from the street. Firefighter Zach Vause was with Engine 21, but he had been detailed to Ladder Co. 7 for the day, and he had arrived at the firehouse only to find the rig had already departed for the Trade Center. He had hopped the subway in full gear, telling everyone who asked that he knew no more than they did about what had happened. He got off at the City Hall stop and waded through the rushing tide of people who were fleeing, many of them crying. He noticed some black specks high above as he neared the North Tower and only realized as he was running toward the lobby that they were falling people.

One firefighter had already been killed by a jumper, and Waugh shouted for Vause to hurry in before he was hit. Vause came huffing in through the shattered window beside the command post a few heartbeats ahead of the next booms.

"You know where Seven Truck is?" Vause asked.

"I don't know where anybody is," Waugh said.

Vause headed around the fire station counter to speak to a chief and passed Judge, who was now silently praying, his eyes half closed. Vause continued up to Chief Stephen King and asked permission to head up alone.

"No, stay here," King said. "I'll find something for you to do."

Vause stood there, feeling useless, fighting an urge to start up whether or not he had approval. The Port Authority official continued working the intercom.

"Sixty-nine car. Anyone in this car? Hello, is there anyone in this car?"

The official showed a list to a fire chief.

"These are the cars with people in them," the official said.

The official pointed to an electronic board. Each of the tiny red lights on the board signified an elevator in which people were trapped.

"If you want to see the floor count, that's basically where they're at."

Chief Ray Downey arrived and conferred with Hayden and Pfeifer.

"We got two fifth alarms and it's chaos out there," Downey said.

Downey advised nobody leave by the side of the tower adjacent to the command post to avoid being hit by jumpers. He also coolly observed, "These buildings can collapse, you know."

A large, institutional white-faced clock was on the inside of the fire station counter, the black hands showing it was 9:50 A.M., just an hour since Judge heard the news. The red second hand continued sweeping into what would be the final minutes for him and Ray Downey and so many others. Downey set off for the central command post established between the two towers on the other side of West Street. A reminder came over the radio of the twin horror in the South Tower.

"Tower number two, nineteenth floor, firefighter down. Tower number two, nineteenth floor, firefighter down."

Waugh double-checked with Pfeifer.

"This is tower one?"

"This is tower one," Pfeifer said.

Pfeifer pointed to the countertop.

"Put a big 'one' here."

Waugh wrote "Tower 1" on the white marble with a black Magic Marker.

A young man in the red helmet of the Fire Patrol, which is usually tasked with securing the premises after a fire, stepped over to Judge. He introduced himself as Michael Angelini, son of Firefighter Joe Angelini, who had been honored at the Holy Name Society Communion Breakfast.

On now hearing the name Angelini, Judge set his right hand on young Michael's shoulder and broke into a smile. He turned somber again as he heard that Michael's father and firefighter brother were both working.

"I'll say a prayer for your family," Judge said.

Michael's partner, Fire Patrol Officer Paul Curran, returned from the mezzanine, where he had gazed out at the plaza adjoining the two towers to see a field of carnage.

"Father, it's devastation up there," Curran said.

"I'm needed up there," Judge said.

"I think you are, Father," Curran said.

"Where are they?"

"At the top of the escalator, Father, and you make a left."

Judge turned to Angelini.

"I have to go."

Curran would remember that Judge did not hesitate before climbing the frozen escalator to the mezzanine. Judge stopped before the big windows. The plaza was littered with bodies and body parts, some charred, many only bloody clumps. Those who had jumped looked like splatters of red mud surrounded by bundles of rags and maybe a shoe or two.

Judge was standing alone, his eyes closed, when fire department photographer Lt. Richard Smiouskas came in. Judge was praying aloud so fervently he seemed to Smiouskas almost to be speaking in tongues.

"Jesus, please end this right now! God, please end this!"

"Hello, Father," Smiouskas said.

Judge opened his eyes, looked at him for a moment, and continued praying.

The big clock in the lobby below read 9:58 and the red second hand swept on around. Brown and Ladder 3 were tending the burned on the thirty-fifth floor. Hatton and Rescue 1 were above them. Stackpole was over by the South Tower.

Judge just kept praying.

"Jesus, please end this right now!"

As if in response, another jumper hit just outside the window. Blood and bits of flesh sprayed onto the plate glass and dripped down as Judge prayed. Smiouskas snapped a couple of quick photos and moved to leave.

"Be careful," Smiouskas said.

Judge's supplications only ceased as the clock below ticked to 9:59.

There came a thundering from above, as loud as the Almighty's own.

29

E verybody all right?"
    "Yeah, I'm okay."
"All right, come on down this way."
"Let's get out the way we came in."
"Come on back."
"Come on, guys."
The noise and a hurricane force wind had pursued Hayden and Pfeifer and Waugh and Vause and young Angelini and the others away from the command post. They had just been reaching the escalators when they were enveloped in the all-eclipsing dust. They were now calling to one another, disembodied voices on a bright morning suddenly turned to a dark and suffocating night.
"You got a light?"
"Come on."
"Over here."
"We got to get everybody out. Let's go."
Pfeifer got on his radio.
"Command Post in Tower 1. All units, evacuate the building."
The radio crackled with voices more urgent and agitated than those that continued calling out in the blackness.
"Where's that flashlight?"
"Where's Chief Hayden?"
"Right here."
"What's the situation outside?"
Neither Hayden nor anybody else could answer that question. None of

them knew exactly what had happened, only that it was bigger than anything they had been in before.

"Can we get out that way?"

"We got to go to the left."

"Come on. This way."

"Where are you going?"

"Up the escalator. Right here."

"Where's the escalator?"

"We can get out maybe. Depending on the debris."

"We came in this way."

"No, we came in the other way."

Hayden stumbled blindly onto a body lying on the floor. The dust was just becoming penetrable by flashlight and a beam fell on the sprawled figure. Angelini knew it was Judge when he saw a flash of white at the neck.

Vause was also there. He had been a paramedic before becoming a firefighter. He knelt down and held his fingertips to the priest's throat. He felt no pulse and he could hear the too familiar wheeze of anginal breathing, the stuttering gasps in the final moments of life. He opened the turnout coat and tore away the white collar and the black shirt, but the neck of the T-shirt seemed to be made of titanium. He gave up and began pushing on the chest. He again checked for a pulse.

"You got something?" a voice asked.

"No," Vause said.

Nobody even thought of leaving Judge there.

"Hey, guys, we need a hand here," Hayden said. "We need a—"

Hayden stopped in midsentence as he tried to lift the priest, who was built more like a firefighter.

"Take his coat off," Hayden said. "This is Father Judge."

Waugh grabbed Judge's belt. Vause took an arm, Angelini one leg, Hayden the other.

"All right, we got four guys," Hayden said.

Judge's feet dangled in the flashlight beam. Black lace-up shoes. Black socks. The four booted men carried him up the escalator as one of their own.

The radios still crackled with urgency, but the figures bearing Judge's body quieted and the even *clump, clump, clump* of their ascent was audible in the hush that followed the thundering. Their boots made prints like those of lunar astronauts in the settling gray dust of a world transformed. They could have been on some other, lifeless planet where morning was indistinguishable from night.

At the top of the escalators, they came to the big windows looking out on the plaza where Judge had stood praying aloud for the horror to stop. The thundering from above had sent him dashing out an adjacent door. He had kept going as Smiouskas shouted, "Don't go out!"

Smiouskas had bolted the other way. Not a living soul seems to have witnessed what happened after Judge ran out onto the field of burned and splattered bodies. He must have suddenly realized that he was actually heading toward the noise, that it was not this tower but its twin. He had turned away from the collapsing South Tower and headed back through the doorway.

The glass up on the mezzanine was still intact, but the blinding dust would have roiled up through the shattered windows of the lobby below, blasting past Hayden and the others and swallowing Judge just about when he reached the escalators, as if the horror he was fleeing had circled around to get him. He either fell or collapsed, ending up where Hayden stumbled upon him. He may have been literally frightened to death.

Judge had no visible injuries as the firefighters now carried him up to that same doorway. They were assisted by two white-shirted police lieutenants, Bill Cosgrove and Marc Stollerman. Judge was six-foot-one and maybe 175 pounds, and they had to sidle and shift to get him out the portal.

They started around Tower 1 under a protective overhang, the light now the gray of a dawn devoid of promise, a choking blankness that settled onto the surrounding devastation. A jumper from the still-standing twin landed unseen, the sound just as shocking as the first.

The men trudged on, slowed by their burden. They could have just left him and fled. Their boot prints formed a trail of devotion in the ash. Angelini saw a two-by-six board from a police barricade and figured the carrying would be easier if he could find another. He had stepped away when the others came upon a broken plastic chair that seemed to have been blown out of the tower. They placed Judge in the chair and descended from the plaza, two in front, two behind, the rest coming after.

Hayden set off to find the other surviving commanders. Waugh and Vause and Cosgrove and Stollerman were by then joined by Kevin Allen of the Office of Emergency Management and a lone civilian who had come to the scene looking to help, business executive and West Point graduate John McGuire. They carried Judge up Vesey Street as the dust continued to settle.

Morning was becoming morning again. The sun began to shine through just as brightly, but the returning clarity made only more unreal the absence where the South Tower had been just minutes before.

So unreal that it did not seem quite possible that the same could happen to the remaining tower. They were struggling on through the debris with Judge when Reuters photographer Shannon Stapleton took a picture that some would later call the modern *Pietà*. The bearers were figures from a maelstrom, their faces straining, urgent as they lugged a figure of perfect peace.

On the next block, the bearers shifted Judge to an abandoned orange backboard. Another block brought them to Church Street. An ambulance was parked on the southeast corner. The crew was busy treating three injured people, but a paramedic took a moment to pronounce Judge dead.

"This man is a priest," Cosgrove called out. "Somebody get this man a priest."

A young uniformed cop named Jose Alfonso Rodriguez came over.

"I know where there's a church," he said.

Still half-choked by the dust and his eyes inflamed by the grit, Rodriguez hurried up the street to St. Peter's Church. The roof of the city's oldest Catholic house of worship had been struck by the landing gear from one of the jetliners, but when Rodriguez entered he found the interior undisturbed. A blind woman was tearing the altar cloth into strips that people could use as masks against the dust.

Rodriguez told the woman he needed a priest to give someone the last rites. She said the priests were all out in the streets assisting people.

"But if you're Catholic, then you can give the last rites," she said.

Rodriguez returned to Cosgrove.

"Are you Catholic?" Rodriguez asked.

"Yes," Cosgrove said.

"Me, too," Rodriguez said.

The two knelt in the gray dust, the North Tower blazing above. Rodriguez took Judge's left hand. Cosgrove set his hands on Judge's head. They said the Our Father and then Cosgrove improvised as best he could.

"Take his soul, please, into heaven . . ."

Cosgrove uttered another phrase as the survivors around them reeled and gagged and fought for breath in this realm of gray ash.

". . . dust to dust, ashes to ashes . . ."

There came a second, equally loud thundering from above. Cosgrove and others dove into a corner deli. Waugh and Vause sought refuge in the lobby of an office building at 30 Vesey Street. The living had to save themselves. Judge lay in the street on the backboard as the second tower collapsed in what seismographs clocked at eight and a half seconds, pancaking at thirteen floors a second, the entire tower now a falling object.

Morning again became night. More dust settled on Judge's lifeless form and on everything around him, a toxic powder of steel and concrete and glass and carpet and office furniture and people who had been alive moments before. A scientific analysis would detect a measurable level of human bone.

The second thundering was followed by another hush. The silence was then broken by the coughing of the survivors, the thump of gas tanks exploding in burning cars, and the chirping of PASS alarms, a device worn by firefighters that emits a distinctive high-pitched sound when it does not detect movement. The sound is supposed to direct rescuers to a trapped comrade, but the alarms were coming from all directions, indistinguishable from one another. A firefighter's air tank popped and whooshed crazily on the ground. The fire radio dispatcher could be heard calling for Paddy Brown's company.

"Manhattan to Ladder Three, K. Three truck. Manhattan to Ladder Three, K. Three?"

When the sun reappeared a second time, the North Tower was also gone. Paddy Brown had still been high above, responding to a mayday from Terry Hatton.

Firefighters who had fled the second collapse started back toward the remains of the two towers. They had only axes and steel bars and a single hose run from a fireboat in the river.

"We're going to regroup," a voice said over the fire radio.

Waugh was on his way to join the firefighters regrouping on Broadway when he saw a fire chaplain from suburban Nassau County. Waugh told Father Kevin Smith that Judge was dead and pointed down Vesey Street toward where he had last seen the body.

"He didn't die in the collapse. He collapsed before the building. We got him out of the building," Waugh said. "He didn't get collapsed on. Now you got to find him. You got to bless him for me."

Smith set off to find Judge. The only body in sight was one he did not recognize that lay covered with debris and dust beside an ambulance. He gave a quick blessing before rescue workers carried away the body under a blood-stained disposable sheet. He registered in the passing moment that the right arm was hanging over the side of the backboard.

Smith continued the search for Judge but paused farther up the street to dissuade a fellow priest who was heading into the zone of wreckage and fire without protective clothing. Waugh then came up, asking if Smith had found Judge.

"Where did you put him?" Smith asked

"I put him next to the ambulance," Waugh said.

Smith then flashed to the backboard and the dangling arm. The sleeve had been black.

"Oh my God, that was Mike Judge," Smith said.

Smith set off down the block, asking other cops and rescue workers if they had seen a body carried past.

"Well, there's been a lot of bodies," a worker said.

Smith described the backboard and the blue sheet.

"Oh, that one."

Smith was directed to the lobby of an office building where the police were establishing a temporary morgue, taping paper over the windows. He re-peated the description to the hulking officers at the door.

"It's right in the corner," the cop said.

Smith went over and pulled back the blue bloodstained sheet. He now recognized the face under dust so thick that the black clerical shirt was almost white. Smith began to break down, and the cop eased him away, comforting him.

As he composed himself, Smith saw that he was standing next to a copy-ing machine that somebody had covered with a white sheet. He returned to Judge and replaced the bloody blue sheet with the white one. He then stepped into the street and called to a squad of firefighters from various com-panies who had met up as they rode toward the burning towers on the Staten Island ferry.

"Come with me," he said. "I want you to do something with me."

Smith brought the firefighters inside and told them the body before them was their own Father Mychal.

"He doesn't belong in a hallway," Smith said.

Firefighter Mark Heintz of Ladder 87 knelt and lifted the sheet. He had never spoken to Judge, but he recognized the face from department ceremonies. The ranking officer, Lt. Ralph Pepe of Ladder 169, said they should tie down Judge's hands so they would not fall over the side of the backboard when they moved him.

The other firefighters lifted the end of the backboard and Pepe slid a rope under the body. Heintz grabbed the end and secured the surprising hands that had come to rest after nearly a half century of giving comfort.

The firefighters positioned themselves around Judge so each could take one of the backboard's handholds. They lifted him in unison. There was more blood on the floor. The most likely explanation was that Judge had been struck in the back of the head by debris as he lay dead in the street during the second collapse.

The firefighters trudged slowly from the building and carried Judge down Church Street. Heintz was one of the two firefighters at the front. The other was Firefighter Marty Fullam of Ladder 87. Fullam was older, and Heintz asked if he wanted to rest.

"Marty said something like, 'Don't worry about me, kid,' and we both shared a needed smile," Heintz would recall. "We got to the corner and I saw St. Peter's Catholic Church across the street and to the left. A few passing firemen asked us who we were carrying, and we told them that it was Father Judge. Firemen stopped in their tracks, removed their helmets, and let us pass by in silent prayer."

Smith led the way into the church and saw a medical team was setting up a triage area by the back pews. The city was still in that brief period after the collapses when it imagined there might be hundreds of injured survivors, before all the empty stretchers and wheelchairs and unused bandages became a terrible sight. Smith continued down the aisle and there was only one place to put Mychal Judge.

"We gingerly laid Father Mike before the altar," Heintz recalled.

Smith fetched a stole from the sacristy and found the FDNY chaplain badge in Judge's back pants pocket. He set these on Judge's chest. The firefighters removed their helmets and knelt.

"As I bowed my head in prayer, the reality of the day started to hit me," Heintz said. "I knew that bringing Father Mike safely into the church was not to be taken lightly. It's hard to explain, but I felt an inner peace. I had a sense of invincibility. I didn't know what the other guys were feeling, but I believed that I would be safe for the rest of the day."

Other firefighters began filing into St. Peter's, ghostly with dust, their eyes red from the irritating grit, but not yet crying, even though most of them were by then all but certain they had lost close friends and, in some cases, their entire company. The weeping started when they saw their chaplain lying before the altar. Their tears left dark tracks in the gray powder on their clenched faces as they, too, removed their helmets and knelt.

After a moment, they departed to resume searching, and others took their place as the word spread through the ruins and beyond. The Lutheran fire chaplain, Everett Wabst, came in to pay his respects as a minister and as a former firefighter. He had been on Staten Island, counseling a fire widow at Judge's request, when he learned the Trade Center had been attacked. He now stood by the body, raising the sheet for those firefighters who wished to gaze upon Father Mychal's serene face.

The assistant pastor at St. Peter's managed to get through on a cell phone and notify the cardinal's office of Judge's death. The vicar general telephoned Father Peter Brophy, the pastor at the Franciscan Friary on West Thirty-first Street.

"Have you heard Mychal Judge has fallen?" the vicar general asked.

Brophy was in street clothes, having just removed his vestments after saying the 12:15 P.M. Mass. He donned the brown habit that would be sure to get him through police lines. He arrived with another friar at St. Peter's Church to see Judge wrapped in what they assumed was the white cloth from the altar. Their habits told the firefighters they were the padre's brothers.

"It's time for us to do whatever you want that helps you with Mychal," one said.

Brophy could summarize what he wanted with the single sentence that any firefighter could understand.

"Bring him home."

Wabst took Brophy to a triage center in an office building around the corner on Broadway to see Dr. Kerry Kelly, the department's chief medical officer. Kelly had arrived at the scene when both towers were still standing, and she had gone through the field of body parts numbly telling herself, "This is an anatomy lesson. There's a hip. There's a spleen . . ." She had been pulled to safety during the first collapse by a fire captain and during the second by a firefighter. She, the captain, and the firefighter had found two other survivors, including one who had lost a thumb as well as his memory. He was the only one of thirteen from his firehouse who was still alive.

Kelly told Brophy that as long as there might be other survivors, she could not authorize the use of a vehicle for the dead, even if it was for Father Mychal.

"He's in a church. What better place than a church?" Kelly remembers saying. "Why don't you just leave him here?"

Brophy was worried the situation downtown would become only more chaotic. He had also heard warnings that the forty-story 7 World Trade Center housing the mayor's aerial bunker was about to collapse and that St. Peter's was in the danger zone.

"No, no, he has to come home," Brophy said.

The firefighters resolved the situation in keeping with their maxim that it is easier to ask for forgiveness than to ask for permission.

"Somehow the men got a wagon to appear for me so I didn't have to carry him on my back," Brophy recalled.

An FDNY ambulance pulled up in front of the church and the paramedics came down the aisle with a black body bag. Captains Mike Currid and Richie Goldstein of the fire officers union were there and said they would be the ones who placed Judge inside.

Goldstein is Jewish, but he had come to consider Judge his kind of holy man. Goldstein stopped at a market on 125th Street in Harlem once a week to bring a special blend of coffee to Judge at the friary. Goldstein and Currid now ever so gently rolled Judge up onto his side and slid the body bag under him.

"Me and Goldstein were crying more than we did the rest of our life altogether," Currid later said.

Currid had performed this ritual with any number of fire victims, but even with children it had never been so wrenching. He began pulling up the long zipper, and there was a rasping that he would describe with two words.

"Very final."

Currid, Goldstein, and Wabst were among those who carried Judge from the church. Wabst had grabbed a fistful of the two thousand cards he happened to have in his car printed with a prayer composed by Judge. The words were inspired by the Prayer of Saint Francis and AA's Serenity Prayer, with a twist of pure Mychal. Wabst had intended to give them to Judge so he could pass them out on his travels.

He now read aloud from one.

> *Lord, take me where you want me to go*
> *Let me meet who you want me to meet*
> *Tell me what you want me to say*
> *And keep me out of your way.*

Wabst stayed on the sidewalk as Currid climbed into the ambulance along with Brophy and a cop. Brophy had already sent the other friar ahead to St. Francis. Currid used a cell phone to call the firehouse.

When the ambulance turned off Sixth Avenue onto West Thirty-first Street, eighteen brown-robed figures were waiting outside the quarters of Engine Co. 1 and Ladder Co. 24, along with the blue-clad figures who had arrived at the firehouse after the towers fell.

The driver backed the ambulance into the open front of the firehouse. The firefighters had curtained off an area at the rear with rope and sheets. They gingerly laid Judge on a bed they had brought down from the sleeping quarters. They rummaged up a candle and placed it beside him. The tiny flame flickered as a symbol of life and sanctity.

The men in blue stepped away to give those in brown some time alone with their comrade. Brophy led the friars in prayer.

After a half hour, some of the firefighters stepped up to pray with the friars. A firefighter paid Brophy what he took as a high compliment.

"You're really like one of us," the firefighter said. "You go get your brother and bring him home."

Currid noted another similarity between firefighters and friars.

"We'll do the job, but we'll do it our way," Currid said.

Brophy hoped to transport Judge directly to a funeral home, but the law required that any victim of a violent death must first go to the chief medical examiner's office. A battered blue morgue wagon pulled up.

"The firemen were like, 'He's not going in that truck,'" Brophy recalled.

The same FDNY ambulance returned, and Brophy and Friar Pat Fitzgerald rode with their friend to a squat brick building by Bellevue Hospital. Judge was wheeled on a gurney into the place where he had so often come to claim the personal effects of the homeless who had listed him as next of kin.

The staff was gearing up to receive hundreds, or maybe even thousands of victims, but only four other body bags were in the giant walk-in freezer. Judge had been preceded by the second in command of the fire department, First Deputy Commissioner Bill Feehan, with whom he had more than once held hands and cried and prayed over a fallen firefighter. There was also the highest uniformed officer, Chief of Department Pete Ganci, who had quit smoking two weeks before with Judge's encouragement. The other two bodies were Joseph Lovero of the Jersey City Fire Department, who had come to assist, and Port Authority Police Officer George Howard, whose shield would later be presented by his mother to President George W. Bush.

The friars blessed the bodies and prayed. Brophy adamantly opposed an autopsy of Judge, but the medical examiner's office continued to insist until one of the firemen had an inspiration that their padre would have loved. He looked the official straight in the eye and said, "He's Jewish. He has to be buried by sundown."

The official relented but said the body still had to be examined and photographed and fingerprinted. Before that began Steven McDonald arrived in his blue van. He had heard from a friend in the police department that Judge had been killed. An attendant led him in his motorized wheelchair into a refrigerated room. The attendant pointed to one of the five bagged bodies.

"Here's Mychal Judge's remains."

McDonald rolled back to his van and sat in shock and grief.

Judge became the first to be processed by a sort of assembly line established in anticipation of the victims to come. He was fingerprinted by NYPD Det. Tom Nerney, who gingerly inked the fingertips and pressed them one by one onto a white card. He had tears in his eyes when he was done.

"It was an honor to do that for Father Mychal," Nerney said.

A clerk began pecking out a death certificate but had to start over after putting down the wrong date for a day that would later be known the world over as 9/11. The clerk typed "blunt trauma to head" in the space for Cause of Death, although an autopsy almost certainly would have shown that Judge died prior to suffering the wound in the second collapse. The clerk seemed unsure what to put down in the space marked Manner of Death for a victim of the biggest mass slaughter in American history.

"Homicide?"

The clerk ended up typing the same word that would apply to a street corner shooting. The certificate was numbered DM0001-01, the DM standing for "Disaster Manhattan."

"You're the first," the clerk said.

A hearse bore Judge's body uptown with a police escort arranged by Brian Mulheren. The former night mayor had Judge's body taken to Frank E. Campbell's, the Upper East Side funeral home that handled so many deceased New Yorkers of note. Brophy explained to the funeral director that however much Mychal Judge might have been a true celebrity, he was first and foremost a Franciscan.

"We're not St. Patrick's Cathedral types," Brophy later said. "Campbell's had never done a Franciscan before."

Brophy emphasized that the Franciscans would abhor any extravagance.

"It would be scandalous to us," Brophy said.

Campbell's had certainly received more onerous requests than simplicity.

The light was blinking on the new answering machine that Currid and his fellow officers had given Judge. It was now full to capacity with anxious messages from callers who had turned to Judge on a day that tested everyone's faith. One of those most in need of his steadying words was Timmy Stackpole's wife, Tara. She had been at her mother's house in Rockaway when news of the attack came on the television. She headed home to her five children, and because a bridge was closed, she was detoured past the very place in Brooklyn where her husband had been burned, the spot now marked by a white cross fashioned by a rental car attendant who lived next door. She raced on to her house and called Judge even though she knew he would not be sitting in his room.

"Father Mike, it's Tara. I know you're very busy. I'm just looking for Timmy. Just call me when you get back and tell me everybody's okay."

The firefighter who had told his wife the only thing he could not do was run had been a few steps too slow in fleeing the falling South Tower. He remained one of the missing as hundreds of rescue workers searched the smoking pile. Hopes dimmed that there might be more survivors. So far only eleven firefighters, one civilian, and a Port Authority cop had emerged alive from the North Tower after it came down.

Among them was Mickey Kross. He had been around the second floor of Stairway B when he heard a roaring that grew ever louder as it drew ever nearer. A fierce wind had lifted him into the air.

"I tried to climb inside my fire helmet," Kross later said.

After thirteen seconds there was total, eerie silence, and Kross was not entirely sure he was alive.

"I had never been dead before," he explained.

He then heard moans and the voices of firefighters who had been around the fourth floor. All of Ladder 6 had escaped serious injury. Ladder 6 had been helping an office worker from the building when they came upon Drennan's old company, Ladder 5, attending to a civilian suffering chest pains.

The South Tower had collapsed by then, and it seemed likely the North might soon do the same. And Ladder 6's officer told the Ladder 5 officer, Lt. Mike Warchola, that it was time to go.

"I know," Warchola said. "We're working on this guy. We'll be right behind you."

After the second collapse, Warchola could be heard calling over his portable radio, "Mayday! Mayday! Mayday! This is the officer of Ladder Company Five. I'm in the B stairway on the twelfth floor. I'm trapped and I'm hurt bad."

Rescue workers were unable to reach Warchola in time. He died along with ten other men from Drennan's firehouse. Only a quirk of luck had saved Craig Monahan, whose helmet Judge had blessed two days before.

Other firehouses lost as many as eighteen. The young fire patrolman who introduced himself to Judge in the tower lobby had lost a father and a brother. A retired captain searched vainly for two sons. Three pairs of brothers were missing. Everybody seemed to have lost a brother or somebody as dear as one. The faces of the firefighters as they searched the ruins were stony with anger and hurt when the Lutheran fire chaplain Wabst handed them one of the cards he had stuffed into his turnout coat pockets. He would watch their expressions change when they saw whose prayer it was and they came to Mychal's last line, "and keep me out of your way."

"They'd smile and laugh and we'd start talking," Wabst recalled. "It just changed the nature of everything right on the spot. Mychal was still up to his impish ways."

When the rescue workers recovered a firefighter's remains, Wabst would invoke the one name he knew that would steady and strengthen the survivors.

"Lord, we commit this firefighter to your kingdom and thank you for absolving all his earthly sins. And we ask that you have Father Judge meet him at the gates and that you have Father Judge help to gird him in armor to do battle with this great evil that has befallen us."

The Protestant Wabst had also taken from his car a small container of holy water blessed by Judge in the event he encountered a Catholic in need. Wabst was now called to bless body after body, and he extended his meager supply by pouring a few drops into bottles of drinking water. The problem was that the minute he put a bottle down a parched firefighter would unwittingly pick it up and take a swallow.

"Hey, you drank his holy water!" somebody would shout.

The firefighter would look at Wabst, and there would be what might be termed a Mychal moment.

"That's fine," Wabst would say, "but if you leave this pile and go mess around, it's going to burn like hell."

The firefighters found no more survivors and few intact bodies. Everything in the towers except steel and paper seemed to have ground itself to dust. One financial form was marked "Attn: R Damani 98th Fl. 1 World Trade Center." A firefighter paused to examine a check from Sumitomo Marine Claims Services of Suite 9035, One World Trade Center. He read aloud the amount with a hollow tone that said this was one day in the financial capital of the world when money meant no more than the Franciscans held it to mean.

"A hundred and seven thousand dollars," he said.

A mass of dollar bills was strewn nearby, improbably pristine atop the ash, all but unnoticed by the passing rescue workers.

What did stop one firefighter was a snapshot of a little girl wearing a white turtleneck with a shamrock on the collar. A sight that commanded all eyes was a flock of orange-and-black monarch butterflies that skirted the smoldering ruins on their annual migration. Several dozen fluttered through a row of saplings from whose branches hung long strips of glazing from the windows of the collapsed towers.

Anyone who had been at John Drennan's burial thought of the monarch that had alighted on his coffin. A friend called Vina from a cell phone on the Brooklyn Bridge to report seeing other butterflies at midspan, bright against the smoke rising from downtown Manhattan.

Vina remembered Judge speaking of his God of Surprises, saying even the most terrible times present us with wonders, that good always arises from bad in the most unexpected ways. The words now returned to Vina as an impossibly delicate thought on a day when Patrick Brown and Terry Hatton and Timmy Stackpole and so many other dear friends had been killed with such astonishing violence. She got a second butterfly call from her daughter, Adrienne, who reported that one of them was banging against her window.

"Well, let it in and give it a beer," Vina said.

30

Two days after the attacks, as ever more monarchs fluttered through the smoke rising from the ruins of the World Trade Center, the remains of Mychal Judge were carried into the lower church adjoining the friary for his wake. Vina Drennan attended. Tara Stackpole was also there, and of course Dympna and Erin.

Judge lay before the altar in an open coffin. He was dressed in his brown habit. The hands that had felt so useless in the tower were folded before him, still surprising in their size, still looking strong. His dress fire department hat and a pair of white gloves were by his head. A fire department honor guard stood in their dress blues, staring fixedly as the mourners knelt in ones and twos, a homeless man, a prominent lawyer, a recovering alcoholic, the sister of an AIDS victim, a company of firefighters dusty from the pile.

Giuliani approached, his face tight.

"How are we going to get through this without him?" Giuliani would remember thinking.

As he knelt before the coffin to say a prayer for Judge, Giuliani was already showing the whole world the truth of what his favorite chaplain had said about him since that first night at Ladder 5. Judge always insisted that despite Giuliani's prosecutorial mania and roughshod narcissism and heedless love life, there could be no better mayor in a time of tragedy. Giuliani was proving this true in the middle of the biggest tragedy the city ever suffered, and as he did so he was asking himself a question again and again.

"What would Mychal Judge do?"

He had been asked on the day of the attacks how many people had died. His reply had made people begin to see him as Judge had seen him.

"The number of deaths will be more than we can bear," he said.

As he now spoke at the wake's concluding service, Giuliani seemed truly to represent the whole city.

"This is the first funeral and we are going to have so many others," he said.

Giuliani spoke of Judge heroically leading the way into heaven. The mourners sat separate in their individual grief for the loss of a man so many thought of as their best friend, one of their very own.

"I even know that up in heaven Cardinal O'Connor is letting Father Judge say Mass," Giuliani then added.

The mourners erupted in laughter and looked at each other, as if surprised that the others got the joke. They had imagined that Judge's conflicts with the late cardinal had been a secret to which only his very closest friends were privy. They realized that this was true, that the real surprise was he had been intimately connected with all of them. A group as diverse as Judge's New York felt itself drawn together in a unifying embrace.

At Bronx Lebanon Hospital, Brathwaite had no TV service and did not know what had happened to Judge until a buddy phoned on September 14.

"He said, 'I think your priest friend died,'" Brathwaite recalled. "I just lay there until the evening came."

Brathwaite finally decided to call the friary and was told Judge had indeed been killed.

"Right then and there I started screaming, asking them to pull out all these tubes and everything," Brathwaite remembered. "I said, 'I have to leave here right now.'"

He tore out the IV tubes himself and got to St. Francis just after the wake. Friars Brian Carroll and Pat Fitzgerald were standing outside.

"They said, 'Your friend is here. He's downstairs.' They said, 'The funeral is tomorrow,'" Brathwaite recalled.

The Lutheran chaplain Wabst had also missed the wake. He had been scheduled to speak, but the firefighters began recovering more and more of their comrades, and he was sure that Judge would not have wanted him to leave the pile. He remained for forty-eight hours, taking only a brief break to wash out his clerical shirt in a sink and get more cards printed with what had become known as Mychal's Prayer.

The firefighters searching the ruins included Liam Flaherty of the pipe band. The Celtic spirit that Judge had invoked now seemed to drive Flaherty and his small crew as they searched through the night, keeping to the dark side of the pile so they would not be spotted by fire chiefs and chased away from the more dangerous places.

By four A.M., the firefighters had found ten comrades. Each time they helped Wabst up over ropes and ladders and across smoky voids. He sometimes was still on his way up when the body had begun to come down, and he would give a blessing as he teetered atop the debris.

"And Father Judge is waiting up there for the guys now," Wabst would say. "He's led the way."

At one point, Wabst peered over the top of the ruins and saw thousands of rescue workers digging by hand, a sight that burned into his memory as both inspiring and heartbreaking. He continued his own efforts past dawn, the rising sun first striking what had been the dark side of the pile.

At eight A.M., the firefighters began to unearth two more bodies. Only the boots were visible when the hour for Judge's funeral neared. Wabst figured that was enough of the bodies for him to bless before he headed uptown. He arrived in time to march in his chaplain's uniform with the procession of friars down the center aisle of the upper church.

Even as they followed Judge's mortal remains up to the altar, several friars could not help but smile on seeing fourteen-month-old Andrew Brautigan grinning from the lap of his grandmother, Vina Drennan. She had gotten him to smile by softly singing "Moonlight Bay" as the church filled. The boy kept smiling as the figures in blue followed the friars.

"See the firemen?" Drennan whispered.

When the boy began to fidget, Mike Currid leaned over from his seat beside Vina and held out his white uniform hat. The boy hushed, his two tiny hands clutching the hat of the man who had so gently placed Judge in a body bag.

Brathwaite arrived on time, only to be stopped by a cop at the end of the block.

He then chanced to see friars Carroll and Fitzgerald again. The friars escorted him in past the guardians at the door and seated him in accordance with Judge's priorities.

"A couple of seats away from the President and the dignitaries," Brathwaite reported.

President Clinton had come with Hillary and their daughter, Chelsea. Hillary had arrived at the church expecting only to pay respects to the priest who had made her smile when she so desperately needed to smile, whose loss brought her to tears. She had not expected to be asked to speak and now faced the surprising prospect of having to be spontaneous. But she felt she could not say no.

"Because he was my friend," she later said.

At the appointed moment, she rose from beside Judge's sisters. She spoke of the shock of hearing of the attack.

"And then I was called and told that Father Mychal Judge had died doing what he was called to do. And all of a sudden the enormity of the tragedy became very personal."

Her voice and expression said this was so.

"What a bearer of light," she continued. "He lit up the White House as he lit up every place where he saw himself. Father, you gave us so many gifts when you were alive: gifts of laughter and love."

She sounded as authentic as anybody had ever heard her, speaking from the core that Judge had recognized, that had made him defend her when firefighters dismissed her as a fake who would say anything. She was as good as she had ever been, as good as Judge saw her.

The homily was delivered by the man Judge had designated in a form filled out by all Franciscans marked "On the Occasion of Your Death." He had chosen fellow friar Michael Duffy.

"After all that has been written about Father Mychal Judge in the newspapers, after all that has been spoken about him on television, the compliments, the accolades, the great tribute that was given to him last night at the wake service, I stand in front of you and honestly feel that the homilist at Mother Teresa's funeral had it easier than I do," Duffy began.

The upper church filled with laughter just as the lower one had the night before, but this time there was no inside joke. Judge had indeed become a kind of international star of the spirit, and the mourners knew he would have found this at once ridiculous and delicious.

The church hushed as Duffy described how he felt when he learned his friend had been killed.

"I felt my whole spirit fall and turn into a pile of rubble at the bottom of my heart," Duffy said.

The hush deepened to stillness as the mourners sat with their own rubbled hearts.

"A very holy friar, whom I have the privilege to live with, Father Charlie Finnegan, just gently slipped a piece of paper in front of me and whispered, 'This was written thousands of years ago in the midst of a national tragedy. It's a quote from the Book of Lamentations.' 'The favors of the Lord are not exhausted. His mercies are not spent. Every morning, they are renewed. Great is his faithfulness. I will always trust in him.'

"I read and thought that the light is better than darkness, hope better than despair. And in thinking of my faith and the faith of Mychal Judge and all he taught me and from Scripture . . . I spiritually began to lift up my head and once again see the stars."

Too many mourners could still see only the people who pitched themselves from the falling towers. Mychal Judge was the one they would have sought out, but he lay in the box before them.

"And so, I had the courage today to stand in front of you to celebrate Mychal's life. For it is his life that speaks, not his death. It is his courage that he showed on Tuesday that speaks, not my fear. It is his hope and belief in the goodness of all people that speaks, not my despair.

"And so I am here to talk about my friend."

Whatever doubts some of the mourners may have been suffering about the Almighty, not a soul was to be found among them who did not retain a total faith in the priest they also called "my friend."

"He was a New Yorker through and through," Duffy said. "As you know, he was born in Brooklyn. . . . Some of you may not know this, he was a twin."

Almost everybody did, for Judge never missed a chance to recount the circumstances that Duffy now related.

"He was born May 11, she was born May 13. Even in birth, Mychal had to have a story."

Again there was laughter, as there had been when he told his stories in the burn unit and at the deathbeds of AIDS patients and other places where laughter had seemed impossible and maybe even inappropriate until it came.

"He just did nothing normally, no."

Still more laughter came at a time when none seemed possible in the whole city. Duffy spoke of the Brooklyn childhood and teenage years in the Franciscan friary and young adulthood as a priest. The mourners sat rapt as Duffy described the man they knew.

"Simple, joyful, life-loving and laughter."

The mourners hushed as Duffy spoke of how Judge loved to bless others.

"And I mean physically. Even if they didn't ask."

The stillness again erupted into laughter. The mourners could not only see the brightness of Judge's eyes and smile, they could feel the power of those hands that had so often blessed and embraced them, as strong and sure as those of a rescuer.

"But what you may not know, and I'd like to tell you today because this may console you a little, it really was a two-way street. You people think he did so much for you. But you didn't see it from our side, we that lived with him. He would come home and be energized and nourished and thrilled and be full of life because of you. . . . I want just to let you know, and I think he'd want me to let you know, how much you did for him. You made his life happy. You made him the kind of person that he was for all of us."

Duffy was solving the prime mystery of Mychal Judge, this being how he kept going as he did year after year, right to the end.

Here was the physics of transcendence, suddenly as understandable as the physics of a falling body.

"You should know how much you gave to him, and it was that love that he had for people, and that way of relating to him, that led him back to New York City and to become part of the fire department. He loved his fire department and all the men in it. He'd call me late at night and tell me all the experiences that he had with them, how wonderful they were, how good they were. It was never so obvious that he loved a group of people so much as his New York firefighters."

In accordance with those sublime physics, it was equally obvious that the firefighters had never loved anyone so much as Father Mychal.

"And that's the way he was when he died."

Just as gravity made the bodies and ultimately the World Trade Center it-self fall, it was love that sent Judge into the North Tower. Duffy described how the survivors had carried Judge out.

"And wouldn't you know it? There was a photographer there."

Duffy then reminded the congregation, "Mychal Judge's body was the first one released from Ground Zero. His death certificate has the number one on the top."

Duffy then asked, "Why was Mychal Judge number one? . . . I think I know the reason."

Duffy spoke of the hundreds of firefighters who had been lost.

"Mychal Judge could not have ministered to them all. It was physically impossible in this life but not in the next. And I think that if he were given his choice, he would prefer to have happened what actually happened. He passed through the other side of life, and now he can continue doing what he wanted to do with all his heart. And the next few weeks, we're going to have names added, name after name of people who are being brought out of the rubble. And Mychal Judge is going to be on the other side of death. . . . And he's going to greet them with that big Irish smile. . . . He's going to take them by the arm and the hand and say, 'Welcome, I want to take you to my Father.' "

Duffy asked everyone to stand.

"We, his family and those who loved him should return the favor that he so often did to us. All of us have felt his big Irish hands at a blessing that he would give to us."

Duffy asked them to raise their right hands.

"Extend it toward my friend Mychal and repeat after me . . ."

The mourners spoke as one.

"Mychal, may the Lord bless you . . . May the angels lead you to your Savior . . . You are the sign of His presence to us . . . May the Lord now em-brace you . . . And hold you in His love forever . . . Rest in peace. Amen."

Duffy stepped down and everyone sat and nobody wanted to believe his vision of heaven more than Vina Drennan. She was beginning to see her hus-band and Paddy Brown and Terry Hatton and Timmy Stackpole and Mychal Judge as all part of one tale. She felt as if it were a single story that began long before it became fashionable to call firefighters heroes, a story that encom-passed the Watts Street fire and the World Trade Center attack, one that was, as her favorite friar once said of her husband's forty days of suffering, as biblical as the Bible. She remembered aloud what Judge had said at her husband's funeral and had so often repeated.

"He used to tell me, 'All is well,'" Vina said. "And I didn't believe him."

She then looked at the child in her lap, as undeniably present as the others were undeniably gone, beginning life when theirs had ended. She suddenly felt this tale had not culminated in the ruin of the Twin Towers, but continued in these two bright blue eyes.

"All *is* well," she said.

The logistics and security for the funeral had been overseen by the one-time night mayor, Brian Mulheren. He knew the upper church could not possibly hold all the mourners, so he had set up a large flat-screen TV in the lower church along with smaller flat-screen TVs and loudspeakers outside. He had posted retired firefighters and cops at the door who had known Judge and "knew what they were looking for."

"Family, friends, dignitaries, all that kind of stuff," Mulheren recalled. "Everybody that needed to get there got in there."

The guardians at the door had not known to look for a slender Filipino who arrived in a dark suit and sunglasses. Mulheren himself would not have imagined that Alvarado was among the very few people who were a constant in the appointment books Judge had kept over the previous decade.

When he learned of the attack, Alvarado had expected Judge to call as he had on the way to TWA Flight 800, as he always did when something big happened. No call came all morning.

"I knew something was wrong," Alvarado later said.

He had a busy day at work to keep him distracted, but he was already certain of the worst when a call did finally come at four P.M. It was a friar Judge had confided in, Brian Carroll.

"I want you to sit down," Carroll said.

His emotion masked by his sunglasses, Alvarado had gone up to Father Peter Brophy as the upper church filled for the funeral. Brophy told him there was no room inside. The night mayor's men were not about to let in just anybody.

Carroll was nowhere in sight. Alvarado was consigned to stand in the street and watch the funeral on one of the monitors.

"I told myself it's not about me, it's about Mychal," Alvarado later said.

He approached a figure in a Franciscan habit who stood in front of the firehouse across the street. The figure was Christopher Keenan, who had not joined the procession of friars into the church because he had to leave early to preside at his niece's wedding in New Jersey. She had considered postponing the wedding, but Keenan had urged her to go ahead. He did not want to suddenly arise from among the friars in the middle of Judge's funeral and depart, so he had remained outside.

"Al came to me and said, 'They won't let me in. I can't get into Mychal's funeral,'" Keenan recalled. "I said, 'Then stand right here with me.'"

Keenan stood with Alvarado on his right, a firefighter on his left, and he placed a hand on each man's shoulder as they watched the Mass on the monitors. A photographer snapped a picture of the three of them standing in shared sorrow.

"It was quite an image," Keenan later said.

Over the speakers, they heard Duffy's call from the pulpit for everybody to raise a hand to bless Judge as he had loved to bless others. Keenan's right hand rose from Alvarado's shoulder. Alvarado's hand also rose, as did that of the firefighter and all the others in the street, the whole magnificently varied crowd now speaking with a single voice, a single love.

Keenan then had to hurry off. Word had spread among the firefighters as to where he was headed, and they offered their good wishes as he passed through the crowd. They seemed to view it as a kind of victory that a couple was starting a new life together in the face of so much death.

"They were saying, 'Tell the couple to have a wonderful life! Tell them to have a *great* life!'" Keenan recalled.

A man whose dearest wish was to have started such a life with Judge remained in front of the firehouse as the funeral ended and the monitors showed the FDNY honor guard escorting the coffin up the aisle. The church door opened and what had been onscreen took substance. The firefighters bore the coffin down the steps. Judge's sisters were directly behind.

The friar Brian Carroll had remained outside the church by choice but only now saw Alvarado standing in front of the firehouse. Carroll went over to invite him to join the friars on a bus going to the Franciscan burial ground in New Jersey where Mychal Judge was to be interred. Alvarado accepted.

The bus followed as the hearse bore the mortal remains of Father Mychal Judge to Holy Sepulchre Cemetery in Totowa. Alvarado stepped out to see that Judge's grave was among those of the friars who had gone before him, each buried in order of demise, each marked by a small, plain stone set flush with the ground.

"I thought they would have sent his remains to Ireland," Alvarado later said.

Alvarado rode the bus back to the city where Judge's spirit had always resided. The spirit remained there, still embraced in New York's darkest time, not only by those who knew him in life, but by multitudes who were coming to know of him in death.

The horrific attack perpetrated in the name of God caused many to question whether there could be a God at all. But in defiance of the evil arose the image of five men bearing a fallen priest from the ruins.

The myth arose that Judge had been killed by falling debris as he knelt to administer last rites to a firefighter who had been struck by a jumper. The story seemed confirmed when it turned out a firefighter named Danny Suhr had indeed been killed by a jumper outside the South Tower and that a radio call had indeed gone out for a fire chaplain and that Judge had indeed been struck in the head by falling debris.

As it turned out, Judge had never been notified of the radio call, and he had left the North Tower only for a terrifying instant, and he had suffered the head injury postmortem. It was he who had been given the Last Rites, or as close an approximation as two cops were able to improvise. But the exact details of Judge's death changed nothing for the firefighters. He had still died among them. He had still lived among them as their priest. A poster went up in firehouses with thumbnail photos of the other fallen 342 members of the FDNY along with a much bigger picture of Judge, as if his were the smiling face of the Almighty Himself.

Judge's good was the firefighters' good, and their good engendered more good, and the whole city filled with wonders, or what he would have called surprises. Firefighters and cops and rescue workers were cheered in the streets. Citizens of all colors and backgrounds united in an effort to do whatever they could to help. Hundreds trooped to the ruins to volunteer. Others donated money and equipment. A group of girls in Judge's native South Brooklyn held a bake sale to benefit Squad 1 on Union Street and raised $2,400 in an hour as passersby kicked in as much as twenty dollars for a brownie. An elderly woman of humble means arrived at a relief station with a plastic bag.

"She said, 'I have no money, but I've been making ice,'" Detective James Nuciforo later reported. "And they were happy to take it."

The Stars and Stripes appeared everywhere, and the devastation at the tip of Manhattan only made the Statue of Liberty's upraised torch seem to shine brighter. President Bush visited the pit and afterward rode up the West Side Highway with Giuliani. The motorcade passed liberal Greenwich Village and people who would have ordinarily cursed both men waved flags and called out, "Thank you!"

As the wonders burgeoned, celebrity and money paled before bravery and devotion. A Concert for New York was held at Madison Square Garden, and the movie stars who appeared onstage were nothing compared to a person who had been laboring on the smoldering mountain of death. Richard Gere seemed incidental beside Firefighter Mike Moran, survivor of Paddy Brown's Ladder 3 and brother of a fallen battalion chief who used to visit the hospital with Judge on Christmas. Moran drew by far the biggest cheer of the night when he made a declaration from the stage.

"In the spirit of the Irish people, Osama bin Laden, you can kiss my royal Irish ass!"

Nobody would have loved that more than Mychal Judge, who had a shamrock tattooed on his. He would have been equally, if more quietly, pleased to see *The New York Times* begin running its "Portraits of Grief," brief hagiographies of those who died at the towers. Nobody was a wife beater or a belligerent drunk or a self-obsessed boob or a bullying boss or a pilfering employee or anything but what their loved ones most fondly remembered.

Among the nearly three thousand dead, the only one who seemed to have anything written he might not have liked was Judge himself. A *Village Voice* writer had "outed" Judge a month after the attack, saying his sexual orientation was widely known in the gay community. The writer cited as a corroborating source none other than the fire commissioner. Von Essen recounted in that and numerous subsequent stories how Judge had confided in him "just to alert me" about his sexual orientation.

The first tiny fracture apparent in the unity following the attack took place among those devoted to the man listed as the first fatality, the man who felt the spanning Brooklyn Bridge was a better representation of his faith than any soaring steeple. The more militant gays sought to make Judge a kind of icon, arguing that the strictures of the Church had forced him to keep the wraps on his sexual identity. The more traditional Catholics insisted that he could not possibly have been gay. Vina Drennan and others for whom Judge had assumed the form they most needed were surprised he might have a private form they had not imagined. Many firefighters were angry because they felt that wherever the truth might lie, Judge had revealed whatever he chose to reveal when he was alive and nobody had the right to go beyond that now that he was gone. His sisters took the position that whatever his inclinations, he had remained celibate. Patti Ann McDonald called Dympna in tears, wanting to know if Judge really was gay and why he had not told her.

And then there was Al Alvarado, who said nothing at all publicly but whose "ALA" appears so often in the appointment books that he almost certainly was as much a part of Judge's life as Steven McDonald and Vina. Yet few people knew of him and he had no official status in relation to Judge. He was not offered the comfort and consolation accorded others who lost a loved one on 9/11.

Alvarado was not at the FDNY memorial service at Madison Square Garden, where Dympna and Vina and Tara and Paddy Brown's brother, Mike, and thousands of others listened to a recitation of the names as the faces of the fallen flashed on big screens and a chill seeped up from the hockey ice below the temporary flooring. White-gloved firefighters presented each family with a polished wooden case containing four medals, including the Medal of Supreme Sacrifice. The panning cameras flashed seven-year-old Terence John Stackpole on the big screens, the very image of his fallen father.

The same sorrowful rain falling outside the Garden during the memorial fell on the Bronx, where Alvarado grieved alone.

"It was a good ten years," he said. "I would have liked another ten years, but it was a good ten years."

Alvarado had heard the talk that Judge had become the first fatality so he could welcome all the others into heaven.

"If there is an afterlife, he'll be surrounded by people, and I'll have to make an appointment," he said. "For now I'll bank on my dreams."

He kept photos on his computer of a small house standing in walled grounds that had the flowering lushness of Eden. This was the house in the Philippines that had been built without a plan, now finished, as perfect as if it had been blueprinted by the heart.

"Big enough for one person and a spirit," Alvarado said.

The same spirit Captain Al Fuentes called on when he came out of an induced coma three weeks after becoming one of a handful pulled alive from the ruins of the towers. He awoke in tears, his wife, Eileen, standing by his bed.

"Eileen, I'm going crazy," he said. "The jumpers. All I kept dreaming was the jumpers. I got to talk to Father Judge."

"Father Judge—" she said.

"Yeah, you got to call Father Judge," he said. "I'm going crazy."

"Father Judge . . . Honey, what do you remember?" she asked.

"No!" he said. He knew. "Father Judge is dead. I need him to talk to me."

The spirit that steadied Tara Stackpole as she waited for the firefighters to find Timmy's body. The spirit that stayed with her through the wake and the funeral, that went with her and Vina to Terry Hatton's funeral, that stood with them afterward by the steps of St. Patrick's Cathedral, down which John Drennan's body had been carried six years before.

The spirit that could be heard with Hatton's widow, Beth, when she got the call on her cell phone from a doctor confirming she was pregnant. She stood in a Manhattan street and cheered.

A coffinless memorial was held for Paddy Brown at the cathedral before a good portion of his body was recovered. His brother, Mike, had the remains cremated and led thirty mourners into Central Park on a cold January night four months after the attack. They stopped at the spot at the top of the Great Lawn where Paddy had once taken Judge so he would know where to go, the spot that Paddy had marked on a map should anything ever happen to him.

Nobody needed to ask why Paddy had chosen this spot. The remaining spires of Manhattan stood beyond the dark trees with incandescent majesty as though they had been constructed to be admired from exactly this spot at precisely this hour.

Paddy had assumed Judge would be there to preside, but they had only his spirit and their own to guide them. Paddy's cremated remains were in a cardboard container that Mike carried down the line of mourners. Most took only a modest handful.

"Anybody need some more?" Mike asked.

Mike went back down the line and each scooped a little more. The gray ash was gritty to the touch and it rested in the palm as if disbelief had taken substance.

Vina was there and joined the others in following Mike's instructions to turn toward the moon that shone big and bright behind them. They cast their handfuls into the icy air and called out in one voice.

"God bless Paddy Brown!"

The breeze caught the ash and it stayed aloft, swirling and sparkling in the moonlight, a kind of magic, heavenly dust. They all were left with gritty ash on their palms and fingers. The one who knew what to do was Beth Hatton. She rubbed her hands on her face in a gesture of pure and perfect love, proof of Judge's long contention that the Church sprang from the hearts of the people and would survive there no matter what.

In a hush, the mourners walked over to a silver maple that firefighters had sneaked into the park to plant in Paddy's memory a few midnights before. They had managed to do so in the middle of a renowned grove of evergreens, and the Parks workers had carefully transplanted it not far from a statue of Alexander Hamilton.

Nobody had wanted to take the last of the ashes from the cardboard container, and Mike gently poured what was left around the base of the tree. Somebody set down a holy card that had a smiling Paddy on the front and a photo of the famous rope rescue on the back in the usual place of a prayer. Somebody else added a small, flickering candle.

With the unadorned, genuine voice of a former grammar school teacher, Vina broke into "The Marine Corps Hymn," an anthem of love to the firefighter who truly had been her best friend. Everybody sang along, and she led them straight into the song Judge had sung at the firehouse Mass the day before 9/11. Their gritty hands remained over their hearts until they ended with

". . . my home sweet home." An airliner flew overhead, as if in a variation of the traditional military tribute.

"The hardest thing was to get that plane to fly over," Mike Brown joked.

The ceremony ended as Judge would have ended it, with a laugh. Everyone then went down the path leading out of the park. They passed the glass pavillion at the Metropolitan Museum of Art, and they could see the Egyptian Temple of Dendur sitting in its ancient stillness.

Later, three coins recovered from the pit were determined to have traces of Paddy Brown's DNA. Mike went with family down by the Hudson River, across West Street from what had been the World Trade Center. They stood where Paddy and Vina had stood when they tossed in their pocket change with the wish that John Drennan would live.

Mike's wife, Janet, now took the quarter and two dimes from the velveteen pouch in which they had been delivered. The Statue of Liberty had her torch upraised in the distance as Janet gave the quarter to his cousin, a California fire captain named Jay Presten. She gave one of the dimes to Mike. She kept the other. Together, they threw the coins into the sunlight. The coins hit the water with three distinct little splashes.

On the way out, family and friends passed a homeless man who sat on a wood bench. Any worry that it might have been better to give the coins to him ended when one of the group went over and presented him with a dollar, folded lengthwise, Mychal Judge's way.

32

Not even a fragment of DNA was identified for more than a thousand of those who perished at the World Trade Center. Among them was Firefighter Michael Ragusa, whose family finally decided to hold a funeral with a coffin containing only a vial of blood he had submitted as a volunteer to a bone marrow transplant registry before the attack. His was the last of four hundred FDNY funerals and memorials in the aftermath of 9/11, and it seemed an ending had come when the band marched slowly away from the church and the last notes were fading in the distance.

Flaherty then signaled with his drum major's staff for the band to turn around. They marched back toward the church playing an upbeat, joyful "Athol Highlanders."

By then the chaplain who had rightly called the band "so fucking good" was being widely spoken of as a candidate for sainthood by people who had heard the many true stories about him. The clamor grew loud enough that New York's head friar, Provincial John Felice, felt compelled to respond when he accepted an award from St. Bonaventure University on Judge's behalf.

"Although that tragic event took the lives of almost three thousand people at the World Trade Center, Mychal became the symbol of our grief as a city and as a nation," Felice said. "His selfless act brought meaning and dignity in the face of the incomprehensible destruction of that day. His actions and those of his beloved firefighters, as well as the police and emergency service workers, gave us something to be proud of at one of our darkest moments. Their stories tug at our hearts to this very day."

Felice seemed to be only reiterating what had been said so often about Judge in the days following the attack.

"I accept this award not because Mychal died an heroic death, a cruel fate of time and place, but because he lived an heroic life," Felice continued. "He made it a point to say yes far more often to life than no, because he believed that a living God wrote the agenda of his day, not himself. In placing himself second, he honored each person he met by putting them first in his time and attention. That is why he is remembered so personally by so many, and so beloved.

"There is a rush to canonize Mychal these days, and I think it is a mistake. In making saints out of people, we often shove them away from our experience and place them on a pedestal. He was a very human, flawed, complex person, just like the rest of us."

Felice stated in words what Judge had said with his life as well as his death.

"His real legacy to each one of us is that such is the stuff of greatness. Mychal Judge's life is not summed up by that terrible moment at the foot of the North Tower of the World Trade Center. He died doing what he loved among those he loved, a privilege not often afforded to most of us. It was just one last example of a generous heart that knew no bounds.

"Greatness of heart to which we are all called."

To answer that call, he needed only to find the goodness inside that he seemed able to see in everybody.

In Judge's view, human frailty and weakness only made that goodness more remarkable. He recognized this in the firefighters and long before 9/11 told them they were holy rascals. They continued to revere him even as they themselves were knocked off the pedestal to which they had been elevated after 9/11. The tabloid newspapers seemed to go out of their way to play up every instance when one of the erstwhile heroes got into a brawl or was arrested for drunk driving. A 9/11 widow was said to have spent the outpouring of financial support on a boob job and fancy clothes. The firefighter son of one of the men who carried Judge from the ruins was fired after being named as one of the men who had consensual sex with a woman in a Bronx firehouse.

FDNY SEX SCANDAL, a front-page headline blared.

At the same time, celebrities who had looked almost ridiculous on stage beside the first responders at the Concert for New York regained their prominence in the public psyche. Money reasserted its preeminence. The

briefly unified nation split back into red and blue states, in part because the
Bush administration used 9/11 as an excuse to invade Iraq, trying to make
the American public believe there was a link between Osama bin Laden and
Saddam Hussein.

The use of our own murdered innocents as an excuse to invade Iraq
also alienated the great majority of the countries that had expressed such
solidarity with America after 9/11. We thereby squandered the global good-
will engendered by the good that rose from the ruins in downtown Manhattan. Ireland had shut down for a national day of mourning following the
attack, perhaps the sole time in the recent history of Judge's homeland
when the pubs were not only officially closed but really did not serve drink.
The war by pretext turned many of those same people against America as
never before.

Even so, the people of the tiny village of Keshcarrigan in County
Leitrim contrived to build a lakeshore memorial to Judge at the edge of the
farm where his father was raised. Dympna rode at the head of a procession
for the unveiling on the fourth anniversary of 9/11, having chosen the
honor over an invitation to the White House that same day to receive the
Medal of Valor on behalf of her twin. She had brought the flag that had
covered Judge's coffin, still folded as it had been by the honor guard after the
funeral. Also present was a fire rig as well as ten members of the Leitrim Fire
Brigade.

"From all five firehouses," a commander noted.

The procession came to a lush expanse of bright green grass and freshly
planted trees at the shore of tranquil Keshcarrigan Lake, the new Father Mychal Judge Memorial and Peace Park.

At the appointed moment, Dympna pulled a black cloth away to reveal a
gray stone bench. Inscribed in the stone was a smiling likeness of the twin she
still called Emmett, along with the prayer he had composed that made the
firefighters smile in the ruins. The woman holding the folded flag set it down
on one end of the bench. Another local woman began to sing, the crowd joining in at the end.

"Hard times, hard times come again no more . . ."

At the end of the song there came a moment of perfect peace. Then the
crowd dispersed. The sun sank behind the hills. The lake went glassy in the
evening calm, just as in the mythic times, just as through the centuries since,

through the time of Saint Patrick and through the Famine and the exodus to America and all that followed.

In New York, Steven McDonald marked the approach of each anniversary of 9/11 by leading a procession in the Stations of the Cross in the way of Mychal, stopping to say a prayer at each firehouse and police station along Judge's route to Ground Zero.

McDonald was in the lower church at St. Francis before the start of the sixth procession when the gay activist Brendan Fay approached. Some of Judge's friends outside the gay community harbored hard feelings toward Fay, believing he had only been furthering his own agenda when he energetically furthered the image of their Mychal as the Gay Priest. They had bristled on seeing the newspaper reports when Fay married Tom Moulton using a Bible that Judge had given them.

Whatever his own feelings may have been, McDonald now set them aside and said the one thing that would be in keeping with Judge's spirit.

"Brendan, you're welcome to walk with us."

Brendan joined a hundred or more others of every type in following the motorized wheelchair of the man whom Judge believed to be as close to a saint as anyone he encountered. They reached the edge of the pit and between breaths from the respirator McDonald led those of every faith and persuasion in Mychal's prayer.

On the actual anniversary, the city marked the day with a reading of the names of the dead. They as always began with Gordon Aamoth and ended with Igor Zukelman, with Patrick J. Brown and Terence Hatton and Mychal Judge in between. There were a total of 2,749 souls in whom people had sought to see only what was best, which is to say what DM0001 would have seen, which might be another way of saying that his spirit did indeed welcome theirs into heaven, if heaven is conceived as a realm of the heart.

"The greatest honor we could do them is to remember them," the new mayor, Mike Bloomberg, said on the fourth anniversary. "The one miracle we can perform is to go on living."

To go on living while remembering is to heed the lessons put forth by the 9/11 Commission and others who investigated how such evil came to be perpetrated in the name of God, evil so monstrous as to make many of us wonder whether the cosmos is governed only by natural laws of absolute and immutable indifference.

To go on living while remembering is also to ponder how such resplendent good manifested itself in the aftermath of such evil. That way we might recapture some of what we have squandered since those days when the fiery pit gave rise to what was the very best in all of us.

"Heaven is here," Judge used to tell Alvarado. "We make our own heaven and we make our own hell."

For however brief a time, so many of us were who we would like to believe ourselves to be, what we imagine is our own true shape, what Father Mychal Judge saw as he assumed a shape to match, the other stanchion in the bridge from one person to another, twinned towers reaching heavenward, heaven being neither up nor down but across.

That true shape is what the jumpers must have felt as they plummeted toward the earth from the upper floors, where the most common word in the final cell phone calls was *love*, the shape that would live through a fall from any height. They must have felt everything in them that most distinguished living weight from dead. That made them more precious than the debris falling with them. That would not just be obliterated when they struck the sidewalk. That was worth cherishing. That was God or at least good.

Good as surprising as those butterflies that appeared after the second collapse, fluttering through the sunlight among the twisted girders, impossibly delicate and intact and perfect in the aftermath of such violence.

"Like souls," a firefighter said.

Good dispersing as if on silent wings, fluttering into what was most like a soul in the survivors.

Good needing only to be seen to become visible again.

Good, or God, visible nearly always and nearly everywhere to Father Mychal Judge, whose own good remains a guide for those who wish to be a little better than they are.

"Sometimes in life we lose someone we love and we don't know what to do. We should just pray and worship," he once said at the memorial for two brothers who had been shunned by the Church after dying of AIDS. "Thank you, Lord, for their lives, for their love, creativity, for their friendship; their good days and bad, for their happiness, for their anger, for everything they brought into our lives."

He went on. "These are things we should say about each other always. If we did, life wouldn't be half bad. I hope someday that someone says things nicely about me as I said about them through the years. I love you, so just love each other. The best you can."

33

O n the first St. Patrick's Day after the attack, the newest members of the FDNY carried 343 American flags onto Fifth Avenue. With them marched 343 firefighters, each representing one of the fallen. Friar Christopher Keenan, having become the new fire chaplain for Manhattan and the Bronx, was there for Judge. Mike Brown was there for his brother Paddy.

At 12:30 P.M., the pipe band went silent as the biggest St. Patrick's Day crowd anybody could remember hushed. The whole broad avenue became quieter than a whispered prayer as all the marchers joined the 343 firefighters in turning about-face toward the place where their comrades had perished.

"Uncover!" a voice called out.

The firefighters removed their hats and stood with the wind at their backs. The air itself seemed to gust downtown with their thoughts and memories. The moment of silence deepened to where the only sound was the snapping of the flags.

Then, almost as if arising from that place of death downtown, a cheer came up the avenue, rolling through the throngs like the force of life itself. The roar reached the firefighters a little earlier than some of them might have wished, but there was no mistaking that the moment had come to turn around and march on uptown.

Earlier losses were not forgotten, and in June Keenan presided at the plaque dedication at Rescue 4 marking the first anniversary of the Father's Day fire. There was a big turnout despite the rain and Keenan asked Tara Stackpole to serve as a Eucharistic minister. She was distributing the Host when a young firefighter stepped before her fresh from battling a blaze. She saw the rivulets of rain that had left tracks in his sooty, youthful face.

"Body of Christ," she said.

She set a wafer in his roughened hand and felt exactly what Judge would have wanted her to feel.

"I knew it was going to go on," she later said. "I knew it was going to be okay."

Marvelous.

Index